Oracle Power Objects Developer's Guide

Rich Finkelstein
Kasu Sista
Rick Greenwald

Osborne **McGraw-Hill**

Berkeley New York St. Louis
San Francisco Auckland Bogotá Hamburg London Madrid
Mexico City Milan Montreal New Delhy Panama City
Paris São Paulo Singapore Sydney Tokyo Toronto

Osborne **McGraw-Hill**
2600 Tenth Street
Berkeley, California 94710
U.S.A.

For information on translations or book distributors outside the U.S.A., or to
arrange bulk purchase discounts for sales promotions, premiums, or fundraisers,
please contact Osborne **McGraw-Hill** at the above address.

Oracle Power Objects Developer's Guide

Copyright © 1996 by McGraw-Hill, Inc. All rights reserved. Printed in the United
States of America. Except as permitted under the Copyright Act of 1976, no part of
this publication may be reproduced or distributed in any form or by any means, or
stored in a database or retrieval system, without the prior written permission of the
publisher, with the exception that the program listings may be entered, stored, and
executed in a computer system, but they may not be reproduced for publication.

1234567890 DOC 99876

ISBN 0-07-882163-0

Acquisitions Editor
Cynthia Brown

Editorial Assistant
Daniela Dell'Orco
Terese Tatum

Copy Editor
Dennis Weaver

Proofreader
Linda Medoff

Computer Designer
Jirka Vcelak

Illustrator
Lance Ravella

Series Design
Jani Beckwith

Quality Control Specialist
Joe Scuderi

Cover Design
Ted Mader Associates

Information has been obtained by Osborne **McGraw-Hill** from sources believed to be reliable.
However, because of the possibility of human or mechanical error by our sources, Osborne
McGraw-Hill, or others, Osborne McGraw-Hill does not guarantee the accuracy, adequacy, or
completeness of any information and is not responsible for any errors or omissions or the results
obtained from use of such information.

Dedication

Richard Finkelstein I would like to dedicate this book to the memories of my beloved parents Harry and Mary Finkelstein, to my dear wife Julie, and to my son David Finkelstein with whom I share all of my aspirations and achievements, and to my brothers Norman and Henry and Henry's wife Shirley.

Kasu Sista To my mother, who passed away while this book was in its final stages, and who I hope is smiling.

Rick Greenwald To my mother, my wife, and my father.

About the Authors...

Richard Finkelstein is an internationally recognized authority on client/server computing and RDBMS. He evaluates and recommends SQL database management systems, and application development and decision support software. He is president of Links Technology Corporation and Performance Computing Inc., in Chicago.

Kasu Sista is a principal at Links Technology Corporation, a consulting firm specializing in client/server systems. Kasu has over 10 years experience in designing and deploying client/server, and the more general, requester/server systems. His interests include relational databases, object-oriented languages, and high speed networks.

Rick Greenwald is a principal at Performance Computing and a recognized authority on client/server computing. He has been active in client/server computing for eight years, and has spoken on application development and database systems throughout the United States, Europe, South America, Asia, and Australia. He has written white papers and articles for many magazines and companies.

Contents At A Glance

Contents

Foreword

The amount of change occurring on our planet has dramatically increased over the past several decades, and it continues to grow at an accelerating rate. With the burgeoning technology industry at its core, the ever-shifting environment is affecting all of us and our organizations. Fortunately, we have the choice to take a proactive role in shaping the change. We all share an innate desire for continuous improvement, for ourselves, our organizations, and our planet. But before we can lead a transformation, we must closely examine our environment and determine where we want to go next. Then, with visionary leadership, the journey of change becomes the path to progress.

Oracle Power Objects is the result of the evolution of technology and a strong commitment to improvement. In the summer of 1993, Larry Ellison and I recognized a problem that inspired a new product solution. At the time, a bifurcation was taking place in the PC client/server marketplace. Application development tools basically fell into two separate categories. They were either singularly powerful or singularly efficient. The high performance client/server tools required complicated and time consuming programming while those that were easy to use were far inferior in terms of capability. Recognizing this, we resolved to create a custom applications tool that would combine the best of both worlds: powerful functionality with simple visual programming.

To achieve our vision, a development effort, known in its early stages as "Project X," was launched. In less that two years, six exceptionally talented engineers created Power Objects, which has become Oracle's flagship development tool for workgroup client/server applications. The product is a direct reflection of the great personal and organizational leaders behind it.

Oracle has been fortunate to have an excellent team on the front lines as well. I am especially proud to have Apple and IBM as partners in the distribution and marketing of Power Objects. This marks an important collaboration that will benefit not just the partners involved, but our customers as well. By working together, we have been able to offer a multi-platform applications tool that is widely accessible in the PC software marketplace.

The business opportunities created by Power Objects extend to our developers as well, with the introduction of the Oracle Object Marketplace. The object marketplace will allow developers to market and sell Power Objects "objects" through the Internet. One of the most important aspects of Power Objects is that it is truly object oriented. This creates an opportunity for developers to reuse a majority of the code that they write. We view this as a significant contribution towards the future of network computing, a marketplace that Power Objects is designed to compete in especially well.

In the technology industry, as in other industries, we need new tools to take us from where we are now to where we want to go. These tools will assist us in leading our way through the coming changes of the 21st century. It is our hope that Oracle's contribution of Power Objects will facilitate many more contributions to come. This book was written to support developers in this endeavor. Our sincere thanks go to its authors.

Marc R. Benioff
Executive Vice President
Client/Server Systems Division
Oracle Corporation

Acknowledgments

I would like to thank my coauthors Kasu Sista and Rick Greenwald for their tireless efforts in creating this book. Special thanks to my partners Julie Finkelstein, Paul Lionikis, and Ilya Movmyga for their encouragement and support, and to Ken Wiegle for his invaluable comments and technical input.

Special appreciation and thanks to Marc Benioff and his organization at Oracle whose efforts and support were critical in making this book possible. I would like to thank Matt Bennett, the first person to propose we write this book, and Laura Pauli who is always there to help.

I would also like to thank the great team at Links Technology including Liliya Kantor, Nitin Potdar, Prabha Ranganathan, Donna O'Barski, and Radka Winwood.

Finally, I would like to thank our editors and support staff at Osborne/McGraw-Hill who helped make this book the best that it could be.

Richard Finkelstein

First of all I would like to thank Marc Benioff and his team for the opportunity to write this book. Special thanks to Matt Bennett who got us involved in the development of this product from the initial stages of Project X. Thanks also go to Leith Anderson for getting us access to the developers during the writing of this book. My thanks to the Oracle Power Objects team, Steve McAdams, Mike Roberts, Adam Greenblatt, Dave Levine, and Jennifer Krauel, and to the product managers Max Schireson, Rick Schultz and Wister Walcott.

Many people worked on this book. It would not have been possible without the help of my partners Rich Finkelstein, Julie Finkelstein, Paul Lionikis, and Ilya Movmyga who took up the slack and kept billing while I was researching and writing this book. My thanks also to the rest of the Links' staff. Special thanks to my coauthor Rick Greenwald who moved this project along with his experience and dedication.

Thanks to Brad Shimmin who gave me his encouragement and constructive criticism; to Cindy Brown for getting the project done; and to Daniela Dell'Orco for keeping us all straight. Thanks also to Tony Kranz who spent many hours making sure that all the material is correct.

Finally I would like to thank my wife Janet and my daughter Saraswathi for their unflagging support and patience. They, more than anyone else, had to put up with long days and even longer nights. Thank god I am still married.

Kasu Sista

I would like to thank all of those at Oracle and Oracle Press who helped me to create this book, especially Mike Roberts, Dabe Levine, Steve McAdams, Rick Schultz, and Max Schireson of Oracle, and Brad Shimmin, Cindy Brown, and Daniela Dell'Orco of Oracle Press.

I would like to thank Lew Kirshner, who gave me my first job in the computer industry; Ray Schwartz, who gave me the initial guidance and encouragement to stick with it; and Rich Heaps, who gave me the opportunity to expand my horizons and abilities and grow to a new level.

Finally, I am very grateful to Rich Finklestein for giving me the chance to help write this book.

Rick Greenwald

Introduction

The client/server marketplace is replete with easy-to-use graphical front-end development tools. Why is there a need for yet another development tool for graphical client applications?

Most of the existing tools fall into one of two categories. Some tools are presented as easy-to-learn-and-use development environments for creating graphical client applications. Although these tools may indeed allow easy development of simple applications, developers often find a steep learning curve and reduced productivity when they attempt to create more complex applications. Many of these tools lack the sort of features, such as object orientation, that experienced developers have come to rely on. And most of these tools have gained their ease-of-use credentials by hiding the complexities of data access and integrity, which leave gaping holes in the resulting applications.

Other tools on the market skip the ease-of-use and proceed directly to a steep learning curve and reduced productivity. It is very difficult for developers to choose to use one of these complex tools while still having to deliver applications on schedule.

Oracle Power Objects raises the bar for client/server development tools by offering the best of both worlds. Oracle Power Objects gives developers the ability to create robust basic applications in a matter of minutes, while still providing them with the architecture and the functionality to grow these applications into sophisticated systems. By doing so, Oracle Power Objects gives developers the tools and the environment they need to address the demands of creating client/server applications.

Oracle Power Objects sets a new standard for combining rapid development, the easy extension of application functionality, and appropriate client/server implementation for developers.

Some of the basic features Oracle Power Objects provides are

- Visual Drag & Drop programming

- A comprehensive set of data aware controls

- An easy-to-use language in the form of Oracle Basic

- The ability to create classes and object-oriented extensions

- A rich event model to help create customized user interfaces

- Dedicated drivers to access major databases

- ODBC access to most other databases

- A small but powerful local engine to facilitate stand alone development

This book aims to help the developer come up to speed quickly, and become proficient in using Oracle Power Objects to develop powerful applications that interface with popular back end databases. It will show how to use Power Objects to rapidly develop prototypes, and then refine the applications with proven techniques to make them production ready. This book comprises several chapters. A high-level summary of these chapters follows.

Oracle Power Objects—Let's Get Started (Chapter 1)

If you are like most developers, you can't wait to get in the driver's seat and take the vehicle for a test drive. So this chapter will do just that. You will be able to build a master detail application with data lookups, integrity controls, and query-by-form capability within minutes. In this chapter you will

- Become familiar with the Oracle Power Objects environment

- Create a basic application in less than five minutes

■ Enhance the functionality and appearance of the basic form with pick boxes, calculated values, radio buttons, and bitmaps

■ Extend the basic form to include a master-detail relationship

Introducing Oracle Basic (Chapter 2)

Most applications require developers to implement application specific logic. Oracle Basic is the programming language that is embedded in Oracle Power Objects. Oracle Basic is modeled on the BASIC programming language and allows many developers to use their existing knowledge of BASIC. For those programmers who have not worked with a form of BASIC, this chapter will teach you everything you need to know. In this chapter you will learn

■ Why, when, and where to use Oracle Basic (OB)

■ Data types, variables, and database objects

■ Functions and subroutines

■ Controlling program flow

■ Using database objects

■ Event processing and order of execution of events

■ Debugging Oracle Basic programs

■ Handling run time errors

Extending Your Application (Chapter 3)

In Chapter 3, you will extend the capabilities of the form you built in Chapter 1. You will learn how to

■ Add descriptive values from other tables in the database

■ Create fields with values automatically set

■ Create fields with calculated values

■ Create fields which display summary information

■ Add a combo box to the application which will allow the user to select from a list of descriptive values that are automatically translated when added to or retrieved from their bound column in the database.

Adding a Sorting Screen (Chapter 4)

In Chapter 4 you will start interacting with the database more. One of features that users ask for most is the ability to sort data retrieved from a database. In this chapter you will

■ Create a form that will allow users to graphically specify columns they wish to use to sort data returned from the database

■ Add push buttons to the default toolbar to call the sort order form

Leveraging Your Work through Libraries and Classes (Chapter 5)

Chapter 5 is an introduction to Objects in Power Objects. The concept of visual classes in Power Objects is a powerful feature. In this chapter you will

■ Learn how to take the sort order form you created in Chapter 4, generalize it so that it can be used in many different applications, and create a library to store the form

■ An introduction to object classes, with an explanation of how they differ from libraries. Also, see how the concept of inheritance between object classes and instances works.

■ Create a simple address class to learn the basics of object classes

Extended Class Functionality (Chapter 6)

Chapter 6 will extend your understanding of objects and classes. In this chapter you will

■ Build an object class that can be added to an application and will allow users to create selection expressions to limit the data returned from the database

■ Learn how and where to create class logic and use many Oracle Power Object functions in creating the class

■ Learn how to create a subclass from an object class and the relationship between classes and subclasses

Business Rules (Chapter 7)

Chapter 7 briefly looks at the three layer client/server architecture. Then it focuses on classifying and implementing business rules in Power Objects. In this chapter you will

- Learn the meaning of business rules and how they fit into a client/server application
- Create a login class to enforce password security
- Look at several examples of referential integrity implementation in Power Objects
- Look at entity level validation features available in Power Objects
- Build an address class that does automatic lookups

Database Server Connections and Client-Side Database Considerations (Chapters 8 & 9)

In Chapters 8 and 9, you will learn about the interaction between Oracle Power Objects applications and server databases. In particular you will

- Create a login screen, different from the one created in Chapter 7, to enforce database security
- Learn about the different ways Oracle Power Objects can retrieve data from the server and the implications of using each method
- Learn how Oracle Power Objects applications work in a multi-user environment and how to guard against the loss of data integrity

Reporting (Chapters 10)

Oracle Power Objects provides an easy to use Report Writer, that can create simple as well as fairly complicated reports. This chapter will explain how to

- Select data, format, and print reports
- Use aggregate functions to create group and grand totals
- Create master-detail reports
- Use charting to highlight important features

■ Use the Form designer to generate mailing labels

■ Create custom menus to enhance forms and reports

Extending the Power (Chapters 11)

No matter how sophisticated the tool, there are always features that cannot be implemented using the tool's native capabilities. That is where external interfaces are important. This chapter looks at three important technologies in this regard. In this chapter you will learn

■ How to use DLL libraries

■ How to use OLE 2.0 technology to take advantage of tools like word processors, spreadsheets, etc.

■ How to use OCX controls to shamelessly extend the functionality of Power Objects

■ How to compile your applications for deployment

Obtaining the Code for this Book

Every attempt has been made to ensure the code listings in this book are correct. If you would like to obtain source code for all of the applications in this book, you can download the code from the Oracle Web site at **http://www.oracle.com** or from the CompuServe Oracle User Group forum in the Power Objects section.

The code available includes an application file with the name "CHAP*n*.POA" for each chapter of the book, where *n* is the number of the chapter. The application file represents the application as it stands at the end of the chapter. For instance, the application file name "CHAP3.POA" represents the application as it stands at the end of Chapter 3.

Some chapters may have two application files associated with them, such as Chapter 4 and Chapter 6. These chapters require slightly different coding depending on whether they are running against an Oracle database or a Blaze database. For these chapters, the "CHAP*n*.POA" syntax will include an "O" or a "B" at the end of the name to indicate which database they will work with. For instance, the application file "CHAP4O.POA" is the application as it stands at the end of Chapter 4 for an Oracle database.

You can examine or run any of these applications by using the Open menu choice from the File menu in Oracle Power Objects, or by clicking on the File Open icon in the standard Oracle Power Objects toolbar.

The files on the bulletin board include a Blaze database that is designed to work properly with the examples in the book. The database is called "ORDERS.BLZ". It is very similar to the MLDB.BLZ database included with Oracle Power Objects with three main differences:

1. The database contains only a subset of the tables in the MLDB.BLZ database which are appropriate to the purposes of the book.

2. The ORDER_DATE, SHIP_DATE, SHIP_METHOD_ID, and ORDER_FILLED columns accept null values.

3. The DISCOUNT column does not contain null values.

You may choose to use the MLDB.BLZ database for the examples in this book. If you do, you may have trouble inserting new rows into the ORDERS table in the early chapters of the book. You may also have incorrect values displayed in the repeater display for the ORDER_ITEMS table, due to the null values for the DISCOUNT field in the MLDB.BLZ database.

To The Reader

This book is the product of many people's efforts. Most of them are mentioned in the acknowledgments. But this book would be nothing but for you, the reader. We as authors can only hope that this book would be helpful to its readers. We are sure that this book will evolve as the product evolves. So if you have any suggestions for additions or improvements, please feel free to drop us a note on Email.

Rich Finkelstein	finkel@links.com
Kasu Sista	Sista@links.com
Rick Greenwald	greenie@interaccess.com

CHAPTER 1

Oracle Power Objects—Let's Get Started

Welcome to the world of Oracle Power Objects. Oracle Power Objects is a development tool specifically designed to allow you to rapidly create robust client/server applications that can run on a variety of operating systems. In the first part of this book, you will learn about Power Objects and create your first application—all within your first hour of work. Let's get started.

Welcome to Power Objects

In this section, you will learn a little about Oracle Power Objects as a product. You will be introduced to the Oracle Power Objects working environment to make sure that you are ready to start developing your first application.

Oracle Power Objects is a unique development tool. Oracle Power Objects gives developers an enormous amount of default functionality that automatically implements the interaction between a client application and server data. You can create applications that can insert, update and delete data, as well as allow you to automatically define simple selection criteria for data retrieval—all by merely dragging and dropping objects (and with no code!). At the same time, Oracle Power Objects gives you a powerful graphical development environment that allows you to easily design and implement user-driven applications across a variety of client platforms. Oracle Power Objects includes a rich procedural language, Oracle Basic, which is based on standard BASIC and allows you to implement virtually any type of functionality in your application. Finally, Oracle Power Objects gives you the ability to use the power of object-oriented programming techniques to create your own object classes to use as building blocks in creating applications.

Oracle Power Objects delivers a unique combination of ease-of-use and power unequaled among existing development tools.

What Is Oracle Power Objects?

Oracle Power Objects is a complete application development environment developed by Oracle Corporation (makers of Oracle, the leading relational database in the world). Oracle Power Objects was created to give developers an easy, graphical tool to create powerful client/server applications. The Oracle Power Objects environment includes tools and methods to create, modify, and manage application components such as applications, forms, and reports. With it, you can create libraries of resources that can be used by many different applications, such as bitmaps and shared forms.

Oracle Power Objects is built around the power of *object orientation*. Object orientation allows a developer to create object *classes* that can be used in many different applications. Object classes can *inherit* capabilities from other object classes. Object inheritance gives developers the power to use existing classes as building blocks for their applications, while easily extending the capabilities of the classes to meet their specific requirements. Objects and classes will be discussed in depth in Chapter 5 of this book, but you do not have to understand objects to start creating powerful applications.

Prerequisites for Your First Application

In order to build the applications in this book, you must have first installed the complete Oracle Power Objects product. If you have not yet installed Oracle Power Objects, you should install it now with the CD included with this book.

You should also have already created the demonstration database that comes with Oracle Power Objects. If you have not yet done this, please see the instructions that come with Oracle Power Objects for details on creating a sample database with the MLBUILD.DMP file included.

You can create all of the applications in this book to run against an Oracle database, a Personal Oracle database, or with a Blaze database. Blaze is the name of the stand-alone database that is included with Oracle Power Objects. Applications built with Oracle Power Objects can run against any database that can be accessed with the standard database drivers included with Oracle Power Objects, or with any ODBC database.

Once you have completed installing Oracle Power Objects and your sample database, you are ready to begin exploring its uses.

Exploring Oracle Power Objects

Let's start by getting familiar with the Oracle Power Objects development environment.

To bring up Oracle Power Objects, double-click on the Oracle Power Objects Designer icon

in the Oracle Power Objects program group. The Oracle Power Objects Designer Environment, shown in Figure 1-1, will open.

The Oracle Power Objects Designer Environment, which will be referred to as simply Oracle Power Objects, is a truly graphical environment. At the top of the main window panel is a *Menu bar*. The Menu bar contains selections that lead to five different drop-down menus, described here.

The File Menu
The File menu controls how Oracle Power Objects handles various types of files. Menu choices in the File menu include *New Application*, *New Library*, and *New*

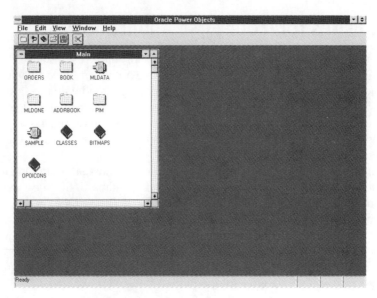

FIGURE 1-1. *The Oracle Power Objects environment*

Session, which create new objects; *Open* and *Close*, which open existing object files and close already open files; *Save* and *Save As*, which allow you to save your work or save your work in another format; *Print*, *Print Setup*, and *Print Preview*, which control output to the printer; *Read from File* and *Write to File*, which allow you to read and write forms, classes, and objects to and from a binary file format; *Import BMP* and *Export BMP*, which allow you to bring bitmaps into Oracle Power Objects and save bitmaps from Oracle Power Objects to .BMP files; and *Exit*, which will close Oracle Power Objects.

The Edit Menu
The Edit menu controls editing within Oracle Power Objects. The first two menu choices, *Undo* and *Redo*, allow you to undo your last action or to redo your last undo. These menu choices will also give a description of your last action, such as *Undo move*, or indicate that you *Can't Undo* your last action. The menu choices *Cut*, *Copy*, and *Paste* work with the Windows clipboard. The menu choices *Paste Special* and *Insert Object* give you the ability to work with OLE objects. The *Select All* menu choice gives you a shortcut to selecting all of the objects in the active window. There may also be other menu choices in the Edit menu, depending on what you are doing in Oracle Power Objects.

The View Menu

The View menu controls what is displayed in Oracle Power Objects. You can always choose to view or hide the *Toolbar, Status Line*, and the *User Properties* dialog box by clicking on the appropriate menu choice. The menu choice will be checked if the object is already visible. There may be other menu choices in the View menu, depending on what you are doing in Oracle Power Objects.

The Window Menu

The Window menu controls how the *child windows* (all open windows in the OPO multiple document interface window) are displayed. You can create a *New Window*, arrange the existing windows in Oracle Power Objects with the *Cascade* or *Tile* menu choices, or *Arrange Icons* in an Oracle Power Objects window with icons. The Window menu also contains a list of all existing windows—you can bring any of these windows to the foreground by selecting the name in the Window menu.

The Help Menu

The Help menu controls the Windows help system. You can call up the *Contents* of the Oracle Power Objects help system or get help on *Using Help* with the appropriate menu choices. The menu choice *About Power Objects* will give you information about the version of Oracle Power Objects you are currently running.

Beneath the Menu bar is the Oracle Power Objects *toolbar*. The toolbar contains buttons that you can use as shortcuts for commonly used actions. The toolbar will dynamically change to reflect the particular task you are doing in Oracle Power Objects. When you start Oracle Power Objects, the toolbar contains six buttons:

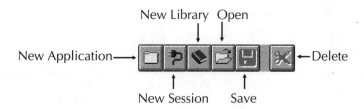

- The New Application button will create a new Oracle Power Objects application.

- The New Session button will create a new Oracle Power Objects database session.

■ The New Library button will create a new Oracle Power Objects library.

■ The Open button will open an existing Oracle Power Object application, class, or library.

■ The Save button will save any changes to the currently active window. This button will only be enabled when the active window has been changed since it has been opened.

■ The Delete button will delete the currently selected object. Whenever you are going to delete an object, Oracle Power Objects will prompt you to confirm that you want to delete the object, since a deletion cannot be reversed.

You can execute all of the functionality triggered by the buttons in the Oracle Power Objects toolbar by using menu choices from the File menu. You can hide the Oracle Power Objects toolbar by unchecking the Toolbar menu choice in the View menu. You might want to do this if you would like a little more screen real estate for your development environment. You will learn how to create toolbars for your own application in Chapter 4.

At the bottom of the Oracle Power Objects environment is a *Status bar,* shown here. Oracle Power Objects use the Status bar to give you messages about its own operations or brief help messages about the objects selected by your mouse movements. The Status bar also contains indicators for CAPS LOCK, NUM LOCK, etc. You can create your own custom Status bar for your Oracle Power Objects applications. You can also hide the Status bar by unchecking the Status line menu chioce in the View menu.

Ready		CAPS	NUMLK	SCRL

Oracle Power Objects is a multiple document interface (MDI) environment. You can have many child windows open within the Oracle Power Objects MDI framework. You can bring different child windows to the foreground or change the arrangement of the child windows with the Windows menu in the Menu bar. You can also maximize, minimize, and resize every child window. When you minimize a child window, the child window becomes an icon at the bottom of the Oracle Power Objects environment.

When you start Oracle Power Objects, a single child window, titled *Main,* is created. The Main window contains several different types of file object icons:

ORDERS   SAMPLE   CLASSES

The icons in the Main window are referred to as *file objects* because each of these objects is stored in a separate operating system file. The folder icon (left) represents an Oracle Power Objects *application*. An application consists of forms, bitmaps, classes, and reports that make up a complete application system. You will be creating your own application in the next few minutes.

The plug icon (center) represents an Oracle Power Objects *session*. An Oracle Power Objects session represents a conversation between an Oracle Power Objects application and a database. The session contains information, such as a user name, a password, and an address of a local or network database, that enables Oracle Power Objects to make a connection to a database, along with different information that can shape the way the database conversation takes place. You will be using a session to connect your application to a database. You can use a single session to provide connection information to one or more applications, and you can use one or more sessions in an application. Using multiple sessions in an application can affect how you will handle database transactions, which we will be discussing in Chapter 8 of this book.

The book icon (right) represents an Oracle Power Objects *library*. A library is a collection of bitmaps or Oracle Power Object classes that can be used in many different applications. Using a library for bitmaps or classes can simplify your maintenance tasks, since you can change an object in a library and all applications that use that object will also change. You will learn more about libraries and classes in Chapter 5 of this book.

When you create a new application, session, or library, an icon is placed in the Main window. When you start Oracle Power Objects, it reads an initialization file that lists the icons that were in the Main window when you closed Oracle Power Objects the last time. If you wish to remove a particular icon from the Main window, select the icon and click on the Delete button in the toolbar. You will remove the icon from the Main window, but the file the icon represented will not be deleted. You can open the file at a later time if you wish with the Open menu choice in the File menu.

Your First Application

Now that you are familiar with the Oracle Power Objects environment, you are ready to build your first application. In this section, you will

- Create an application
- Create a form
- Add the ability to read, select, update, insert, and delete rows on the form

- Enhance the appearance of the form's titles, fonts, colors, and backgrounds
- Add a master-detail relationship to the form

Of course, you will also get familiar with using Oracle Power Objects as you create your first application. You will be able to implement all of this functionality without writing a single line of code! In later sections, we will improve the appearance and functionality of the application, and extend the database access to handle a master-detail relationship.

Creating Your Application

You must start your development process by creating an application folder, which will contain all of the components of your application.

Creating an Application Folder

You can create a new application folder by using the New Application menu choice in the File menu, or by clicking on the button on the left of the toolbar that creates a new application. Once you have done one of these things, you will be presented with a standard file creation dialog box. The dialog box will prompt you for the name of your Oracle Power Objects application file, which must follow the standard naming restrictions of your environment and have a file extension of .POA. If you would like your application to follow the example in this book, you should give your application the name of "ORDERS.POA."

After you give your application a name, Oracle Power Objects will automatically create a window that represents your application and a Properties sheet window for the application, shown here:

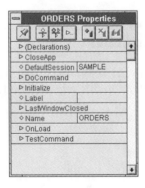

Every object in Oracle Power Objects, including applications, sessions, and individual objects in an application, has a Properties sheet. The Properties sheet contains a list of the *properties* of the objects, which are values that are used to control the activities of the object, and *methods*, which are functions that affect the object. Properties are preceded by a diamond shape, while methods are preceded by an arrow. You will learn more about the Properties sheet, properties, and methods as we build our application, and much more about these subjects in Chapter 2. You will not have to modify many of the values on the Properties sheet for your application.

Creating a Form

Once you have created an application, you can start creating objects in the application. You will notice that there are some additional buttons in the toolbar, shown here. You can create your first form window by clicking on the Form button shown on this toolbar:

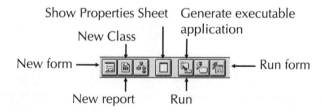

Oracle Power Objects will create a new window that contains the window you have just created in Design mode and change the Properties sheet to display the methods and properties of your newly created form, which is now the active object. Your first form window is shown in Figure 1-2.

Oracle Power Objects gives a default name (frmOrders) to your Form window. It is helpful if you give the objects you create in Oracle Power Objects meaningful names, since you will be using these names whenever the objects are referenced by other objects. Most objects in Oracle Power Objects also have a label. The name of an object is used to identify the object in the application. When you are writing Oracle Basic code, the name of the form identifies the form and is often necessary to qualify the identification of objects in the form. An object's label is used as a means of displaying an identifier for some Oracle Power Objects; for instance, the label of a Form window appears in the title bar of the Form window when the form is running, while the label of a radio button object appears next to the radio button.

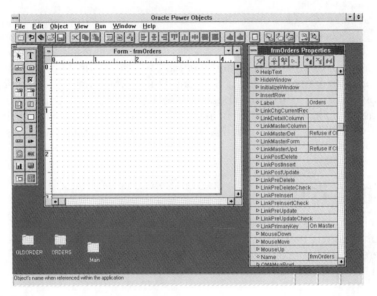

FIGURE 1-2. *Your first Form window*

■ Scroll to the Name property in the Properties sheet. Click in the data entry space to the right of the Name property label, which will highlight the entire value for the Name property. Delete the default value and enter 'frmOrders'. Press either the ENTER key or the ESC key to leave edit mode.

You should use a convention to name your objects, such as placing the 'frm' prefix in front of each of your forms, since you will be using that name in any code that you write that accesses the object.

■ Scroll to the Label property in the form's Property sheet. Change the label of the form to 'Orders'.

You can use a more understandable label for objects, since the application user will see the label.

You do not have to give your form the name and label of 'Orders', but all of the examples in this book will use this name for the form. It is helpful to give an object a similar name and label, since it will help in identifying objects in the form; but, since object names do not allow spaces, you may have to have some differences in your naming schemes.

The Tool Palette

Whenever your active window contains a form in Design mode, the Oracle Power Objects *Tool palette* is visible:

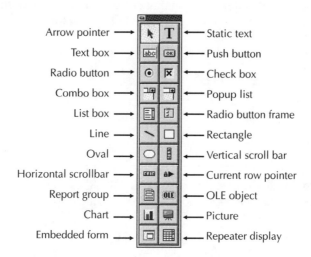

Arrow pointer ⟶ ◄ Static text
Text box ⟶ ◄ Push button
Radio button ⟶ ◄ Check box
Combo box ⟶ ◄ Popup list
List box ⟶ ◄ Radio button frame
Line ⟶ ◄ Rectangle
Oval ⟶ ◄ Vertical scroll bar
Horizontal scrollbar ⟶ ◄ Current row pointer
Report group ⟶ ◄ OLE object
Chart ⟶ ◄ Picture
Embedded form ⟶ ◄ Repeater display

   The Tool palette contains a number of buttons with icons that represent the objects that you can use in a form. The type of object that each button represents is displayed in the Status bar when you position the mouse over the button. When you click on one of the buttons, your mouse cursor changes into the icon on the button, and you can add objects to your form by clicking the mouse in the form where you want the object to appear. You can return the mouse cursor to the pointer tool by clicking on the pointer icon, which is in the upper-left corner of the Tool palette. You will learn more about the objects in the Tool palette as you build your application.

TIP
You can move the toolbar by clicking on the heading at the top of the Tool palette, holding down the mouse button, and dragging the Tool palette to a new location. The Tool palette will always be the "top" object in the Oracle Power Objects environment, so you may wish to hide it at times to make it easier to navigate. You can hide the Tool palette by clicking on the small box at the upper-left corner of the Tool palette. You can bring the Tool palette back by clicking on the Tool palette menu choice in the View menu of the main Menu bar.

Connecting to Your Database

You have created the first form for your application. In order to add data access capabilities to your form, you must first create a connection to your database. For this, you will use the ORDERSES session that came with the code for this book. Please refer to Appendix A for information about obtaining this code.

1. Click on the Main window to bring it to the foreground.

2. Click on the ORDERSES session icon:

ORDERSES

Clicking on the session icon will tell Oracle Power Objects to establish a connection to the database specified in the ORDERSES session. If you get an error when you attempt to establish a session, refer to the following table for potential causes and solutions.

Error	Solution
Oracle not running	Start your version of Personal Oracle or your networked version of Oracle.
Database not found	The DesignConnect property of the ORDERSES session contains an incorrect database name. Refer to your Oracle Power Objects documentation for details.
Invalid user/password— logon denied	The DesignConnect property of the ORDERSES session contains an incorrect user name or password. Refer to your Oracle Power Objects documentation for details.

Once you have successfully connected to the database through the ORDERSES session, the icon representing the ORDERSES session will change to show the power cord plugged into the database schematic and the ORDERSES window will fill with a series of icons that represent the database objects in the database, as shown in the next illustration.

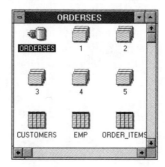

Database Object Types

There are four basic types of objects in a database, the icons of which are shown here:

A *table* (the first icon shown) is the basic structure in a database for holding data. A database table can contain many different pieces of information in its *columns*. You will be using the data in tables and columns as you create your application.

The Sequence icon (second from the left) represents a special type of object called a *sequence*. A sequence is a means by which a database can deliver unique sequential numbers to applications. When an application asks for a value from a sequence, the database gives the application an integer that is one greater than the last sequence delivered by the object. Oracle and Blaze databases both support sequence objects, but some databases do not. Your application will use several sequences to assign unique identifiers to table entries.

The View icon (third from the left) represents a database *view*. A database view is an alternative way of seeing data in the database. A database view can contain columns from one or more tables and can limit the data in the view by selection criteria. You will not be using any views in the application you will be building, but you can learn more about views by consulting the documentation for your database server. Be aware that many databases limit your ability to insert or update data through a view.

The Index icon (fourth from the left) represents a database *index*. A database index is a structure attached to a table that provides rapid access to the data in the table. For instance, the ORDERS table may have an index on the ID column. For more information on indexes and their use, please refer to the documentation for your database.

■   Double-click on the ORDERS table.

After you double-click on the ORDERS table icon, Oracle Power Objects will open the Table Description window with the descriptions of all of the columns in the table.

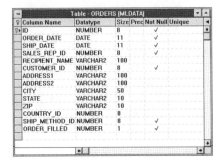

Each column has a number of attributes, such as the data type of the column, the size of the column, the precision of numeric columns, whether a column allows missing (or null) values, and whether the value in a column must be unique. You can see a small arrowhead that points toward the center of the table description window on the right side of the table window, just below the resizing buttons in the upper-right corner. If you click on this button, the table window will only show the column names and data types.

■   Click on the Run button in the toolbar to see the data in the ORDERS table.

Oracle Power Objects gives you an easy way to verify the data in a database table. You may have noticed that some new buttons appeared in the toolbar when you opened the ORDERSES session. The Run button will allow you to view the data from the table in the active window.

TIP

When you position your cursor on one of the Oracle Power Objects buttons, a single-line description of the button appears in the status line.

When you click on the Run button, Oracle Power Objects will retrieve data from the ORDERS table and display it to you in a Table window, similar to the one shown in Figure 1-3.

You could modify data in this table by simply editing the data in any cell in the table, but this is not recommended as a general practice since the data window in the session object does not gracefully handle any integrity constraints imposed by the database server.

- Click on the Stop button in the toolbar or close the data window to return to the table description.

If you have modified any of the data in the data window, you will be prompted by Oracle Power Objects to either save or discard the changes you have made to the database.

Adding Data Access to Your Form

When you return to the table description window, you are ready to add data fields, labels, and data access to your form in a single action.

- Select the columns you wish to display in your form by clicking the selection box on the left-hand side of the table description window.

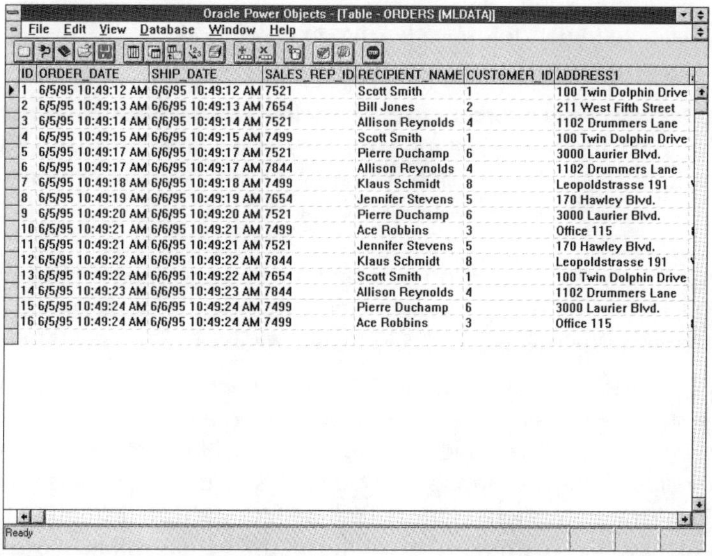

ID	ORDER_DATE	SHIP_DATE	SALES_REP_ID	RECIPIENT_NAME	CUSTOMER_ID	ADDRESS1
1	6/5/95 10:49:12 AM	6/6/95 10:49:12 AM	7521	Scott Smith	1	100 Twin Dolphin Drive
2	6/5/95 10:49:13 AM	6/6/95 10:49:13 AM	7654	Bill Jones	2	211 West Fifth Street
3	6/5/95 10:49:14 AM	6/6/95 10:49:14 AM	7521	Allison Reynolds	4	1102 Drummers Lane
4	6/5/95 10:49:15 AM	6/6/95 10:49:15 AM	7499	Scott Smith	1	100 Twin Dolphin Drive
5	6/5/95 10:49:17 AM	6/6/95 10:49:17 AM	7521	Pierre Duchamp	6	3000 Laurier Blvd.
6	6/5/95 10:49:17 AM	6/6/95 10:49:17 AM	7844	Allison Reynolds	4	1102 Drummers Lane
7	6/5/95 10:49:18 AM	6/6/95 10:49:18 AM	7499	Klaus Schmidt	8	Leopoldstrasse 191
8	6/5/95 10:49:19 AM	6/6/95 10:49:19 AM	7654	Jennifer Stevens	5	170 Hawley Blvd.
9	6/5/95 10:49:20 AM	6/6/95 10:49:20 AM	7521	Pierre Duchamp	6	3000 Laurier Blvd.
10	6/5/95 10:49:21 AM	6/6/95 10:49:21 AM	7499	Ace Robbins	3	Office 115
11	6/5/95 10:49:21 AM	6/6/95 10:49:21 AM	7521	Jennifer Stevens	5	170 Hawley Blvd.
12	6/5/95 10:49:22 AM	6/6/95 10:49:22 AM	7844	Klaus Schmidt	8	Leopoldstrasse 191
13	6/5/95 10:49:22 AM	6/6/95 10:49:22 AM	7654	Scott Smith	1	100 Twin Dolphin Drive
14	6/5/95 10:49:23 AM	6/6/95 10:49:23 AM	7844	Allison Reynolds	4	1102 Drummers Lane
15	6/5/95 10:49:24 AM	6/6/95 10:49:24 AM	7499	Pierre Duchamp	6	3000 Laurier Blvd.
16	6/5/95 10:49:24 AM	6/6/95 10:49:24 AM	7499	Ace Robbins	3	Office 115

FIGURE 1-3. *Data in the ORDERS table*

You can select multiple columns for your form by holding down the CTRL key and clicking on multiple columns. The first form of our Orders application will use the following columns from the ORDERS table:

```
ID
SALES_REP_ID
RECIPIENT_NAME
CUSTOMER_ID
ADDRESS1
ADDRESS2
CITY
STATE
ZIP
COUNTRY_ID
```

You can also select the consecutive columns from the list of columns by clicking first on the ID column, holding down the CTRL key, and then clicking on the selection box for SALES_REP_ID and holding down the mouse button as you drag the mouse down the selection box list to the COUNTRY_ID field. You can also select a number of consecutive columns by clicking on the first column and then holding down the SHIFT key when you click on the last. For the first step of our application, we will not have to use the SHIP_DATE, ORDER_DATE, or SHIP_METHOD_ID column.

■   Activate the Orders form by clicking on its window.

This will bring the window with the Orders form to the foreground. Move the form toward the lower-right corner of your Oracle Power Objects workspace, since you will have to be able to see it at the same time as the table description window for the ORDERS table for the next step. You may have to resize the Property sheet in order to have enough room in your work area.

■   Click on any of the selection boxes for the columns selected in the ORDERS table and hold down the mouse button. Drag the mouse to the upper-left corner of the Orders form and release the mouse button.

When you release the mouse button, Oracle Power Objects will put a data field object and a static text object on your form for each column you had selected in the table description window. Oracle Power Objects will give the static label the name of the data column and arrange the data fields by default. Oracle Power Objects will use the system font as the default font for the data fields and static text objects. The spot where you have released the mouse button will be the upper-left corner of the block of data fields.

Oracle Power Objects will also automatically set the RecordSource property of the form to the ORDERS table and the RecSrcSession property of the table to ORDERSES. (The RecordSource property indicates which table the form will access and the RecSrcSession property indicates the session to use to access the RecordSource table.) The RecordSource property is available for any *container* object, which is an object that can contain other objects. When Oracle Power Objects interacts with a database, it uses the session of the container form to connect to the database and uses the RecordSource property of the container form to determine the table or view that the objects in the container refer to.

NOTE
You may have released the mouse button toward the middle of the form. When the data fields are first dropped onto the form, they are all selected by default, so you can move the entire block of data fields by clicking on any one of them and holding the mouse button down as you drag them to the desired position.

Don't worry if your form is not as beautiful as you would like at first. You will learn how to easily enhance the appearance of your form later in this chapter.

■   Close the table description window for ORDERS.

Once you have created the data fields in your form, you will not need to use the table description window for ORDERS any more for the time being, so you can close the window. When you dragged the column names to your form, Oracle Power Objects automatically set the RecSrcSession property of the form to ORDERSES, so the session will be automatically used whenever the frmOrders form is active.

■   Resize your form to hold the data fields.

You may find that your form is not big enough to hold all of the data fields. You can resize your form by moving the mouse to one of the edges of the form. When the mouse is over one of the edges of the form, the pointer will change into an arrow pointing in the directions that you can resize your form. When the mouse pointer changes into an arrow, click the mouse button and hold it as you drag to resize your form.

■   Select a horizontal scroll bar from the Tool palette. Drop the scroll bar into the Orders form.

You have created data field objects for all of the columns you will need in your initial form, but you still need a way to navigate through the rows in the table. You can add data navigation to your basic form by adding a scroll bar to the form. You can resize the scroll bar to any length or width. Notice how the scroll buttons and scroll bar automatically resize themselves as you resize the object, giving you a choice of different styles of scroll bar. You can also make a horizontal scroll bar into a vertical scroll bar by grabbing one of the corners of the scroll bar and dragging it to give the scroll bar a vertical orientation.

When you add a scroll bar to your application, Oracle Power Objects automatically sets the ScrollObj property of the scroll bar to the Name property of the form. This enables the scroll bar object to scroll through the rows of the *recordset* associated with the session associated with the form. You will learn more about recordsets in Chapter 8.

■   Save your work by clicking on the Save button in the toolbar.

You may have noticed that when you made changes to your application, the Save button was enabled. You can also save your work with the Save menu choice in the File menu. It never hurts to occasionally save the work you have done. Your form, at this point, should look like this:

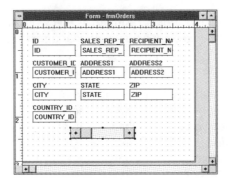

Believe it or not, you have already created a functional application that will allow you to read, navigate through, modify, insert, and delete data, or even use selection criteria on the data without writing a single line of code. In the next section, you will run your application and explore the default functionality.

Running Your Application

To appreciate the power of Oracle Power Objects, you can run your application and see all of the functionality that has been automatically built into your form.

■   Click on the Run button in the toolbar to run your application.

When you click on the Run button, you create and run a version of the active application. Oracle Power Objects will create a connection between your application and the database according to the specified ORDERSES session properties and retrieve the first row of data into your form.

■   Use the scroll bar to navigate through the rows in the database table.

You can scroll forward and backward through your rows by dragging the scroll bar handle in the scroll bar, by clicking on the buttons at either end of the scroll bar, which will retrieve the next or previous row, or by clicking in the scroll bar to either side of the scroll bar handle. This will retrieve the next or previous page of records. Scroll bar navigation will be discussed in depth in Chapter 6 of this book.

■   Click on the QBF button, shown below, to bring up the Query by Form window. Enter the number '7499' in the SALES_REP_ID field. Click on the Apply Conditions button to select rows that meet the selection criteria. Click on your original form to scroll through the selected rows.

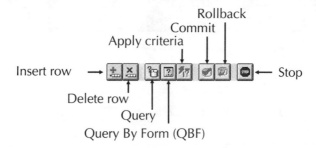

The QBF form looks like the form you have designed, with the static text fields being disabled, as shown in Figure 1-4. You can add selection criteria to any object on the QBF form. The QBF form assumes that any values you list are to be used as equivalents unless otherwise indicated. For instance, entering the value '7499' in the SALES_REP_ID field will create a selection where only those rows with the SALES_REP_ID = 7499 are selected. If you wanted to get all rows where the SALES_REP_ID was greater than 7499, you would enter '> 7499' in the SALES_REP_ID QBF data field. Conditions on different data fields are compounded with **AND**; in other words, a row would have to meet the criteria specified for all data fields in the QBF form to be selected. For more details on the QBF capabilities of applications built with Oracle Power Objects, please refer to the Oracle Power Objects online help.

You will notice that the QBF form remains "on top" of the standard form even after you have queried the database. You can use the Window menu in the Oracle Power Objects Menu bar to easily select the active window as your standard form.

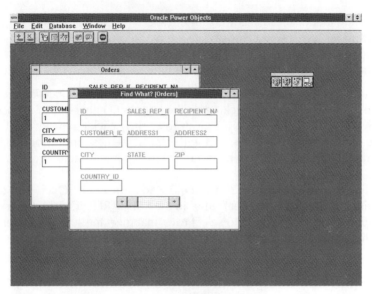

FIGURE 1-4. *Your application with QBF form*

■ Click on the Query button in the toolbar to retrieve rows without the selection criteria.

When you click on the Query button or choose the Query App menu choice from the Database menu, your Oracle Power Objects application requeries the database without the selection criteria described in the QBF form. The selection criteria remain in the QBF form, so you can requery the database with the same query criteria by simply clicking on the Apply Criteria button.

■ Modify the name of a customer by clicking in the RECIPIENT_NAME data field.

By default, all of the data fields in your form allow user modification, although you can change this by changing the properties of a data field, as we will discuss later in the book. Notice that when you make any changes in a form, the Insert and Rollback buttons in the toolbar are automatically enabled.

■ Restore the data to its original state by clicking on the Rollback button in the toolbar.

Any changes that you have made to data in your application have only been made in the copies of the data that are being used by the application, not in the data on the server. In order to apply the modifications you have made in an application, you must either commit the changes by using the Commit button in the toolbar or remove the modifications by clicking on the Rollback button.

- Insert a row into the database by clicking on the Insert button in the toolbar. Cancel the insertion by clicking on the Rollback button.

- Scroll to the end of the rows by moving the scroll bar all the way to the right. Insert a new row into the database by entering data into the "empty" row at the end of the scroll range. Cancel the insertion by clicking on the Rollback button.

By default, Oracle Power Objects give you an "extra" blank row at the end of your scroll range that can be used to insert new data. You can easily modify your form to disable the appearance of this extra row, which we will learn about later in the book.

- Delete a row by clicking on the Delete button in the toolbar. Cancel the deletion by clicking on the Rollback button. Stop the application by clicking on the Stop button.

Throughout this chapter, you have been instructed to roll back any changes that you make to the database so that your database can remain "in sync" with the database examples used throughout this book. The way in which your application makes changes to the database has an enormous impact on the performance of your application, the performance of the database, and the correctness (or integrity) of your data. We will be looking at the issues surrounding database access at length in Chapter 8.

Enhancing Your Application

Your application was created with just a few mouse movements and contains a large amount of functionality. But a good client/server application not only performs effectively, but looks good. You will dramatically improve the appearance of your basic application in the next section.

Rearranging the Data Fields

You have been able to rapidly create an application with a great deal of functionality built into it. But the application is not very attractive, and you know that your users want something pretty! This section will show you how to change your drab-but-powerful application into a thing of beauty.

Changing the Placement of Objects

The first step to a beautiful form is to change the placement of the data fields and labels in your form. Start by enlarging your form. You will need real estate on the form to rearrange the objects attractively.

■ Drag the sides of the form until it is 5 inches wide and 3 1/2 inches high.

The Oracle Power Objects Designer Environment allows you to easily see the size of the form by referencing the rulers along the top and left sides of the form design environment.

TIP
The Properties sheet appears on top of all objects in the Oracle Power Objects environment except the Tool palette. You can close the Properties sheet by clicking on the System menu box in the upper-left corner of the sheet and selecting the Close menu choice, or you could use the ALT-F4 key combination under Windows while the sheet is active. You can redisplay the Properties sheet by clicking on the Property Sheet button in the toolbar.

■ Move the scroll bar to the bottom of the form. Select the scroll bar by clicking on it, and then move it by placing the mouse over the selected scroll bar, holding down on the mouse button, and dragging the scroll bar to a new location.

■ Select the COUNTRY_ID data field by clicking on it. Hold down the SHIFT key and also select the COUNTRY_ID static text object by clicking on it. Grab both of the objects and drag them to the lower-right corner of the form, leaving room on their left for the CITY, STATE, and ZIP objects.

You can select any number of objects together by holding down the SHIFT key and clicking on the objects. If you want to select a group of objects that are situated next to each other, the next step provides an even easier way to accomplish this.

■ Move the mouse to a space below the data field in the lower-left corner of the block of remaining data fields and above the scroll bar. Click on the mouse button and hold it down. As you continue to hold the button down and move the mouse, a dotted-line box will appear. Drag the mouse so that it covers parts of the CITY, STATE, and ZIP data fields and static text objects.

When you release the mouse button, all of the objects in your form that were completely or partially in the box will be selected, as shown in Figure 1-5. Move the selected objects down the form and to the right of the COUNTRY_ID data field and static text object.

■   Rearrange the rest of the fields on the form.

Don't worry about lining up the objects now. Oracle Power Objects gives you tools to align objects in your form, and you will be using those tools later in this section.

■   Select the ADDRESS2 data field and static text object and place them just above the lowest line of data fields.

■   Move the ADDRESS1 data field and static text object to position them just above the ADDRESS2 data field and label.

■   Select the RECIPIENT_NAME and CUSTOMER_ID data fields and static text objects and position them just above the ADDRESS1 data field and label.

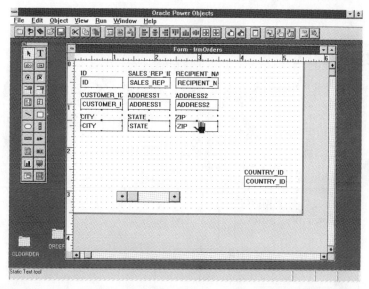

FIGURE 1-5.   *Selecting a group of objects with the selection rectangle*

When you have finished moving the objects, your form should look like this:

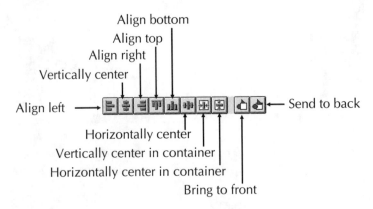

TIP
You may have noticed that when you position or size objects in a Form window, the objects automatically snap to a grid. This powerful feature of the Oracle Power Objects environment makes it easy for you to align objects in a form. If you would like to override the automatic grid alignment, simply hold down the CTRL key while you are placing or sizing an object.

Aligning Objects

Oracle Power Objects makes it easy for you to align objects in your forms. You will be able to align the leftmost objects in your form and each of the objects in a line by simply selecting the objects and making a single mouse click. The Alignment buttons in the toolbar are shown here:

Align bottom
Align top
Align right
Vertically center

Align left ───▶

Horizontally center
Vertically center in container
Horizontally center in container
Bring to front

─── Send to back

■ Select the ID, RECIPIENT_NAME, ADDRESS1, ADDRESS2, and CITY fields and static text labels. Click on the Align Left button in the toolbar to align the left edge of the selected objects.

The toolbar includes six different buttons to align objects and two buttons to center objects horizontally and vertically in your form. You can move the mouse over each button and the button's function will appear in the Status bar. The first object you select will serve as the guide to aligning the rest of the objects you select.

■ Select the CITY, STATE, ZIP, and COUNTRY_ID data fields in the bottom row. Click on the Vertically Center button in the toolbar to align the data fields. Follow the same procedure with the static text objects for the four data fields and the objects in the rows that contain the RECIPIENT_NAME and CUSTOMER_ID objects and the ID and SALES_REP_ID objects.

Changing the Data Field Labels

Now that the fields are arranged more nicely in the form, the data field labels seem to be even more misplaced. As mentioned earlier in this chapter, Oracle Power Objects will create a static text field label for each data field window dropped onto the form from a session and use, by default, the name of the database column. Many database column names use underscores instead of spaces, and many column names are totally in uppercase. To improve the appearance of your form, you will want to change the default labels that Oracle Power Objects created for you.

■ Click on the static text object above the CITY data field. Click on the text of the object to highlight the entire text of the label to enable editing of the label. Delete the entire label and enter 'City' for the label. To leave edit mode, press the ENTER key.

When you are editing the text of a static text object, you can move to the beginning of the text by pressing the ESC key and navigate around the text with the standard Windows arrow keys.

■ Click on the static text object above the STATE data field. Click in the field for the Label property for the object. Delete the existing label and enter a label of 'State'. You can leave edit mode for the property by pressing either the ENTER key or the ESC key.

You can change the label of a static text object either by editing the object directly in the form or by changing the property of the object.

■ Change the rest of the static text objects, using either method on the following labels:

COUNTRY_ID to 'Country'
ADDRESS1 to 'Address'
CUSTOMER_ID to 'Customer ID'
RECIPIENT_NAME to 'Recipient'
SALES_REP_ID to 'Sales Rep'
ID to 'Order ID'

You do not have to change the static text object above the ZIP data field. Since the ADDRESS2 data field is just the second part of the address, you can simply delete that static text object and adjust the position of the data fields on the form.

Changing the Size of Objects

By default, Oracle Power Objects creates all of the data field objects the same size. Since the data in the fields are different lengths, the form would appear more attractive if the data field objects were proportional to the data they will contain.

■ Run your application to get an idea of the best length for the data fields.

■ Adjust the size of the data fields:

■ Make the CITY data field larger.

■ Make the STATE data field smaller, since it will only contain 2 characters.

■ Make the ZIP data field smaller.

■ Make both ADDRESS data fields longer.

■ Make the RECIPIENT_NAME data field larger.

■ Make the CUSTOMER_ID data field smaller.

■ Make the ID data field smaller.

When you have completed modifying the static text objects and the data field object sizes, your form should look like the following illustration:

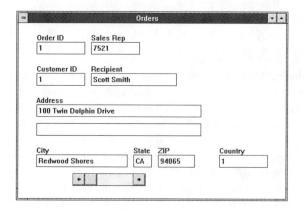

Your form now looks much more presentable. You will only need to add a few finishing touches to make it really good-looking.

Changing Fonts and Colors

You could improve the appearance of your form by displaying the static text objects with a nicer font than the default system font. Oracle Power Objects gives you the ability to change the properties of many objects at the same time.

■ Select all of the static text objects by clicking on each of the objects while holding down the SHIFT key. The Properties sheet, shown here, will change to display the properties shared by all the objects selected.

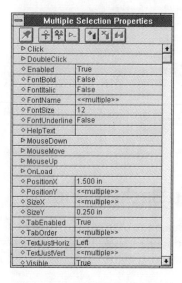

You could also choose all the objects on the form, but the sample application displayed in this book will leave the data field objects displayed with the default system font.

■ Click on the FontName property. A list box will open up below the property with the available fonts on your system. Change the font to a more "friendly" font by clicking on the name of the font of your choice. To closed the list box, click on the FontName property again.

You could double-click on the font name to select the font and close the list box in one action. If you want your application to look the same as the sample application, you should choose the Times New Roman TrueType font.

■ To make the static text objects a little more visible, change them to a bold font. Click on the value in the field to the right of the FontBold property. When you click on the value, it toggles from False to True.

■ To make the static text a little more noticeable, click on the ColorText property. A list box will open up with a selection of font colors. Select a different color and close the list box by double-clicking on the color.

We will be adding a gray background pattern to the form in the next section, so you might want to choose a contrasting color, such as dark blue, for the static text objects. When you have finished changing the font, highlights, and color of the static text objects, your form should look like this:

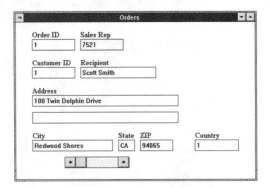

Adding a Bitmap Background

The final appearance enhancement for our form will be to change the form background from plain old white to a pattern. Oracle Power Objects will allow us to add a bitmap to the background of the form with a single drag-and-drop operation.

■ Click on the Main window to bring it to the foreground. Click on the BITMAPS library. Scroll to the bitmap labeled bmpCrystBG.

■ Grab the bmpCrystBG bitmap by clicking on it and holding down the mouse button. Drag the bitmap to a blank spot on your Orders form and release the mouse button.

This action will drop the bitmap onto the background of the Orders form in its normal size.

■ To tile the bitmap on the background of the form, click on the form background to change the Properties sheet. Click on the value for the BitmapTiled property to change the value to 'True'.

When you have completed this section of the chapter, your form should look like this:

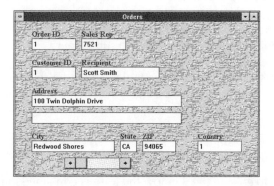

Run the form to see how much better your application looks. When you try to do a QBF, you can see that the QBF parameter form also looks a lot better.

You have made your form much more attractive, but you have not added any functionality to the form. You will be adding a master-detail relationship to your form in the next section.

Adding a Master-Detail Relationship to Your Form

Many applications use data from more than one table. The data from one table in an application is often related to the data in another table in an application. The most common type of relationship is the *master-detail* relationship. A master-detail relationship is a one-to-many relationship, where each member of the master table, such as the ORDERS table in our application, can have one or more related members of another table, such as the ORDER_LINES table. Tables in a master-detail relationship are usually linked by having a common column in both tables and linking on the value of the column.

For many development tools, handling a master-detail relationship in an application calls for a significant amount of coding. In Oracle Power Objects, you can add a master-detail relationship to a form with a few simple operations, as you will see in the final section of this chapter.

The Repeater Display

Oracle Power Objects provides a powerful control called a *repeater display* as a standard object. A repeater display, as the name implies, can display repeated occurrences of a set of objects that generally map to multiple related detail rows in a master-detail relationship. You define a repeater *panel* that will be repeated when the form containing the repeater display is run. You simply add the objects you wish to repeat to the *primary panel* at design time, and Oracle Power Objects will automatically populate the repeater display at run time.

You will use the repeater display to display the data in the detail table and link the retrieval of the rows of the detail table to a master row you have already placed in the form. You should start by enlarging your form to make room for the repeater display.

■ Enlarge the form until it is 5 1/8 inches tall by grabbing the bottom edge of the form and dragging it down.

You may have to enlarge the window the form is contained in to enlarge the form itself. If you drag the bottom edge of your form below the edge of the window that contains the form, the window will scroll down to accommodate the larger form. Remember that when you run the form, the Oracle Power Objects Designer Environment will disappear, which will give you more screen real estate to use for the form.

■ Select the repeater display button from the bottom-right corner of the Tool palette. Drop a repeater display into your form by clicking where you want the upper-left corner of the form and holding down the mouse button as you drag the lower-right corner of the form to its appropriate location. For this application, your repeater form should look like this:

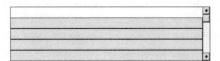

You will notice that the number of repeated panels in the repeater display automatically adjusts itself to fill the space of the repeater display. The top panel in the repeater display is white and referred to as the *primary panel*. You will place the objects you wish to have in each panel in the primary panel.

You can resize the primary panel to change the way the repeater display will display the repeated panels.

■ To resize the primary panel, click on the repeater display to select it, and then click on the primary panel to select it. When the primary panel is selected, you can grab one of the handles on the sides and at the corners of the panel.

The repeated panels will change in size to reflect the size of the primary panel. If you reduce the width of the primary panel, Oracle Power Objects will automatically create multiple panels in each row:

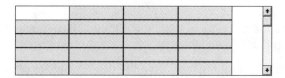

If you increase the height of the primary panel, Oracle Power Objects will automatically reduce the number of repeating panels:

Adding Data Access to the Repeater Display

You can now add data access to your repeater display. Adding data access to a repeater display is just as easy to do as adding data access to your basic form.

■ Open the ORDERSES session. If the session is not connected to the database, double-click on the ORDERSES icon to establish the connection.

■ Open the ORDER_ITEMS table by double-clicking on the ORDER_ITEMS table icon. Select the PRODUCT_ID, QUANTITY, and DISCOUNT columns from the ORDER_ITEMS table.

You will not have to worry about creating an ORDER_ID when you add new rows to the ORDER_ITEMS table. The ORDER_ID column is connected to a sequence object, which will automatically generate a unique number. The use of the sequence object will be further explained in Chapter 3.

■ Click on the selection box in the ORDER_ITEMS table and hold down the mouse button as you drag the columns to the primary panel of the repeater display. When you release the mouse button, Oracle Power Objects will automatically place data field objects into the primary panel. Your repeater display should now look like this:

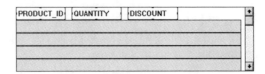

■ Run your application to see how the form you have created retrieves data from two different data tables.

You will notice that all of the rows from the detail table are retrieved when the form is first run and do not change when you move through the rows in the master table. In the next section, you will correct this situation.

NOTE
You will not be able to insert detail rows through your form just yet. You will also see that if you use the QBF capability of the form by specifying values for a detail row, all of the master rows will be retrieved, but only the detail rows that match the selection criteria will be displayed. You will change your form to allow insertions and more flexible QBF in Chapter 3.

To improve the appearance of your form, you might want to place some titles above the data field objects in the repeater display.

■ To add titles, click on the Text icon in the upper-right corner of the Tool palette and drop in a text title above the PRODUCT_ID data field object. Enter the text 'Product' for this static text object. Follow the same procedure for the QUANTITY and DISCOUNT data field objects.You might also want to set the TextJustVert property to Bottom to set the static text closer to the repeater display.

■ To improve the appearance of the data in the repeater display, select the QUANTITY data field in the primary panel by clicking on the object once to select the repeater display, a second time to choose the primary panel, and a third time to select the QUANTITY data field object. Scroll to the TextJustHoriz property and select Right to align the data in the center of the column. Follow the same procedure to center the data in the DISCOUNT data field.

Your form should now look like the one depicted in Figure 1-6. Don't be concerned that there is quite a bit of unused space in your repeater display. You will be adding objects to the primary panel to take up all the remaining space, and then some, in Chapter 3.

Linking Your Detail Row Retrieval to Your Master Row

You have added the ability to retrieve rows from a detail table to your form, but you have not linked the retrieval of the rows in the repeater display to the master row in the form. You can link the two tables together by modifying three properties of the repeater display.

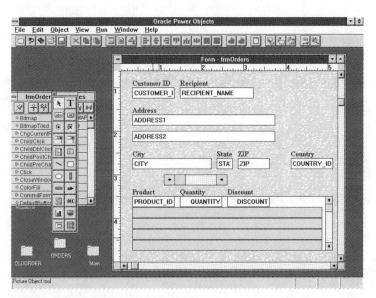

FIGURE 1-6.   *Your updated ORDER form*

■ Select the repeater display in your form. Go to the Properties sheet (shown here) for the repeater display and scroll to the area where the Link... properties are displayed. Make the value for the LinkMasterForm property the name of the master form, 'frmOrders'.

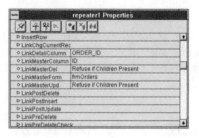

NOTE:

Names in Oracle Power Objects are not case sensitive, so you could enter 'frmOrders', 'FRMORDERS', or 'frmorders'—they would all work properly.

■ Make the value for the LinkMasterColumn the name of the column in the master table that will be used to establish the link, 'ID'.

The ID column in the ORDERS record is the identifying field for each order.

■ Make the value for the LinkDetailColumn the name of the column in the detail table that will be used to establish the link, 'ORDER_ID'.

In the detail table ORDER_LINES, the ORDER_ID column will contain the identifying order number for the member of the ORDERS table that represents the order that the ORDER_ITEMS row is associated with.

■ Run the form and see how your application will retrieve the correct ORDER_ITEMS for each ORDER.

Your completed form should look like the one shown in Figure 1-7.

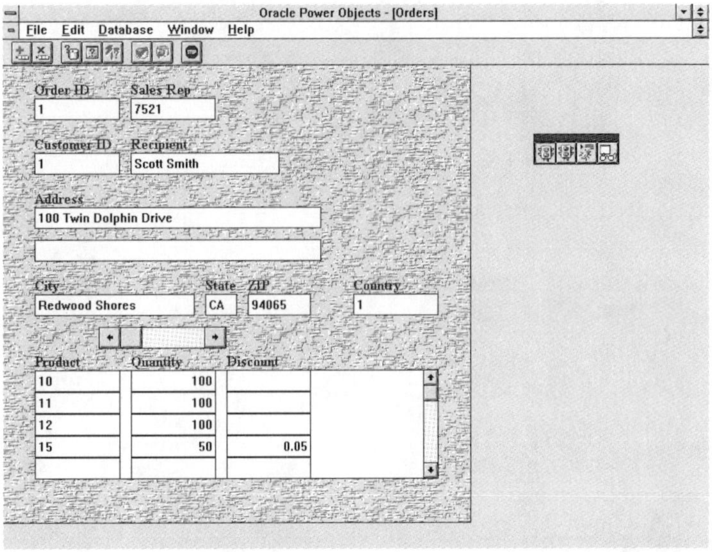

FIGURE 1-7. *Your completed form*

You have created an attractive master-detail form with complete Query-By-Form capabilities and the ability to insert, delete, and modify data. Your form is not yet complete. You would like to add the ability to display lookup texts, to limit the choices a user can make, to be able to properly add detail rows, and to query on the basis of the presence of a detail row value. You will be adding all of these features, and more, in Chapter 3 of this book. But before you can accomplish this, you will have to learn a little bit about the Oracle Power Objects programming language in Chapter 2.

CHAPTER 2

Introducing Oracle Basic

In the first chapter you have learned how to build your first form. You connected it to a database, and were able to inquire, add, update, and delete records. Most applications will require additional functionality. Oracle Basic is a language that allows you to extend your application's functionality; do specific processing with data; and add other features to your default application. In this chapter you will learn the fundamentals of programming in Oracle Basic and also how you can use Oracle Basic with Oracle Power Objects to enhance your application.

Oracle Basic is an ANSI-compliant version of the Basic language with extensions to handle data access. If you are familiar with any of the dialects of Basic—such as Visual Basic, Access Basic, VBA, or Quick Basic—you will feel instantly at home with Oracle Basic. If you are not familiar with Basic, then it might take you a little longer.

Your primary challenge will be to design the logic for your application, since Oracle Basic is fairly easy to learn. Chapters 3 through 11 of this book will focus on creating the appropriate logic for your application. This chapter will focus on the syntax and use of Oracle Basic. In this chapter, you will learn about

- Why, when, and where to use Oracle Basic
- Typographic and naming conventions
- Functions and subroutines
- Datatypes, variables, and database objects
- Controlling program flow
- Manipulating database objects
- Event processing
- Debugging Oracle Basic
- Run-time error handling

Why, When, and Where?

There are three major reasons for using Oracle Basic. These are

- Implementing business rules
- Performing complex calculations
- Customizing the user interface

Oracle Basic is a flexible and rich language that will give you the power you need to address these areas.

Implementing Business Rules

When you are building an application, there are many instances when you would have to do some special processing to guide the user, so that he or she can navigate the application without having to memorize a lot of rules. Some examples in an order entry system are

■ Ensuring that all orders are at least $10.

■ Ensuring that certain products are not shipped out of state.

■ Checking that the full nine-digit ZIP code is entered and giving a warning message to the user if it is not.

In design parlance, these are called business rules. Oracle Power Objects provides for several ways to implement these business rules. You can implement these types of rules either in the front end application or on the back end database server. The recommended procedure is to implement these types of rules in the application for the following reasons:

■ User will get immediate feedback since the validation can be done at field level.

■ Validation is kept off of the server, leaving the server to more important tasks that are specific to database functions.

Implementing business rules in the application reduces network traffic, thus improving overall performance.

Performing Complex Calculations

Every business function involves some calculations. Something as simple as computing the sales tax or a discount could involve an algorithm with several parts. Some statistical analysis problems involve intricate mathematical manipulations. You can use Oracle Basic to perform these calculations.

Customizing User Interface

The most obvious use for Oracle Basic is to customize the user interface so that users can intuitively navigate through the functions of the application. For example, certain data entry fields in a form could be disabled based on the user's security. The user could then look at the data, but could not modify it. You can easily implement customizations to your application's user interface with Oracle Basic.

Typographic and Naming Conventions

The following conventions are used for the code examples in this chapter.

■ Monospace is used for code examples such as variable names.

■ Bold monospace capital letters is used for Oracle Basic type declarations, standard commands, and standard functions, such as, **CONST**, **WHILE**, and **CURDIR**.

■ Italic monospace is used for items that are replaced, such as **Dim** *item* **As Integer.**

■ Bold italic monospace is used for reserved words that are replaced. For example, **Const** *item* **As** *datatype*, where *datatype* is replaced by the required Oracle Basic reserved word.

■ Optional elements are included in square brackets.

■ An ellipsis (...) is used to indicate code that is not shown.

Objects

The following sections will give an overview of objects in general and Oracle Power Objects in particular. The rest of the book will further explain objects in depth along with the related concepts. We will touch upon enough here so that the succeeding Oracle Basic concepts will make sense.

Figures 2-1 through 2-4 show the object hierarchy in Power Objects. There are three classes of objects at the highest level. They are

■ Application

■ Database session

■ Library

Each of the objects is by nature an instance of a class of objects. For example, when you create a table, you are creating an instance of the class of tables. Since it is part of a class of objects, the new instance will inherit all the properties and methods of the class from which it was created. Chapter 6 will examine object classes in depth.

Oracle Basic deals with application objects. It also interacts with the database objects via the Record Manager.

In Oracle Power Objects, there are two modes to an application object: design mode and run mode.

In the design mode, you are actually building the application by using Oracle Power Objects–provided components, as well as components you have built yourself. In the run mode, the application is executing, presenting the user with a set of screens to collect, add, modify, delete data, or run reports.

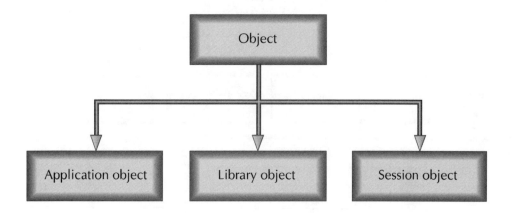

FIGURE 2-1.   *Object hierarchy*

At design time, you can edit or override the properties and methods of an object, as well as add new properties and methods. At run time, you can modify many of an object's properties.

You can define your own class in Oracle Power Objects, then add instances of this class to forms and reports. Generally, you create a user-defined class for a set of controls that you plan to reuse throughout an application.

Application Objects

In Oracle Power Objects, you develop forms in a designed window. Figure 2-2 shows the application objects available in Oracle Power Objects. Three of these objects—Form, Report, and Class—have their own designer windows. While in the designer window, several different types of objects can be placed on a form, a report, or a class. These objects are collectively called the designer objects.

Library Objects

Library objects are collections of bitmaps, forms, and classes that are available for general use. In a sense, they are like a dynamic link library (DLL) in the windows environment and a shared library in the Macintosh environment. The objects defined

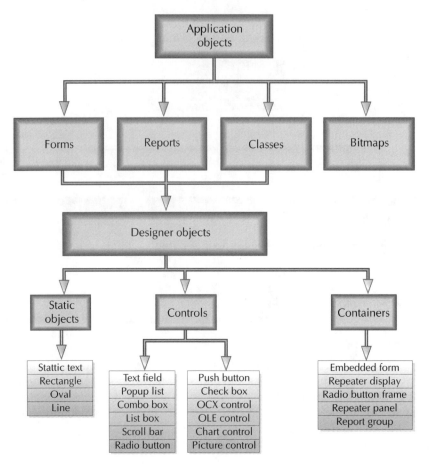

FIGURE 2-2. *Application objects*

in a library can be used by several applications. As in the case of a DLL or a shared library, an Oracle Power Objects library object cannot be run by itself. It can only be used in the context of an application. Figure 2-3 shows the library object hierarchy.

Session Objects

Session objects link the Oracle Power Objects front end application to the database. Session objects can access the tables, views, indices, and sequences that are stored and maintained in the database. Figure 2-4 shows the session objects and the database objects.

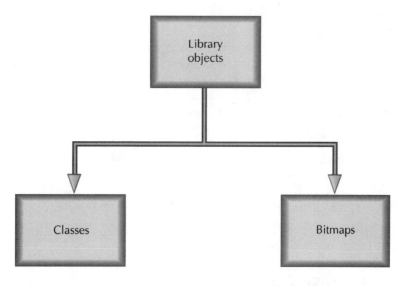

FIGURE 2-3. *Library objects*

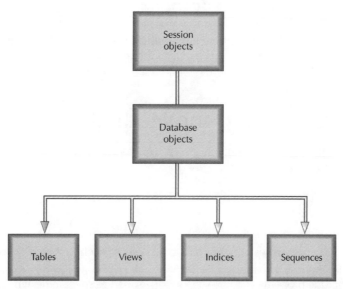

FIGURE 2-4. *Session objects*

Database Objects

Database objects are named structures stored in relational databases. Database objects can be accessed through database session objects, and are represented by icons in a database session window. In developing applications with Oracle Power Objects, you connect database objects with application objects. Linking a database object to a control or container in an application is called *binding*.

There are four types of database objects in Oracle Power Objects. They are

- Tables, which are the database objects that actually store data.

- Views, which are customized presentations of the data in one or more tables.

- Indexes, which provide fast access to individual data elements in a table.

- Sequences, which generate a series of integers that can be used to provide unique identifiers for the rows of a table.

Other Database Objects

Remote databases (such as Oracle7 Servers) can contain many additional types of objects—such as clusters, packages, snapshots, and roles. These database objects are frequently used to provide extra security or performance enhancements. To access these objects, you must execute Structured Query Language (SQL) commands using the Oracle Basic **EXEC SQL** command.

The properties and methods of database objects depend on the database engine in which they are stored. This is unlike the application objects that are created and stored by Oracle Power Objects. You cannot add properties or methods to database objects. Most of the properties of database objects cannot be changed.

Properties, Events, and Methods

Oracle Power Objects objects can have properties, respond to events, and execute logic through methods.

Properties

Properties are variables that are associated with an object. Every object has its own set of properties. Some properties are common to all objects, such as Name. Some properties are unique to certain objects, like the ConnectString property of a database session. Most of the properties can be seen in the Properties sheet in design mode (see Figure 2-5). There are, however, some that are not shown on the property sheet, such as the Container property, which is only available through Oracle Basic.

FIGURE 2-5.   *Properties sheet in design mode*

All properties have a DataType that corresponds to an Oracle Basic data type. You can set a property for an object at design time via the Properties sheet, or you can set it at run time using Oracle Basic code. Not all properties can be changed at run time.

Events

An event is an action that occurs on a particular object, which can respond to the event. For example, clicking on an object triggers the **Click( )** method for that particular object.

Events occur in one of the following three ways:

User Action
The user takes an action that the application recognizes, such as a mouse click.

Application
The application performs a task that it recognizes as an event, such as triggering the methods necessary for deleting master and detail records.

Environment
Something occurs in the environment that the application recognizes, such as an error returned from a remote server.

Methods

A method is a procedure that is executed in response to an event or by calling the method in Oracle Basic. Oracle Power Objects supports two types of methods. Standard methods are supplied by Oracle Power Objects, which often provides default processing for events that occur within an object's context. You can override the default processing of a method by placing Oracle Basic code in the method. Figure 2-6 illustrates the code that overrides the default processing for the **OnLoad( )**. Not all standard methods have default processing. For example, the **Click( )** method normally does nothing unless you add method code to it. If you need the default processing performed in addition to the custom code, you would include the statement

```
Inherited.Method_name()
```

in the code for the method. For example, the code:

```
Inherited.OnLoad()
```

will call the **OnLoad( )** method that was inherited from the base class. (You will learn more about object classes and inheritance in Chapters 5 and 6.)

In addition to standard methods, you can also add your own methods to any application object. User-defined methods never have any default processing associated with them; instead, you must write method code to define the action to be taken when triggered.

Events and Methods

Events trigger methods defined for an object. For example, when you tell the application to open a form, the event (loading the form into memory) automatically triggers several methods, such as the **Query( )** method, which queries records from a table or view to populate the form. Methods normally have default processing associated with them. To add functionality, you can attach your own code to the method.

Often, several methods call each other in sequence. Method-calling sequences are used throughout Oracle Power Objects for many common tasks. However, method code added to one method may prevent it from calling another method, unless the method code includes the statement Inherited.*Method_name*( ).

The names of many methods suggest the events that trigger them. For example, giving the application the command to open a window will trigger the **OpenWindow( )** method. This method, in turn, performs the processing necessary to load and display the form. For example, Figure 2-7 shows the Properties sheet for a form. Notice the method names. The method **ChildClick( )** is executed

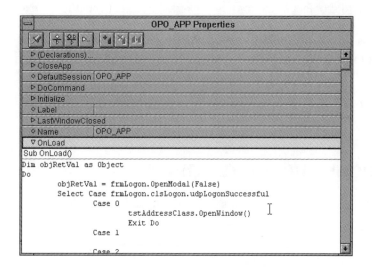

FIGURE 2-6. *Code to override default processing*

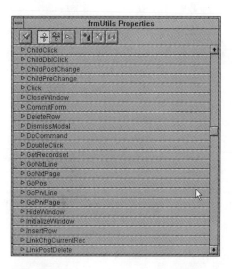

FIGURE 2-7. *Properties sheet for a form*

whenever a child object in the form is clicked. The **Click( )** method is executed when the mouse is clicked anywhere on the form where an object does not appear.

Methods can be called from other methods. The **CloseWindow( )** method is triggered whenever the user closes a form, and can also be called programmatically to close a form.

However, be careful not to confuse an event with a method. Although **OpenWindow( )** sounds like an event, it is in fact a method triggered by an event. Think of events as *actions* and methods as *reactions* to an event.

Functions and Subroutines

You can use functions and subroutines to implement the extended logic in your application.

Functions

A function is an Oracle Basic method that returns a value. You can define your own functions to use in your application. Before defining a function, you must declare it as part of an application. You can then write the Oracle Basic code that defines the function. All user-defined functions have the following components:

Component	Description
Name	A unique name used to call the function.
Arguments	Variables passed either by reference or by value when the function is called. You can have functions that do not require arguments.
Return value	A value returned from the function. Some variable in your Oracle Basic code must capture this value when you call the function.
Method code	The code that defines what the function does.

See Figure 2-8 for an example of a user-defined function. It shows the function definition for **udmStrStrip( )** and the method code defined for it.

Function Declarations

To declare a function, follow these steps:

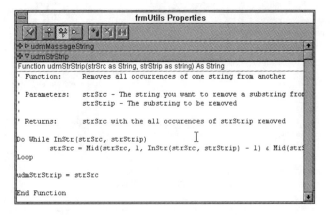

FIGURE 2-8. *Function definition for **udmStrStrip( )***

1. Open the User Properties window (See Figure 2-9).

2. Scroll to the bottom of the user properties table window.

3. On the blank line at the end of the list of user properties, enter the name of the new function in the Name column.

4. Select "Function" from the pop-up list in the Type column.

5. Select the data type for the return value in the Datatype column.

6. Enter any arguments for the function in the Arguments column.

Function Arguments

You can pass arguments to a function either by reference or by value. When you pass an argument by reference, any changes made to the variable while the function is executing affect all instances of the variable outside the function. In contrast, when you pass an argument by value, you merely pass the value assigned to the variable, not a reference to the variable itself. The function cannot change the value for a variable passed by value to a function.

Adding a Function to an Application

Before you can call a function, you must add it to your application. You can add a function to any application object from a class or form to an individual object.

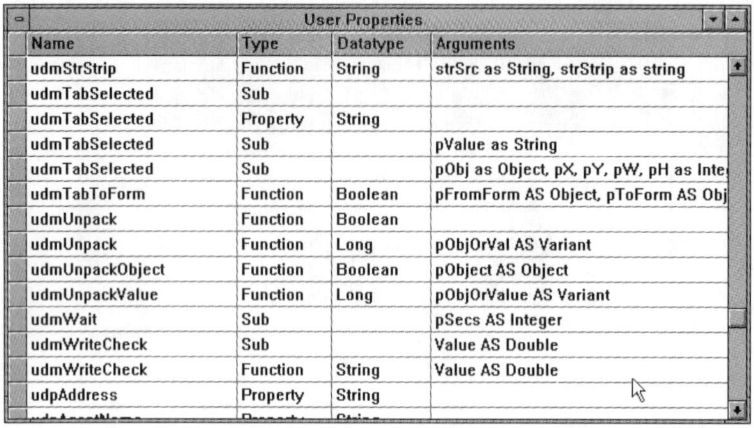

Name	Type	Datatype	Arguments
udmStrStrip	Function	String	strSrc as String, strStrip as string
udmTabSelected	Sub		
udmTabSelected	Property	String	
udmTabSelected	Sub		pValue as String
udmTabSelected	Sub		pObj as Object, pX, pY, pW, pH as Inte
udmTabToForm	Function	Boolean	pFromForm AS Object, pToForm AS Obj
udmUnpack	Function	Boolean	
udmUnpack	Function	Long	pObjOrVal AS Variant
udmUnpackObject	Function	Boolean	pObject AS Object
udmUnpackValue	Function	Long	pObjOrValue AS Variant
udmWait	Sub		pSecs AS Integer
udmWriteCheck	Sub		Value AS Double
udmWriteCheck	Function	String	Value AS Double
udpAddress	Property	String	

FIGURE 2-9. *User Properties window*

To add a function to an application object, follow these steps.

1. Open the User Properties window.

2. Click the button to the left of the function description, the selection rectangle, to select the function.

3. Holding down the mouse button, drag from the selection rectangle to the application object that you want to hold the function description. Optionally, you can drop the user-defined method on the Properties sheet for an object. The function then appears as part of the Properties sheet.

4. In the code window for the function, enter the Oracle Basic code defining what the function does. The return value is defined through the following statement:

```
Function_name() = Assignment
```

Calling Functions
Whenever you call a function, you use the following syntax:

```
Target = Object.Function_name(arguments)
```

In this syntax, *Target* is a property or variable that captures the return value, *Object* is the object that contains the method, and *arguments* are the arguments passed to the function. To call a function and capture the return value, you would enter the following code fragment:

```
RECIPIENT_NAME.Value = Orders.GetName(OrderID)
```

In this example , the function **GetName( )** is associated with the Orders object, which is a form. It returns the name of the order recipient, which is assigned to the text box RECIPIENT_NAME.

There are two ways to define functions for global use. You can create a dummy form and attach all the functions and subroutines to that form. Then, when you run the application, you load the form and hide it so that it is not visible. This will make all the functions and subroutines available to the application. The preferred method is to place all the functions and subroutines that are global in scope into a library. These functions and subroutines are then available to multiple applications.

Subroutines

A subroutine is an Oracle Basic method that, unlike a function, does not return a value. Before defining a subroutine, you must declare it as part of an application. You can then write the Oracle Basic code that comprises the subroutine.

All user-defined subroutines have the following characteristics:

Component	Description
Name	A unique name used to call the subroutine.
Arguments	Variables passed either by reference or by value. You can have a subroutine that does not have any arguments.
Method code	The code that defines what the subroutine does.

Subroutine Declarations

To declare a subroutine, follow these steps.

1. Open the User Properties window.

2. Scroll to the bottom of the User Properties window.

3. On the blank line at the end of the list of user properties, enter the name of the new subroutine under the Name heading.

4. Select "Sub" from the pop-up list in the Type column.

5. Since a subroutine does not have a return value, you cannot define a data type for a subroutine.

6. Enter the arguments passed to the subroutine in the Arguments column.

Subroutine Arguments

You can pass arguments to a subroutine either by reference or by value. When you pass an argument by reference, any changes made to the variable while the subroutine is executing are returned to the variable at the conclusion of the subroutine. In contrast, when you pass an argument by value, you merely pass the value assigned to the variable, not a reference to the variable itself. Therefore, the subroutine cannot change the value in a variable that is passed by value and have that value returned at the conclusion of the subroutine.

Adding a Subroutine to an Application

Before you can call a subroutine, you must add it to your application. You can add a subroutine to any application object.

To add a subroutine to an application object, follow these steps.

1. Open the User Properties window.

2. Click on the rectangle to the left of the subroutine description, the selection rectangle, to select the subroutine.

3. Holding down the mouse button, drag from the selection rectangle to the application object that you want to hold the subroutine description. Alternatively, you can drop the user-defined method on the object's Properties sheet. The subroutine then appears as part of the Properties sheet.

Calling Subroutines

When you call a subroutine, you must use some version of the following syntax:

```
Object.Sub_name(arguments)
```

In this syntax, *Object* is the object that contains the method, and *arguments* are the arguments passed to the subroutine. If you want to call a subroutine, you might enter something like the following code fragment:

```
Orders.GetName(OrderID)
```

Function and Subroutine Declarations

After you have declared a function or a subroutine within the User Properties window, you can add the procedure as a user-defined method to any application object. After adding the procedure to the Properties sheet of an object, you can enter Oracle Basic code for the function or subroutine. To call the procedure, use the syntax *object*.**Sub_name( )** or *object*.**Function_name( )**. For example, to execute a subroutine named MySub, defined on Form1, that does not have any arguments, you would enter the statement Form1.**MySub( )** in Oracle Basic code.

You must name the object containing the code for the procedure when calling a user-defined function or subroutine, unless the call occurs within the object where the code resides. In the example of Form1.**MySub( )**, the Form1. portion of the call would be optional if you called the subroutine from method code attached to Form1. For example, Figure 2-10 shows how the user-defined method **udmStrStrip( )** is called from the **PostChange( )** method of the text field called txtPhone.

Dynamic Link Library (DLL) Procedures

Before you can use a procedure defined in a dynamic link library, you must declare the DLL procedure in the Declarations section (see Figure 2-11) of the

```
Sub PostChange()
' This procedure formats a phone number entered in this text box.
Dim strTmp as String

strTmp = Self.Value

' Strip unwanted characters
strTmp = frmUtils.udmStrStrip(strTmp, "-")
strTmp = frmUtils.udmStrStrip(strTmp, "/")
strTmp = frmUtils.udmStrStrip(strTmp, " ")
strTmp = frmUtils.udmStrStrip(strTmp, "(")
strTmp = frmUtils.udmStrStrip(strTmp, ")")
strTmp = frmUtils.udmStrStrip(strTmp, "E")
strTmp = frmUtils.udmStrStrip(strTmp, "X")
strTmp = frmUtils.udmStrStrip(strTmp, "T")
strTmp = frmUtils.udmStrStrip(strTmp, ":")
```

FIGURE 2-10. *Calling a user-defined function*

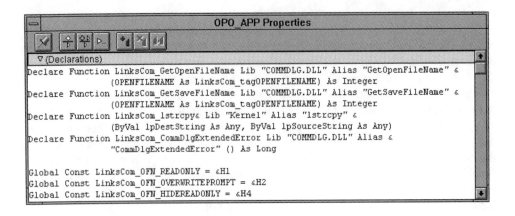

FIGURE 2-11. *Declaration section of Property sheet*

application's Properties sheet. After declaring a DLL procedure, you can call it without having to identify the object where the procedure is defined. Chapter 11 will explain in detail the process of using DLLs with Oracle Power Objects.

Variables

Variables are placeholders. Variables represent data that can be changed during the execution of a program. Variables have names that consist of a sequence of letters, digits, and the underscore (_) character. All variables must begin with a letter and can be up to 39 characters long. Spaces are not allowed.

Examples of valid variable names are

```
abc, a123456, ThisIsaVariable, user_name
```

Examples of invalid variable names are

```
1abc, This is not a variable, user-name
```

Oracle Basic is not case sensitive. Using upper- and lowercase letters to make the names more readable is recommended.

Declaring Variables

Variables are declared explicitly by using them with a declarative statement, such as **DIM**, **GLOBAL**, **REDIM**, and **STATIC**. For example,

```
DIM abc As Integer
```

Variables are declared implicitly by using them in an assignment statement. For example,

```
abc = "this is a variable"
```

In the preceding example, the variable *abc* will be typed as a variant. A variant variable can hold values of any data type. Variables are declared implicitly, but can have explicit type declared by using them as follows:

```
abc$ = "this is a string variable"
```

In the preceding example, the variable *abc* will be typed as a string.

The only way variables should be declared is explicitly. It is a good programming practice to declare your variables and assign them a data type before you assign values to those variables. Do not forget to initialize your variables explicitly, instead of depending on the compiler to do it for you. If you depend on the compiler to create and type your variables, the results may be unexpected and cost you time and effort to debug.

Scope and Duration of Variables

Variables have two levels of scope in Oracle Power Objects: global and local. A global variable is available to all Oracle Basic method code at all times. A local variable can be accessed only within the method code in which it is defined. Oracle Basic commands are listed in Appendix A.

To define a global variable, you must declare it in the Declarations section of the Properties sheet for the application. Global declarations use the following syntax:

```
GLOBAL variable_name As datatype
```

To define a local variable, declare it within method code using the following syntax:

```
DIM variable_name As datatype
```

User-defined properties provide an alternative to global variables. By adding a property to an object, you can make values assigned to that property accessible to all application objects, as long as the object to which the user-defined property has been added currently exists. You use the syntax

```
Object.Property
```

to access the value assigned to a user-defined property from any other portion of an application.

Variables also exist in time, as well as location. Global variables are created with the application and remain active as long as the application is active. Local variables are created and destroyed as the method that contains them becomes active or inactive. To preserve the values of variables between instances, you can declare them as **STATIC**. Static variables have the same lifetime as global variables, but their scope remains local. They cannot be accessed outside the method in which they are declared.

Symbolic Constants

Symbolic constants are names that are used instead of literal values—the value of the symbolic constants is represented by the value specified at declaration time. A constant name follows the same rules as the variable name. It must begin with a letter and can be up to 39 characters. Any letter, number, or underscore (_) character is allowed. All other characters are prohibited.

Declaring Constants

Constants are declared as follows.

```
CONST    Eof = 1
CONST    Myname = "Kasu Sista"
CONST    MaxValue = 300000
```

A constant's data type is determined by the value assigned to it. A constant cannot be of type *variant*.

Scope of Constants

Constants have two levels of scope in Oracle Power Objects, global and local. A global constant is available to all Oracle Basic method code at all times. A local constant can be accessed only within the method code in which it is defined.

A constant declared in the Declarations section of the application is global in scope. A constant declared anywhere else is local in scope.

Data Types

Variables in Oracle Basic have associated data types. A data type indicates the internal representation of data. An untyped variable has a default data type of *variant*. Oracle Basic data types are the same as most of the other dialects of Basic, except for date, variant, and object.

Traditional Basic dialects use type suffixes to explicitly designate a data type. Oracle Basic supports those type suffixes in addition to allowing you to type variables explicitly. It is recommended that the reader only use one method of declaring variables as shown in the following examples.

```
DIM intI As integer, strTemp As string, lngNum As long
```

An alternative way using type suffixes would be

```
DIM intI%, strTemp$, lngNum&
```

NOTE
You can declare multiple variables with a single statement or use multiple statements.

The following table summarizes Oracle Basic data types and their characteristics.

Oracle Basic Type	Suffix	Minimum Value	Maximum Value
Null		Indicates the absence of a value	
Integer	%	–32,768	+32,767
Long	&	–2,147,483,648	+2,147,483,647
Single	!	–3.402823E38 –1.401298E-45	1.401298E–45 3.402823E38
Double	#	–1.79769313486232E308 4.9406564841247E–324	+4.9406564841247E–324 1.79769313486232E308
String	$	0 characters	65,500 characters (+/–)

Oracle Basic Type	Suffix	Minimum Value	Maximum Value
Variant	None	Can store values of any type	
Date		Jan. 1, 100 A.D.	Dec. 31, 9999 A.D.
Object		Reference to an object, such as Form or Textbox	

Database Object Types

Oracle Basic differs from other dialects of Basic in respect to object types. The following table lists the various object types that can be manipulated using Oracle Basic.

Object Type	Description
1	Visible object
2	Record set
3	Bitmap resource
5	Application
7	Session

Arrays and Subscripts

Arrays are variables that hold multiple values of the same data type. Each value in the array is called an element. You reference the elements in an array using subscripts. Arrays can have more than one dimension.

You declare an array with the **DIM** command. For example, the declaration

DIM A(5) **As Integer**

declares an array A with 6 elements. The implied lower bound is 0. The elements of this array can be accessed as A(0), A(1), A(2), A(3), A(4), A(5). This is a single-dimensioned array of type integer.

The declaration

DIM B(5,2) **As Integer**

declares an array A with 18 elements, and two dimensions. The elements of this array can be accessed as B(0,0), B(0,1), B(0,2), B(1,0), B(1,1), B(1,2).

Notice that the numbers in the parenthesis, called subscripts, define the lower and upper bounds of the array. If a single number is specified, it is always assumed to be the upper bound, and 0 automatically is assumed to be the lower bound. This can be changed by using the **TO** modifier. For example, the declaration

DIM A(1 **TO** 6) **As Integer**

declares an array that has 6 elements as before. The lower bound here is explicitly specified as 1, so that the first element in the array is referenced as A(1) instead of A(0). The value A(0), in this case, would produce a "Subscript out of range" error.

Negative subscripts are allowed, provided that the lower bound is algebraically lower than the upper bound. For example,

DIM A(–6 **TO** –1) **As Integer**

would be valid, but

DIM A(–1 **TO** –6) **As Integer**

would be invalid.

Dynamic Arrays

Sometimes you do not know at declaration time exactly how many dimensions are needed. Then you could declare a dynamic array, and redimension it at run time using the **REDIM** statement. For example, the declaration

DIM A( ) **As Integer**

declares a dynamic array A.

REDIM A(2,2) **As Integer**

redimensions the array for 2 dimensions with 3 elements each.

You can redimension an array as many times as you want. Each time you **REDIM** an array, all the elements are initialized to their default value, determined by their data type. Here, they will be initialized to 0. To prevent this initialization, the **PRESERVE** keyword is used. If you want to redimension the array A in the preceding example again and preserve any values, you would use

REDIM PRESERVE A(2,3) **As Integer**.

Operators

Oracle Basic provides all the standard operators for constructing arithmetic, string, relational, and logical expressions. These operators are grouped into the following categories:

- Arithmetic operators
- String operators
- Comparison operators
- Logical operators
- Date operators
- Object operators

Operator Precedence

Operator precedence determines the order in which the operators are executed in an expression. The operators listed in each category are listed in the order of their precedence. Highest precedence operators are listed first.

Arithmetic Operators

Arithmetic operators are used to create numeric expressions. They return numeric values upon evaluation.

Operator	Description	Example
^	Exponentiation	3^3 = 27
–	Negation-unary operator	–(3 + 3 – 2) = -4
* , /	Multiplication and division	12*12/2 = 72
\	Integer division	20.3\5 = 4
Mod	Modulo operator	13 Mod 3 = 1
+ , –	Addition and subtraction	2 + 2 – 2 – 2 = 0

String Operators

String operators operate on strings and return string values.

Operator	Description	Example
&	Concatenation—automatically converts all operands to string before concatenation	"Kasu" & "Sista" = "Kasu Sista" "Variable" & 1 = "Variable1" "Variable" & Null = "Variable"
+	Concatenation—does not convert operands to strings	"Kasu" + "Sista" = "Kasu Sista" "Variable" + 1 = Error "Variable" + Null = Null

Relational Operators

Relational operators manipulate many different data types and always return a Boolean value represented as a *Long Integer.* The values returned represent True as –1 and False as 0.

Operator	Description	Data Types Supported	Example
=	Equality	All	1 = 1 returns True
<>	Inequality	All	1 <> 1 returns False
<	Less than	All except object	"ABC" < "abc" returns True
>	Greater than	All except object	12.3 > 0.00001 returns True
<=	Less than or equal to	All except object	5 <= 5 returns True 6 <= 5 returns False 5 <= 6 returns True
>=	Greater than or equal to	All except Object	5 >= 5 returns True 6 >= 5 returns True 6 >= 7 returns False

Logical Operators

Logical operators act on numeric values and return a Boolean value of True, –1, or False, 0.

Operator	Description	Example
NOT	Negation	NOT(2 = 2) returns False NOT(1 = 2) returns True

Operator	Description	Example
AND	Conjunction	(2 = 2) AND (3 = 3) returns True (2 = 3) AND (3 = 3) returns False
OR	Disjunction	(2 = 3) OR (3 = 3) returns True
XOR	Exclusive Or	(2 = 2) XOR (3 = 3) returns False (2 = 3) XOR (3 = 3) returns True
EQV	Equivalence	(2 = 2) EQV (3 = 3) returns True (2 = 3) EQV (3 = 3) returns False
IMP	Implication	(6 < 2) IMP (2 < 3) returns True

Date Operators

Date operators operate on date and numeric values and return a date value.

Operator	Example
Date – date	4/20/95 – 4/17/95 = 3
Date – number	4/20/95 – 3 = 4/17/95
Date + number	4/20/95 + 13 = 5/3/95

Object Operators

Object operators, shown here, return an object value. Only "in memory" objects can be created with the NEW operator.

Operator	Description	Example
NEW	Creates a new object	mbrMenuBar1 = **NEW** MenuBar

Expressions

Oracle Basic expressions can be formed using any of the following elements. You can use the elements alone or combine them with the appropriate operators.

- Literals
- Constants
- Functions

- Object properties
- Variables

Some examples of expressions are

"My Name"

666

3.1416 * 2 ^ 2

False OR 3 > 2

"You" & " are a " & " great person"

frmOrders.cmdClose.Value * 1.25

Expressions are evaluated to arrive at the resultant value. If a function is used as a part of an expression, then the function is replaced with its return value in the expression. When expressions are evaluated, they result in a value of a certain data type. This depends on the values within the expression. Oracle Basic performs implicit data type conversions.

Operator	Conversion Performed
&	Converts all data types to string
^, *, /, +, –	Converts to the lowest precision used in the expression
\, Mod	Always returns long integers

When a floating value is assigned to an integer type, the fractional part is truncated. If the value is too large to fit in the integer part, then an error occurs. Several Oracle Basic functions are available for explicit conversion. These are described later in this chapter.

Controlling Program Flow

As previously mentioned, Oracle Basic is used to implement business rules—logical operations that affect either the user interface or the data. For an Oracle Basic method to be useful, it must be able to make decisions based on the values of variables and then act on those decisions to perform specific actions. In addition, the method should be able to handle any errors that occur to provide feedback to the user.

The two primitives required for controlling program flow are test and branch. All control structures are based upon these primitives. Oracle Basic provides four ways of controlling program flow:

- Branching using the **GOTO** statement

- Conditionals such as **IF...THEN...ELSE, SELECT...CASE**

- Repetition in the form of **WHILE...LOOP** and related statements

- Terminations in the form of **END** and **EXIT**

Branching and Labels

If you have programmed in Assembler or in an older Basic dialect, you are aware that the only form of flow control was using either a **JUMP** or **GOTO** label. In early Basic, every line was required to be numbered. These numbers were used as labels for branching.

Procedural Basic introduced labels that replaced line numbers. There is no need to number each line anymore. Oracle Basic's **GOTO** label causes execution to continue from the statement where the label is located. A Label is a variable with a colon (:) suffix. Labels must start in column 1 of the statement.

We strongly recommend not using **GOTO** labels in the programs. The **GOTO** label makes for unreadable code that is difficult to maintain. You may use a **GOTO** label for error handling; but aside from this, if you must use **GOTO** labels, then make them forward only. You might use a forward **GOTO** to jump to an exit point so that any cleanup code can be executed before exiting.

The following is an example of a forward **GOTO**:

```
'      This procedure checks for valid ranges of a passed in variable.
DIM    vIntRetVal As Integer
vIntRetVal = True
IF vIntCheck = 0 THEN
    vIntRetVal = False
    GOTO Exit_checkRange
END IF
If   vIntCheck > 1000 THEN
    vIntRetVal = False
    GOTO Exit_checkRange
END IF
```

.
.
.

```
Exit_checkRange:
    checkRange = vIntRetVal
```

Conditional Statements

Conditional statements are used to cause different code to be executed based on a logical condition.

IF...THEN...ELSE

Conditional statements either skip or execute statements based on a conditional expression that must evaluate to True or False. There are two variations of syntax for this statement.

Type 1 (all on one line):

```
IF condition GOTO line_num [ELSE { line_num ¦ statements } ]
```

A type 1 statement is formatted on a single line without the **THEN** or the closing **END IF**. Notice in the code that follows a **GOTO** replaces the **THEN**. The **ELSE** section can either have a branch to a line number or a block of statements to execute. The next example will illustrate this type of **IF...** statement.

```
IF x > y GOTO 1111 ELSE 2222
```

This code will branch to line or label 1111 if the condition is True, and will branch to line or label 2222 if the condition is False.

```
IF  x > y GOTO 1111 ELSE x = y - 1
```

Notice that you are restricted to a **GOTO** after the **IF**, but not after the **ELSE**.

Type 2 (all on one line):

```
IF  condition  THEN {line_num | statements} [ELSE {line_num | statements} ]
```

Type 2 gives you the option of executing a block of statements or branching to a line number if the condition is True. Notice in the following example that the keyword **THEN** is now required. You are not restricted in your choice of statements that can appear after **THEN** or **ELSE**. Again, the closing **END IF** is not required.

```
IF x > y THEN x = y + 1 ELSE x = y - 1
```

Type 3 (multiline):

```
IF condition_1 THEN
          statements
[ ELSE[IF condition_2 THEN ]
        statements  ]
END IF
```

Type 3 is the format that should be used normally. Coding with line numbers is not recommended since it leads to unreadable programs and makes maintenance difficult. The type 3 format allows you to format your conditionals legibly, so that each set of statements are grouped together under the True or False conditional paths.

A type 3 **IF** must be the first statement on a line. The test for type 3 is the absence of any executable statements on the same line as the keyword **THEN**. If any executable statements are found on the same line after **THEN**, Oracle Basic executes the line as a type 2 **IF** statement.

The **ELSEIF** and **ELSE** clauses are optional, but if both appear, **ELSE** must be last. **END IF** is required to end type 3 construction. Each of these three keywords must be the first element on a line, except for an optional line number or label. Note that because one of the statements can be a **GOTO** command, type 3 is both an extension and combination of the capabilities offered by types 1 and 2.

The next example checks for three conditions and prints a message indicating the condition that was True.

```
IF x > y THEN
          MSGBOX " X is Greater Than Y "
      ELSEIF x < y THEN
          MSGBOX "X is Less Than Y "
      ELSE
          MSGBOX " X is Equal to Y"
      END IF
```

SELECT...CASE...END SELECT
When you have a choice to make among many alternatives, the **IF...THEN...ELSE** structure can become cumbersome and complicated. The **SELECT...CASE..END SELECT** structure simplifies this process. The **SELECT** statement can test for True or False conditions, as well as examine variables for ranges and execute statements based on those ranges. The syntax of a **SELECT** statement is

```
SELECT CASE selector
    CASE Expression1[,Expression2, ...]
```

```
        [ statements ]
    [ CASE Expression2 TO Expression3
        [ statements ] ]
    [ CASE IS RelationalExpression
        [ statements ] ]
    [ CASE ELSE
        [ statements ] ]
END SELECT
```

SELECT CASE evaluates the *selector*, which can be a numeric variable, a string, or an expression. It then tests each **CASE** expression in sequence. As shown in the syntax, the **CASE** can take the following four forms:

- A single or a list of values separated by commas. The *selector* is compared with all the values in the list and the results are ORed together to evaluate to True or False. If the expressions evaluate to True then the corresponding statements are executed.

- A range of values specified by the keyword **TO.** The value to the left of the keyword **TO** must be less that the value to the right of the keyword **TO.** Strings are compared using the ASCII value of their first character.

- A relational expression using the keyword **IS**. The keyword is followed by a relational operator and either a variable or a literal.

- The keyword **ELSE**. This is the catchall condition. If none of the conditions are satisfied, then the statements following this **CASE ELSE** are executed. It is a good programming practice to always have a **CASE ELSE** to catch unexpected conditions. In the absence of a **CASE ELSE**, the statement following the case is executed, possibly leading to unwanted results.

Let us look at some examples of the **SELECT CASE** usage:

```
DIM vNumber As Integer
SELECT CASE x
    CASE    1,2,3
        MSGBOX "X IS 1 or 2 or 3"
    CASE    4 TO 7
        MSGBOX "X IS in the range 4 thru 7"
    CASE    Is = 8
        MSGBOX "X IS equal to 8"
    CASE ELSE
        MSGBOX "X IS Greater Than 8"
END SELECT
```

This example uses a numeric selector to illustrate the four cases discussed previously. The following example uses a string selector.

```
DIM vstrStatus As String
    CASE SELECT vstrStatus
        CASE    "A", "S"
            MSGBOX "Employee is Absent or Sick"
        CASE    "C" TO "E"
            MSGBOX "Employee is of status C thru E"
        CASE     IS < "G"
            MSGBOX "Employee Status is Less than G"
        CASE ELSE
            MSGBOX "Employee Status is >= G"
    END SELECT
```

Repetition

Application logic often involves performing a task repeatedly until a particular condition is met. Looping constructs of a language are used to implement repetitive tasks. There are three basic types of looping: loops that repeat 0 or more times, loops that repeat 1 or more times, and loops that execute a specific number of times.

0 or More Times Loop

These are loops where the testing is done at the beginning of a loop. If the condition of the loop evaluates to True, the statements within the loop are executed. Otherwise, the statements are skipped and execution is transferred to the statements following the loop. The **WHILE...LOOP** syntax is used to implement this type of loop. The syntax for a **WHILE...LOOP** is

```
WHILE condition
    [ statements ]
WEND
```

The statements between the condition and the **WEND** are executed only while the condition evaluates to True. When the condition evaluates to False, the statements are skipped and execution continues to the statement following the **WHILE...WEND** structure.

For example:

```
DIM X As Integer, Y As Integer
X = 2
Y = 10
```

```
WHILE X < Y
X = X + 1
WEND
```

This loop increments X until it is equal to Y. One of the problems with this structure is that you cannot exit out of the loop with an **EXIT** statement. An alternative solution would be to use the **DO...WHILE...LOOP** structure, which is identical but allows an exit.

The syntax is

```
DO [ ( WHILE ¦ UNTIL ) condition ]   ]
    [ statements ]
    [ EXIT DO ]
    [ statements ]
LOOP
```

An example of a **DO...WHILE...LOOP** is

```
DO WHILE X < Y
    X = X + 1
    IF X = 7 THEN
        EXIT DO
    END IF
LOOP
```

This structure has similar looping capabilities, but allows for the loop to terminate on special conditions.

1 or More Times Loop

These are loops where testing is done at the bottom of the loop. The statements within the loop are executed at least once. A **DO...WHILE** or **DO...UNTIL** construct is used to implement this type of loop.

The syntax for a **DO...WHILE/UNTIL** is as follows:

```
DO
    [ statements ]
    [ EXIT DO ]
    [ statements ]
LOOP [ ( WHILE ¦ UNTIL ) condition ]   ]
```

As you can see, the statements are executed at least once. The test is performed at the bottom of the loop. If the condition evaluates to False, then the loop is exited. Execution can also be transferred out of the loop by an **EXIT DO** statement anywhere in the loop.

For example:

```
DO
    X = X + 1
    IF X = 7 THEN
        EXIT DO
    END IF
LOOP WHILE X < Y
```

Another example of this construct is

```
DO
    X = X + 1
    IF X = 7 THEN
        EXIT DO
    END IF
LOOP UNTIL X >= Y
```

Notice that the construct **LOOP WHILE** tests for the truth of a condition (X < Y) while the construct **LOOP UNTIL** tests for the failure of the same condition, **NOT**(X < Y), which translates to the condition X >= Y.

Loop for a Specified Number of Times

This type of loop executes a set of statements based on a control variable that is tested for a limit each time through the loop. A **FOR...NEXT** construct is used to implement this type of loop. The syntax is

```
FOR Counter =  BeginValue TO EndValue [ STEP Increment ]
    [ statements ]
    [ Conditional Statement
        EXIT FOR
      End Condition Statement]
NEXT [ Counter ]
```

You establish the number of iterations for the block of statements in the **FOR** loop by specifying the beginning and ending values for a counter. The number of iterations is then *EndValue – BeginValue* + 1 unless you also specify the optional *Increment*. If *Increment* is specified, the number of iterations is the integer value of the expression (*EndValue – BeginValue* + 1)/*Increment*

Execution of the block of statements begins with the counter set to *BeginValue*. When the code reaches a **NEXT** statement, the *Increment* value is added to the counter and execution returns to the first statement in the block. In Oracle Basic, *Increment* can be a negative or floating point number, including fractional numbers.

When the counter is greater than *EndValue*, execution of the **FOR** loop ceases and control transfers to the statement after the corresponding **NEXT** statement. The following example initializes an array with contiguous numbers:

```
DIM vIntIndex As Integer, vIntArray(10) As Integer
DIM vIntSize As Integer
vIntSize = (UBOUND(vIntArray) - LBOUND(vIntArray)) + 1
FOR vIntIndex = 0 TO vIntSize - 1
    vIntArray(intIndex) = vIntIndex
NEXT vIntIndex
.
.
.
```

Using Oracle Basic to Manipulate Objects

The power in Oracle Power Objects comes from three sources. The first is its object orientation, which will be discussed in detail in Chapters 5 and 6. The second is the capability to manipulate the properties of the types of objects we have discussed in the preceding sections. The third is a rich set of built-in functions, which will be discussed throughout the book where appropriate. Oracle Basic provides extensions that allow the developer to access, add, and modify properties of objects. You would do this by writing methods that are normally triggered by events. These events can be generated either by the user or by the program.

Object Names

Most of the objects in Oracle Power Objects have a name, specified by the object's Name property. The naming conventions vary based on the type of object. Application objects, which Oracle Basic is mostly concerned with, use the same rules defined for variables previously. By naming an object, you give the object an identity. The object name must be unique within the application. This does not mean you cannot have two text fields with the same name in two different forms. The complete hierarchical names, as defined below, must be unique.

Hierarchical Names
The concept of hierarchical names is similar to locating a file in a DOS or UNIX directory structure. You would fully qualify the directory path and the file name to identify a file. You would refer to an object on a form by qualifying the object's name with the form's name. You use the dot notation to form the hierarchical name. For example, consider the form in Figure 2-12. This form is called frmObject and it contains a text field called fldField and a push button called btnButton.

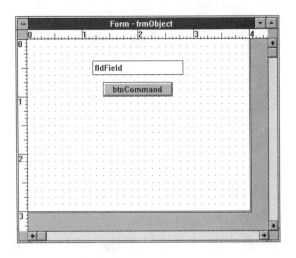

FIGURE 2-12. *frmObject form*

Let's look at how many different ways the object fldField can be referenced.

External to the Form   If this object fldField is to be referenced from outside the form, then you would refer to it as Application.frmObject.fldField, or frmObject.fldField. The first reference is called the full hierarchical name, since **Application** is a keyword that is the container for all application objects. The second reference is called a relative reference, since it assumes that the form exists in the current application. Most of the references you will use in Oracle Power Objects are relative references.

From Within the Form   If this object fldField is to be referenced from the form, you would refer to it as fldField.

From the btnButton   If the object fldField is to be referenced from the object btnButton you could reference it as frmObject.fldField.

Oracle Power Objects provides several keywords, properties, and methods for addressing objects. They are

Name	Type	Description
Self	Keyword	Refers to the object from which this reference originates.

Name	Type	Description
Container	Keyword	Refers to the parent of the object from which this reference originates. Notice this only goes up one level of containment. It can be used at design time.
TopContainer	Keyword	Refers to the top-level container of the object from which this reference originates. It can be used at design time.
GetContainer( )	Method	Refers to the object's parent. Same as Container, but cannot be used at design time.
GetTopContainer( )	Method	Top level container of the object. Same as TopContainer, but cannot be used at design time.
NextControl( )	Method	Returns a reference to the next child of the object. With each invocation, it steps through the children of the object, until none are left when it returns a null.
FirstChild	Property	Refers to the first child of the object. Oracle Power Objects sets this property randomly.

Now, let's apply these operators to the example form and see how the references are resolved.

1. 'Self' in the btnButton returns the object handle for btnButton.

2. 'Container' in the btnButton returns the object handle for the frmObject.

3. 'btnButton.TopContainer' returns the object handle for the frmObject form.frmObject.

4. 'btnButton.**GetContainer( )**' returns the object handle for the frmObject form.frmObject.

5. 'btnButton.**GetTopContainer( )**' returns the object handle for the frmObject form.frmObject.

6. 'frmObject.FirstChild' returns the object handle for the btnButton pushbutton.btnButton.

7. 'btnButton.**NextControl( )**' returns the object handle for fldField... The **NextControl( )** function returns a null when called from the last object in a form.

Using relative references can generalize your code and make it more resistant to changes in the names of other objects in your application. If you are unsure how a reference will resolve, it is recommended that you first figure out each reference and check it with the Debugger to make sure that you are referencing the object you want.

Event Processing

Graphical user interface environments are driven by events caused by user interactions. Applications in GUI environments operate by responding to events.

What Is Event-Driven Processing?

Event-driven processing is the basis for user-driven graphical applications. Most of us are used to procedural, sequential processing-type applications. These applications run on character-mode terminals where all the required data is entered on the screen, and the data is collected in one big chuck and then sent to the application at one time. The application would then examine the data, apply validation criteria, and notify the user of either the success or failure of an operation. This is what is called a synchronous, sequenced operation.

In contrast, the new GUI-based client/server applications work asynchronously. They do this by monitoring the resources and reacting to events as they occur. An event is some action within the application that the application itself recognizes and to which it can respond. Events always occur in the context of a particular object, which can respond to the event.

Event Hierarchy

Preceding sections of this chapter discussed the object hierarchy in Oracle Power Objects, as well as the containment hierarchy of the application objects. Events, and event methods, also apply to the application objects. The events happen in a certain sequence. As events occur they trigger methods that will do the necessary processing.

Consider the previous form in Figure 2-12 and examine the events that occur when loading and interacting with the form.

Opening a Form
When the form is opened for display, the following events occur in order. The method **Query( )** gets executed, which retrieves the records needed for display. This in turn triggers the **QueryMasters( )** method, which determines the top-level containers in the form and calls the **Query( )** method for each of the bound

containers. Once all the querying is done, the **OnLoad( )** method is triggered to do any custom processing necessary.

Clicking the Mouse

When the right button of the mouse is pressed first, the **MouseDown( )** method is triggered. If you move the mouse while the button is pressed, the **MouseMove( )** method is triggered as long as the mouse is moving. When you stop the mouse and release the button, the **MouseUp( )** method is triggered. This is immediately followed by the triggering of the **Click( )** method.

Editing a Control

As you tab into the Text field or when you click the mouse on the field, the **FocusEntering( )** method is triggered. If you either tab out of the field or click the mouse elsewhere in the form, the **FocusLeaving( )** method is triggered. While you are in the field, if you change the value and press ENTER, the methods **Validate( )** and **PostChange( )** are triggered in sequence. Be very careful in using the **PostChange( )** method. It is triggered no matter how the changes are made. If, for instance, you decide to change the value of the text field in the **PostChange( )** method, it might put you into an infinite loop. At the container level, the methods **ChildPreChange( )** and **ChildPostChange( )** get triggered.

These are only a few of the sequences that occur while interacting with forms in Oracle Power Objects. The best way to determine the sequence of events is to place **MSGBOX** statements in the methods that you think will get triggered, and then watch the sequence in which they get triggered. This is the most foolproof way of placing code in the methods.

Debugging Oracle Basic

It was E. W. Dijkstra who said, "You can only prove the presence of bugs, not the absence of them." If you have been programming for any length of time, then you know the truth of the statement. Bugs are a fact of life. The categories of bugs are

- Compile-time errors
- Run-time errors
- Logic errors
- Design errors
- External errors

The following sections will explain each of these in more detail.

Compile-Time Errors

Compile-time errors occur because of syntax errors. These errors could be a missing parenthesis, incorrectly paired **IF...END IF** statements or **WHILE...WEND** statements, or incorrectly spelled names. Oracle Basic detects these errors and places you at that point in the code where the error has occurred. You can then correct the error and proceed with running the application.

Run-Time Errors

Run-time errors occur while the application is running. These are detected by Oracle Basic and you are automatically placed in the Debugger at the point where the error has occurred. Notice that this happens only when you are in the development environment. When you deploy the application, you have to trap the errors and recover from them gracefully, without inconveniencing the user too much. An example of a run-time error would be an invalid column reference. A column value in a table can be modified through the Record Manager or an SQL statement. When you are modifying the column value, you can specify the name of the column you are modifying in a statement. If this column name is mistyped you will get an error at run time when the statement is executed.

Logic Errors

Logic errors cannot be detected by Oracle Basic. Logic errors come in two varieties: program logic errors and business logic errors. Both types of errors will compile and run, but will produce inconsistent results.

Program logic errors are incorrectly constructed statements that compile and run. For example, look at the following **FOR** loop.

```
FOR I = 0 TO 100
    x(i) = I
    I = I + 1
NEXT I
```

This snippet of code is modifying the control variable. Instead of initializing every element to its index value, it will initialize every other element. This is a perfectly valid piece of code, but it does not perform the required function. These types of errors produce side effects that could create some nasty results and can be extremely hard to find.

Business logic errors are a different beast altogether. Consider the following example:

```
FOR I = 0 TO vIntNumEmployees
    IF vOvertime(i) < 40 THEN
        AwardBonus()
    END IF
NEXT I
```

You want to pay overtime to all those employees that have worked for more than 40 hours. Because of a typing mistake, you end up giving bonuses to those employees who have worked less than 40 hours. Come payroll time, there will be an uproar. These types of errors can be caught only by a business analyst working with a programmer. The need here is for a knowledge of the business as well as the program.

Design Errors

Design errors have huge ramifications. These errors could occur at any time during the life cycle of a project. They could be at the functional design, detail design, program design, or module design level. The earlier an error occurs, the larger the impact is on the system. These types of errors are not usually detected until it is too late. Then some type of workaround is fabricated to keep the system going. These types of errors are identified by design reviews, code walkthroughs, and implementing a test plan as early as possible in the life of a system. Decisions such as creating normalized table structures, parameterized user preferences, and global error-handling routines must be made at design time. Wrong decisions at design time will lead to a lot of redesigning and rewriting of code later.

External Errors

These are the worst kind of errors you will encounter as a programmer. These errors have nothing to do with your program, your business logic, your boss, or whatever. You are in the unfortunate position of trying to interface to another system through a layer provided to you by someone else. You try to use it and get an error that makes no sense. This is when you will become a diplomat, a tyrant, or a beggar to try to get the error identified and solved so that you can continue with your development. All you can do is maintain good relations with whoever it is you have to deal with.

Guidelines

A majority of the debugging process involves reproducing errors under controlled conditions so that the source of the bug can be identified and corrected. Program bugs are like diseases. They have a source and a symptom. Most of the time you will only know the symptom. You have to go through a debugging process to identify the source of the bug. It is possible to fix the symptom, but the source of the bug will still lurk within the program only to raise its ugly head at some other time.

Because debugging is an art instead of a science, you can make your life easier by designing programs that are easier to debug as well as maintain. It is a well-known fact that 80 percent of the life of a program is spent in maintenance. That means you or some other programmer will be modifying, enhancing, and debugging the program once it is done. So, it makes sense to follow some rules while developing programs.

Use a Naming Convention

It is absolutely imperative that you follow a naming convention. Use one that is given in the book, or develop your own. Be consistent in your use of it.

Make Your Programs Modular

This is pretty much done for you in Oracle Basic. There is still a need for planning your methods—where to place them and how to use them. Break up the methods into functional units and try to get as much reuse out of them as possible. Chapter 5 will discuss reuse in more detail.

Use Comments

This is a necessity. Develop the habit of commenting as you go along. If you wait to comment until you are done, then you will never find the time to go back. You must make sure your comments are accurate. When you modify any portion of your program, you may have to update the comments. There is nothing worse than misleading comments to a frustrated maintenance programmer.

Declare All Your Variables

Do not use implicit variable and data-type declarations. Make them explicit. In the preceding pages, we talked about how Oracle Basic will automatically type any variables used in the code if they are not declared already. Avoid this practice and declare all your variables explicitly.

Debugger

Even if you follow all the preceding rules and spend enough time planning your application, you will still run into errors. That is why Oracle Basic provides you with a Debugger. The goal of a debugging session is to locate the source of a problem and fix it. This is not always easy, but the Debugger makes the process easier.

The Debugger lets you debug your Oracle Basic code, interrogate the values assigned to variables and properties, and control the execution of your application during testing.

When you run an Oracle Power Objects application, form, or report in run-time mode, the Debug palette appears. The Debug palette, shown here, lets you halt and resume program execution, as well as open the Debugger (Main) and Debugger (Expressions) windows.

The Debugger Window

By opening the Debugger window (see Figure 2-13), you can view all of the properties and methods of objects currently loaded into memory, including the method code added to a method. The Debugger window has the following components.

Object List   Objects currently loaded into memory appear here.

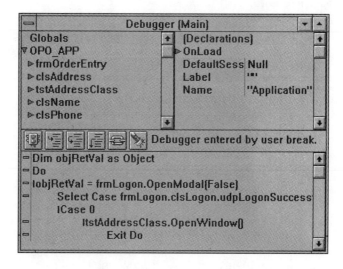

FIGURE 2-13.   *Debugger window*

Property/Method List   Properties and methods for the currently selected object appear here.

Code Stepping Controls   The icons here control execution of the Debugger as you step through code.

Code Area   Method code that has been added to a method that is currently selected in the Property/Method list appears here. In the code area, you set breakpoints, step through method code, and move execution to any point in the code.

To view the objects within a container, click on the arrow to the left of the name of the container from the Object pane of the Debugger window. The objects within the current application and container appear in a hierarchical list, following the object containment hierarchy.

To view the properties and methods of an object, click on the name of the object. The complete list of properties and methods, both standard and user-defined, then appears in the Properties pane of the Debugger window. A method appears in this list only if you have added method code to it.

To control the execution of code, use the Code pane of the Debugger window. In this section of the Debugger window, you can set breakpoints, step through method code, and move execution to any point within the code.

The Debugger Expressions Window

The Debugger Expressions window (shown here) lets you interrogate the values assigned to variables and properties, as well as evaluate the result of an expression.

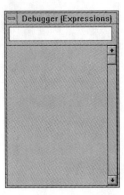

In addition, you can also trigger a method through the Debugger Expressions window by entering the standard object reference used for triggering a method, *object*.**method( )**. You must include any arguments that need to be passed to the method.

Interrogating Values Through the Debugger

To interrogate values through the Debugger Expressions window, you enter an expression in the Expression field. For example, to evaluate the Enabled property of the Field1 object, you would enter the following expression in the Debugger (Expressions) window:

```
Field1.Enabled
```

After you press ENTER, the result of the expression appears in the Result field, immediately below the Expression field.

Expressions entered in the Debugger Expressions window must follow these rules:

- Expressions can use Oracle Basic operators and functions, except for the EXEC SQL command.

- An expression can be no longer than 1,024 characters.

NOTE
If you get a series of question marks (???) in the Return field, it means that the Debugger Expressions window was unable to evaluate the expression.

You can also interrogate the return value of a standard method or a user-defined method through the Debugger Expressions window. By entering the object reference to the method, using the syntax *object.method( )*, you can then see the return value of the method in the Result field.

Setting a Breakpoint

To set a breakpoint, follow these steps.

1. Open the Debugger Main window.

2. Select an object, and then select a method you want to debug.

3. Click to the left of the line where you want to set the breakpoint. A red circle appears to the left of the line of code, indicating that a breakpoint has been set there.

```
Dim objRetVal as Object
Do
objRetVal = frmLogon.OpenModal(False)
    Select Case frmLogon.clsLogon.udpLogonSuccess
    lCase 0
        ltstAddressClass.OpenWindow()
        Exit Do
```

NOTE

If you open a method and do not see the thin rectangle to the left of the code, it means that Oracle Power Objects was unable to compile the method code. You will not be able to set breakpoints for this code and will get an error when your application attempts to execute it.

4. Resume program execution by pressing the Continue button on the Debugger palette.

The method code will halt execution when it reaches the breakpoint. You can resume execution by pressing the Continue button. You can also step through the method code using several buttons appearing in the Debugger Main window.

Setting a Watchpoint

When you set a watchpoint in Oracle Basic method code, the application automatically stops executing and Oracle Power Objects displays the Debugger Expressions window. You can then interrogate values before resuming the execution of the method code.

To set a watchpoint, follow these steps.

1. Run a form, report, or application.

2. Open the Debugger and the Debugger Expressions windows.

3. Interrogate the value for a variable or property through the Debugger Expressions window.

4. Click to the immediate left of the name of the variable or property in the Debugger Expressions window. An icon for the watchpoint appears next to the variable or property name in the window.

5. Continue execution.

As the value assigned to the property or variable changes, the Debugger Expressions window continues to display the new values. To remove the watchpoint, click again to the left of the property or methods name. The watchpoint icon then disappears from the window.

Stepping Through Code

To step through method code, you must first set a breakpoint. Once the breakpoint has been reached, you can then use several buttons in the Debugger window to step through the code:

Button	Button Name	Description
	Resume	Resumes execution, moving execution through all methods called.
	Step Into	Steps through the code one line at a time.
	Step to End	Moves execution to the end of the current method.
	Step Over	Continues execution of the current method. In this case, the application does not branch into any methods called from the current method.
	Call Chain	Moves to any method in the call chain. When you press this button, a list of methods appears, representing the chain of methods called, one after the other. You can then move to a different method in the call chain by highlighting its name in the list.
	Clear All Breakpoints	Clears all breakpoints set in the application, form, or report being tested.

Additionally, you can move execution to any line within the current method by clicking on the line currently being executed (marked by a green line) and dragging up or down to the new point of execution. This technique lets you move the point of execution within a single method. You cannot move execution to a different method, however.

Handling Run-Time Errors

The Debugger works well during the development stage. Unfortunately, most end users do not want to debug the program when they run into an error at run time. They want to be notified of the error, what has caused the error, and a possible resolution so that they can continue with their work. Part of your task as a developer is to get the user to report all the errors and the operations that were being performed at the time the error occurred so that you can reproduce the error under controlled conditions.

As much as you debug your program and get that last bug out, there are still those external errors that are caused by agents beyond your control. These are the type of errors you need to predict and trap, and then provide a graceful way to recover without inconveniencing the user. This is where you need to have error-handling routines. In this chapter, we will develop a simple error-handling routine that you can include in each of your functions and subroutines.

You do not have to include an error handler with every function or subroutine you write. It is a good idea to include one whenever the application is interacting with something external, like a database, a file system, or another application. Oracle Power Objects provides an error-handling statement that can be included with a function or a procedure. It is **ON ERROR GOTO** <*Label*>. This statement turns on the Oracle Power Objects error-trapping facility. If your function/subroutine does not have this statement, then the default Oracle Power Objects message is displayed to the user. If you trap the error, then you can display your own message to the user and continue processing if the error is recoverable or close the application gracefully if necessary. The following is typical error-handling code you may want to include with your function code.

```
SUB InsertRow()
ON ERROR GOTO Err_InsertRow
Inherited.InsertRow()     ' Performs default processing
   .
   .
   .
' Performs specific processing
Exit_InsertRow:
      EXIT SUB
Err_InsertRow:
  MSGBOXERROR$
      RESUME Exit_InsertRow
END SUB             ' Optional, but recommended.
```

In this piece of code, **ON ERROR** turns on the error handling. If an error occurs anywhere in the subroutine, the execution branches to the Err_InsertRow label. At this point, use the Error$ function to get the error message to display, and then **GOTO** the Exit_InsertRow label by using the **RESUME** statement. The **RESUME** statement jumps to the specified label.

Another way to use the error handler is to anticipate certain errors and take corrective actions. Examine the following routine.

```
DIM vstrFileName As Integer, vIntRetVal As Integer
CONST FILEALREADYOPEN = 1063, OK = 1, CANCEL = 2
CONST FILEDOESNOTEXIST = 1067
ON ERROR GOTO Err_OpenSpecifiedFile
```

```
' Get the file name from the user.
vstrFileName = INPUTBOX("Please Enter File Name to Open: ")
OPEN vstrFileName FOR INPUT As #1
    .
    .
    .
' Read and process lines from the file
Exit_OpenSpecifiedFile:
    EXIT SUB
Err_OpenSpecifiedFile:
    IF   ERR = FILEALREADYOPEN THEN
        MSGBOX "Specified File Already open, Continuing with processing"
        RESUME NEXT
    ELSEIF ERR = FILEDOESNOTEXIST THEN
        vintRetVal = MSGBOX ("Specified File Does Not Exist. Try Again?" , &
MB_OKCANCEL, MBICONQUESTION)
        IF vintRetVal = OK THEN
            vstrFileName = INPUTBOX("Please Enter File Name to Open: ")
            RESUME 0
        ELSE
            RESUME Exit_OpenSpecifiedFile
        END IF
    ELSE
        MSGBOX "Error " & STR(Err) & " Occurred: " & Error$
        RESUME Exit_OpenSpecifiedFile
    END IF
```

The preceding error-handling code checks for specific errors and takes specific action. The function opens a file that is specified by the user via the **INPUTBOX( )** function. If the file is opened without any errors, then it is read and processed. If there is an error on opening it then the execution transfers to the error handler that is at the label Err_OpenSpecifiedFile.

The error handler checks the error for two specific codes. If the file is already open, then it warns the user and continues processing the file. If the file does not exist, then it gives the user a choice to specify another file or exit the function. If the error code is different from the preceding two, then it displays the error number and the message, and exits.

You may notice the different uses of **RESUME** in the function. It is used three ways.

■ **RESUME** Exit_OpenSpecifiedFile transfers control to the label.

■ **RESUME NEXT** transfers control to the next statement after the statement that has caused the error.

■ **RESUME** 0 transfers control to the statement that has caused the error (in this case, the OPEN statement).

Summary

That was a lot of material to cover in a chapter. In this chapter, you have learned some basic constructs of Oracle Power Objects and Oracle Basic. This chapter covered the following:

- The concepts of events and methods
- Functions and subroutines, which are used to write method code
- Constants, variables, and data types of Oracle Basic
- Control structures of Oracle Basic
- Object hierarchy, and object addressing
- Some fundamental concepts of errors and error handling
- Use of the Debugger to debug your Oracle Basic programs

This gives you a pretty solid foundation to build your Oracle Power Objects expertise on. In the following chapters, you will be revisiting most of these concepts time and again. You are on your way to becoming an Oracle Power Objects expert!

CHAPTER 3

Extending Your
Application

You have seen in Chapter 1 how easy it is to create a functional application
using Oracle Power Objects. In this chapter, you will extend the basic
functionality of your application and make your application easier to use, more
informative, and more powerful. Before you begin to make all of these
improvements, it is worthwhile to spend a little time discussing the overall goals of
a good client/server application.

Client/server Computing

Client/server computing has come to prominence in the decade of the 1990s, although the introduction of the components of client/server computing occurred throughout the 1980s. Client/server systems are distinguished by graphical applications, running on personal computers, and accessing data in database servers or local database engines. The storage and manipulation of data is separate from the applications that access the data.

But client/server applications are more than just putting a pretty face on legacy systems and running them in a local area network. The primary impetus behind the growth of client/server systems is the *user's need for access to corporate data*. This is a dramatic change from the philosophy behind legacy systems. In a legacy system, the application system was designed around the storage of data on a mainframe. The applications were driven by the needs of the systems rather than the needs of the users.

In a client/server system, the user is in control. A graphical environment, such as Windows or the Macintosh operating environment, lets the user drive through the system with a mouse. Similarly, in a client/server application, a user must be able to easily find, retrieve, add, and modify their data. And, just as in the graphical environment, users should be able to make their way through a system without a great deal of training.

Although the basic design of the client application may change in a client/server system, developers and data administrators must still utilize proper design principles if the systems are to deliver adequate performance and maintain the integrity of the data. For instance, according to the principles of good relational design, all rows in a table must have a unique identifier. The unique identifier may be meaningless or even confusing to a user, but crucial to the proper functioning of the application system.

In a well-designed database, data is kept in *normalized* tables, where only data that directly relates to the database key is kept in the table. Many applications, such as the order entry system we are designing, will need data from more than one table. But users have no interest in, and may have little understanding of, the need to maintain data in related tables to allow the related members of each table to be linked together.

As a database is normalized, database designers will often implement a system of *referential integrity* constraints. A referential integrity constraint automatically forces a value that is entered into a column in one table to exist in another table. For instance, the ORDER_ID of an ORDER_ITEMS row must exist as the ID in the ORDERS row. The referential integrity in a database helps to ensure that only correct data is stored. Referential integrity can also help to reduce the size of the data in a row of a table by using a code to refer to another value. In the data you have used, you can see this in the ORDERS table, where both customers and sales representatives are referred to by their numeric code rather than by their names, which exist in separate tables. Although this is an efficient and powerful database design, it makes the data more difficult for a user to understand.

There are many data attributes that are essential to maintaining correct data on the server that are of no interest to an application user. In the user-driven client/server system, a key function of a client application is to automatically handle these issues without interfering with the ease of use of an application. In other words, a client application in a client system can seamlessly mediate between the demands of data integrity and user demands of ease of use.

Adding Data-Related Features

In this section, we will add functionality to handle

- Automatically assigning values to fields
- Limiting the data choices available to a user
- Giving a user an online list of available data values
- Deriving values from existing values
- Adding mandatory data column values to your form
- Controlling the way data is presented to the user

At the end of this section, you will have an application that is easier to use and understand and that will guard against invalid data being entered into the database. You will have added additional data field objects to your form that will allow you to properly insert rows into the ORDERS table.

Assigning Default Data Values

In most application systems, there is some data that is created or assigned by the system. Sometimes system-created data is used to establish relationships between different tables or to establish unique identifiers, both of which will be discussed later in this chapter. Sometimes you will just want to make your application easier to use by having the application automatically create values and spare the user the trouble of having to continually re-enter the values.

In the order entry system you are designing, there is a column in the ORDERS table for the ORDER_DATE. The ORDER_DATE is the date the order was entered. As mentioned in Chapter 2, Oracle Power Objects provides many functions, including data functions. You will now modify your application to make it automatically assign the order date.

■ You must first add a data field to your form for the ORDER_DATE column. Choose the data field object push button from the toolbar. Add a data field to your form to the right of the top row of data field objects and set the Name property to 'ORDER_DATE'. Add a static text object with a Label of 'Order Date' just above the data field object.

■ Position the ORDER_DATE data field and static text objects in the top row of data fields, but all the way to the right since you will be adding a field to display the name of a sales representative later in this chapter.

Your form should now look like this:

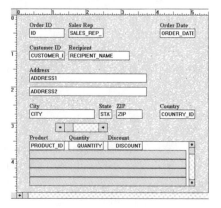

■ Since this data field is going to be connected to the ORDER_DATE field, enter 'ORDER_DATE' for the DataSource property in the property sheet.

This is the first time you have had to explicitly assign a data source to one of your data field objects. When you created the other data fields in your application by dragging them to your form from the ORDERSES session, Oracle Power Objects automatically assigned a data source to the data field objects for you. Oracle Power Objects uses the value in the DataSource property of the data field objects in your form to create the underlying SQL statements that the application uses to interact with the database. You must spell the name of the DataSource properly or your application will have run-time errors as Oracle Power Objects attempts to execute improper SQL statements.

■ Change the DataType property of the ORDER_DATE data field to 'Date'.

By default, Oracle Power Objects assigns a data type of 'Long Integer' to data field objects. When Oracle Power Objects automatically creates data field objects, the proper data type is set for you.

■ Bring up the property sheet for the Orders form by clicking on the form background. Open the code window for the **InsertRow( )** method. Enter the code

```
ORDER_DATE.Value= NOW
```

to set the default value for the ORDER_DATE for a new order to today's date.

Adding a new row to the ORDERS table is controlled by the overall form. The **InsertRow( )** method for the form is triggered whenever you add a new row to the form, either by clicking on the Insert push button in the toolbar or by beginning to enter data in the blank row at the end of the table. Note that you must set the Value property of a data field object. The value of the data field object is kept in the Value property, so you must set the ORDER_DATE value to the date returned by the NOW date function.

NOTE
Oracle Power Objects code is not case sensitive. You could use the code

```
order_date.VALUE = NOW
```

in place of the above code. All the code examples in this book will use standard conventions for case—the same case for referenced objects as the name of the object and lowercase for properties. For functions, capitalization will be consistently used to provide the most comprehensible form of the function—for instance, SqlLookup instead of SQLLOOKUP or sqllookup.

■ In order to have the default processing for the **InsertRow( )** function execute, insert the underlined code at the beginning of the function:

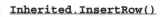

```
Inherited.InsertRow()
ORDER_DATE.Value = NOW
```

Oracle Power Objects is an object-oriented development environment. Whenever you enter code for an object, it replaces any code that was inherited from an object class. The **Inherited** keyword calls the default processing inherited from the master form class. You have to call the default **InsertRow( )** method before setting any values, since part of the default **InsertRow( )** method processing initializes all of the values in a form. You will learn all about classes and object orientation in Chapter 5.

■ Run the form to see the default value in action. Start to insert a new row into the ORDERS table by either entering data in the blank row at the end of the data or by clicking on the Insert push button in the toolbar. Notice the appearance of today's date in the ORDER_DATE data field. Roll back the new row by clicking on the Rollback push button. Stop the application by clicking on the Stop button.

As you saw today's date appear in the ORDER_DATE data field, you probably realized that you would only like to see the date portion of the time and date, rather than the default display of the complete date and time. To change the appearance of the date value, you will have to change the date's display format.

■ Bring up the property sheet for the ORDER_DATE field. Click on the FormatMask property to bring up a list of available date formats. Double-click on the "Short Date" entry to change the date format for the object and close the list of formats.

You have now enhanced your application to automatically enter the current date as the ORDER_DATE for a new order. To ensure data consistency, you should prevent a user from being able to change the date.

■ Scroll to the ReadOnly property of the ORDER_DATE data field object. Click in the value box to the right of the property name to change the ReadOnly property to 'True'.

A user will only be able to read the date in the ORDER_DATE data field. The user will be able to enter a value or a condition via the QBF facility to see the orders from a particular date, but he or she will not be able to change the system-generated value.

Calculating Default Values

You have been able to automatically assign the date an order is placed. Your application could also assign a default shipping date, since orders normally go out three business days after they are entered into the system.

In Chapter 2, you learned how to use a date function to determine the day of the week of a particular date. You will be able to use this function to determine the date that falls three business days after the order date.

■ Add a data field object for the SHIP_DATE to your form, in the row below the ORDER_DATE data field. Make the DataSource property for the data field 'SHIP_DATE', the DataType property for the field 'Date', and the FormatMask for the data field 'Short Date'. Add a static text object for the SHIP_DATE with the text 'Ship Date'.

The values for these properties are all identical to the values for the ORDER_DATE data field object. You could have selected the ORDER_DATE data field and static text objects, copied them using the Copy push button, and pasted a copy of each of them into the application using the Paste push button in the toolbar. You would then have to go back and change the DataSource property, the Name property, and the ReadOnly property for the data field and the text of the static text object. In Chapter 5, you will learn how to define object classes that can be repeatedly used.

Your form should now look like this:

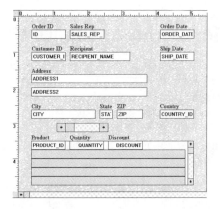

■ Bring up the property sheet for the Orders form. Return to the **InsertRow( )** method, which now is labeled as the **InsertRow...** method to indicate that code exists for the method. Add the following code between the code to set the ORDER_DATE data field and the call to the inherited **InsertRow( )** function:

```
IF WEEKDAY(NOW)) > 3 THEN
    SHIP_DATE.Value= DATEADD("d",5,NOW)
ELSE
```

```
    SHIP_DATE.Value= DATEADD("d",3,NOW)
END IF
```

This code checks today's day of the week. If the day of the week is not a Monday, which returns a 2 from the **WEEKDAY** function, or a Tuesday, which returns a 3 from the WEEKDAY function, the SHIP_DATE is set for five calendar days in the future, to allow for the weekend. If today is a Monday or a Tuesday, the SHIP_DATE is set for three calendar days in the future.

The default value for the ORDER_DATE was fixed—you did not want to allow a user to change the date. Since you did not change the ReadOnly property of the SHIP_DATE data field object, the default date for the SHIP_DATE data field object can be modified by the user, if necessary.

NOTE
You may wonder why you couldn't enter the **NOW** function as the default value for the ORDER_DATE data field object. In Oracle Power Objects, an object can have a property, which is a constant value, or a method. A property is not evaluated, so you cannot include functions in a property value.

Automatically Generating Sequence Numbers

One of the principles of good relational database design is to provide a unique identifier for every row in a table. There are many times when your data will require a generated sequence number to uniquely identify each new row. Oracle Power Objects give you an easy way to generate sequence numbers for new rows in your database, whether you are using a database, such as Oracle or Blaze, that support sequence objects in the database, or a database that does not offer sequence objects.

■ Select the ID data field. Change the ReadOnly property of the data field object to 'True'.

Sequence numbers are automatically assigned to rows in the ORDERS table. You do not want users to be able to change these sequence numbers, since they are used to uniquely identify a row and changing the identifying number of a row may interfere with the relationships between a row and rows in other tables.

■ Click on the CounterType property label to drop down the list of values and double-click on the 'Sequence' value to select the value and close the list box.

You have three types of counters you can use to implement automatic sequence generation. If you are using Oracle or Blaze, both of which support sequence objects, you can choose a Sequence type of counter. Oracle Power Objects will automatically interact with the sequence object you will specify in the next step to derive a unique sequence number.

If you are working with a database that does not support a sequence object, you can choose the 'Table, MAX() & CounterIncBy' counter. For this type of counter, Oracle Power Objects will automatically query the table that contains the column specified by the DataSource property for the maximum value in that column. Oracle Power Objects will set the value of the data field object to the maximum value retrieved plus the amount specified by the CounterIncBy property. This type of counter requires a database query for each new sequence number, so it tends to be more resource intensive.

If you choose to use the User Generated counter, Oracle Power Objects will call the **CounterGenKey( )** method whenever a new row that contains the data field object is added to the database. You might want to create your own routine to generate a unique sequence number, but Oracle Power Objects makes it easy for you to integrate your routine into an application.

■   Set the CounterSeq property to 'ORDER_ID_SEQ'.

ORDER_ID_SEQ is a sequence object in your Oracle or Blaze demo database.

■   Set the CounterTiming property to 'Immediate'.

You have two options for CounterTiming. Immediate counter timing will request a sequence number as soon as you start to insert a row. Deferred counter timing will request a sequence number when you actually commit a new row to the database. If you use Immediate timing, you can display the sequence number in the application while the user is entering data, or use the sequence number elsewhere in the application. If you use the Deferred timing, you will avoid requesting a sequence number for rows that are rolled back and not added to the database.

Both timing methods have pluses and minuses. It is a good idea, though, to be consistent in your timing method for any particular database sequence.

You have been able to add automatic sequence generation by changing just a few properties with Oracle Power Objects. Your next step will be to add more information to help your users understand their data better.

Providing User Feedback

In the application you have built, customers and sales representatives are indicated with their unique identification codes rather than something more understandable to users, such as their names. As discussed earlier in this chapter, good relational database design will deliver good database performance and data integrity, but it does not by itself necessarily offer the most user-friendly structure for data. The names of the sales representatives and customers exist, but in another table.

In this section, you will learn how you can easily display descriptive information from other tables. You will include the display of a sales representative's name in your application.

- Reduce the size of the SALES_REP_ID data field object to make room for the customer name object.

- Draw a data field object to the right of the SALES_REP_ID data field. Set the Name property of the data field object to 'SALES_REP_NAME'. Change the DataType property to 'String' and make the ReadOnly property 'True'.

Since the display of the customer name is only to give a user more information about the customer, the SALES_REP_NAME data field should be read only.

- For the DataSource property, enter the following code:

```
=SqlLookup(ORDERSES,"select ENAME from EMP where EMPNO =" &&
    SALES_REP_ID)
```

NOTE
You can specify the session name as the first parameter in the **SqlLookup( )** function or omit it. If you omit the session name, Oracle Power Objects will use the session specified as the DefaultSession property in the application property sheet. If you are only going to use a form against the same session, you should include the session name for documentation purposes. If you are creating a form for use in a library or a class, which is discussed in Chapter 5, you might want to omit the session name so that you will not have to modify your code when you use the form in different applications with different sessions.

The **SqlLookup( )** function retrieves the sales representative's name from the EMP table. The first parameter of the **SqlLookup( )** function is the name of the database session, ORDERSES. The second parameter is a string that is the SQL statement necessary to retrieve the sales representative's name, which is the ENAME column in the EMP table.

You have used the & character to concatenate a numeric value and a string. You could also concatenate the SALES_REP_ID object with the + concatenation operand. The advantage of using the + as the concatenation operand revolves around the possible use of a null value. The + operand will return null for any concatenation that includes a null, while the & operand treats a null as a zero-length string. Oracle Power Objects will not execute a **SqlLookup( )** function call if the comparison value is null, so the + operand tends to work better with string comparisons. The **SqlLookup( )** code in this book will use the & operand for concatenation in **SqlLookup( )** function calls, since all of the calls will be using numeric values.

■   Run the form to see the action of the lookup.

Your form should now look like this:

In the next section, you will modify your application to allow a user to not only display a sales representative's name, but also to allow users to select sales representatives by their names rather than their identification numbers.

Handling New Rows with SqlLookup( )

The **SqlLookup( )** code you entered in the previous section works fine when retrieving rows from the database. A value for the SALES_REP_ID is retrieved, and then the **SqlLookup( )** function does its work. However, if you are entering a new row, **SqlLookup( )** will not work properly. The **SqlLookup( )** function will try to use the null value in the SALES_REP_ID field, which will result in the SQL statement being "select ENAME from EMP where EMPNO =", which is invalid.

You can fix this function by deriving the value used in the lookup with the **IIF( )** function. The **IIF( )** function has three parameters: a logical test that returns a True or False result, the value to return from the function if the test is True, and the value to return from the function if the test is False. The logical test you will have to use is the **ISNULL( )**, which returns True if the tested value is null and False if it is not.

■ Modify the code you have in the DataSource property of the SALES_REP_NAME data field object to

```
=SqlLookup(ORDERSES,"select ENAME from EMP where EMPNO =" &
        IIF( ISNULL(SALES_REP_ID), 0, SALES_REP_ID))
```

NOTE
A property value must be on a single line. The above code is shown on two lines due to the formatting limitations of this book. This convention is used throughout the book.

If the value of the SALES_REP_ID data field is null, the modified function will give the SALES_REP_NAME data field the value of the SALES_REP_NAME for sales rep '0', which is null also.

Translating User Choices

When you added the lookup of a sales representative's name from a customer ID in the previous section, you provided information to the user that makes the application more comprehensible when it is returning data. But if the user chooses to add a new order or change the sales representative for an existing order, he or she will still have to know the sales representaive's ID, even though the sales representaive's name is immediately associated with a particular ID.

There very well may be only a few sales representatives for a company, but, hopefully, there are many customers. Although a user could know the IDs of a few sales representatives, they probably won't be able to memorize the identification numbers of all of the customers.

Oracle Power Objects gives you the ability to automatically translate a descriptive value to its corresponding code value. You will implement this functionality in the next section and also use a *pop-up list* for the first time.

■ Modify the Label property of the static text object over the CUSTOMER_ID data field to 'Customer'. Delete the CUSTOMER_ID data field object. Reduce the size of the RECIPIENT_NAME data field object and move it to the right.

You will be replacing the CUSTOMER_ID data field object with a *pop-up* list object that will display the customer name.

■ Select the pop-up list icon from the Tool palette. Draw a pop-up list object to where the CUSTOMER_ID data field used to be and extend the width of the pop-up list, since the customer name will be a bit longer than the ID. Set the Name and Label properties of the pop-up list object to 'CUSTOMER_ID'. Set the DataSource property of the pop-up list to 'CUSTOMER_ID'. Set the DataType property of the pop-up list to 'String'.

A pop-up list object is a special type of compound in Oracle Power Objects with some of the qualities of a list box object and some of the qualities of a data field object. The pop-up list box gives a user a set of choices. A user can click on the drop-down button to see the choices and click on a choice to set the data field portion of the pop-up list to the selected value. A user can only select one of the values in a pop-up list. A *combo box* gives a user a list of values, but also allows a user to enter a value in the data field area of the object.

The Oracle Power Objects pop-up list and combo box include the ability to display a list of values and automatically translate a value to another corresponding value. In the application you are building, you will be displaying the name of a customer but using the corresponding identification number of the customer as the data to be retrieved or inserted into the CUSTOMER_ID column of the ORDERS table. You will accomplish this by setting the Translation property of the pop-up list.

■ Click on the Translation property of the CUSTOMER_ID pop-up list object. Enter the following code in the code window.

```
= AT ORDERSES select distinct customers.NAME, customers.ID from
    CUSTOMERS order by .NAME
```

NOTE
As with the **SqlLookup( )** function discussed earlier in this chapter, you can specify the session in the Translation property or omit the "**AT** *session* clause. If you omit the session clause, Oracle Power Objects will use the session specified in the DefaultSession property of the application.

■ Close the code area by clicking on the Translation property label again.

The Translation property controls the action of the pop-up list box object. You must first specify the database session you will be using for your translation. If you do not specify an **AT** *session* phrase in a Translation property, Oracle Power Objects will use the session specified in the DefaultSession property of the application. If there is no value in the DefaultSession property, Oracle Power Objects will use a session from the Main window. It is always good programming practice to specifically document aspects of your code when you are coding specific screens rather than depending on a proper setting in another object's property. The exception to this guideline is when you are creating a general-purpose library or class, which will be discussed in Chapters 5 and 6.

The **AT** *session* clause is followed by the SQL statement that will retrieve the display value and the corresponding data value from the database. In this case, you will be displaying the NAME column from the CUSTOMERS table and using the ID column from the CUSTOMERS table as the data value for the pop-up list object. The "order by" clause will establish the order the customer names are displayed in the pop-up list.

NOTE
Some portions of Oracle Power Objects require the use of SQL. If you are unfamiliar with the SQL language, you might want to refer to the documentation for your database or get an introductory book on SQL.

The Translation method used for this pop-up list object is one of three translation method styles. You may also *hardcode* translation values, such as

```
One=1
Two=2
Three=3
```

to display the names of numbers rather than the figures.

You may also set up *table column mapping* if the display value and the corresponding value are in the same table. For instance, if you want to display the employee name instead of the employee number, the Translation property would be

```
ENAME=EMPNO
```

Since the translation values are coming from a different database table than the data source, you have to use the *queried values* method for your pop-up list.

The values in the pop-up list are automatically filled when your application starts. You can programmatically repopulate a pop-up list by using the **UpdateList( )** method.

NOTE
You must specify a Translation property for a pop-up list or combo box. If you do not, no values will show in the object.

Your form should now look like this:

Order ID	Sales Rep		Order Date
1	7521	WARD	5/20/95

Customer	Recipient	Ship Date
CandleSellers	Scott Smith	5/21/95

Address
100 Twin Dolphin Drive

City	State	ZIP	Country
Redwood Shores	CA	94065	1

Product	Quantity	Discount
10	100	
11	100	
12	100	
15	50	0.05

You have used a pop-up list to make it easier for a user to work with data. The pop-up list object also limits the values that a user can give to a piece of data. You will be able to limit a user's choice of data values by using radio buttons and check boxes, which will be explained in the next section.

Limiting User Choices of Data

In the previous section, you used a pop-up list object to give the application users more descriptive data. The pop-up list also limited the users to choosing one of the listed values—the users could not enter a value on their own. The pop-up list object can display many values, so the pop-up list is a good way to limit the values a user might enter if there are many acceptable values. The pop-up list object populates itself with values when the application is started by querying the database, so it is also a good method to use if the acceptable values for a column will be frequently changing.

You can also limit the values for a column in the database by using *check boxes* and *radio buttons*. A check box is a graphical object that can have two states: checked or unchecked. Radio buttons can be combined in a group, and only one radio button in a group can be "on," or selected, at a time. The SHIP_METHOD_ID column in the ORDERS table can have a value of '1', which indicates standard shipment, or '2', which indicates overnight shipment. You will be able to use a check box to graphically represent the two choices available to the user.

■ Select the check box icon from the Tool palette. Drop and size a check box to the right of the scroll bar. You can immediately enter 'Overnight Delivery?'as the Label property for the check box.

■ Change the Name property of check box object to 'cbOvernight', the ColorText and FontName properties to the same color and font as your other labels, and the FontBold property to 'True'.

The standard Windows naming convention for check boxes is to preface the name of the check box with the prefix "cb." You do not have to adhere to the standard, but when you start to reference objects in the method code of other objects, it is helpful to stick to a naming standard to save you the trouble of having to constantly check your object names.

■ Set the DataSource property of your check box to SHIP_METHOD_ID. Set the ValueOn property of your check box to '2' and the ValueOff property to '1'. Set the DefaultValue to '1'.

All you have to do is to set the ValueOn and ValueOff properties of your check box, and Oracle Power Objects will handle setting the check box and assigning a value to the SHIP_METHOD_ID column. You should set the default value of the check box to '1', since overnight delivery is not the standard option.

■ Run the form to see the operation of your check box.

Your form should now look like this:

Your next step is to add a group of radio buttons to specify the country.

■ Delete the COUNTRY_ID data field and static text objects, since you will be replacing them with a group of radio buttons.

■ Select the radio button group icon from the Tool palette. Draw a radio button group from the right of the ADDRESS2 data field object down to the bottom of the ZIP data field. Set the Label property of the radio button to

'Country'. Set the ColorBrdr property to the same color as the static text objects in your form.

In a graphical application, you can use graphical features to help describe the function of different objects in your form. All of the data in the form is black, while all of the descriptive titles are blue in the form illustrated. It is not necessary that you follow this suggestion, but an application can be both more attractive and better understood by your users if you can fully use the graphical capabilities of your application.

■ Set the Name property of the radio button group box to 'rbfCountry', the DataSource property to 'COUNTRY_ID', and the DefaultValue to '1'.

The default prefix we recommend for a radio button frame is "rbf." Notice that you are assigning the data source of the radio button frame to COUNTRY_ID. The Value property of the radio button frame will automatically be set by Oracle Power Objects to the ValueOn property of the selected radio button.

■ Select the radio button icon from the Tool palette. Drop a radio button at the top of the radio button frame and set the Label property to 'U.S.'. Set the Name property of the radio button to 'radUS' and the OnValue of the radio button to '1'.

The value of the rbfCountry is automatically set to 1 when this radio button is selected. Oracle Power Objects will turn this radio button on when the retrieved value of COUNTRY_ID is 1.

■ Drop a radio button in the middle of the radio button frame and set the Label property to 'Canada'. Set the Name property of the radio button to 'radCanada' and the OnValue of the radio button to '2'.

The value of the rbfCountry is automatically set to 2 when this radio button is selected. Oracle Power Objects will turn this radio button on when the retrieved value of COUNTRY_ID is 2.

■ Drop a radio button at the bottom of the radio button frame and set the Label property to 'Europe'. Set the Name property of the radio button to 'radEurope' and the OnValue of the radio button to '5'.

The value of the rbfCountry is automatically set to 5 when this radio button is selected. Oracle Power Objects will turn this radio button on when the retrieved value of COUNTRY_ID is 5.

■ Select the radio button frame and the three radio buttons. Change the FontName property to the font you have used in the rest of the application, the FontColor of the objects to the same color as the fonts in the rest of the form, and the FontBold property to 'True'.

■ Run the application to see how your radio buttons operate. Notice that selecting any of the radio buttons automatically turns off all of the other radio buttons.

Your form should look like this:

Once again, all you had to do was to set the ValueOn property of each of the radio buttons and set the DataSource of the radio button frame to a database column and Oracle Power Objects took care of the rest.

You have now created screen objects for all of the required fields for the ORDERS table. You can use the form to properly insert new rows into the database for the ORDERS table.

You will adjust the way your application delivers data to the user in your final modification of the functionality of your form for the master table ORDERS.

Controlling the Display of Master Table Data

You might want to adjust the way the rows from the master table, ORDERS, are presented to the user. In this section, you will change the order the rows are returned and eliminate the blank row that appears at the end of the scroll range.

■ Click on the background of the Orders form to bring up the Property sheet for the form. Scroll to the OrderBy property. Enter 'CUSTOMER_ID, ORDER_DATE' so that the form will return rows from the ORDERS table sorted by the CUSTOMER_ID first and the ORDER_DATE second for each customer.

You can specify as many columns as you like in the OrderBy property. The first column name entered is the highest level of sort, and all columns are sorted in ascending order. The OrderBy property will sort the rows returned to the application whenever rows are retrieved, either by default or through a QBF query.

The OrderBy property can be set at run time. You could set the OrderBy property at run time by including check boxes, radio buttons, or a separate form window, which would allow a user to select the columns to sort results by setting the OrderBy property and re-executing the query. You will be learning how to use properties set at run time in Chapter 4.

■ Scroll to the HasExtraRow property and set it to 'False'.

Some users find the extra row at the end of the scroll range confusing, especially since there is an Insert Row push button. When you change the HasExtraRow property to 'False', the extra row at the end of the scroll range will no longer appear. The user will be able to use the InsertRow push button to add new rows to the ORDERS table, and your form will no longer contain the blank row at the end of the scroll range.

You have really refined the interaction with the ORDERS table in your form. In the next section, you will take the techniques you have learned and apply them to the repeater display containing the ORDER_ITEMS data.

Putting It Together in the Repeater Display

You may have noticed a problem with the repeater display in your form. If you tried to add new rows to the ORDER_ITEMS table, you have received an error message informing you that some non-null columns did not contain data.

Your repeater display could also contain more useful information. In this section, you will correct both of these problems.

Adding a Sequence Counter for the ORDER_ITEMS Table

The ORDER_ITEMS table contains a unique identifier called ID. You have not bound an object to this field, which accounts for the error when you try to insert a new row. The database you are using has a sequence object that is used to assign a sequence number to the ID column, so you will be able to add a sequence number to your form.

■ Start by reducing the size of the existing PRODUCT_ID, QUANTITY, and DISCOUNT data field objects to make room for some of the data fields you will be adding to the primary panel. For the time being, move the data field objects toward the right side of the primary panel of the repeater display.

Remember that you will have to click on the data field object three times to select it—once to select the repeater display, once to select the primary panel, and once to select the data field object. You will be in edit mode when you select the data field object, so press the ENTER key to select the object.

■ Add a data field object to the far left of the primary panel. Give the data field object a Name property of 'ID' by entering it in the highlighted area that appears when you add the data field. Set the value of the DataSource property as 'ID' to bind it to the ID column in the ORDER_ITEMS table.

Since the ID column is a number, you do not have to change the DataType property of the data field object from its default value of 'Long Integer'. Data field objects do not have a label.

■ Make this data field a sequence by adding the database sequence object 'ORDER_ITEMS_ID_SEQ' as the CounterSeq property. Set the CounterType property as 'Sequence' and the CounterTiming property as 'Immediate'.

If you are using a database that does not support sequence objects, you should use the 'Table, MAX( ) & CounterIncBy' sequence counter type. You will be using the 'Immediate' sequence timing in this application, but you could set the sequence timing differently in other applications.

■ Move the PRODUCT_ID data field object to the left so that it overlaps the right end of the ID data field. Click on the Bring To Front push button in the toolbar to move the PRODUCT_ID data field in front of the ID data field. Move the PRODUCT_ID field to the left so that it hides the ID data field object.

The ID column of the ORDER_ITEMS table does not have a meaning to the end user of the application, so there is no need to have this item visible in the application. You could move an object to the front by selecting the object and choosing the Bring to Front menu choice from the Object menu.

You could also set the Visible property of the ID data field object to 'False'. This would hide the data field when the application is running, but leave it visible while you are in design mode.

Adding the Product Description

The repeater display currently shows the product identification number. The repeater display would be more comprehensible if it also displayed a description of the product.

- Since you will be adding more fields to the repeater display, you should enlarge your form to make it 6 1/4 inches wide and 5 1/2 inches tall.

- Reduce the size of the PRODUCT_ID data field until it is 3/8 inches wide. Move the QUANTITY and the DISCOUNT data fields to the right of the primary panel. Add another data field object to the repeater display and set the Name property to 'PRODUCT_DESCRIPTION'. Make this data field 2 3/4 inches wide, since it will be displaying long descriptions.

- Set the DataType property of data field to 'String'. Set the DataSize property to '100'. Set the ReadOnly property to 'True'.

By default, the DataSize property is 0. The 0 value for the DataSize property will allow any size data up to 41 characters. Since the description of a product could be up to 100 characters, you will have to explicitly set the length of the data field object.

This data field will be used to display a lookup value, so you should not allow a user to edit the field.

- Set the DataSource property for the PRODUCT_DESCRIPTION data field object to the following **SqlLookup()** function:

```
=SqlLookup(ORDERSES, "select DESCRIPTION from PRODUCTS where ID = " &
PRODUCT_ID)
```

NOTE
As with the earlier **SqlLookup( )** function, all of the above text must be on the same line in your Oracle Power Objects code.

The **SqlLookup()** function will retrieve the DESCRIPTION column from the PRODUCTS table where the ID column is equal to the value in the PRODUCT_ID data field.

Your form should now look like this:

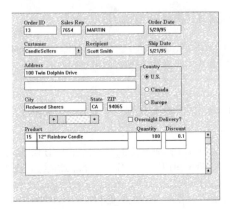

Adding the Price of an Item

The information in the primary panel is more useful for the user of the application. It is amazing, however, how important the price of an item can be to customers. You will use the same lookup function you have used to supply description information to add the price of an item to an order line.

■ To make room for the rest of the fields that you will add to the repeater display, enlarge the repeater display until it almost goes to the right border of the form.

■ To improve the appearance of the form, change the static text Label of 'Discount' to 'Disc' and change the FormatMask property of the DISCOUNT data field object in the repeater display to 'Percentage'.

■ Move the QUANTITY and DISCOUNT data fields so they are just to the right of the PRODUCT_DESCRIPTION data field in the primary panel of the repeater display. Move the static text objects so they are over their respective data fields.

■ Add a data field object to the right of the existing fields in the primary panel of the repeater display and set the Name property to 'UNIT_PRICE'. Set the FormatMask property to 'Standard' and the ReadOnly property to

'True'. Set the TextJustVert property to 'Right' to display the value left justified in the data field object. Add a static text object with a Label property of 'Price' over the UNIT_PRICE data field. Make the static text field the same font and color of the other labels in the form.

Oracle Power Objects uses the default currency format as established in your operating system. If you are in the United States, there will be a $ at the front of the number; a comma (,) to separate thousands, millions, etc. to the right of the decimal; and a period (.) as the decimal marker.

■ Set the DataSource property to the following **SqlLookup( )** function:

```
=SqlLookup(ORDERSES, "select UNIT_PRICE from PRODUCTS where ID = " &
    IIF(ISNULL(PRODUCT_ID),0,PRODUCT_ID))
```

NOTE
Once again, the above text should be on a single line in your Oracle Power Objects code.

You should use the **ISNULL( )** function for the same reason you used the function to look up the SALES_REP_NAME in the main part of the form.

■ Run your application to see the unit prices of each item in the repeater display.

Your form should now look like this:

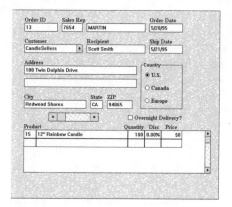

Calculating the Price of an Order Line

You have all of the data you will need to calculate the price of a single line in your order. In this section, you will calculate the final price of the items ordered in a single order line with some basic calculations.

- Add the final data field object to the far right of the primary panel of the repeater display. Set the Name property of the data field 'LINE_TOTAL'. Set the FormatMask to 'Standard', and set the ReadOnly property to 'True'.

You may have noticed that Oracle Power Objects automatically aligns the dimensions of any object in a design window to a grid. This can create some sizing problems, such as the difficulty in making the rightmost data field object, LINE_TOTAL, extend to the edge of the scroll bar of the repeater display. To size an object without having it snap to the grid, select the object and grab one of its sizing handles while holding down the CTRL key. You can now size the object to a nongrid position.

- Add two static text objects stacked over each other above the LINE_TOTAL data field. Set the top static text object's Label property to 'Line' and the bottom text object's Label property to 'Total'. Select both text objects and set the FontName, FontBold, and ColorText objects to match those of the other text objects. Set the TextJustHoriz property to 'Center' and center the two fields together to improve their appearance.

You might also want to set the TextJustVert of the top text object to 'Bottom' to bring the two lines of text closer together.

- You will want to display the calculated total of the items in the order line. You can derive this by multiplying the QUANTITY of an item by the UNIT_PRICE and subtracting the DISCOUNT. Since you will be doing decimal arithmetic, you must set the DataType of all fields involved in the calculation to 'Double'. Select the QUANTITY, DISCOUNT, UNIT_PRICE, and LINE_TOTAL data field objects and change their DataType property to 'Double'. To make your primary panel easier to understand, set the FormatMask of the DISCOUNT data field object to 'Percent'.

If you were to leave the data type of any of these fields as the default 'Long Integer', Oracle Power Objects would use integer arithmetic in your calculation. Integer arithmetic would automatically truncate any digits to the right of the decimal, so any value less than 1 would be truncated to 0. Since you are using a decimal calculation to assign a discounted value by multiplying the total price by the discounted amount (1– DISCOUNT), this would result in any order line that had a discount having a LINE_TOTAL of 0, since any discount would result in a multiplier less than 1.

■ Set the DataSource property of the LINE_TOTAL data field to

```
=(QUANTITY * UNIT_PRICE)*(1 - DISCOUNT)
```

■ Run your form to see the calculated price of each order line.

Your form should now look like this:

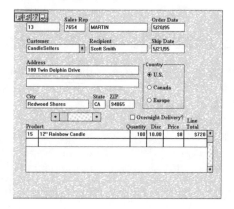

Your form may not have a LINE_TOTAL for any order line that does not have a discount. (If you are not using the ORDERSES session or the ORDERDB database described in Appendix A, this will occur.) If there is no DISCOUNT, the value of the DISCOUNT column is not 0, but null. A null value is different from a 0 in that it indicates an absence of value. Any arithmetic that includes a null value will give a result of null, regardless of the other numbers involved.

You can address this problem by using the Oracle Power Objects **IIF( )** function. The **IIF( )** function takes three parameters: the first is a Boolean condition that returns a True or False, the second is the value to return if the Boolean condition is True, and the third is the value to return if the Boolean condition is False. You can also use the Oracle Power Objects function **ISNULL( )** to determine if the value in the DISCOUNT data field is null. The modified DataSource for the LINE_TOTAL field will now be

```
=(QUANTITY * UNIT_PRICE) * (1 - (IIF(ISNULL(DISCOUNT), 0, DISCOUNT))
```

If DISCOUNT is null, the **IIF( )** function will return 0; if DISCOUNT is not null, the **IIF( )** function will return the value in DISCOUNT.

You can prevent this problem in new order lines with the following modification.

- Select the DISCOUNT data field object in the primary panel of the repeater display. Set the DefaultValue property to '0'.

This will give all new rows in the ORDER_LINES repeater a default value of 0 for the DISCOUNT field. You will notice that this causes the DISCOUNT column in the blank row at the end of the repeater to display a 0.

Calculating the Total Price of the Order

The final piece of information for your screen is the calculation of the total price of all of the items in an order. You will be able to easily calculate the total price of the order with an Oracle Basic function.

- Add a data field object below the repeater display. Set the Name property of the data field to 'TOTAL'. Set the DataType property of the data field to 'Double' and the FormatMask property of the data field to 'Standard'.

- Set the DataSource property of the TOTAL data field object to

```
=SUM(LINE_TOTAL)
```

The Oracle Basic function **SUM( )** returns the sum of all of the instances of the data field objects referenced. You should be aware of the fact that a data field object with the **SUM( )** function cannot be a part of the same container as the fields that are to be summed. In other words, you could not have used this function call within the repeater display, which is the container for the LINE_TOTAL data field object. Any data field objects used with the **SUM( )** function must be repeated as a data field in a repeater display and must be numeric.

- Add a static text object to the left of the TOTAL data field. Set the Label property of the static text object to 'Total price of Order:'. You should set the TextJustHoriz property to 'Right' and line the static text object up just to the right of the TOTAL data field.

- Run your form to see the total price of the order.

Your form should now look like this:

You have added a great deal of functionality to your form. All that remains for you to do in this chapter is to modify some of the ways that you handle your master-detail relationship.

Master-Detail Enhancements

In this final section, you will make a few changes in the way that the master-detail relationship is handled in your application.

Enabling Master-Detail Query-By-Form

If you have not yet attempted to use QBF with your master-detail form, you should try it now.

■ Run your form. Click on the QBF push button in the toolbar. Enter **'10'** in the PRODUCT_ID of the repeater display. Click on the Apply Criteria push button in the toolbar to retrieve rows that match the values specified. Stop the application by clicking on the stop push button.

You will notice that the results returned may not be exactly what you were expecting. All of the orders are returned, but only the order lines with a PRODUCT_ID value of 10 are displayed.

■ Select the repeater display. Change the value of the LinkPrimaryKey property to 'Here (on detail)'. Run the form again and try the same QBF condition.

This time, your form should only return those rows in the master ORDERS table that have an associated row in the detail table that contain a PRODUCT_ID of 10.

Ensuring the Master-Detail Integrity

The relationship between the rows in the master table and the associated rows in the detail table is maintained by having the same value in the ID column of the ORDERS table and the ORDER_ID column of the detail table. Oracle Power Objects makes it easy for you to maintain the integrity of the relationship between a master row and its associated row in the detail table. In this section, you will look at the choices you have for maintaining coordination between a master table and a detail table.

■ Click on the background of the form to bring up the properties sheet for the frmOrders form. Scroll to the LinkMasterUpd property of the form. Click on the value area to drop down a list of the available choices.

You will see that you have three choices for implementing master-detail integrity:

1. *Refuse if Children Present* If you choose this option, Oracle Power Objects will not allow you to update the linking column in the ORDERS table, ID, if there are child records present on the form. This will take place whether there are children in the room the application is being run in or not. (joke)

2. *Update Cascade* If you choose this option, Oracle Power Objects will automatically update the value in the linking column, ORDER_ID, in the ORDER_ITEMS detail table if you change the value in the linking column, ID, in the ORDERS master table.

3. *Orphan Details* If you choose this option, Oracle Power Objects will not change the value of the linking column in the detail table. The detail items will now be "orphaned"—they will not have a master row to link to.

For this form, choose "Update Cascade."

■ Move to the LinkMasterDel property of the form. Click on the value area to see a list of your valid choices. For this form, choose "Refuse if Children Present."

By choosing "Refuse if Children Present," you are preventing a user from deleting a row from the ORDERS table if there are children present, *in this form only*. It is very common to enable this restriction and give the user a different way of deleting a master row and its associated details, such as choosing a menu option, using a different push button, or using a different form.

The issue of synchronizing the master and detail rows is one of many validation, or integrity, issues. You will learn a lot more about this later in this book.

You have made a lot of progress with your application. The application you have rapidly created is highly functional. The next few chapters will add some features to your form, and they will also go into some depth on the action "behind the scenes"—how your database operates, how to coordinate your client application with your database, how Oracle Power Objects handles database issues by default, and how you can create mission-critical applications that will perform well in multiuser environments.

CHAPTER 4

Adding a Sorting Screen

In Chapters 1 and 3, you created a nicely functional single-screen application. Your application can insert, modify, and delete rows from two related tables; it can even selectively retrieve rows from the tables. In the real world, most of your applications will be more than a single screen or form.

In this chapter, you will be adding another form to your application. The form will give your users the ability to dynamically select the way they want the rows returned to their application from the database. You will not only learn how to create and call another form, but you will also learn how to add a dynamic toolbar to a form, how to use list boxes, and how to dynamically modify properties used by Oracle Power Objects at run time.

There's a lot to learn, so let's get started!

An Overview of Your Task

In Chapter 3, you learned how you could specify the order that rows returned from the database server would be displayed in an Oracle Power Objects form. You did this by setting the OrderBy property of the form to use the sort columns of the master table.

Client-server applications should be able to flexibly address the needs of the user. There may be times when the user would like to view the data in a different order. As explained in Chapter 1, Oracle Power Objects uses the values of the properties of objects to control the way an application operates. You could give a user the ability to change the sort order of rows in the application easily by creating a process where the user could modify the value of the OrderBy property and the application would refetch rows from the database server using the new sort columns.

In this chapter, you will design a form that presents the user with the columns in the ORDERS table that could be used for sorting. The user will be able to select the columns to use for sorting and the application will automatically retrieve rows in the specified order. You will also learn how to call this form from the frmOrders form through a push button on a toolbar. You might want to use this type of functionality in many of your applications, so you will learn how to generalize the functionality of the form window and make it available through a library.

Create a Form to Specify Sort Order

In this section, you will create a form that you will be able to attach to your frmOrders form that will allow users to dynamically specify the columns they want to use to sort the data returned from the server, as well as how the data is to be sorted.

Creating a New Form

You will start by creating a new form window and adding the specific objects from Oracle Power Objects that you will need in the form. The form will include a list box for displaying the columns available to sort by, push buttons to select and deselect columns, and push buttons to close the form window and return to the Main Form window. When you have created the form and added all of the necessary objects, your form will look like this:

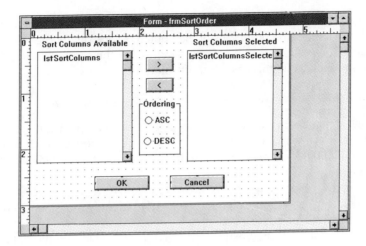

■ If you are still using the frmOrders form of the application, return to the Application window by closing the form window.

You could also make the Application window the active window by selecting it from the list of existing windows from the Windows menu in the Menu bar.

■ Create a new form window by clicking on New Form pushbutton in the Application toolbar. Set the Name property of the Form window to 'frmSortOrder' and set the Label property of the form to 'Specify Sort Order'. Make the form 4 3/4 inches wide.

■ Select the list box icon from the Tool palette and draw a list box that takes up about three-fourths of the form window's length and about one-fourth of the width of the form window in the upper-left portion of the form window. Make the list box 1 3/4 inches wide so that it will be able to hold the longest column name expected. Set the Name of the list box to 'lstSortColumns' and the Datatype to 'String'.

The "lst" prefix is a useful standard to use so that you will be able to reference the list box object easily in your Oracle Basic Code.

■ Create another list box in the upper-right portion of the form. You can either draw the list box in the same manner as you did the first list box or you could select the first list box, click on the Copy menu item in the Edit menu, paste a copy of the object using the Paste choice in the Edit menu, and move the list box to the appropriate position in the form.

When you paste a copy of an object, Oracle Power Objects creates a new object with all of the same properties of the copied object, but with a different name. Oracle Power Objects will append a number to the end of the original object's name, such as (in this case) 'lstSortColumns2'.

■ Give the new list box the Name of 'lstSortColumnsSelected'.

Although it may seem excessive to give objects in your application long names, using descriptive names for objects is well worth the extra few characters of typing. A consistent naming convention and descriptive names act as documentation for your application.

Add static text objects over the list boxes to identify them. Use the titles "Sort Columns Available" and "Sort Columns Selected" to identify the lstSortColumns and the lstSortColumnsSelected, respectively.

You might want to set the TextJustVert property to 'Center' for the static text objects, and you might have to use the CTRL-drag method of changing the size of an object without using the grid to properly size the static text objects.

■ Drop a push button onto the form between the two list boxes. Give it a Label of '>' by entering the character on the push button. Set the Name of the push button to 'btnSelect'. Add a second push button below the btnSelect push button and give it a Label of '<' and a name of 'btnDeselect'.

By using the ">" and the "<" labels for the push buttons, you are providing valuable information to the application users as to the purpose of the push buttons.

■ Add two more push buttons at the bottom of the Form window. Give the one on the left of the form the Label of 'OK' and the Name of 'btnOK'. Give the push button on the right the Label of 'Cancel' and the Name of 'btnCancel'.

It is good programming practice to always give your users the option of canceling any changes they have made in a particular form. In a graphical application, it is usually necessary to have a user indicate when he or she has finished using a form, given the modal nature of graphical systems, which is discussed later in this chapter. It is also good processing practice to give a standard name to these push buttons. Many graphical applications use the "OK/Cancel" labels for these push buttons.

■ Add a radio button frame between the two list boxes and below the push buttons. Give the radio button frame the Label of 'Ordering' and the Name of 'rbfOrdering'.

You should use the "rbf" prefix for a radio button frame to avoid confusing it with the "frm" prefix for a form.

■   Add a radio button to the rbfOrdering radio button frame. Give the radio button the Label of 'ASC' and the Name of 'btnAsc', a DataType of 'String', and a ValueOn of 'ASC'. Add a second radio button to the frame. Give the radio button the Label of 'DESC', the Name of 'btnDesc', a DataType of 'String', and a ValueOn of 'DESC'.

The user will select one of these radio buttons to determine whether a selected column will be used to sort the returning data in ascending (ASC) or descending (DESC) order.

■   Change the DataType of the rbfOrdering radio button frame to 'String' and set the DefaultValue to 'ASC'.

You must make the datatype of the radio button frame 'String' so that it can properly interact with the btnAsc and btnDesc radio buttons, which have string values for their ValueOn properties. You have already learned that Oracle Power Objects will automatically turn on the radio button whose ValueOn property corresponds to the value for the radio button frame. Since you have not connected the rbfOrdering frame with any particular piece of data, you should set the default value for the frame to 'ASC' so that Oracle Power Objects will initially turn on the btnAsc radio button.

You have now created the form and all the objects necessary to let your users specify the columns they wish to use to sort. All you have to do now is to add functionality to the form.

Your next step will be to populate the lstSortColumns list box with a list of the columns in the ORDERS table.

Populating a List Box with Table Column Names

The OrderBy property of your master form can use any column that is a part of the ORDERS table, the RecordSource for the master form. You will want to give your users the same options for sorting, so you will have to get a listing of all of the columns that are in the ORDERS table.

Oracle and Blaze, like all relational databases, keep track of the database objects in a database by using *system tables*. System tables are internal tables consisting of meta-data (or data that describes other data) that describes the objects in the database. Oracle has created a set of views that present this data to database administrators in an easy-to-use-and-understand format. You will use one of these system tables to populate the lstSortColumns list box.

NOTE
You can create, delete, and modify database objects and structures with SQL Data Definition Language (DDL), which your database will use to modify its own system tables. You will not be able to use SQL statements directly on the systems tables to accomplish this purpose.

■ Select the lstSortColumns list box to bring up the Properties sheet for the list box. Click on the Translation property to open up the Code window. If you are using an Oracle database, enter the following code:

```
= at ORDERSES select COLUMN_NAME, COLUMN_NAME from ALL_TAB_COLUMNS
where TABLE_NAME = 'ORDERS'
```

Note: All of this code should be on a single line in the code window.

All list boxes in Oracle Power Objects give you the ability to have one column's value displayed and another column's value, which contains the corresponding value, used for the value of the bound column. For this list box, the display column and corresponding column should have the same value since there is no translation necessary. The COLUMN_NAME column contains the names of the columns, and the TABLE_NAME column specifies the name of the table a column belongs to. Both of these columns are in the ALL_TAB_COLUMNS view, which contains all the relevant information for the columns in the database.

If you are using a Blaze database, the code should look like this:

```
= at ORDERSES select COLUMN_NAME, COLUMN_NAME from
SYS.ALL_COLUMNS, SYS.ALL_OBJECTS WHERE ALL_COLUMNS.ID =
ALL_OBJECTS.ID and ALL_OBJECTS.NAME = 'ORDERS'
```

Note: All of this code should be on a single line in the code window.

In a Blaze database, the system tables are laid out a bit differently than in an Oracle database. The ALL_COLUMNS table and the ALL_OBJECTS table are both owned by the user SYS, so you must qualify the name of the table with the owner's name. The ALL_OBJECTS table contains the names of tables in its NAME column. The ID column in the ALL_OBJECTS and the ALL_COLUMNS tables refers to the ID number of a table and acts as a link between the two tables.

You should have the name of the table ORDERSES in capital letters, since your SQL database may be case sensitive with regard to string values. Oracle Power Objects uses the single quote as the string delimiter in any SQL statements.

■ Run the form by clicking on the Run Form push button in the toolbar.

The Run Form push button is different from the Run push button you used in previous chapters. The Run Form push button runs only the active form, not the entire application. In previous chapters, the application only had a single form, so you could use either push button for the same effect.

If you use the Run Form push button to launch a form that contains references to other forms, you will have errors and be unable to run the form. When you have run your form, it should look like this:

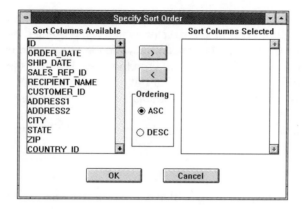

Moving a List Box Value to Another List Box

You have successfully created a list box that contains all the columns in the ORDERS table for your users to select. The next step is implementing a way to move a value from the lstSortColumns list box to the lstSortColumnsSelected list box.

You will be adding Oracle Basic code to your btnSelect push button. You will add the Oracle Basic code to the **Click( )** method for the push button. The **Click( )** method for a push button is automatically executed whenever a user clicks on the push button. You can also execute the function by calling it from another method.

As mentioned in Chapter 3, there are three methods you can use to populate values into a list box. You have used SQL statements to populate list boxes and combo boxes up until now. For the lstSortColumnsSelected list box, you will use a text list for the Translation property. The text list format for the Translation property takes the form

display_column = corresponding_column

- Click on the btnSelect push button to bring up the Property sheet. Click on the **Click( )** method to open a Code window for the push button. Enter the following code:

```
lstSortColumnsSelected.Translation = lstSortColumnsSelected.Translation &&
    lstSortColumns.Value  & "=" & lstSortColumns.Value & CHR(13) & CHR(10)
```

With this code, you concatenate a new string onto the existing Translation property. The selected value in the lstSortColumns list box can be referenced by using the Value property of the object. The string you add to the Translation property, for a selected column name of ID, would be

ID=ID

The **CHR( )** function is used to add nonprintable characters to a string. In this case, you are adding the New Line character, which is represented by the ASCII code of 10, and the Carriage Return character, which is represented by the ASCII code of 13. This will act as if the user had used the ENTER key after the entry.

You have modified the value of the Translation property, but you have to get the lstSortColumnsSelected list box to repopulate itself using the new value.

■ Add the following code to the **Click( )** method of the btnSelect push button below the previous code:

```
lstSortColumnsSelected.UpdateList()
```

The **UpdateList( )** method is associated with list boxes, pop-up lists, and combo boxes. The **UpdateList( )** method causes the object associated with the method to repopulate itself based on its Translation property.

■ Run your form. Click on the btnSelect push button to add a column to the lstSortColumnsSelected list.

When you have run your form and moved some values to the lstSortColumnsSelected list box, your form should look like this:

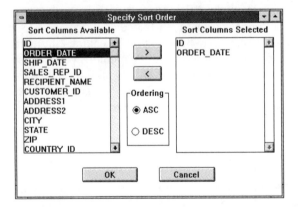

Adding the Ordering of a Selected Column

You have been able to add a selected column from the lstSortColumns list box to the lstSortColumnsSelected list box. You must also add the ordering information that the user has indicated by using the btnAsc and btnDesc radio buttons.

■ Add the underlined code to the code in the **Click( )** method for the btnSelect push button:

```
lstSortColumnsSelected.Translation = lstSortColumnsSelected.Translation &&
    lstSortColumns.Value & " " & rbfOrdering.Value & "=" &
    lstSortColumns.Value &  CHR(13) & CHR(10)
lstSortColumnsSelected.UpdateList()
```

The new code will add the value for the rbfOrdering radio button frame.

■ Run your form. Click on the btnSelect push button to add a column to the lstSortColumnsSelected list.

When you have run your form and moved a value to the lstSortColumnsSelected list box, your form should look like this:

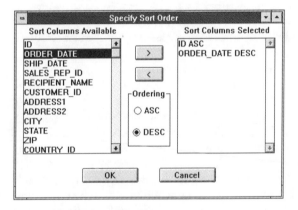

Deleting a Value from a List Box

Your next step is to add Oracle Basic code to the btnDeselect push button to enable the user to remove a sort column from the lstSortColumnsSelected list box. You can do this by modifying the Translation property of the lstSortColumnsSelected list box in a different way. You will delete the value from the Translation property by concatenating the portion of the Translation property string that comes before the value to be deleted with the portion of the Translation property string that comes after the value to be deleted.

■ Open the Property sheet for the btnDeselect push button. Open the Code window for the **Click( )** method. Enter the following code:

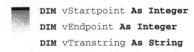

```
DIM vStartpoint As Integer
DIM vEndpoint As Integer
DIM vTranstring As String
```

For this method, you will need to use some variables in your Oracle Basic code. The *vStartpoint* variable will be used to find the starting point of a value in the Translation property for the lstSortColumnsSelected list box. The *vEndpoint* variable will be used to find the end point of a value in the Translation property for the lstSortColumnsSelected list box. The *vTranstring* variable will hold the Translation property of the lstSortColumnsSelected list box while you are manipulating it in the method.

■ Enter the following code after the previously entered code:

```
vTranstring=lstSortColumnsSelected.Translation
vStartpoint=INSTR(1,vTranstring,lstSortColumnsSelected.Value)
vEndpoint=INSTR(vStartpoint,vTranstring,CHR(10))
vTranstring = LEFT(vTranstring,vStartpoint - 1) & RIGHT(vTranstring,&
    LEN(vTranstring) - vEndpoint)
lstSortColumnsSelected.Translation=vTranstring
lstSortColumnsSelected.UpdateList()
```

The first and next-to-last lines of this section of code copy the value of the Translation property of the lstSortColumnsSelected list box to the internal variable *vTranstring* and from the variable back to the Translation property of the list box.

The second and third lines of the code section use the **INSTR( )** function. The **INSTR( )** function searches a string for another string. The first parameter of the **INSTR( )** function indicates the place where the search should start, the second parameter of the function identifies the string that is to be searched, and the third parameter identifies the string that is to be searched for. The *vStartpoint* variable is set to the position of the first letter of the value of the selected column name in the lstSortColumnsSelected list box in the Translation property. The *vEndpoint* variable is set when the Translation property string is searched, starting from the beginning of the selected column name in the Translation property to find the line feed character (**CHR**(10)), which is the final character in a line of the Translation property. The fourth line of code in this section recreates the Translation string by using the **LEFT( )** function, which extracts a substring starting at the left side of a string, to extract the portion of the Translation property before the start of the selected column name (vStartpoint –1) and the **RIGHT( )** function, which extracts a substring starting at the right side of the string, from the end of the string rightward until the end of the selected column name. You determine the number of characters to extract by determining the length of the trailing string. This is done by subtracting the position of the end of the string (*vEndpoint*) from the overall length of the string, which you derive by using the **LEN( )** function. The **LEN( )** function returns the length of a string.

When you have created a new Translation property for the lstSortColumnsSelected list box, you repopulate the list box with the **UpdateList( )** method.

- Run your form. You should be able to add a column to the lstSortColumnsSelected list box and remove it from the list box.

Handling User Errors

It has not been too difficult to move values from one list box to another and to delete values from a list box, but good applications do more than just enact desired functionality. A good application will also foresee and prevent common usage errors. In the next section, you will add Oracle Basic code to the btnDeselect push button to prevent a user from trying to delete a column name without having selected a column name in the lstSortColumnsSelected list box.

Preventing User Errors–NULL Values

You may have run across an error in using your application. If you clicked on the "<" push button without having first selected a value from the lstSortColumnsSelected list box, you will get an execution error in your code. When you have not selected a value in the lstSortColumnsSelected list box, the lstSortColumnsSelected list box Value property is null. Your Oracle Basic code will try and use the **INSTR( )** function on a null value and you will get an error.

It is easy to imagine a user mistakenly clicking on the < push button without selecting a value from the list box, and it is not readily apparent from the running application that this would result in an error. One of the guiding principles of client-server application design is that the application should be intuitive—that a user should not be required to have a lot of training to successfully use an application.

You need to add a little bit of Oracle Basic code to handle this situation.

- Open the Code window for the **Click( )** method for the btnDeselect push button. Add the underlined code after the code already in the **Click( )** method:

```
DIM vStartpoint As Integer
DIM vEndpoint As Integer
DIM vTranstring As String
IF ISNULL(lstSortColumnsSelected.Value) THEN
    MSGBOX("There is no value to delete.")
```

```
ELSE
vTranstring=lstSortColumnsSelected.Translation
vStartpoint=INSTR(1,vTranstring,lstSortColumnsSelected.Value)
vEndpoint=INSTR(vStartpoint,vTranstring,CHR(10))
vTranstring = LEFT(vTranstring,vStartpoint - 1) & RIGHT(vTranstring,
    LEN(vTranstring) - vEndpoint)
lstSortColumnsSelected.Translation=vTranstring
lstSortColumnsSelected.UpdateList()
```

You have used the **ISNULL( )** function before in Chapter 3. These three lines of
code check to see if the lstSortColumnsSelected.Value property is null, which will
be the case if the user has not selected a column name from the list box. If the
Value property is null, you will inform the user of the source of the problem and
skip the execution of the rest of the code. The **MSGBOX( )** function opens a modal
message box with the message as the parameter of the function. Note that Oracle
Basic uses double quotes to indicate a string value. Make sure that you have the
THEN at the end of the same line of code as the **IF**; you will get a syntax error if
you don't.

Whenever you have an **IF...ELSE** clause, you must have an **END IF**.

■ Add the following code to the end of your code for the **Click( )** method of
the btnDeselect push button:

```
END IF
```

In Oracle Power Objects, the Value property of a list box maintains its previous
value if a selected entry is deleted. After you have repopulated the
lstSortColumnsSelected list box, you do not want to have a value in the
lstSortColumns list box selected so that the user will be forced to act to select a
value. You can remove a selection from a list box by setting the Value property of
the list box to null.

■ Add the underlined code to the code in the **Click( )** method for the
btnDeselect push button:

```
DIM vStartpoint As Integer
DIM vEndpoint As Integer
DIM vTranstring As String
IF ISNULL(lstSortColumnsSelected.Value) THEN
    MSGBOX("There is no value to delete.")
ELSE
vTranstring=lstSortColumnsSelected.Translation
vStartpoint=INSTR(1,vTranstring,lstSortColumnsSelected.Value)
vEndpoint=INSTR(vStartpoint,vTranstring,CHR(10))
```

```
vTranstring = LEFT(vTranstring,vStartpoint - 1) & RIGHT(vTranstring, &
            LEN(vTranstring)  - (vEndpoint+1))
lstSortColumnsSelected.Translation=vTranstring
lstSortColumnsSelected.UpdateList()
lstSortColumnsSelected.Value=NULL
END IF
```

You will also want to deselect the value in the lstSortColumns list box after it has been added to the lstSortColumnsSelected list box.

■ Add the underlined code to the code in the **Click( )** method for the btnSelect push button:

```
lstSortColumnsSelected.Translation = lstSortColumnsSelected.Translation & &
    lstSortColumns.Value & " " & rbfOrdering.Value & "=" & lstSortColumns.Value &
    CHR(13) & CHR(10)
lstSortColumnsSelected.UpdateList()
lstSortColumns.Value = NULL
```

■ Run your form. Try to use the < push button when you do not have a value selected in the lstSortColumnsSelected list box to see the message box work.

Your application with the message box showing will look like this:

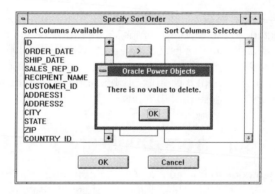

Now that you have added code to handle a null value for the lstSortColumnsSelected list box, you should go back and add similar code for the lstSortColumns list box, since that list box may also not have a value selected.

■ Open the Properties sheet for the btnSelect push button. Open the Code window for the **Click( )** method. Add the underlined code to the code already in the Code window:

```
IF ISNULL(lstSortColumns.Value) THEN
    MSGBOX("There is no value selected to add.")
ELSE
lstSortColumnsSelected.Translation = lstSortColumnsSelected.Translation & &
    lstSortColumns.Value  & "=" & lstSortColumns.Value & CHR(13) & CHR(10)
lstSortColumnsSelected.UpdateList()
lstSortColumns.Value = NULL
END IF
```

With this message box showing, your application should look like this:

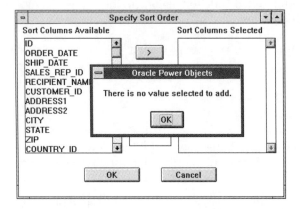

When a user first enters your application, the lstSortColumns list box will not have an entry selected, so the lstSortColumns.Value property will be null. Since you do not delete values from this list box, an entry will normally always be selected after a user selects the first entry. You could set a flag or check to see if an entry had been selected yet, but it is probably better programming practice to use a similar method for both of these push buttons.

Preventing User Errors—Duplicate SORT Columns

You have just written code to intercept a potential run-time error in your application. In this section, you will anticipate and compensate for a condition that would not result in a run-time code error, but would result in a logical error.

The lstSortColumns list box contains a complete list of all the columns in the ORDERS table. When you add a column name to the lstSortColumnsSelected list box, you do not delete the added column name from the lstSortColumns list box. (You could not delete the column name even if you wanted to, since the list box is linked to a column in a system view that is not editable.) This would allow a user to potentially add the same column name to the lstSortColumnsSelected list box twice. Although specifying the same column name twice would not result in an error, it wouldn't make any sense.

You already have learned all of the Oracle Basic functions and syntax you will need to prevent this condition.

■ Click on the btnSelect push button to bring up the Properties sheet and open the **Click( )** method Code window. Add the underlined code in the following example:

```
IF ISNULL(lstSortColumns.Value) THEN
    MSGBOX("There is no value selected to add.")
ELSE
    IF INSTR(1,lstSortColumnsSelected.Translation,lstSortColumns.Value) > 0 THEN
        MSGBOX("You have already added the " & lstSortColumns.Value & & 
        " column.")
        lstSortColumns.Value = NULL
    ELSE
        lstSortColumnsSelected.Translation=lstSortColumnsSelected.Translation & & 
            lstSortColumns.Value & "=" & lstSortColumns.Value & CHR(13) & CHR(10)
        lstSortColumnsSelected.UpdateList()
    END IF
lstSortColumnsSelected.Value = NULL
END IF
```

You use a new **IF...ELSE** clause and the **INSTR( )** function to test the existing Translation property to see if the column name is already in the list. If it is, the program displays a message box to the user explaining the problem and does not add the column name to the lstSortColumnsSelected list box. Notice that you have concatenated the column name selected, lstSortColumns.Value, into the message in the message box to give clear feedback to the user.

You have to indicate the end of the second **IF...ELSE** clause with another **END IF**. In the above code example, the interior **IF...ELSE** clause is indented for clarity, a practice that the authors of this book strongly recommend. When you are creating an application, it is tempting to enter code as rapidly as possible and not worry about formatting the code. After all, only wimps write pretty code. But try and remember that you may have to come back to this code at some time in the future when you don't remember it quite as well, and well-formatted code is much easier to understand. And even if you don't have to maintain the application, show a little compassion for those poor programmers who may come after you. (If your code is poorly documented, they actually MAY come after you!)

■ Run your application. Try to add a column name that has already been added. When you do this, your application should look like this:

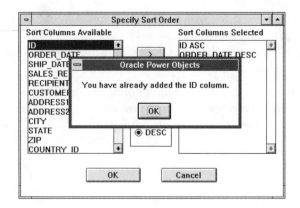

User Feedback

Your selection form is working very well—no run-time errors will occur and you have prevented the user from accidentally causing some logic errors. However, you could enhance the operation of this form and improve the productivity of your user by making the operation of the form a little more graphically intuitive for your user.

Visible User Feedback–Enabling and Disabling a Push Button

Graphical user interfaces have become very popular because applications that use these interfaces can be easily learned by their users. As a developer, you have a number of ways you can graphically illustrate the way an application can work.

In the form you are creating, the user can always add a column name to the selection list box. The user can only delete a column name from the selection list when the selection list box contains values. The selection list box will not contain values when the form first appears, and it may not contain values if the user has deleted all the column names from it.

You can *enable* and *disable* the push button that allows users to delete selected column names. When a push button is disabled, it will not receive a message when the user clicks on it, and the **Click( )** method for the push button will not execute. More importantly, the appearance of the push button changes when it is disabled, so the user will immediately know that the push button cannot be used. You will not have to explain this to the user—the conventions of the graphical user interface will make this functionality abundantly clear.

In this section, you will enable and disable the btnDeselect push button at the appropriate times. Click on the btnSelect push button and open the Code window for the **Click( )** method. Add the underlined code to the existing code:

```
IF ISNULL(lstSortColumns.Value) THEN
    MSGBOX("There is no value selected to add.")
ELSE
    IF INSTR(1,lstSortColumnsSelected.Translation,lstSortColumns.Value) > 0 THEN
        MSGBOX("You have already added the " & lstSortColumns.Value & &
            " column.")
    ELSE
        lstSortColumnsSelected.Translation=lstSortColumnsSelected.Translation &
            lstSortColumns.Value & "=" & lstSortColumns.Value & CHR(13) & CHR(10)
        lstSortColumnsSelected.UpdateList()
        btnDeselect.Enabled = True
    END IF
    lstSortColumnsSelected.Value = NULL
END IF
```

Whenever you successfully add a column name to the lstSortColumnsSelected list box, the list box will contain at least one value, so you will want to enable the btnDeselect push button. Although you may call this function when the push button is already enabled, it will not cause any problems to set the property again, so there is no need to check the value of the Enabled property before you set it again.

■ Open the Property sheet for the btnDeselect push button. Set the Enabled property to 'False'.

Since the btnDeselect pushbutton will be enabled whenever a value is added to the lstSortColumnsSelected list box by clicking on the btnSelect push button, your form should initially have the btnDeselect push button disabled, since you will not be able to remove a value from the selected columns list box until one has been added to the list.

The next step will ensure that the btnDeselect push button is disabled if the user removes the last column from the lstSortColumns list box.

■ Select the btnDeselect push button and open up the Code window for the **Click( )** method. Add the underlined code to the existing code:

```
DIM vStartpoint As Integer
DIM vEndpoint As Integer
DIM vTranstring As String
```

```
IF ISNULL(lstSortColumnsSelected.Value) THEN
    MSGBOX("There is no value to delete.")
ELSE
vTranstring=lstSortColumnsSelected.Translation
vStartpoint=INSTR(1,vTranstring,lstSortColumnsSelected.Value)
vEndpoint=INSTR(vStartpoint,vTranstring,CHR(10))
vTranstring = LEFT(vTranstring,vStartpoint - 1) & &
    ((RIGHT(vTranstring, & &
    LEN(vTranstring)  - (vEndpoint+1))
lstSortColumnsSelected.Translation=vTranstring
lstSortColumnsSelected.UpdateList()
lstSortColumnsSelected.Value=NULL
IF LEN(vTranstring) = 0 THEN Self.Enabled = False
END IF
```

Whenever you delete a column name, you will check the *vTranstring* variable, which is the internal storage variable for the lstSortColumnsSelected.Translation property, to see if there are no column names remaining in the list box. If this is true, then you will disable the btnDeselect push button. Notice that this form of the **IF...ELSE** clause is self-contained and does not require an **END IF**.

The Self qualifier refers to the object that is executing the method. You could use either the Enabled property without the Self qualifier, since a method will always take the most local version of a property, or you could have specifically qualified the property name by calling it btnDeselect.Enabled.

When you run your form and there are no values in the lstSortColumnsSelected list box, your form should look like this:

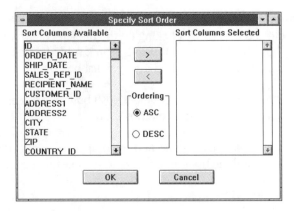

Notice that the btnDeselect push button is disabled.

You should follow the same procedure to appropriately enable and disable the btnSelect push button.

■ Open the Properties sheet for the btnSelect push button. Set the Enabled property to 'False'.

As with the btnDeselect push button described previously, your form should begin with the btnSelect push button disabled.

■ Open the Properties sheet for the lstSortColumns list box. Add the following code to the **Click( )** method:

```
btnSelect.Enabled = True
```

This code will enable the btnSelect push button whenever you have selected a value in the lstSortColumns list box.

■ Open the Properties sheet for the btnSelect push button. Add the underlined code to the existing code for the **Click( )** method:

```
IF ISNULL(lstSortColumns.Value) THEN
    MSGBOX("There is no value selected to add.")
ELSE
    IF INSTR(1,lstSortColumnsSelected.Translation, lstSortColumns.Value) > 0 THEN
        MSGBOX("You have already added the " & lstSortColumns.Value & &
            " column.")
    ELSE
        lstSortColumnsSelected.Translation=lstSortColumnsSelected.Translation & &
            lstSortColumns.Value & "=" & lstSortColumns.Value & CHR(13) & CHR(10)
        lstSortColumnsSelected.UpdateList()
        btnDeselect.Enabled = True
    END IF
lstSortColumnsSelected.Value = NULL
        btnSelect.Enabled = False
END IF
```

The line of code you have just added will disable the btnSelect push button after you have successfully added a value to the lstSortColumnsSelected list box. The btnSelect push button will be enabled as soon as the user selects another value in the lstSortColumns list box.

You may have realized that with these last few lines of code you have prevented the user from using the btnSelect push button if a column is not selected from the lstSortColumns list box. If you have successfully prevented the user from trying to add a sort column when there are none to add, you can eliminate the code that checks to see if a value has been selected, since this problem condition will never occur.

■ Delete the underlined code from the **Click( )** method of the btnSelect push button:

```
IF ISNULL(lstSortColumns.Value) THEN
    MSGBOX("There is no value selected to add.")
ELSE
    IF INSTR(1,lstSortColumnsSelected.Translation,lstSortColumns.Value) > 0 THEN
        MSGBOX("You have already added the " & lstSortColumns.Value &
            " column.")
    ELSE
        lstSortColumnsSelected.Translation=lstSortColumnsSelected.Translation & &
            lstSortColumns.Value & "=" & lstSortColumns.Value & CHR(13) & CHR(10)
        lstSortColumnsSelected.UpdateList()
        btnDeselect.Enabled = True
    END IF
    lstSortColumnsSelected.Value = NULL
    btnSelect.Enabled = False
END IF
```

For the sake of readability, you should probably redo the indentation of the code for the **Click( )** method of the btnSelect push button so that it looks like this:

```
IF INSTR(1,lstSortColumnsSelected.Translation, lstSortColumns.Value) > 0 THEN
    MSGBOX("You have already added the " & lstSortColumns.Value & &
        " column.")
ELSE
    lstSortColumnsSelected.Translation=lstSortColumnsSelected.Translation & &
        lstSortColumns.Value & "=" & lstSortColumns.Value & CHR(13) & CHR(10)
    lstSortColumnsSelected.UpdateList()
    btnDeselect.Enabled = True
END IF
lstSortColumnsSelected.Value = NULL
btnSelect.Enabled = False
```

Since you have also prevented the user from trying to delete a value from the lstSortColumnsSelected list box after the last value has been deleted, you could also eliminate the message box for that error in the btnDeselect push button's **Click( )** method. It is your choice as to whether you want your application to intercept possible errors or just prevent them. The authors of this book advocate preventing errors if possible, since the user will not have to interrupt the flow of their work to correct an error. The authors also advocate giving the user a visual representation of capabilities of objects, such as disabling push buttons, as a way of helping the user to understand how the application works.

By enabling and disabling push buttons, you have conveyed a certain type of graphical message to your users. When a push button is disabled, it indicates that the push button is not operable now, but will become operable when the user takes certain actions. When the push button is enabled after the user selects a value in the lstSortColumns list box, it serves to train the user in the correct operation of the application without having to interrupt the workflow with a message box.

Application Toolbars

You have successfully created a form that allows a user to select their own sort order. The frmSortOrder form prevents run-time and logical errors and can be easily understood by providing visual feedback to the user. The form is functionally complete within itself, but you have not added any functionality to close the form or to take the selected sort columns and apply them in your frmOrders form. Before you can create that functionality, you should return to your frmOrders form and create a means to call this screen from your frmOrders form.

Calling the Sort Order Form from the Main Form

Your Sort Order form is now ready to be integrated into your application. Your next task is to give the user the ability to call the form from the Main form.

Choosing an Interface to Call a Form

It is fairly easy to open another form from a form. You will simply call a method in the Sort Order form from the Main form. Since the method can be called in a number of ways from the Main form, you should spend some time thinking about the best user interface to call the form.

You could cause the form to be automatically called based on some action in the Main form. For example, you could decide that every user would have to specify a sort order before they used the form at all, so you could call the method from the **OpenWindow( )** method of the Main form. This would not be the best choice, since there is no absolute need for a user to specify a sort order, and the user may get frustrated by having to navigate through a superfluous screen when they enter the Main form.

You could have a push button on the form that would call the screen. The user would have to click on the push button to call the screen and could simply ignore the push button if they chose to. This is a better interface since it is less intrusive to the user, but placing a push button on the form itself takes up some precious real estate in the form.

The best way to call the Sort Order screen would be to use a menu choice or a push button on a toolbar. This allows the user to explicitly call the screen if desired and makes the ability to call the screen apparent, but not intrusive. Oracle Power Objects uses very similar methods to create menus and toolbars. For the purposes of this application, you will create a push button in a toolbar to call the Sort Order screen. For this application, it makes sense to use a toolbar for two main reasons: the other push buttons on the toolbar all relate to data access, so including the Sort Order screen push button would make logical sense; and it will be easy to put a descriptive graphic on the push button.

Toolbars

Oracle Power Objects give you a great deal of power in creating toolbars for your application. You have already seen how Oracle Power Objects automatically provides a default toolbar for your application, which contains push buttons relating to data access. You can easily add your own push buttons to the default toolbar, replace the default toolbar with your own toolbar, and dynamically change the toolbar for your form while the form is running. In addition, Oracle Power Objects allows you to globally define command codes for your toolbar push buttons and menu choices, so you could have a menu choice or toolbar push button on many different menus or toolbars throughout your application that all execute the same functional code.

You will be going through seven steps in defining a toolbar. You will

1. Create a toolbar object.

2. Associate the toolbar object with a form.

3. Initialize the toolbar with the default toolbar push buttons provided by Oracle Power Objects.

4. Create a constant, which represents the push button command.

5. Add the push button to the default toolbar.

6. Add Oracle Basic code to enable the push button on the toolbar.

7. Add Oracle Basic code for the actions of the push button.

Creating a Toolbar

Your first step is to create a toolbar object for your frmOrders form. You have two options for the location of the code that will create your toolbar. You could create the toolbar locally in the **InitializeWindow( )** method of the Main form, or you could create the toolbar in the **OnLoad( )** method for the application. If you create the toolbar in the application method, you will have to qualify some of the Oracle Basic code with the name of the form, but you could conceivably use the Menu bar in more than one form in the application.

For the purposes of this book, you will be using the **OnLoad( )** method of the application to create and manipulate the toolbar. For more information on using the **InitializeWindow( )** method to create a toolbar for a form, please refer to the documentation set for Oracle Power Objects.

■ Return to the application window of your application to bring up the Property sheet for the application. Open the Code window for the **OnLoad( )** method. Declare a variable to hold the handle of the toolbar object with the following code:

```
DIM vtbrMyToolbar As Object
```

The handle of an object gives you a way to identify an object in Oracle Basic code.

■ Create a toolbar object by adding the following code after your variable declaration:

```
vtbrMyToolbar = NEW Toolbar
```

The **NEW** command creates a new Oracle Power Object of the type specified by the qualifier following the function. You can create many types of object at any time with this function. This gives you an enormous amount of flexibility and power in creating your applications. For instance, you could dynamically create a toolbar only when the conditions in your application dictate.

Associating the Toolbar with a Form

Once you have created a toolbar object, you can associate it with one or more of the forms in your application.

■ Add the following code to the end of the **OnLoad( )** method code:

```
frmOrders.SetToolbar(vtbrMyToolbar)
```

This code causes the **SetToolbar( )** method to be called for the frmOrders window. You could add the vtbrMyToolbar toolbar to additional forms in your application by calling the **SetToolbar( )** method for the forms.

If you do not have a **SetToolbar( )** method defined for a form, Oracle Power Objects will use the default toolbar for that form. If you do not wish to have a toolbar on a particular form, you can call the **SetToolbar( )** function with null as the parameter.

Defining the toolbar in the **OnLoad( )** method of the application makes it easy to use the toolbar on several different forms within the application.

Initializing a Toolbar

Once you have created a toolbar and associated it with your frmOrders form, you can initialize the toolbar to contain the default push buttons used by Oracle Power Objects forms.

■   Add the following code to the end of the **OnLoad( )** method code:

```
frmOrders.DefaultToolbar(vtbrMyToolbar)
```

The code in the **OnLoad( )** method for the Orders application should now read

```
DIM vtbrMyToolbar As Object
vtbrMyToolbar = NEW Toolbar
frmOrders.SetToolbar(vtbrMyToolbar)
frmOrders.DefaultToolbar(vtbrMyToolbar)
```

The **DefaultToolbar( )** method exists for both Form windows and Report windows.

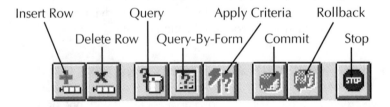

For a Form window, the **DefaultToolbar( )** method will add push buttons to add and delete rows, to query the data source, to call the query-by-form screen and use the query-by-form conditions, to commit and roll back changes, and to stop the application.

The **DefaultToolbar( )** method works transparently whether the toolbar is for a Form or a Report window. You can create a single toolbar object, add your own push buttons and functionality to it, and use it in all of your forms, regardless of whether the form is a standard Form window or a Report window. For instance, you could create a push button that would give your user the ability to access an E-mail system and easily include the push button throughout your application.

Since you now have more than one form in your application, you will have to explicitly open one of the forms in the **OnLoad( )** method of the application.

■ Add the underlined code to the code for the **OnLoad( )** method of the Orders application:

```
DIM vtbrMyToolbar As Object
vtbrMyToolbar = NEW Toolbar
frmOrders.OpenWindow()
frmOrders.SetToolbar(vtbrMyToolbar)
frmOrders.DefaultToolbar(vtbrMyToolbar)
```

The **OpenWindow( )** method opens its parent window.

■ Run your application by clicking on the Run Application push button in the Oracle Power Objects development toolbar.

You currently have the Properties sheet open for the application; you cannot use the Run Form push button, since there is no form as the active window.

You can delete any of these push buttons explicitly by calling the **TBDeleteButton( )** function. In the next section, you will be adding a push button to the default push buttons in the toolbar.

Creating a Constant for the Push Button Command

Oracle Power Objects uses an integer to identify a menu choice or toolbar push button. You will have to create a constant that will be used in other methods that interact with your push button.

■ Add the following code to the code for the Declarations section of the Orders application:

```
CONST cmdCallSortWindow = Cmd_FirstUserCommand + 1
```

As discussed in Chapter 2, you can declare a constant with the **CONST** command. Since you will be using this constant throughout your application, you should declare it in the Declarations section of the application to make it global in scope.

You should give your identifying constant a descriptive name, since you will be using it in several other methods. The Cmd_FirstUserCommand constant is defined by Oracle Power Objects. Since Oracle Power Objects supplies a number of default push buttons and menu choices, you would not want to use an identifying constant that is the same as one of the internal constants used by Oracle Power

Objects. Oracle Power Objects provides the Cmd_FirstUserCommand to allow you to safely define your own command constants that will be higher than any command constants used internally. Since future revisions of Oracle Power Objects may provide additional default commands, you should use the Cmd_FirstUserCommand constant to set your own command constants to ensure that there will never be any conflict between your command constants and internal Oracle Power Objects command constants.

Adding the Push Button to the Default Toolbar

Now that you have defined your toolbar, associated it with a Form window, and added the default push buttons to it, you can add your own push button to the toolbar.

▪ If you want to use a bitmap on your toolbar, you must first add it to your application. Open the Main window for the Orders application. Select Import BMP... from the File menu and use the file dialog box to import the SORTORD.BMP bitmap that is included in the files described in Appendix A of this book. The bitmap will appear in your application window with the title of SORTORD.

▪ Add the underlined code to the code for the **OnLoad( )** method of your application:

```
DIM vtbrMyToolbar As Object
vtbrMyToolbar = NEW Toolbar
frmOrders.OpenWindow()
frmOrders.SetToolbar(vtbrMyToolbar)
frmOrders.DefaultToolbar(vtbrMyToolbar)
vtbrMyToolbar.TBAppendButton(cmdCallSortWindow, SORTORD, ToolbarStyle Pushbtn, 0)
```

There are four parameters for the **TBAppendButton( )** function. The first parameter is the command code constant you have previously defined. The second parameter is the name of the bitmap you want on the push button. If you do not want a bitmap, you can use the null keyword for this parameter. The third parameter is an internally defined constant that represents the style for the push button. You can also define a push button with a ToolbarStyle_Toggle style that will maintain an on/off state or you can specify a style of ToolbarStyle_Separator that will place 10 pixels of space after the last push button in the toolbar. The final parameter is an integer that is passed to your local help system. If you specify a 0 in this parameter, online help will not be invoked from this push button.

You have used the **TBAppendButton( )** function to add a push button to the end of the existing toolbar. You could also use the **TBInsertButton( )** to place a push button in a specific location on the toolbar. Oracle Power Objects also gives you functions to get and set any of the parameters of a push button, as well as the ability to delete individual push buttons from a toolbar or to clear all the push buttons from a toolbar. Please refer to the Oracle Power Objects documentation set for further information.

Notice that you qualified the **TBAppendButton( )** function with the name of the toolbar, rather than any particular form that contains the toolbar. The toolbar object exists independent of any particular form, which also allows you to make changes to a toolbar in one specific place that can affect the toolbar wherever it appears. This is one of the strengths of the object-oriented nature of Oracle Power Objects, which will be explored at great depth in later chapters.

Enabling the Pushbutton on the Toolbar

As stated above, one of the principles of client/server application design is to have the application be graphically self-documenting. A user should be able to look at the objects on a form and intuitively know how to use them. One of the visual clues you can use is to enable and disable push buttons to indicate when they are available. Oracle Power Objects provides a method that will automatically enable, disable, and mark the push buttons in your toolbar according to the logical conditions you specify. The same method will work with either toolbars or menus.

■ Open the Property sheet for the Orders application. Open the Code window for the **TestCommand( )** method.

The **TestCommand( )** method is used to set the state of the push buttons in a toolbar or the menu choices in a menu. There is a **TestCommand( )** method for the application, as well as any of the forms or reports in the application. Since you have defined the push button at the level of the application, you should use the **TestCommand( )** method at the same level.

■ Add the following code to the **TestCommand( )** method for the Orders application:

```
SELECT CASE cmdCode
    CASE cmdCallSortWindow
        TestCommand=TestCommand_Enabled
END SELECT
```

The **SELECT CASE...CASE...END SELECT** construct allows you to specify a variety of actions based on the value of a variable. The *cmdCode* variable is an internal variable used by Oracle Power Objects to hold the command code of a particular toolbar push button or menu choice.

You test the *cmdCode* variable for each potential value with the **CASE** statement. The **TestCommand( )** method is a function—it returns a value on completion. You set the value it returns by making the name of the function equal to a specified value. When the **TestCommand( )** function returns, Oracle Power Objects uses the returned value to set the state of a push button.

The **TestCommand( )** function is iteratively called for all visible push buttons and menu choices at regular frequencies. Oracle Power Objects uses this function to constantly monitor and set the state of toolbar push buttons and menu choices. You have enabled your push button, but you could also set the state of the push button to TestCommand_Checked, TestCommand_Disabled, or TestCommand_Disabled_Checked. All the TestCommand_ values are constants, internally defined by Oracle Power Objects.

Although you have only defined a single push button in this application, you will typically have many toolbar push buttons and menu choices, so a **SELECT CASE** construct is much more efficient that using an **IF...ELSE** chain.

For this application, you are simply enabling your push button. For many push buttons, you would set the state of the push button differently depending on the logical state of your application with **IF...ELSE** logic.

NOTE:
Oracle Power Objects automatically processes the **TestCommand( )** and **DoCommand( )** (see following section) for all default push buttons.

■ Run your application. Click on the new push button in the toolbar. The main form of your application should appear as in Figure 4-1.

Coding the Actions of the Push Button

Oracle Power Objects uses the **TestCommand( )** method of a form to set the state of the push buttons in a toolbar. A form also has a **DoCommand( )** method that is used to specify the actions performed when a push button is pushed.

■ Open the **DoCommand( )** method Code window for the Orders application.

■ Add the following code to the **DoCommand( )** method:

```
SELECT CASE cmdCode
    CASE cmdCallSortWindow
        frmSortOrder.OpenModal(0)
END SELECT
```

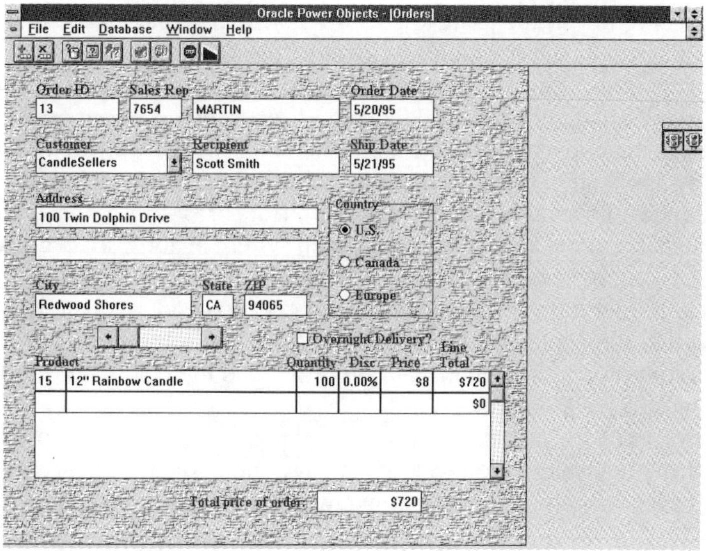

FIGURE 4-1. *The frmOrders form with a customized toolbar*

The **DoCommand( )** method is called whenever a user clicks on a menu choice or a push button in a toolbar. The **SELECT CASE** construct is used to determine the push button that has been clicked or the menu choice that has been selected.

You can call a number of different methods to create a window. If you use the **OpenPrint( )** method, you will open a window and print its contents. Using the **OpenPreview( )** method will open a window in Print Preview mode. If you were to use the **OpenWindow( )** method, you would open a standard window.

The **OpenModal( )** method causes a *modal window* to be created. A modal window assumes control of an application until the window is closed. Modal windows play an important role in client-server applications. One of the strong points of a graphical application is that the application is controlled by actions of the user. As an application developer, you can no longer force a user into a particular course of action by limiting his or her choices. The application is driven by the user. (If you are new to the client-server application world, you may react negatively to this concept and try to control the user. Don't bother. You will spend more time trying, unsuccessfully, to limit an open environment than you will creating applications, and your users will be unhappy to boot.)

The modal window gives you one of the few control mechanisms in an application. When a modal window is created, the user cannot use any of the other windows in an application until the modal window is closed. You can ensure a particular logical condition has been resolved by using a modal window to establish the condition and refusing to let a user close the window and return to the main application until the condition is resolved. The sole parameter of the **OpenModal( )** method indicates whether the modal window is *application modal* or *system modal*. An application modal window keeps the user from doing anything else in the application, while a system modal window prevents any actions in any application in the environment. A value of 0 indicates an application modal window, while a value of more than 0 indicates a system modal window. For this application, there is no need to block all system actions, so an application modal window will be good enough.

The frmSortOrder form is an example of a good choice for a modal window. When a user tells the application he or she wants to set a sort order, you want them to set a sort order properly, establish the sort order, and then close the window before returning to the Main form.

One of the problems with modal windows comes about because closing the window destroys any values the window may have held. Oracle Power Objects gives you an easy way around this dilemma, which will be discussed later in this chapter.

■ Run your application. Click on the new push button in the toolbar. The application with the Sort Order window open should look like Figure 4-2.

■ Stop the application by clicking on the Stop push button.

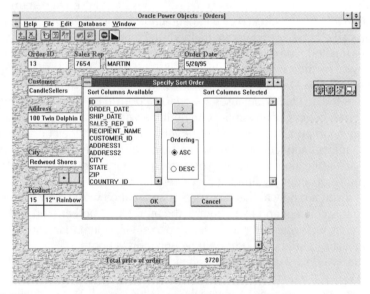

FIGURE 4-2. *The frmOrders form with the frmSortOrder form active*

You will add the code to return to the frmOrders form from the frmSortOrder form in the next section.

You have successfully created your first customized toolbar! You can call your Sort Order form easily with a push button in the toolbar of your Main form. But you may have found that although you can easily get to your Sort Order form, you have not yet added the functionality to properly set the sort order of the frmOrders form, refetch the rows in the new sorted order, or even close the modal Sort Order form. You will be implementing all of this in the final section of the chapter.

Implementing the New Sort Order

You now can call the sort order from your frmOrders form, and the Sort Order form works in a way that allows your users to easily specify the columns they wish to use to sort. To complete this portion of your application, you will need a way to take the selected sort columns, set the appropriate property of the frmOrders form, return to the frmOrders form, and requery the database with the new sort order.

Passing the Sort Columns to the Main Form

Your user has indicated the columns to be used for sorting in the frmSortOrder window. In this section, you will use the list of selected columns to set the OrderBy property of the Main form.

■   Open the frmSortOrder form and select the btnOK push button. Open the Code window for the **Click( )** method and enter the following code:

```
DIM vOrderBy As String
DIM vTranstring As String
vTranstring=lstSortColumnsSelected.Translation
```

The *vOrderBy* variable will hold the string that will be used to set the OrderBy property of the frmOrders form. As with the earlier code, the *vTranstring* variable will be initialized with the value of the Translation property of the lstSortColumnsSelected object.

■   Add the underlined code to the code for the **Click( )** method of the btnOK push button:

```
DIM vOrderBy As String
DIM vTranstring As String
vTranstring=lstSortColumnsSelected.Translation
DO WHILE LEN(vTranstring) > 0
```

```
        vOrderBy=vOrderBy & LEFT(vTranstring,INSTR(1,vTranstring, "=") - 1) & ","
        vTranstring = RIGHT(vTranstring, LEN(vTranstring) - INSTR(vTranstring, &
           CHR(10)))
   LOOP
   IF LEN(vOrderBy) > 0 THEN
        frmOrders.OrderBy = LEFT(vOrderBy, LEN(vOrderBy) - 1)
   ELSE
        frmOrders.OrderBy=NULL
   END IF
```

As discussed in Chapter 2, the **DO** construct lets you repeatedly execute code. The **DO WHILE** construct will repeat the code between the **DO WHILE** and the **LOOP** statement an infinite number of times until the condition specified in the **DO WHILE** statement is true. When you use the **DO WHILE** form of the construct, you will be executing the code 0 or more times. Since the lstSortColumnsSelected list box may not contain any entries, using the **DO WHILE** construct is appropriate.

All entries in the Translation property take the form of

   column_name=column_name

followed by a line feed and carriage return character. As you go through the *vTranstring* variable searching for column names, you remove the line of the string once you have extracted the property. When you have extracted all the column names, there will be nothing left in the *vTranstring* variable, so you can use the length of this variable as a test for completion.

You extract the column name from the *vTranstring* variable by finding the position of the first "=" and extracting the characters to the left of that character. You concatenate this new value with the existing *vOrderBy* variable and add a comma "," as a separator to the end of the string. Once you have added the column name, you remove the line from the *vTranstring* variable by finding the final carriage return character and extracting the portion of the string to the right of that character with the **RIGHT( )** function.

When you have completed going through the *vTranstring* variable, you are ready to return the list of sort columns to the frmOrders form. You will use the **LEFT( )** function to remove the trailing "," separator from the string and use it to set the OrderBy property of the frmOrders form. Since the user may not have selected any columns, the *vOrderBy* variable may be empty. You would get a run-time error if you used the **LEFT**(*vOrderBy*, **LEN**(*vOrderby*)–1) code on an empty string, so you have to use a final **IF...ELSE** construct to properly handle all possible cases.

The OrderBy property of the frmOrders form has been properly set. Your next small task is to leave the Sort Order form and return control of the application to the frmOrders form.

Closing the Sort Order Form

As discussed earlier in the chapter, a modal window maintains control of an application until it is closed. But when you close a window, all values associated with the window are destroyed.

This could present a problem in your application. A user goes to the Sort Order screen to specify columns for sorting. The user closes the window and returns to the Main form. Later, the user wants to add another column to the sort order, so he or she returns to the Sort Order form. The form will open with no sort columns selected, so the user will have to reselect the previously selected columns. This is at best a hindrance, and at worst the user could make errors in reselecting the columns, which would interfere with the successful use of the application.

You could handle the situation by writing code to go through the OrderBy property of the Main Form window to initialize the form. However, Oracle Power Objects gives you another option.

■   Select the btnCancel push button. Click on the value section of the IsDismissBtn property to set the value of the property to 'True'.

In Oracle Power Objects, you have the ability to "dismiss" a modal window rather than just close it. When you dismiss a modal window, the window is hidden and control returns to the window that called the **OpenModal( )** function for the modal window. The modal window remains in memory, so you can restore it to the state it was in when it was dismissed by opening it again.

■   Select the btnOK push button. Add the underlined code to the code in the **Click( )** method Code window:

```
DIM vOrderBy As String
DIM vTranstring As String
vTranstring=lstSortColumnsSelected.Translation
DO WHILE LEN(vTranstring) > 0
    vOrderBy=vOrderBy & LEFT(vTranstring,INSTR(1,vTranstring, "=") - 1) & ","
    vTranstring = RIGHT(vTranstring, LEN(vTranstring) - INSTR(vTranstring,
        CHR(10)))
LOOP
IF LEN(vOrderBy) > 0 THEN
    frmOrders.OrderBy = LEFT(vOrderBy, LEN(vOrderBy) - 1)
ELSE
    frmOrders.OrderBy=NULL
END IF
frmOrders.Query()
btnCancel.Click()
```

You have given the btnCancel push button the ability to dismiss the frmSortOrder modal window. Rather than adding the code to the btnOK push button, you can just call the **Click( )** method for the btnClick push button from the btnOK push button.

The **Query( )** method for the frmOrders form will cause the query that retrieves information from the database for the form to be re-executed. The **Query( )** method is executed when a form is initially created and whenever a user clicks on the Query push button in the run-time toolbar. You can also call it explicitly in your code, as you are doing here. If the user clicks on the btnOK push button, you will want to run the query with the new OrderBy property in place. If the user clicks on the btnCancel push button, you will just want to close the dialog box without running the query for the frmOrders form again.

The ability to call methods that belong to other objects is one of the powerful features of using objects to build applications. The OK push button and the Cancel push button are meant to perform the same action, except that the OK push button will set the OrderBy property of the Main form and the Cancel push button will not. If you later decide to add any additional functionality that you want to have executed whenever the user leaves the Sort Order form, you can add it to the **Click( )** method of the Cancel push button and it will automatically be called by the OK push button also.

Congratulations! You have given your users the ability to specify whatever sort order they wish for their order information. And you have given them the ability to specify any sort order they wish without the possibility that they could create an improper sort order and get an error at run time. By delivering an application with this type of built-in functionality, you will find yourself with happy users, who are the greatest reward for a developer.

Possible Enhancements for the Sort Order Screen

In this chapter, you have learned a great deal about working with Oracle Power Objects. You have learned how to use and manipulate list boxes, how to call windows from other windows, and how to execute database queries from a form. You have also gained a lot more experience in working with Oracle Basic and using the functions and constructs to implement functionality.

There are some additional enhancements you might make to improve your application. As you learned in Chapter 3, you can assign a default OrderBy property to a Form window. You might want to have your Sort Order screen use the values in the OrderBy property to initialize the columns selected in the Sort Order form. You could use the string parsing functions, such as **INSTR( )**, **LEFT( )**, and **RIGHT( )** to derive the column names from the OrderBy property and then call the **Click( )** method of the btnSelect push button to add them to the lstSortColumnsSelected list box.

The current implementation of the lstSortColumnsSelected list box automatically adds a new column name to the end of the list of columns selected. You could add push buttons to the form to allow a user to move a sort column name up or down in the list of sort columns, which would affect the order the columns were used for sorting. You would use the string parsing functions to manipulate the Translation property, along with some logic to determine if a column name was the first or last column name in the list, which would affect how column names were moved.

You could also make the push button in the toolbar a toggle push button that would allow the user to impose a selected sort condition or revert to the default sort order, similar to the way a user can use QBF selection conditions or not when retrieving data. In doing this, you would have to store the default sort order in a variable and check the state of the push button to determine the type of action taken.

As mentioned at the beginning of this chapter, the Sort Order form you have described could be used in many different applications. In the next chapter, you will learn how to create libraries and user classes to make it easier for you to use forms, objects, and functions in many different applications.

CHAPTER 5

Leveraging Your Work Through Libraries and Classes

You have spent the first four chapters of this book developing a basic order entry system. Some of the work that you have done for your application could be used in other systems that you will build in the future. This chapter will introduce you to two methods of improving your productivity by leveraging your work: libraries and object classes.

Improving Productivity

Computer programming is an iterative task. As a programmer, every new project presents a learning challenge. At the same time, each new project is also similar to many other projects you have already done. You can dramatically improve your productivity if you can find ways to leverage the work you have already done.

In one sense, all programmers are already doing this. As you create an application, you have solved a number of development problems, and you can use the knowledge gained in solving the problems to tackle new problems you face. You could become more productive, however, if you could find a way to not only use the knowledge you have gained, but to reuse the actual functionality you have implemented.

Oracle Power Objects provides two different ways to reuse your previous work. Libraries and object classes will give you the power to dramatically improve your productivity with Oracle Power Objects.

You have probably noticed that your workload is constantly growing. With the reusability provided through Oracle Power Objects, you have a chance to stay even with the challenges ahead of you — or even get ahead!

Libraries

You have already seen that Oracle Power Objects supports a top-level application object called a library. The first section of this chapter will introduce you to the concept of libraries and help you to modify the Sort Order form you created in Chapter 4 to be used as a library.

A *library* is a top-level Oracle Power Objects object you can use to share form windows and bitmaps between different applications. You can easily copy a form window or bitmap to an application from a library. You have already copied a bitmap from a library of bitmaps to use as the background for your Main form in Chapter 1. The rest of this section will show you how to modify your sort order form to make it easier to share with other applications, how to create a library, how to add your form window to the library, and how to reuse your form window in your application.

Making a Form Generic — Creating a User Property

When you created your Sort Order form, you designed the form so that it would work well within the context of the ORDERS application. If you would like to share the Sort Order form with other applications, you will have to modify the form so that it can be used generically by many other forms.

■ Select the Sort Order form. Click on the New Property/Method push button in the toolbar of the Properties sheet to call the User Properties screen.

Name	Type	Datatype	Arguments
__Comment	Sub		
_CreateTbl	Sub		strTblName as String, intDebug as integer
_ReDimColArrays	Sub		
_ResultCompare	Sub		
_SavLast2	Sub		strTblName as String
_SavLast2	Sub		strTblName as String, intDebug as integer
_Value	Property	String	
a	Property	Long	
a	Function	Long	
a6	Property	Long	
About	Sub		
AboutBox	Sub		
actOnOCX	Sub		
addItem	Sub		item as string

To generalize your form, you will have to create a new property for the frmSortOrder.

■ Scroll to the bottom of the User Properties table window in the User Properties screen. Click on the Name, or leftmost column in the blank row at the bottom of the window and enter the name of the new property as 'udpCallingScreen' (short for user defined property calling screen).

You insert new properties into the User Property screen by using the blank row at the end of the table window. Spaces are not allowed in property, function, or subroutine names, so you should use a naming convention, such as capitalizing the first letter of each word of the name, to make your names more understandable.

■ Click in the Type column to the right of the Name column. When you enter the column, a drop-down list appears with the valid types of Property, Function, or Sub. Select the Property type.

The User Properties screen is also used to define the calling interface to functions and subroutines, which were introduced in Chapter 2. You will be defining your own functions later in this book.

■ Click in the Datatype column to the right of the Type column. When you enter the column, a drop-down list appears with valid data types. Select the Object data type.

CallingScreen	Property	Object	

The udpCallingScreen property is a variable that will be used to hold a *handle* that identifies the screen that will be calling the Sort Order form. Object handles are unique identifiers assigned by your operating system for every visible object in your application. You do not generally have to worry about the actual value of a handle, since you can refer to an object handle by using the name of the object; but since your Sort Order form will be called by different form objects, you will use a variable to reference the calling screen.

■ Open the Sort Order window in your Orders application. Arrange the open windows in the Oracle Power Objects development environment so that you can see both the User Properties screen and the Properties sheet for the frmSortOrder form. Click on the box to the left of the udpCallingScreen property. Hold down the mouse button and drag the property from the User Properties screen to the Properties sheet for the frmSortOrder form.

Dragging a property from the User Properties screen to a Properties sheet will add the property to the Properties sheet. Notice that the udpCallingScreen property has a + icon to the right of the diamond property indicator. The + icon indicates that a property, function, or subroutine has been defined by a developer and added to the Properties sheet. A user-defined property, unlike a standard Oracle Power Objects property, can be deleted from a Properties sheet with the Delete Property/Method button in the toolbar of the Properties sheet. You can also sort the items in a Properties sheet to show the user-defined properties and methods at the beginning of the property list. As you add functionality to your applications and create your own reusable libraries and classes, you will be using your own properties, functions, and subroutines to implement your application logic, so you might want the user-defined properties, functions, and subroutines to be readily accessible at the beginning of a Properties sheet.

Once you close the User Properties screen, your property will be automatically added to Oracle Power Objects internal list of properties, functions, and subroutines, so the next time you open the User Properties screen, the udpCallingScreen property will appear mixed in with all the other values in the User Properties screen in alphabetical order.

The udpCallingScreen property will be used to hold the handle of the screen that calls the frmSortOrder form. Your next step will be to modify the code in your form to use the new property.

Making a Form Generic – Modifying Your Code

The next step is to return to the code in the Sort Order form that refers to the specific frmOrders screen and replace the references with references to the udpCallingScreen property variable.

■ Open the code window for **Click( )** method for the pbOK push button in the frmSortOrder form. Modify the code for the **Click( )** method by replacing the references to frmOrders with the udpCallingScreen property, as indicated by the underlined portions of the code below.

```
DIM vOrderBy As String
DIM vTranstring As String
vTranstring=lbSortColumnsSelected.Translation
DO WHILE LEN(vTranstring) > 0
    vOrderBy=vOrderBy & LEFT(vTranstring,INSTR(1,vTranstring, "=") - 1) & ','
    vTranstring= RIGHT(vTranstring, LEN(vTranstring) - INSTR(vTranstring, &
    CHR(13)))
LOOP
IF LEN(vOrderBy) > 0 THEN
    frmSortOrder.udpCallingScreen.OrderBy = LEFT(vOrderBy, LEN(vOrderBy) - 1)
ELSE
    frmSortOrder.udpCallingScreen.OrderBy=NULL
END IF
frmSortOrder.udpCallingScreen.Query()
pbCancel.Click()
```

When you created the Sort Order form, you only referred to the main screen of the Orders application when you were setting the OrderBy property of that form upon leaving the Sort Order form. Since you only referred to the Main form in this single function, it is easy to modify the form so that it will work with any calling form.

The udpCallingScreen is a property of the frmSortOrder form, so you will have to qualify the references to it in your function with 'frmSortOrder'.

You have modified all the code you need to change in the Sort Order form that refers directly to the calling screen. You will now have to change some of the code you have written to use the udpCallingScreen property to generalize the functionality of the form.

Making a Form Generic – Using the User Property

In order to have your newly modified Sort Order form work properly with your Orders application, you will have to change the way the lstSortColumns list box populates itself.

The Translation property of the lstSortColumns list box currently uses an SQL statement to retrieve the columns from the ORDERS table. If you want to use the frmSortOrder form with other forms, you will have to dynamically set the Translation property of the list box when the form is created.

In Chapter 5, you learned that you can open a modal dialog box by using the **OpenModal( )** method for the form. The **OpenModal( )** method calls a specific method in the form. You can add your own code to the **OpenModal( )** method of a form to implement any specific functionality you need when the form is created with the **OpenModal( )** method.

■ Open the frmSortOrder form window. Open the code window for the **OpenModal( )** method. If you are using Oracle as your database server, enter the following line of code:

```
lstSortColumns.Translation = "=select COLUMN_NAME, COLUMN_NAME from &

    ALL_TAB_COLUMNS where TABLE_NAME = '" & udpCallingScreen.RecordSource & "' "
```

If you are using Blaze as your data source, enter the following line of code:

```
lstSortColumns.Translation = "= at ORDERS select COLUMN_NAME, COLUMN_NAME from &
    SYS.ALL_COLUMNS, SYS.ALL_OBJECTS where ALL_COLUMNS.ID = ALL_OBJECTS.ID and &
    ALL_OBJECTS.NAME = '" & udpCallingScreen.RecordSource & "'"
```

NOTE
A property in Oracle Power Objects cannot be continued from one line to the next by adding the & continuation character, so you will have to fit all of the above text on a single line. The text is shown on multiple lines because of the format of this book's page.

Each of these lines of code sets the Translation property of the lstSortColumns list box to populate itself with the column names of the columns for the record source of the form that is specified in the udpCallingScreen property of the frmSortOrder form. You have to set the Translation property to be an appropriate translation string, so you have to include the = sign at the beginning of the property and you have to surround the name of the udpCallingScreen's RecordSource property with single quote marks.

Since you are referring to the udpCallingScreen property in the **OpenModal( )** method of the frmSortOrder form, you do not have to qualify references to the property.

Notice that the new Translation property of the form does not include the **AT** *session* clause. The frmSortOrder form will use the default session for the

application, which you should always specify in the DefaultSession property of the
Properties sheet for the application.

■ Add the following line of code to the code in the **OpenModal( )** method of
the frmSortOrder form:

```
Inherited.OpenModal(0)
```

You are adding code to the **OpenModal( )** method. The code that you add to
this method will be executed instead of any default code that is included with
Oracle Power Objects as part of that method. You have to call the original code for
the **OpenModal( )** method by calling the method name with the Inherited qualifier.
You will learn more about the use of inherited methods later in this chapter in the
discussion of object classes.

■ Set the udpCallingScreen property of the form to "frmOrders".

■ Run the Orders application to verify the Sort Order form is working properly.

Now that you have modified your application to work with the new, generic
version of the Sort Order window, you have one final task to complete before you
make your Sort Order form a library object.

Making a Form Generic – Documenting
the Library Form

Although some programmers don't document their code, kind and compassionate
individuals understand that making life miserable for the programmers who will
have to maintain programs after their author has moved on is not a very charitable
attitude. Moreover, many programmers occasionally have to return to code they
have written quite a while before, so they can actually experience some of the
problems of maintaining "perfectly understandable but undocumented code."
Because of this, you should always make sure that you properly document
your code.

Documenting your code is even more important when you are improving your
productivity through the use of libraries and object classes. You will be designing
your libraries and classes to be reused in a wide variety of known and unknown
situations, so you want to make sure that you do not lose any of the productivity
you have gained by failing to properly document your reusable objects.

■ Open the User Properties screen. Scroll to the bottom of the User
Properties table window and add the Name '__Documentation'.

You will be using the __Documentation subroutine to document the way your Sort Order form works. Oracle Power Objects sorts the items in a Properties sheet in alphabetical order, and the underscore character comes before any of the letters of the alphabet. By using two underscore characters at the beginning of the __Documentation subroutine, you are ensuring that the documentation for an object will appear early in the Properties sheet and mark the subroutine as an "artificial" routine.

■ Set the Type of __Documentation as 'Sub'.

__Documentation is not really a subroutine. Oracle Power Objects does not use a subroutine until it is called in application code, which you will not be doing, so no errors will result from this slightly inaccurate declaration. By specifying __Documentation as either a function or a subroutine, you can open up a code window for it, rather than just having a single line to enter a value. Since you should document your objects thoroughly, it will be useful to display the documentation in a code window in a more readable manner.

A subroutine does not return a value, and a subroutine does not need to have parameters defined for it, so you do not have to define anything else for the __Documentation subroutine.

■ Add the __Documentation subroutine to the Properties sheet for the frmSortOrder. Open the code window for the __Documentation subroutine and add the following documentation:

```
The frmSortOrder can be used to set the Sort Order for another
window. When the window is opened, a list of the columns for the
RecordSource of the calling screen are listed in the lefthand
list box. A user can select a column to be used to sort by
clicking on the column name in the lefthand box and clicking on
the push button labeled > to move it to the righthand list box of
columns. When the user clicks on the OK push button, the form
will set the OrderBy property of the calling form, re-execute the
query, and dismiss the form. If the user clicks on the Cancel
push button, the form will be dismissed without changing the
OrderBy property of the calling form.

To call this form, use the following code :

frmSortOrder.OpenModal(0)

You will have to set the udpCallingScreen property of the form to
the name of the form that is calling the frmSortOrder form.
```

When it comes to documentation, the more complete, the better. Your next step is to take the generic Sort Order form you have created and move it to a library object.

Creating a Library Object

Now you will create a library that can be used to hold the form window that you are going to use in multiple applications and to add the Sort Order form to the library.

Since a library will hold form windows and bitmaps that can be used in multiple applications, library objects are created in the Main window, at the same level as application objects and session objects.

■ Make the Main window your active window. Click on the New Library push button in the toolbar or the New Library menu choice in the File menu. Enter the name 'GENFORMS.POL' as the file name of the library. Click on the OK push button to create the library.

The default extension for Oracle Power Object libraries is .POL, for Power Object Library.

■ Open the Orders application while keeping the GENFORMS library object visible. Click on the frmSortOrder object and, while holding down the mouse button, drag the form to the GENFORMS library.

A library can contain form windows or bitmaps. To add a bitmap to a library, use the Import BMP menu choice from the File menu. Once you have imported a bitmap into a library, you can copy it to an application in the same way that you copy a form window.

■ Click on the frmSortOrder form in the GENFORMS library and drag it, while holding down the CTRL key and the mouse button, into the Orders application.

Most libraries begin their lives as part of an application, as your Sort Order form did. To use the form in another application, you would copy it from the library to an application using the same technique that you used to copy it to the library.

With only a few small modifications, you have made it possible to use the Sort Order form in any future application you design. Of course, you could have also written your Sort Order form as a generic library form initially, but it is often easier to implement a library form window within the context of an application, so you can easily test the form.

Oracle Power Objects gives you an even more flexible and powerful way to increase your productivity by using object classes.

Classes

You can use a library to improve your productivity by reusing your previous work. However, libraries have some limitations.

As mentioned above, a library object can only be a form window or a bitmap. You can only use one library object to create a form window, so any functionality or objects you wish to reuse in multiple applications must be contained in the same library form window. There are many different functions and objects you might want to include in your applications, and many different combinations of these functions and objects you might want to use in any particular application. A library form window is monolithic — you must include everything you will want to use in a form within a single library form window.

This can lead to very complex form window library objects that contain all of the functionality you might ever need in your application. You could then use these large form window objects to create your form windows, and possibly delete those objects and functions you do not need in your specific application. This approach creates its own problems, though. Adding a library to an application is similar to pasting text into a word processing document. When you drag a form window or a bitmap from a library to an application, you are copying the complete object into the application. If you were to make changes to the library form window or bitmap, you would have to go to the applications that use the library, delete the library from the application, and copy the new library object into the application. If you have changed any part of the library object, you will lose those changes when you recopy the object. You can see that this could rapidly create major maintenance headaches.

It would be very useful if you could create your own application "building blocks" that could be combined in a number of ways to create different combinations within your applications. Oracle Power Objects gives you the ability to create these building blocks in the form of object classes. You have already been using object classes, unbeknownst to you, since all of the objects you have been using to build your application, from the form window to data fields, push buttons, and radio buttons, are instances of the standard object classes included with Oracle Power Objects. Oracle Power Objects also lets you define your own object classes, which gives you an enormous amount of power and flexibility in creating your applications.

What Is a Class?

An *object class*, also referred to as a *class*, is a complete description of an object or group of objects. An object class describes the way an object or group of objects appear, how they interact, and how they interface with the rest of an application. A class specifies the values for all of the properties and methods of all of the objects in a class.

The object class itself is essentially a recipe for creating an object or group of objects. You can create an *instance* of a class, which is a particular copy of an object class that is created in an application. The object class itself exists independent of any particular application, and the instances of an object class are all linked to the class.

A class is merely a description. This seems rather ephemeral — shouldn't there be a more concrete definition of a class? In fact, the architecture of object classes creates their enormous flexibility. The description of a class exists separately from an instance of the class. You can change the class, or description, and the concrete instances of the class will also change. In this way, object classes can not only improve your productivity, but they can have a dramatic impact on the way you handle maintenance. If the functionality of a class has to be modified or enhanced, you can modify the class and simply recompile any applications that use that class. The object class acts as a repository for functionality.

You can have a class that is a single object, or dozens of objects. You can add properties to a class or methods. You can create an instance that is an exact implementation of a class, or extend or override any of the functionality of the class. You can even create a class that is made up of other classes. In the rest of this chapter and the next, you will learn much more about object classes and how they work.

How Is a Class Different from a Library?

Earlier in this chapter, you learned how to reuse form windows from libraries in your applications to improve your productivity as a developer. You can use instances of object classes to also reduce your development effort. How are object classes and libraries different?

First of all, the instance of a class is dynamically linked to the object class. This means that when you change any of the properties, methods, or composition of a class, the instances of the class will, with a single exception described and illustrated in the next section, automatically also change. If you change an object class, you merely have to recompile the application containing the class and the changes will be automatically included in the recompiled application. This means that it is much easier to make changes to your object classes and maintain the applications that use the classes than it is to delete and recopy changed versions of library objects.

As mentioned above, a library object can only be a form window or a bitmap. An object class can be any combination of standard Oracle Power Objects objects or user-defined classes. An object class could be as small as a single data field or static text object, or a virtual form with dozens of objects and hundreds of properties and methods.

Because you have control over the scope of an object class, you can modularize the functionality of a class. If you want to create a set of push buttons to replace the standard data navigation scroll bar, you can create an object class with four push buttons, for next, previous, and first and last row, and all of the methods necessary for these push buttons to work generically with a form window. When you or another developer add the class to a form, all of the objects and methods would automatically be added to the form.

The ability to define the scope of an object gives an object class designer a great deal of flexibility in making changes to the object class. The functionality of an object class is *encapsulated* within the class. This means that the functionality is completely contained within the class, so a developer can make any changes to that functionality without disturbing the relationship between instances of the class and the applications they are in. For instance, suppose you had designed the set of navigation push buttons mentioned in the previous paragraph. You decided that you would like to supplement the push buttons with a progress gauge that would show the relative position of the displayed row in the result set. You could add a new object, the progress gauge, to the class and all of the code to properly set the gauge. The interface to the database session would remain the same, as would the user interface through the push buttons. All you would have to do is to recompile any applications that used the class to add the new functionality.

Finally, object classes support the concept of *inheritance*. As mentioned above, you can create an object class from another object class. When you create a child class like this, the class inherits all of the methods and properties of the parent class. You have the ability to selectively extend or replace the properties and functionality of a parent class in the child class. Oracle Power Objects will also let you have an unlimited number of levels of parents, or ancestors, so you can create base object classes that implement wide-ranging functionality and build more specific implementations of this basic functionality in descendant classes. For instance, you could create a standard object class to handle the display of run-time errors in an application. You could create a variety of descendant classes to handle different types of run-time errors, and use the standard mechanisms in the parent class to display the errors. One of the properties of the parent class might control whether errors are written to a log file or displayed to the user. By setting the property in the parent class, you could route all the errors from all the child classes without modifying any of them. You could even add additional options for displaying errors, such as sending E-mail messages to the developers, to the parent class without touching any of the child classes.

The concept of inheritance is at the root of the power of object classes to create larger, more powerful classes. Changes in a parent class at any level roll down through its descendant classes according to a set of powerful standard rules. The next section will give you a hands-on demonstration of how inheritance works.

Exploring Inheritance – Properties

In this section, you will use an existing object class to explore the composition of classes and how inheritance works between object classes and their instances.

- Create a new form in your application. Set the the Name property of the form to 'frm1'. Size the form so that it is 2 1/2" wide and 3" tall.

You will be using this form for demonstration purposes only, so you can give the form a nondescriptive name. Reducing the size of the form will make it easier to see the effect that changes in an object class have on the instances of the class.

- Open the MLDONE application. Scroll to the clsLogoClass object class. Click on the class and drag it to your application folder while holding down the CTRL key and the mouse button.

When you are copying an object, you must hold down both the CTRL key and the mouse button. Any class that you will be using in your application must either be in the application or in a library.

- Click on the clsLogoClass and drag it into the frm1 form.

When you are creating an instance of an object class and not copying an object, you do not have to hold down the CTRL key.

- Create another instance of the clsLogoClass by dragging from the class to frm1. The second instance will be placed, by default, in the upper-left corner of the form. Click on the instance and drag it down below the first instance.

As discussed earlier in this chapter, an instance inherits all the properties and methods of the object class. This includes the default location of the class, which for the clsLogoClass is the upper-left corner of the form.

Each instance of the class is given a default name. The first instance of a class in a form is given the name of the class. Subsequent instances of a class are given the default name of the class followed by an integer, such as 'clsLogoClass2'.

You will be using these two instances of an object class in the same form to demonstrate the way inheritance works, but the inheritance scheme would work the same way for any number of instances on any number of forms. The inheritance scheme would also work the same way between child classes and their parent classes at any level.

■ Open the clsLogoClass in your application.

Your Oracle Power Objects development space should look like this:

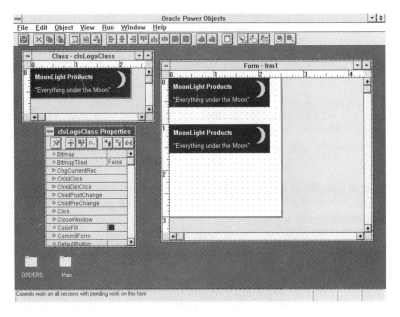

■ Click on the first instance of the clsLogoClass in the frm1 form window to select the instance. Click on the four objects that are part of the class in turn:

■ The 'MoonLight Products' static text object

■ The 'Everything under the Moon' static text object

■ The yellow oval that is overlaid to create a crescent moon

■ The blue oval overlaying the yellow moon to create the crescent

To select the yellow crescent, click directly on the crescent. To select the overlaid blue oval, click just to the left of the yellow crescent.

■ Click on the crescent moon in the second instance of the logo class. Click on the ColorFill property of the object and change the color of the crescent to green.

Notice that the property diamond for the ColorFill is now filled in. Whenever you change the value of an inherited property or method, the indicator is filled in for easy identification.

■ Open the clsLogoClass object class in your application window. Select the crescent moon in the class. Change the ColorFill property of the crescent moon to white.

Your form should now look like this:

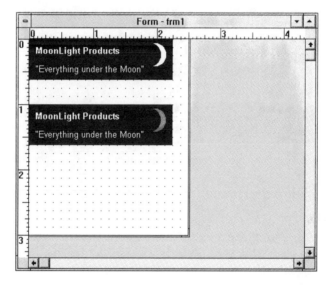

Notice that the crescent moon in the first instance of the logo class changes to white along with the crescent moon in the parent class. Once you change the value for a property or method in an instance of an object class, changes in the property or method are no longer inherited by the instance.

■ Select the crescent moon in the second instance of the logo class. Change the ColorFill property to white so that the crescent moon in the second instance of the logo class is now the same color as the crescent moon in the clsLogoClass. Select the crescent moon in the clsLogoClass and change the ColorFill property to green.

Notice that the color of the crescent moon in the second instance of the logo class still does not change when you change the property of the clsLogoClass object class, even though the crescent moon in the second instance and the parent class have the same value for the ColorFill property. Once you change the value of a property or method in an instance, the link between the instance and its parent class is broken, regardless of the value in the instance.

■ Select the ColorFill property for the second instance of the logo class. Click on the Reinherit push button in the toolbar of the Properties sheet. Select the crescent moon in the clsLogoClass and change the ColorFill property of the class to white.

Your form should now look like this:

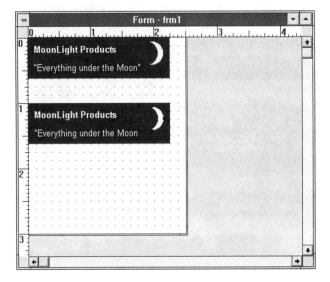

When you reinherit a property from an object class, the link between the object class and the instance is re-established, and any future changes to properties or values in the object class will be inherited by the instance of the class.

Inheriting Methods

You have been able to see how instances of a class can inherit changes in the value of properties from their parent classes, how to override property inheritance, and how to re-establish inheritance for properties. The inheritance scheme for properties is very straightforward, since a property can only have a single value.

Inheritance works slightly differently for methods than for properties. If you change a method in an instance of a class, you override the default method code for that class, in the same manner that changing the value of a property will override the default value of the property. Changing the value for a method in an instance will also break the linkage between the instance method and the object class.

However, you can also call the method in the parent object class from an instance of the class. To call a method in a parent class, you would use the syntax

```
Inherited.Method_name()
```

This syntax calls the method in the parent object class. You have already used this syntax in your application. When you set default values for the ORDER_DATE and SHIP_DATE data field objects in the Main form, you added the code to set these values in the **InsertRow( )** method of the form. You had to add the code

```
Inherited.InsertRow()
```

at the end of your method code.

As mentioned earlier in this chapter, all of the objects you have been using are actually instances of Oracle Power Objects standard object classes. The default **InsertRow( )** method for a form implements a great deal of functionality, from preparing the recordset for a new row to initializing all the objects on the form. If you had not specifically called the **inherited** method, the method code you added to your form would have replaced the default method.

The ability to call an **inherited** method gives an enormous amount of flexibility in using object classes. You can easily replace any particular method in an instance of a class, or you could call the **inherited** method at any point in your additional code. This allows you to supplement the functionality in a particular object method while still inheriting any changes in the class method code.

For instance, suppose you had created a **Validate( )** method that tested a data field for a particular value using a **SELECT CASE** construct. You wanted to create an instance of this class that would test for an additional value, such as 'X'. You could replace the **Validate( )** method with the following code:

```
IF Self.Value = 'X' THEN

    . . . . .

ELSE

    Inherited.Validate()

END IF
```

if you wanted to test for the value of 'X' first. You could also write the code to call the **inherited** method first and test for the value of 'X' last.

Remember that the rules for inheriting methods also apply to a parent class and a child class. In the above example, you could create a base class that tested for a number of values, and a child class that tested for all of those values and 'X'. Any changes to the method in the parent class would be automatically inherited in the child class. When you multiply this scenario with the ability to have many generations of class inheritance, you can begin to see how you can create an entire hierarchy of object classes to implement many different varieties of classes. You will be creating a hierarchy of complex classes in Chapter 6 of this book.

You have now learned enough about the basis and use of object classes to create your own class. The remainder of this chapter will walk you through the creation and use of an object class.

Creating and Using an Object Class

Now that you have learned how classes operate, you are ready to create an object class that you can use in your Orders application.

You will be creating a *complex* class. A complex class is an object class that contains multiple child objects. The ability to create a complex class gives you a great deal of power and flexibility.

Your complex class will contain window objects for all of the different pieces of information that are part of an address. Once you have created this class, you will be able to drop it into any application or form that will have address information and get all the window objects you need with a single action. In addition, you will be able to supplement the functionality of the class by adding validation and other logic and have the instances of the class automatically inherit the additional functionality.

Creating Your Object Class

Your first task will be to create your object class.

■ Open the window for the ORDERS application. Click on the New Class push button to create a new object class. Set the Name property to 'clsAddress'.

Oracle Power Objects are created at the form level. When you create a class, Oracle Power Objects will give you a workspace that looks like a form. The object class has all of the properties and methods of a form.

■ Add data field objects for two lines of address information, and set the Name properties of the objects to 'fldAddress1' and 'fldAddress2', respectively. These two data field objects should be 3 3/8" wide. Add a data field object for the city information and set the Name property to 'fldCity'. Add a data field object for the state information and set the Name property to 'fldState'. Add a data field object for the ZIP code information and give it the name of 'fldZIP'. These three data fields should be in a horizontal line below the dfsAddress2 data field.

When you created similar data field objects for the frmOrders form by dragging and dropping the column names from the database session, the data fields were given the names of the columns. By giving the names of the data fields in the class names beginning with the prefix "fld," you clearly mark them as data field objects that were not created by dragging and dropping columns. Since you may want to look at these types of data fields differently than automatically created data fields, the lack of consistency in the naming scheme can serve as an easy-to-see marker of difference.

■ Select all of these objects by clicking on one and then clicking on the others while holding down the SHIFT key. Change the DataType property of all of the selected fields to 'String'.

Whenever you want to show the address of an individual or a business, you will want to show these five pieces of information. All of the information is kept as strings. If you should use this class for address information where the ZIP code is stored as a number, you could change the data type of the instance of the class for that specific information.

When you have added the data field objects to the class, your class should look like this:

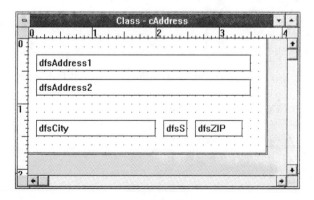

■ Add static text objects with Label properties of 'Address', 'City', 'State', and 'ZIP' in their appropriate positions. Select all of the static text objects and set the FontBold, FontName, and FontColor properties of the objects to match the properties of the static text objects in the frmOrders form. Resize the form so that it is 3 3/4" wide and 1 3/4" high.

NOTE
You are creating an object class to use instead of the five data field objects used for address information in the frmOrders form. As a shortcut, you could open the frmOrders form, select the data field objects and the static text objects, copy them using the Copy menu choice and the Paste menu choice in the Edit menu. You would then have to change the names of the data fields so that they had the "fld" prefix.

You are creating this class for use in the frmOrders form. If you use this class in another form and want to change any of the properties of the objects in the class, you can easily override the properties in the class instance.

When you have added the static text objects to the class, your form should look like this:

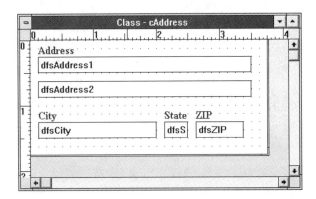

■ Set the DataSource property of each of the data field objects as follows:

```
dfsAddress1.DataSource = 'ADDRESS1'

dfsAddress2.DataSource = 'ADDRESS2'

dfsCity.DataSource = 'CITY'
```

```
dfsState.DataSource = 'STATE'

dfsZIP.DataSource = 'ZIP'
```

As with the properties mentioned above, you can always change the DataSource of any particular object in the clsAddress class in any one of its instances. If the databases you are working with are named consistently, you will not have to do this very often; but you will still be able to use the clsAddress class productively even if you do, since you will be able to drop appropriately spaced and named objects into forms and reports, as well as any validation or logic that you may choose to add to this class.

■   Open the properties sheet for the clsAddress class. Set the Transparent property to 'True'. Set the Has Border property to 'False'.

These two properties will allow you to seamlessly integrate an instance of this class into any form or report. When the Transparent property of a form or class is set to 'True', the form or class will automatically assume the same background color or bitmap as the form that it is embedded into. With the frmOrders form, the complicated bitmap that is used as a background will not be disturbed by using an instance of the clsAddress class.

Setting the Has Border property of the class to 'False' will eliminate the border that normally surrounds any form-level object.

■   Set the RecordSource of the clsAddress class to '=**container**'.

Oracle Power Objects supports *shared recordsets*. As mentioned above, and as will be further explained in Chapter 9, Oracle Power Objects uses a recordset to act as the intermediary between the database and an Oracle Power Objects application. The recordset holds the data that has been retrieved from the database server, as well as acting as a buffer for any changes to the data or for any new records that have been added until they are committed to the database server.

The RecordSource property can be set to a specific record, or you can indicate that the recordset for a form-level object is to be shared with another form by using the = and the name of the form that has the recordset that will be shared. When you indicate that a recordset will be shared by using the = at the beginning of the RecordSet property, you eliminate the need to specify a RecSrcSession, since the form-level object will automatically be sharing the record source session when it shares the recordset.

Remember that an object class is a container object that will be embedded into some other form or report. You use the keyword **container** to indicate that the recordset for this particular class will be shared with any form that contains the instance of the class. By using **container**, you have indicated that the class will share a recordset and generalized the reference to the recordset, which makes it much easier to use the class.

Documenting Your Class

As mentioned above, you should always document your code. With object classes, this is especially important, since an object class may be widely used by many different developers.

■ Open the Properties sheet for the clsAddress class. Open the User Properties dialog box by clicking on the User Properties push button in the Properties sheet toolbar. Select the __Documentation subroutine in the user properties dialog box and drag it to the Properties sheet for the clsAddress object class.

If you have been using this guide sequentially, you created the __Documentation user property in Chapter 4. If you have not, please refer back to Chapter 4 for information on creating user properties, subroutines, and functions.

■ Add the following text into the __Documentation subroutine:

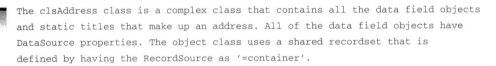

```
The clsAddress class is a complex class that contains all the data field objects
and static titles that make up an address. All of the data field objects have
DataSource properties. The object class uses a shared recordset that is
defined by having the RecordSource as '=container'.
```

Adding an Instance of Class to a Form

Your final step is to add an instance of the object class to your frmOrders form. Before you can add the instance to the form, you should get rid of the window objects and text that will be replaced by the instance of the object class.

■ Open the frmOrders form. Select the data field objects and static text objects for the ADDRESS1, ADDRESS2, CITY, STATE, and ZIP data fields. Delete the objects from the form by clicking on the Delete push button in the toolbar or using the Cut menu choice from the Edit menu.

■ Reduce the size of the frmOrders form so that you can see the window for the ORDERS application at the same time. Click on the clsAddress class icon and drag it to the frmOrders form.

Just as with the clsLogoClass, you do not have to hold down the CTRL key while you drag from the class icon, since you are creating an instance of the class rather than copying the entire class.

- ■ The class instance will appear in the upper-left corner of the frmOrders form. Move the class to the appropriate spot on the form.

Since the class is a container object, you can move the class and all of the objects in the class by simply clicking on any part of the class. As with the repeater display container object, you will have to first select the class instance and then the individual objects in the class with successive clicks if you want to select an object within the class.

- ■ Run your frmOrders form. Scroll through some of the data until you get to at least the fourth row so that you can see that the clsAddress class provides the proper address information.

Since you have specified that the data will appear in the form sorted by customer name, the first three rows are all for the same customer, so they will all have the same address. By scrolling to at least the fourth row, you can verify that the linkage between the instance of the clsAddress class and the frmOrders form is correct.

Adding a Class to a Library

Since an object class is designed to be used with many different forms, you may also want to use instances of an object class over many different applications. To enable this ability, you should move your clsAddress class to a generalized library object.

- ■ Open the GENFORMS library. Arrange the GENFORMS library and the ORDERS library so that both are visible on the screen. Click on the clsAddress object class and the CTRL key and copy it to the GENFORMS library.

Once the clsAddress object class is in a library object, you can add an instance of the class to any form in any other application by clicking on the class and dragging it to the form while holding down the CTRL key. If the class is not in the application when you run the application, Oracle Power Objects will ask you which library the class resides in.

NOTE
You should keep all of your object classes in a library, especially if they use a shared recordset. If you try and compile an application that has an object class as part of the application, the '**=container**' phrase in the RecordSource property of the object class will result in an error in Oracle Power Objects version 1.0. By moving the class object to a library, Oracle Power Objects only tries to compile the instance of the object class, where the '**=container**' will be properly compiled.

Congratulations once again! You have created a class that will allow you to add complete address information to any form or report in the future by simply dragging and dropping an instance of the class.

You have learned a great deal in this chapter. You have learned how to use libraries and object classes to leverage your productivity. You have learned how to create a class object and how to create an instance of a class in a form. You have also learned how inheritance works between object classes and their instances.

You have taken the first few giant steps in learning how to use classes and libraries to make you much more productive. In the next chapter, you will build a complex class that will allow you to create selection conditions for any form, just as you created sort conditions for a form in Chapter 4, but with even more functionality and flexibility.

CHAPTER 6

Extended Class Functionality—Creating an Expression-Creation Class

In Chapter 5, you learned how you can improve your productivity by leveraging your work through the use of classes. You learned about the implications of inheritance and how to create a class. In this chapter, you will be going through the entire process of creating a useful class. The class you will create will allow a user to create expressions where a data column can be compared with a value. You will be able to drop this class into your order entry application and give your users an easy, graphical way to specify selection conditions.

The class you create will also be usable for any purpose where you need to allow a user to create an expression where a value is compared to a selected value, column, or variable.

In creating you class, you will

■ Create a form class with the objects necessary to implement the functionality

■ Implement the basic functionality required in the class

■ Add logical integrity features to the class

■ Add user features to the class

■ Create an instance of the class in your application and test the class

■ Modify the functionality of the class

■ Create a subclass with slightly different functionality

■ Generalize the base class to enable it to work seamlessly in a wider variety of situations

You will be accomplishing a lot in this chapter, so let's get right to it!

Creating Your Class and Its Objects

You can describe the functionality of this class with a few sentences: This class will allow a user to graphically create an expression composed of a column name, an operand, and a value. The user will be able to build an expression of the form

```
column_name operator condition
```

such as ORDER_DATE < 1/1/95. The user should also be able to build compound expressions composed of several expressions like this and join them with conditional operators, such as AND or OR.

In order to accomplish this purpose, you will need to add objects to your form that can

■ Display the column names

■ Specify the operand of the expression

■ Enter the value for the right side of the expression

■ Store the compound expression as it is built

■ Specify the conditional operators AND or OR

■ Add an expression clause to the compound expression

■ Return to the form or container that has called the instance of the class

In this section, you will create your form class. You will also determine the appropriate type of object for each of the purposes listed above and add the object to your form.

Adding a Column Name Listing to Your Class

Since different tables will have different numbers of columns, the column names will be loaded dynamically each time the user opens an instance of this class, and the user should only be allowed to pick a valid column name, a list box is the most appropriate visual object to display the column names.

■ Open the Orders application window. Add a new class object to the application by clicking on the New Class push button in the toolbar and setting the Name property of the class to 'clsExpression' and the Label property of the class to 'Expression Builder'.

You will not need to specify a RecSrcSession or a RecordSource property. Oracle Power Objects will automatically use the session specified in the DefaultSession property of the application.

■ Set the Transparent property of the class to 'True' and the HasBorder property of the class to 'False'.

Specifying a form as transparent will allow the form to visually integrate with the form that contains it by allowing any objects, bitmaps, or colors "behind" the form to show through. Setting the HasBorder property to 'False' will eliminate the border of the form. These two property settings will let you drop an instance of this class into any form without worrying about the background color or bitmap of the form.

■ Add a list box toward the upper-left corner of the form 1 5/8" high and 1 3/8" wide. Set the Name property of the list box to 'lstColumns' and add a static text object with a Label property of 'Columns' above it.

At this point, your class window should look like this:

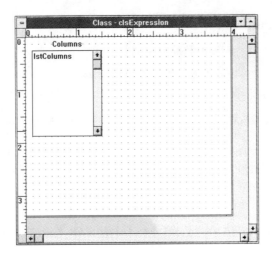

Adding an Operator List to Your Class

There are not many operators that can be used in your expression clause. The most common operators are

```
=
<
>
<=
>=
<>
```

The number and type of operators will not change very often, so you do not need a dynamic display object like a list box. You could use a set of radio buttons in a frame to display the operand choices to the user. The only problem with using radio buttons is that you would have to use six different buttons, which could make an unattractive form.

You can come up with an optimal solution by looking at the operators themselves. The "<=", ">=", and "<>" operators can also be expressed as "NOT >", "NOT <", and "NOT =", respectively. You can use three radio buttons and a check box to indicate a NOT prefix.

It doesn't really matter if the expression you are building allows the "NOT" string in operators. You can always convert the logical indication in the form to the appropriate string. It is important to have a clean and clear graphical representation in your class.

NOTE
You may decide that you wish to use a list box instead of this combination of radio buttons and a check box. Using a list box is probably just as good as the solution proposed; but for the purposes of this book, it is instructive to work with different combinations of objects.

■ Add a narrow radio button frame to the left of the lstColumns list box 1 1/4" high and 7/8" wide. Set the Label property of the radio button frame to 'Operators' and the Name property to 'rbfOperators'. Set the DataType property of the radio button frame to 'String'. Add three radio buttons to the frame. The first will have a Label property of '=', a Name property of 'radEquals', a DataType property of 'String' and a ValueOn property of '='. The second radio button will have a Label and ValueOn property of '<', a DataType property of 'String' and a Name property of 'radLessThan'. The third radio button will have a Label and ValueOn property of '>', a DataType property of 'String', and a Name property of 'radGreaterThan'. Arrange the radio buttons within the radio button frame.

If you make the radio button frame narrow, you will find that the default size of the radio button itself will fill the entire frame. Before you can center the radio buttons in the frame, you will have to reduce the size of the radio button's label area.

■ Add a check box below the radio button group. Set the Label property and the ValueOn property to 'NOT', set the Name property of the check box to 'cbNot', and set the DataType property to 'String'.

Your class should now look like this:

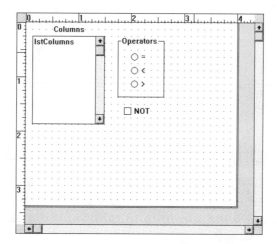

Adding a Value to Your Expression-Making Class

The right side of the expression clause will be a value that will be compared with the value in the column specified in the left side of the expression clause. You should use a data window object to capture the value for the right side of the expression clause.

■   Add a data field object to the class in the upper-right portion of the class form window. Set the Name property of the data field object to 'fldValue' and set the DataType property of the field to 'String'. Add a static text object with a Label property of 'Value' centered over the data field.

NOTE
An easy way to center a static text string over a window is to make the static text object the same width as the window and choose the Center option for the TextJustHoriz property.

Although the value in the expression clause might be a string, a number, or a date, the expression clause itself will be a string, so the value must be entered as a string.

Your class should now look like this:

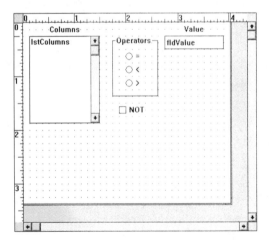

Adding an Expression Holder to Your Class

Your user may wish to build an expression that consists of multiple expression clauses. Your expression-making class should have an object that can hold your complete expression as the user is building the individual expression clauses.

■ Enlarge your Class window to a height of 3 3/8". Add a data field object to the lower left-hand corner of the window. Make the data field 2" wide and 1 1/8" high. Set the Name property of the data field to 'fldExpression', the Datatype property to 'String', and the MultiLine property to 'True'. Set the DataSize property to 400. Add a static text object with a Label property of 'Expression:' over the data field object.

When you set the value of the MultiLine property to 'True', the data field object will automatically allow multiple lines of data and word wrap if the length of the value exceeds the width of the object.

NOTE

When you click on an object and hold down the mouse button in the Oracle Power Objects, the size and position of the object is shown as a black bar in the rulers at the top and left of the form design area.

Your class should now look like this:

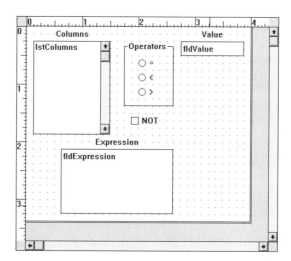

Adding a Conditional Operator Indicator to Your Class

When adding more than one expression clause to an expression, a user will have to specify how additional classes will be tested in the overall expression by using a conditional operator, AND or OR, to link the clause to the expression.

Since there are only two valid conditional operators, and since the user will have to use one of them, a radio button group is appropriate for the conditional operator.

■ Add a radio button frame, 1" high and 7/8" wide, to the lower-right portion of your class window. Set the Name property of the radio button frame to 'rbfCondition' and the Label property to 'Condition'. Set the DataType property of the radio button frame to 'String'. Add two radio buttons to the frame: one with a Label and ValueOn property of 'AND' and a Name property of 'radAnd', and the other with a Label and ValueOn property of 'OR' and a Name property of 'radOr'. Set the DefaultValue property for the radio button frame to 'AND'.

NOTE
Oracle Power Objects automatically sets the state of a radio button based on the Value property of the frame that contains the radio button. By default, the Value property is initialized to null, so no radio button in a frame will automatically be selected. Typically, you would use a group of radio buttons to force a user to choose one and only one value, or radio button, so you will want to initialize a group of radio buttons so that one of them is initially selected.

Your class should now look like this:

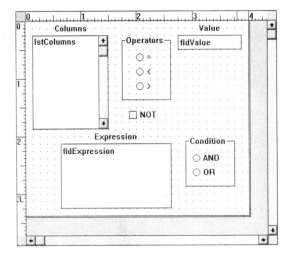

Adding User Function Objects to Your Class

A client/server environment is a user-driven environment. You should provide visual objects in an application to allow a user to add an expression clause to an expression or to leave the expression-making class.

You could use menu choices for this functionality. But since your class will be used in widely different situations, you won't be able to predict how adding a menu will affect the application environment. It will be easier to add push buttons to your class to implement the user-driven functionality.

■ Add a push button below the fldValue data field. Set the Label property of the radio button to 'Add' and the Name property to 'btnAdd'. Add a push button below the rbfCondition radio button frame. Set the Label property of the push button to 'Exit' and the Name property to 'btnExit'.

You have now created all of the objects you will need in your class. Your completed class should look like this:

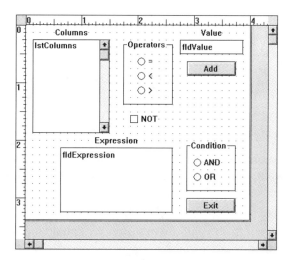

Adding Basic Functionality to Your Class

Now that you have designed the visual objects in your class, you can add the basic functionality needed in your class. The basic functionality required in your class will

■ Populate the leftmost list box with a list of column names

■ Check the validity of the expression

■ Process the NOT operand, if necessary

■ Move the expression clause to the multiline expression holder

■ Leave the class and set a property of the calling class or container

■ Document how the class should work

As you implement this class, you should try to segregate the different logical steps into individual methods of class objects. In this way, you can make your class more flexible by allowing descendant classes or class instances to override or add to each individual logical step without disturbing the rest of the logic. For instance, you should design the way you display column names so that you could display something other than column names and still be able to use the rest of the class unmodified. By *encapsulating* the different logical steps in your class, you make it easier to replace or supplement any step or steps without having to reimplement other steps.

Populating the Column List Box

You have already populated a list box with a list of columns that are in a table in the sort order window. You will follow the same procedure in your expression-making class.

■ Open the property sheet for the clsExpression class. Add the udpCallingScreen property to your class by opening the User Properties window and dragging the udpCallingScreen property to the Properties sheet for the class.

As you did in Chapter 5, you will use this property to hold the object handle of the container of an instance of the class. You will also want to populate the list box with the names of the columns in the table that is the RecordSource of the udpCallingScreen. You will have to set the Translation property for the lstColumns list box in the **OnLoad( )** method of the class, depending on whether you are using an Oracle database or a Blaze datastore.

■ If you are using an Oracle database, add the following code to the **OnLoad( )** method of the class:

```
lstColumns.Translation = "=select COLUMN_NAME, COLUMN_NAME from " & &
"ALL_TAB_COLUMNS where TABLE_NAME = '" & updCallingScreen.RecordSource & "'"
```

```
Inherited.OnLoad()
```

If you are using a Blaze datastore, add the following code to the **OnLoad( )** method of the class:

```
lstColumns.Translation = "=select COL_NAME, COL_NAME from SYS.ALL_COLUMNS," & &
    "SYS.ALL_OBJECTS where ALL_COLUMNS.ID = ALL_OBJECTS.ID and ALL_OBJECTS.NAME ="& &
    "'" & udpCallingScreen.RecordSource & "'"
Inherited.OnLoad()()
```

Each of these SQL statements queries the system tables of their respective databases to retrieve the columns that belong to the RecordSource table of the calling screen.

You must set the Translation property of the lstColumns list box in the **OnLoad( )** method of the form since a property cannot include any concatenation or functions. The & concatenation operator would be interpreted as part of the string in a property, so to generalize the use of a class or library, you have to specifically set any property that might be different under different circumstances.

Adding an Expression Clause to the Expression Holder

Once having specified an expression clause to add to the expression holder multiline text field, a user can add the expression by clicking on the btnAdd push button. There are three logical steps that have to take place to add an expression clause:

- The expression clause must be concatenated from the column name, the operand, and the value.

- The conditional operator must be added to the expression clause.

- The expression clause must be added to the expression holder.

You will add code to the btnAdd push button and the radio button frame rbfOperators to implement this functionality.

- Open the code window for the **Click( )** method of the btnAdd push button. Add the following code to create a variable to hold the expression clause:

```
DIM vExpression As String
```

■ Add the following code to concatenate the expression clause:

```
vExpression = lstColumns.Value & " "& cbNot.Value & " " & &
    rbfOperators.Value & &
    " " fldValue.Value & " "
```

This code will take the value for the column name selected in the lstColumns list box, concatenate it with a space, the value for the cbNot check box, another space, and the value for the fldValue data field object.

If the expression clause you are adding to the expression holder is the first clause to be added, you do not want to include a conditional operator. In all other situations, you do want to include the conditional operator. You can easily determine if the clause you are adding is the first clause by testing the expression holder to see if it is null.

■ Add the underlined code to the **Click( )** method of the btnAdd push button:

```
DIM vExpression As String
vExpression = lstColumns.Value & " " &cbNot.Value& " " &rbfOperators.Value & &
    " " & fldValue.Value & " "
IF NOT ISNULL(fldExpression.Value)THEN vExpression=rbfCondition.Value &" " & &
    vExpression
```

You will concatenate the string in the fldExpression multiline data field if the fldExpression data field is not null. Since there is a single result based on the **IF** condition, you do not need to use the **END IF** clause as long as all of your **IF...ELSE** expression is part of a single line. You can now add the expression clause to the expression holder by adding the underlined code to the **Click( )** method of the btnAdd push button:

```
DIM vExpression As String
vExpression = lstColumns.Value & " " &cbNot.Value& " "& rbfOperators.Value & &
    " " & fldValue.Value & " "
IF NOT ISNULL(fldExpression.Value)THEN vExpression=rbfCondition.Value &" " & &
    vExpression
fldExpression.Value = fldExpression.Value & vExpression
```

Processing the NOT Operand

The code you have written will use the selected values to build an expression clause. Although the code is clean and logical, there will be something wrong in the expression clause built with this code, since the resultant clause will not work properly in a selection clause in an SQL statement against either Blaze or Oracle. Blaze and Oracle do not support the NOT qualifier to a conditional operator in an SQL statement.

You should always try to make your class as generic as possible. Some logical statements require the "!" operator to signify a NOT condition, such as "!=", which translates as "not equals." Some logical statements don't accept any NOT conditions, and so would require the operand "<>" for the "not equals" condition. Because of this, you should create a function in the rbfOperators object that will return the appropriate string to implement the user-specified logic.

This is an example of encapsulating logic in an object. It is the responsibility of the rbfOperators object to deliver a string that represents an operand to the class. If you use this class in a situation where you have to change the way an operand is created, you can simply replace the code in the **udmGetOperator( )** method and leave everything else in the class untouched.

■ Open the property sheet for the rbfOperators radio button frame. Click on the User Properties push button in the toolbar to go to the user properties list. Scroll to the bottom of the list box to add a new method. Add a method with the Name property 'udmGetOperator', a Type property of 'Function', and a DataType property of 'String'. This method will not require any parameters. Click on the box on the left of the entry and drag the method to the property sheet for the rbfOperators object.

■ Add the following code to the **udmGetOperator( )** method of the rbfOperators radio button frame:

```
IF cbNot.Value = "NOT" THEN
    SELECT CASE Self.Value
        CASE "="
        udmGetOperator = "<>"
        CASE "<"
        udmGetOperator = ">="
        CASE ">"
        udmGetOperator = "<="
    END SELECT
ELSE
    udmGetOperator = Self.Value
END IF
```

This method code will examine the value represented by the cbNot push button and the value represented by the radio button selected in the rbfOperators radio button group and return the appropriate comparison operator.

The keyword **Self** identifies the current object. In this particular code, the keyword **Self** is primarily used to document the reference.

You can use the **SELECT CASE** construct for situations where you want to evaluate a variable or property that will have one of several different values. The name of the object property or variable follows the **SELECT CASE** statement. Each potential value of the property or object is listed beneath the **SELECT CASE** statement with the word **CASE** preceeding it, and the code that should be executed if the variable or property matches the value in the preceding **CASE** statement follows. You can also use a **CASE END** statement to specify code that should be executed if the variable or property does not match any of the listed values. You end the **SELECT CASE** construct with the **END SELECT** phrase.

If an instance of the class is used in a situation where the "NOT" string is either not allowed or must be formatted in a different way, you can simply modify the **upmGetOperator( )** method. Even if you decide to delete the cbNot check box in an instance of the class, you can simply modify the **updGetOperator( )** method and still have the rest of the class operate properly. By encapsulating the parsing of the operator, you have made the class much more flexible.

When you want to return a value from a function, you set the function name to the value you wish to return.

■ Open the **Click( )** method for the btnAdd push button. Modify the underlined portion of the code to read:

```
vExpression = lstColumns.Value & " " & &
    rbfOperators.upmGetOperator() & " " & &
     fldValue.Value & " "
```

In the modified code, the return value of the **upmGetOperator( )** method will serve as the appropriate value for the operand. Using the **upmGetOperator( )** method will also eliminate the problem of having excess spaces if the cbNot check box is not checked. Of course, it makes more sense to have the function that delivers an operand string be a part of the object where a user specifies the operand string, so including the function as a method of rbfOperators will make the class easier to understand and maintain.

Exiting the Class

The final piece of basic functionality you need to add to your class is the ability to exit the class container when the user has finished defining the expression.

■ Open the property sheet for the btnExit push button. Enter the following code for the **Click( )** method:

```
clsExpression.updCallingScreen.QueryWhere( &
    fldExpression.Value)
```

The **QueryWhere( )** method forces a bound container to requery its data source and uses the string passed as a parameter to replace the DefaultCondition property of the container. Since this class may be used with containers that have a DefaultCondition already specified, you might want to concatenate the DefaultCondition of the container with the new conditions.

Since the updCallingScreen property is associated with the class, you have to qualify a reference to it with the clsExpression qualifier when using it in methods in the btnExit push button.

■   Add the the following code to the the **Click( )** method for the btnExit push button:

```
DIM vTop As Object
vTop = GetTopContainer()
clsExpression.updCallingScreen.QueryWhere(" " & fldExpression.Value)
vTop.DismissModal(Self)
```

The **GetTopContainer( )** function will return the handle of the form that contains the the instance of the class. The **DismissModal( )** method of a form is called whenever the IsDismissBtn property of a push button that is directly on the form is set to 'True' and the push button is clicked. Since the btnExit push button is part of the clsExpression class and not a particular form, you will have to call the **DismissModal( )** method of the form that it is on rather than designate it as the dimiss push button. The **DismissModal( )** method takes the handle of the object that calls it as a parameter, so you can use the **Self** keyword to indicate the handle of the calling push button.

You used the IsDismissBtn property of the btnCancel push button in the frmSortOrder form. Either clicking on the push button or calling the **DismissModal( )** method of a form that was opened as a modal dialog box will close the form, return control of the application to the calling screen, and keep an image of the modal dialog box in memory. The next time you use the **OpenModal( )** method to open the dialog box, the stored image will be recreated. This is handy for a form like the expression builder form, since you will normally want to reopen the form with the objects in the dialog box retaining the same values they had when the dialog box was closed.

If an instance of this class is used in a form that is not a modal dialog box, the **DismissModal( )** method will not have any effect.

When you close the form, you requery the rows in the calling form. If the user of an application that uses an instance of this class chooses to leave the dialog box that contains an instance of the class without setting a selection condition, the calling screen should not have to requery the rows.

■ Add the underlined code to the code in the btnExit push button:

```
DIM vTop As Object
vTop = GetTopContainer()
IF NOT ISNULL(fldExpression.Value) THEN&
    clsExpression.updCallingScreen.QueryWhere(&
    fldExpression.Value)
vTop.DismissModal()(Self)
```

Since the **IF** condition will only require a single function if it is true, you can use the **IF...THEN** clause without requiring the **END IF** condition.

Documenting Your Class

Earlier in this section, we suggested calling a function to return the operand based on the states of the rbfOperators radio button frame and the cbNot check box. Using a function in this way will make the class more understandable, which is important for all programmers who will be using or maintaining this class in the future. You should also add some documentation to this class using the same __**Documentation** subroutine that you created to document the sort order window library.

■ Add the __**Documentation** subroutine to the clsExpression class by opening the user properties window and dragging the property to the clsExpression property sheet. Add the following documentation in the __**Documentation** code window:

```
This class will allow a user to create a compound selection expression.
Drop the class into its own form and call it with the following code:
```

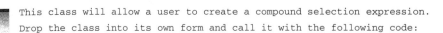

```
form_name.OpenModal(0)
where form_name is the name of the form that contains the class and calling_form
is the name of the form which is calling the form that contains the class.

You will have to set the updCallingScreen property of the class to the handle of
the screen that calls the form that contains the instance of the class.

This class will use the session specified in the DefaultSession property of your
application.
```

You have added all the basic functionality to your expression-making class. Your next step is to create an instance of the class and test it.

Testing Your Class

As discussed in Chapter 5, a class is a description, not an object. You can compile your class by compiling the file object that contains the class, but to test the operation of your class you will have to create an instance of it in an application.

Adding an Instance of Your Class

In order to test the operation of your class, you will have to create an instance of the class in your application.

■ Return to the application window for the Orders application. Create a new form with either the New Form push button or the New Form menu choice in the File menu. Enlarge the size of the form that was created until it is at least 3 1/2 " high. Set the Name property for the form to 'frmSelectionClause' and the Label property to 'Create Selection Criteria'.

Since the class you created was in a window that was 4" wide and 3 3/8" high, the form that will contain an instance of the class must be at least that size to properly hold the instance of the class. It is helpful to make your form a little bigger than the class, so you will be able to bring up the property sheet for the form by clicking on the area of the form that is not also part of the class instance.

■ Bring the window for the Orders application to the top by selecting it in the Window menu. Click on the clsExpression class and hold down the mouse button while you drag it into the frmSelectionClause form. Release the mouse button to create an instance of the class in the form.

Since you are creating an instance of a class, rather than copying the class, you do not need to hold down the CTRL key. Since you have set the Transparent property of the class to 'True' and the HasBorder property of the class to 'False', the objects in the class will appear to be directly placed into your form window. Remember, however, that the class still acts as a container for the objects in the instance of the class, so you will have to qualify references to them with the name of the class. The Name property of the class instance is set by default to the name of the class.

■ Set the updCallingScreen property of the instance of the clsExpression class to 'frmOrders'.

Adding a Push Button to Call Your Class

You have easily created a form that will allow you to create selection expressions by simply dropping an instance of the class into a form. To integrate the form into your application, you could create a push button or menu choice to call the form. Since you already have a push button to call the sort order screen, it would make visual sense to include another push button for the selection expression form.

■ Bring the application window for the Orders application to the top and select the Import BMP menu choice from the File menu. Import the EXPRESS.BMP bitmap that is described in Appendix A, or a bitmap of your own.

You will use the EXPRESS.BMP bitmap on the push button that will call the frmSelectionClause form.

■ Bring the application window for the Orders application to the top. Add the following line to the Declarations section of the property sheet:

```
CONST cmdCallSelectionWindow = Cmd_FirstUserCommand + 2
```

The cmdCallSelectionWindow constant will be used to add a push button to the toolbar and in the **TestCommand( )** and **DoCommand( )** methods of the frmOrders form.

■ Add the underlined code to the **OnLoad( )** method of the application:

```
DIM tbrMyToolbar As Object
CONST cmdCallSortWindow = Cmd_FirstUserCommand + 1
tbrMyToolbar = NEW Toolbar
frmOrders.DefaultToolbar(tbrMyToolbar)
frmOrders.SetToolbar(tbrMyToolbar)
tbrMyToolbar.TBAppendButton(0,NULL, ToolbarStyle_Separator, 0)
tbrMyToolbar.TBAppendButton(cmdCallSortWindow, SORTORD,
ToolbarStyle_Pushbtn, 0)
tbrMyToolbar.TBAppendButton(cmdCallSelectionWindow,EXPRESS, &
    ToolbarStyle_Pushbtn,0)
```

The first underlined piece of code adds a 10-pixel separator between the standard push buttons on the default toolbar and the push buttons to call the sort order and selection forms. When you are specifying a separator, you can use 0 as the value of the command code and null to indicate that there is no bitmap for the separator.

NOTE
You might want to use the **TBInsertButton( )** function to put sort order and selection push buttons between the QBF push buttons and the push buttons that control commit and rollback and exit the application.

The second piece of code adds a push button to call the selection form.

- Add the underlined code to the **TestCommand( )** method of the application:

```
SELECT CASE cmdCode
    CASE cmdCallSortWindow
        TestCommand = TestCommand_Enabled
    CASE cmdCallSelectionWindow
        TestCommand = TestCommand_Enabled
END SELECT
```

The **SELECT CASE** construct allows you to easily add additional command codes to the **TestCommand( )** method.

- Add the underlined code to the **DoCommand( )** method of the frmOrders form:

```
SELECT CASE cmdCode
    CASE cmdCallSortWindow
        frmSortWindow.OpenModal(0)
    CASE cmdCallSelectionWindow
        frmSelectionClause.OpenModal(0)
END SELECT
```

The frmSelectionClause will be opened as a modal window, in the same manner as the frmSortWindow, since you want the user to stay in the screen until the user either creates a complete selection expression or decides to return to the main form without designating a selection expression.

You are now ready to give your new selection clause form a whirl.

- Run your application. Click on the push button to call the frmSelectionClause form. Create a simple selection expression and return to the main form. Call the selection form again and add another selection clause to the expression.

Your main form, with the new push button and the selection form visible, should look like this:

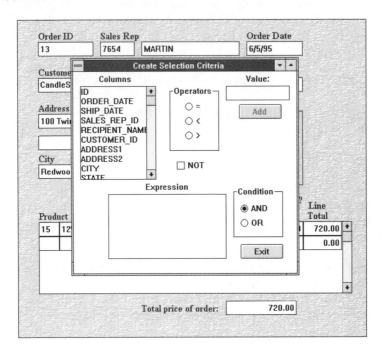

You may have found that your selection form could be improved in a number of ways. You may have found that it is very easy to design an invalid selection statement with your form, or that it is easy for a user to make mistakes when they are trying to use the form. You could also improve the readability of a compound selection expression. You may also have thought of ways to add useful functionality to the form. You will address each of these areas of concern in the next three sections of the chapter.

Adding Logical Integrity to Your Class

Although the expression-making class that you have designed is very useful, it is easy for a user to create invalid expressions when using a form based on the class. You could add *logical integrity* to the class by making it difficult, or impossible, for a user to leave a form based on the class unless the user has created a valid selection expression. If you can add logic to your class to prevent errors, you will make developers using the class more productive, since they will not have to add error checking to the form. Even more important, if you create a logically complete class, you can reduce the amount of time that developers and users will have to spend testing the applications that contain instances of the class.

Testing an Expression Clause

You may have found that it is easy to pass an invalid selection clause from the frmSelectionClause form to the main form. This will result in run-time errors, the bane of all application developers. You could address this problem by training users how to avoid creating invalid selection expressions; but since user training is costly and not guaranteed to be effective, and since users will still occasionally make mistakes, it would be much better if you could check the validity of a selection expression before you left the selection form.

Oracle Power Objects gives you a function that allows you to run any SQL statement, the **EXEC SQL** command. A foolproof way to guarantee the validity of a selection expression would be to use it as the **WHERE** clause in an SQL statement. If the statement executed successfully, you could be relatively sure that the selection expression would work properly with the SQL statements automatically created by Oracle Power Objects.

■   Open the clsExpression form window. Open the **Click( )** method for the btnExit push button. Add the underlined code to the existing code:

```
DIM vTestWhere As String
DIM vTop As Object
vTop = GetTopContainer
IF NOT ISNULL(fldExpression.Value) THEN
    vTestWhere = " WHERE " & fldExpression.Value
    clsExpression.updCallingScreen.QueryWhere(&
    fldExpression.Value)
    END IF
vTop.DismissModal(Self)
```

The additional code creates a string that you can use to create a **WHERE** clause to be tested and adds the SQL keyword **WHERE** to the beginning of the string stored in the fldExpression multiline text field. Since you are now executing more than one statement after the **THEN** clause, you will have to add an **END IF** clause and take out the continuation character.

Your next step is to create an SQL statement that will use the **WHERE** clause. You have already ensured that there will only be columns that are from the RecordSource table in the calling screen. You want to test the **WHERE** clause against the RecordSource table, but all you know about the table is its name and the columns in the table. If the table is very large, selecting even a single column could be very time consuming.

You want to use an SQL statement that will work with any table and not return too much data. The SQL statement **SELECT COUNT(*)** returns the number of rows that satisfy the selection conditions in the rest of the statement. Using **SELECT COUNT(*)** will return a single value, and most relational databases can process the **COUNT( )** function quite rapidly.

■ Add the underlined code to the existing code in the **Click( )** method of the btnExit push button in the clsExpression class:

```
DIM vTestWhere As String
DIM vTop As Object
vTop = GetTopContainer()
IF NOT ISNULL(fldExpression.Value) THEN
    vTestWhere = "SELECT COUNT(*) FROM " & &
    clsExpression.updCallingScreen.RecordSource & &
    " WHERE " & fldExpression.Value
    clsExpression.updCallingScreen.Query Where( &
      fldExpression.Value)
END IF
    vTop.DismissModal(Self)
```

The SQL statement will use the table specified in the RecordSource property of the calling screen to build the appropriate SQL statement.

Now that you have built an SQL statement, you can use the **EXEC SQL** command to test it.

■ Add the underlined code to the **Click( )** method for the btnExit push button:

```
DIM vTestWhere As String
DIM vTop As Object
vTop = GetTopContainer()
If NOT ISNULL(fldExpression.Value) THEN
    vTestWhere = "SELECT COUNT(*) FROM " & &
        clsExpression.updCallingScreen.RecordSource &
        " WHERE " & &
            fldExpression.Value
    EXEC SQL :vTestWhere
```

```
clsExpression.updCallingScreen.QueryWhere(&
        fldExpression.Value)
END IF
   vTop.DismissModal(Self)
```

The **EXEC SQL** command will execute the SQL statement stored in the vTestWhere string. As with many other database-oriented functions and commands in Oracle Power Objects, the **EXEC SQL** command can have a session specified; but if the session is not specified, the command will use the default session.

The **EXEC SQL** will attempt to execute the SQL statement stored in the vTestWhere variable. You need to prefix the name of the vTestWhere variable with the colon (:) character. The : character indicates that the value following the character is a *bind variable.* A bind variable is a variable that is bound to the **EXEC SQL** statement at run time from Oracle Power Objects.

The execution of the statement in the **EXEC SQL** command generates a return code. The return code does not contain the results of the query, but rather the results of the execution of the query. The return code will be 0 if the statement executed without errors, and an error code if errors were encountered in the execution of the statement.

You can check the return code with the **SqlErrCode( )** function. The **SqlErrCode( )** function will return the result code from the last **EXEC SQL** command.

■ Add the underlined code to the existing code in the **Click( )** method for the btnExit push button:

```
DIM vTestWhere As String
DIM vTop As Object
vTop = GetTopContainer()
IF NOT ISNULL(fldExpression.Value) THEN
   vTestWhere = "SELECT COUNT(*) FROM " & &
   clsExpression.updCallingScreen.RecordSource & &
      " WHERE " & fldExpression.Value
   EXEC SQL :vTestWhere
   IF SqlErrCode() = 0 THEN
   clsExpression.updCallingScreen.QueryWhere(&
   clsExpression.updCallingScreen.DefaultCondition & &
         " " & fldExpression.Value)
   END IF

   vTop.DismissModal(Self)
```

Whenever an SQL statement is executed by Oracle Power Objects, the result code can be retrieved with the **SqlErrCode( )** function. If the **SqlErrCode( )**

function returns a value of 0, the SQL statement executed successfully. The underlined code checks to see if the **EXEC SQL** command executed without any errors. If the command did complete successfully, the class will call the appropriate **QueryWhere( )** function and dismiss the form. If the code did not complete successfully, you will have to inform the user there is a problem, and hopefully offer some default remedies.

You should try and indent your **IF** clauses in such a way so that the statements that are parts of the **IF** clause are easily identifiable.

The code as outlined will avoid the problem of returning to the calling screen and having an invalid SQL statement executed. You could improve the usability of this class by having the class react to any errors, informing the user that errors occurred, and giving the user the option of taking some action to correct the error. You could add the error-handling code in this method; but since another developer may want to modify the way that errors are handled, it would increase the flexibility of the class if you were to call a method to handle the errors. That way another developer could just modify the error-handling method and not have to touch any of the rest of the code.

■ Add the underlined code to the existing code in the **Click( )** method for the btnExit push button:

```
DIM vTestWhere As String
DIM vTop As Object
vTop = GetTopContainer()
IF NOT ISNULL(fldExpression.Value) THEN
    vTestWhere = "SELECT COUNT(*) FROM " & &
    clsExpression.updCallingScreen.RecordSource & &
    " WHERE " & fldExpression.Value
    EXEC SQL :vTestWhere
    IF SqlErrCode() = 0 THEN
    clsExpression.updCallingScreen.QueryWhere( &
     fldExpression.Value)
    vTop.DismissModal(Self)
    ELSE
        Self.udmErrorRoutine()
    END IF
    ELSE
    vTop.DismissModal(Self)
END IF
```

You have to add the earlier *vTop.**DismissModal(Self)*** to the code, since you want to dismiss the dialog box if the selection is correct or if there is no selection condition. You will now have to create a function called **udmErrorRoutine( )** and add it as a method to the btnExit push button.

■ Call the user properties screen. Scroll to the bottom of the table window and add a new function with a Name property of 'udmErrorRoutine', which will have a Type property of 'Function' and Datatype property of 'Long'.

The difference between a function and a subroutine is that a function can return a result, while the subroutine cannot. Although it is not necessary for the **udmErrorRoutine( )** function to return a value in this application, you may want to return a value in other situations or instances of this class, so it does not hurt to make the **udmErrorRoutine( )** a function.

■ Drag the **udmErrorRoutine( )** function to the btnExit push button in the clsExpression class.

By creating a separate function to handle errors, you give a developer an easy way to substitute their own error handling without having to modify other portions of the class. If you had left the error handling in the **Click( )** method and a developer wanted to change the way errors were handled, they would have to rewrite all of the other code in the **Click( )** method, since they would not want to call the inherited **Click( )** method with the inappropriate error handling. You have allowed the **udmErrorRoutine( )** function to return a Boolean value to use for further actions.

The final step in this validation process is to write code for the **udmErrorRoutine( )** method.

■ Open the **udmErrorRoutine( )** method for the btnExit push button. Add the following code:

```
IF MSGBOX("The selection expression you have created is not valid" & &
    "Would you like to erase the selection condition?", 4 + 48, &
    "Invalid Selection Expression") = 6 THEN
        fldExpression.Value =""
ELSE
    MSGBOX("You can edit the selection condition directly")
END IF
```

There are a number of new facets in this use of the familiar **MSGBOX( )** function. First of all, there are three parameters, instead of the one you are used to.

The first parameter is the text of the message box. The second parameter is made up of numbers that indicate the number of buttons in the message box, the icon used in the message box, and other options. The number "4" indicates that this message box will have a Yes and a No push button. The number 48 indicates that the message box will have an exclamation mark icon in it, which will draw attention to the fact that an error has occurred. The third parameter in the function is the title of the message box.

The **MSGBOX( )** function also returns a result code. The result code for the "Yes" push button is 6. The **IF** construct tests to see if the user wishes to erase the existing selection condition, in which case the selection is cleared and the user is returned to the expression-building form. If the user clicks on the No push button, another message box informs the user that the expression can still be edited directly.

This is far from the best way to handle errors. The user may want more information about the error, or be given more options than to just delete the condition or try to fix it. You might want to give more descriptive error messages based on the value returned from the **SqlErrCode( )** function.

The **EXEC SQL** can be used in many other ways. Whenever you wish to access data in your database server, you can use the **EXEC SQL** command. It has served us well in handling invalid selection conditions.

NOTE
You can specify that any errors that occur in the execution of the **EXEC SQL** command automatically raise a user notification with the WHENEVER clause. To cause any **EXEC SQL** errors to bring up a message box, use this code:

```
EXEC SQL WHENEVER SQLERROR RAISE
```

To disable this notification, use this code:

```
EXEC SQL WHENEVER SQLERROR CONTINUE
```

By default, the **EXEC SQL** command does not notify users of errors. The clsExpression class will not affect the way that your application handles **EXEC SQL** errors.

Initializing Selections After Adding an Expression

You may have noticed that it is a little difficult to use the selection condition form when you are making an expression from multiple conditions. After you have added a clause to the expression, the column name and operand remain selected, and the value remains in the Value data field. It is easy to forget to change one of the portions of the expression.

You can add code to the btnAdd push button to reinitialize the objects used in building an expression.

■ Add the underlined code to the existing code in the **Click( )** method of the btnAdd push button in the clsExpression class:

```
DIM vExpression As String
vExpression = lstColumns.Value & " " & rbfOperators.udmGetOperator() & " " & &
    fldValue.Value & " "
IF NOT ISNULL(fldExpression.Value) THEN
      vExpression=rbfCondition.Value &" " & & vExpression
      fldExpression.Value = fldExpression.Value & vExpression
      lstColumns.Value= NULL
      rbfOperators.Value = NULL
      cbNot.Value = NULL
      fldValue.Value = NULL
END IF
```

This code will clear the list box entry and the radio button selected in the operand frame. The fldValue data field will be cleared and the cbNot check box will be unchecked. Since you added more than one line of code after the **THEN** clause, you have to add an **END IF** clause at the end of the code.

You have been able to prevent some of the errors that a user might make in using a selection form based on the clsExpression class. All of the enhancements you have made in the class have been automatically made in every instance of the class. To implement the new class functionality, you merely have to recompile an application that contains an instance of the class.

■ Run the application and use the new selection form. Test the enhancements you made to the class.

■ Select a column name and click on the Add push button.

Notice that there is nothing to stop you from adding an incomplete clause to the expression. In the next section, you will add some functionality to the class that will not only help prevent user errors, but give graphical hints to the user about how to use the form.

Preventing User Errors with Graphical Indicators

In the previous section, you enhanced the clsExpression class to prevent some errors that a user might accidently make. You cannot assume that a user will necessary understand the correct form for an expression, or that the user will properly understand and use the form you deliver to create correct expressions. In this section, you will prevent more user errors, but you will also make your class graphically reflect the proper way to use a form based on your class. In this way, a form based on your class will help to train users how to use the form.

Preventing Users from Adding Incomplete Expression Clauses

In the clsExpression class, it is very easy for a user to add an incomplete expression clause to the expression, either by accident or because the user does not understand when to add an expression clause. You can add a function that will prevent a user from adding an incomplete expression clause and graphically indicate this to the user.

- Select the clsExpression class and call up the User Properties sheet. Scroll to the bottom of the user properties table window and add a new subroutine. Give the subroutine the **Name** of 'udmEnableAdd' and set the **Type** to 'Sub'. Add the subroutine to the property sheet of the class.

Since you will be calling this function from several different objects in your class, you should place the subroutine in the class property sheet, rather than attaching it to any one specific object in the class.

- Open the code window for the **udmEnableAdd( )** method of the clsExpression class. Add the following code:

```
IF ISNULL(lstColumns.Value) OR ISNULL(rbfOperators.Value) OR&
    ISNULL(fldValue.Value) THEN
        btnAdd.Enabled = False
ELSE
        btnAdd.Enabled = True
END IF
```

If any of the three portions of the expression clause are null, this code will disable the btnAdd push button. When the btnAdd push button is disabled, it gives the user a graphical indication that new expression clauses cannot be added to the expression.

■ Select the lstColumns list box, the rbfOperators radio button frame, and the fldValue data field. Enter the following code as the **PostChange( )** method in the Multiple Selection Properties sheet:

```
clsExpression.udmEnableAdd()
```

Since all three objects have a **PostChange( )** method, you can select them all and change the method through the Multiple Selection Properties sheet. Using the 'clsExpression' qualifier before the **udsEnableAdd( )** method will correctly call the method that is in the clsExpression class.

The **PostChange( )** method is called for an object whenever a value for the object is changed. Since the **Click( )** method of btnAdd push button changes the value of the lstColumns list box, the rbfOperators radio button frame, and the fldValue data field object, each of these objects will call the **udmEnableAdd( )** function, which will properly disable the btnAdd push button.

Your final step is to initialize the btnAdd push button to a disabled state.

■ Select the btnAdd push button. Set the Enabled property to 'False'.

You have now made sure that the Add push button will be disabled unless the user has specified a complete expression clause. You have not only prevented the user from adding an incomplete expression clause to the expression, you have also been able to give a visual indication that the push button cannot be used by disabling it.

The **PostChange( )** method for the fldValue data field object will only be triggered when the user leaves the data field. As you may have already noticed, tabbing out of the fldValue data field puts the cursor into the fldExpression data field. Since the user may very well be adding the assembled expression clause to the fldExpression data field after adding a value in the fldValue data field, tabbing immediately to the fldExpression field may be confusing. To avoid this problem, you can prevent the user from tabbing into the fldExpression field.

■ Open the properties sheet for the fldExpression data field object. Set the TabOrder property to '0'.

Your next step is to give the user a visual indication that conditional operators should only be used when you are adding a new expression clause to an existing expression. You will also use visual tactics to help users understand how an application works.

Preventing Users from Adding Conditional Operators for the First Clause

You have already included the appropriate code to automatically add the selected conditional operator to an expression when an expression clause is added to an expression. A novice user, however, might be confused as to why he or she was selecting a conditional operator for the first expression clause and the operator was not being added to the expression. You could make the operation of the class clearer by giving the user a visual indication when a conditional operator was going to be added to the expression. You will do this by hiding the radio button frame and its radio buttons until the conditional operator is necessary.

■ Select the btnAdd push button. Add the underlined code to the existing code in the **Click( )** method:

```
DIM vExpression As String
vExpression = lstColumns.Value & " " &
rbfOperators.upmGetOperator() & " " & &
    fldValue.Value & " "
IF NOT ISNULL(fldExpression.Value)THEN
    vExpression=rbfCondition.Value &" " & & vExpression
    fldExpression.Value = fldExpression.Value & vExpression
    lstColumns.Value= NULL
    rbfOperators.Value = NULL
    cbNot.Value = NULL
    fldValue.Value = NULL
    Self.Enabled = False
    rbfCondition.Visible = True
```

When you set the Visible property of the rbfCondition radio button frame, Oracle Power Objects automatically shows the frame and all the radio buttons in the frame.

Since an instance of the class will begin without a value in the expression multiline data field, you will have to hide the radio buttons and their frame when the form is created.

■ Select the rbfCondition radio button frame. Set the Visible property to 'False'.

You have hidden the conditional operator radio buttons when the form first appears, and you have added code to show the radio buttons once the user adds an expression clause to the expression. However, the expression data field can still be edited by the user, or cleared if the validation fails on the selection condition. You want to hide the radio buttons whenever the expression data field is cleared.

■ Select the fldExpression data field object. Add the following code to the **PostChange( )** method:

```
IF ISNULL(Value) THEN rbfCondition.Visible = False
```

The **Validate( )** method is only activated when the user changes the value of an object. The **PostChange( )** method activates when the value of an object changes, through user interaction or programmatic interaction.

You have made the operation of your class clearer by adjusting the appearance of some of the visual objects in the class. You could make the information the class contains clearer by modifying the way expressions are displayed in their multiline data field object.

Making the Expression Easier to Read

You may have noticed that an Oracle Power Objects multiline data field does not wrap long lines to the next line. Because of this, a compound expression can rapidly become unreadable. You can add a little code to the Add push button to improve the readability of the expression clause by starting each expression clause in the expression on a new line.

■ Open the **Click( )** method for the btnAdd push button. Add the underlined code to the existing code:

```
DIM vExpression As String
vExpression = lstColumns.Value & " " &
rbfOperators.upmGetOperator() & " " & &
    fldValue.Value & " "
IF NOT ISNULL
    (fldExpression.Value) THEN & vExpression = CHR(13) & CHR(10) & &
    rbfCondition.Value & " " & vExpression
fldExpression.Value = fldExpression.Value & vExpression
lstColumns.Value= NULL
rbfOperators.Value = NULL
cbNot.Value = NULL
fldValue.Value = NULL
```

```
Self.Enabled = False
rbfCondition.Visible = True
```

Whenever you add an expression clause to an expression, you should start the new expression clause on a new line. Since you are already testing the fldExpression multiline data object to see if there is already an expression, you simply have to use the **CHR( )** function to add a new line character and a carriage return.

Your selection form should now look like this when it is running:

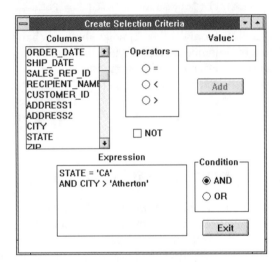

◼ Run the application and call the frmSelectionClause form to see enhancements you have added to your class.

You have improved the functionality of your class and made it more understandable to the end user. There is still one major way the user can unintentionally make mistakes in creating expressions, which you will fix in the next section.

Preventing Errors in Data Typing

Someone who is using an application that includes a form created with the clsExpression class is not necessarily aware of the internal structures involved with computers. To some users, the only difference between a number and a string and a date is their values. Some users may be unaware that a computer stores these different types of data in dramatically different ways, so it may be difficult for these users to remember that a string value requires single quotes, or that a date must fall in a certain valid range.

In this section, you will add data type validation to your class.

Determining the Data Type of a Column

The first step in adding data type validation to your class is to determine the data type of a selected column.

- Select the **PostChange( )** method in the lstColumns list box. If you are using an Oracle database, add the underlined code to the existing code:

```
DIM vDatatype As String
DIM vColValue As String
DIM vTableName As String
vTableName = clsExpression.updCallingScreen.RecordSource
clsExpression.udsEnableAdd()
```

The *vDatatype* variable will hold the data type of a selected column and the *vTableName* variable will hold the name of the table that is the RecordSource of the calling screen.

- For a Blaze database, the code will look a little bit different. Add the underlined code to the existing code for the **PostChange( )** method:

```
DIM vDatatype As Integer
DIM vTableID As String
DIM vItemName As String
vItemName = clsExpression.udpCallingScreen.RecordSource
clsExpression.udsEnableAdd()
```

In order to ensure that you retrieve the right data type for a selected column, you will have to use the name of the column and the name of the column's table—since there may be more than one column with the same name, and the different columns may have different data types. In Oracle, you can simply select from the ALL_TAB_COLUMNS table using the table name as one of the selection criteria. In Blaze, the ALL_COLUMNS table recognizes the table by the ID of the table, which is a number. In Blaze, the data type is also a number, so the variable declarations are a little different if you are using a Blaze database or an Oracle database.

■ If you are using an Oracle database, add the following code to the end of the **PostChange( )** method of the lstColumns list box:

```
vColValue = Value

EXEC SQL select DATA_TYPE into :vDatatype from ALL_TAB_COLUMNS where  &
    COLUMN_NAME = :vColValue and TABLE_NAME = :vTableName
```

If you are using an Oracle database, you can select the data type from the ALL_TAB_COLUMNS system view into the string variable *vDatatype*.

■ If you are using a Blaze database, add the following code to the end of the **PostChange( )** method of the lstColumns list box:

```
EXEC SQL select ID into :vTableID from SYS.ALL_OBJECTS where NAME = &  :vItemName
vItemName = Value
EXEC SQL select TYPE into :vDatatype from SYS.ALL_COLUMNS where COL_NAME
    = & :vItemValue and ID = :vTableID
```

If you are using a Blaze database, you will have to use the *vItemName* variable to first hold the name of the table while you are selecting the ID of the table from the SYS.ALL_OBJECTS system table. You can then reset the value of the *vItemName* variable to the value selected in the lstColumns list box to select the data type into the *vDatatype* variable.

Both of these sets of SQL statements query the system tables of their respective databases to retrieve the data type of the select column name into the *vDatatype* string variable. Notice that you precede both the *vDatatype* variable name and the lstColumns.Value property name with a colon (:) to indicate that these values are coming from the Oracle Power Objects environment. You can use bind variables in an **EXEC SQL** command that uses a string, rather than a string variable. The **EXEC SQL** command will bind the values from a variable or property in Oracle Power Objects at compile time, but it cannot do this when a string is the parameter, since any ":" characters that are in a string variable will be treated as simple characters, rather than as bind variable indicators.

You cannot use the Value property of an object as a bind variable, so you have to declare a local variable, set it to the value of the Value property and use it in the **EXEC SQL** command.

■ Call the User Properties window. Scroll to the bottom of the user properties list box and add a new property. Give it the Name property of 'udpColumnDatatype', give it a Type property of 'Property', and give it a DataType property of 'String'. Add the udpColumnDatatype property to the clsExpression class.

In Oracle Power Objects, you can declare variables at the level of the application or within a method. Variables declared within methods only exist while the method is executing. If you want to access a value within the scope of a form, you can declare a property and set the value of the property within the method.

■ If you are using an Oracle database, add the following code to the end of the **PostChange( )** method of the lstColumns list box:

```
SELECT CASE vDatatype
    CASE "DATE"
        clsExpression.udpColumnDatatype = "DATE"
    CASE "NUMBER", "INTEGER"
        clsExpression.udpColumnDatatype = "NUMBER""
    CASE ELSE
        clsExpression.udpColumnDatatype = "STRING"
END SELECT
```

You can test for multiple values in a **SELECT CASE** clause by separating the values in the **CASE** statement with a comma. This code will set the value of the udpColumnDatatype, which can be referenced from anywhere in the form.

If you are using a Blaze database, add the following code to the end of the existing code in the **PostChange( )** method of the lstColumns list box:

```
SELECT CASE  vDatatype
    CASE 4
        clsExpression.udpColumnDatatype = "DATE"
    CASE 1, 3
        clsExpression.udpColumnDatatype = "NUMBER""
    CASE ELSE
        clsExpression.udpColumnDatatype = "STRING"
END SELECT
```

Since the data type of a Blaze column is returned as a number into the *vDatatype* variable, you will test for the appropriate numeric values. As with string values, you can test for multiple values in a **CASE** clause by separating the values with a comma.

Whether you are using a Blaze database or an Oracle database, the udpColumnDatatype property will be set to the appropriate string value, so that all the other code in the class can simply reference the value of the property.

NOTE
You will notice that all columns that do not have a data type of DATE, INTEGER, or NUMBER are assigned as strings. This logic will

identify data types such as LONG and RAW as strings. In reality, a user should not be creating expression clauses with LONG or RAW columns, since most databases either cannot evaluate these data types in an expression or incur significant performance penalties when doing so. To make the clsExpression class work even better, you could modify the Translation property of the lstColumns list box to exclude listing any columns that had LONG or RAW data types.

Now that you have identified the data type of a selected column name, your next step is to validate the entry in the fldValue data field.

Validating the Selection Value

Your class can prevent a lot of user errors by ensuring that the value entered in the fldValue data field has the same data type as the column with which the value is being compared.

Although you are validating the value in the fldValue data field, it is not appropriate to put the code that will check the value in the **Validate( )** method for that object. Remember, in a client/server application, the user can roam through a form at will. There is no guarantee that the user will enter a value after having selected a column name. If a user wants to enter a second expression clause, he or she may choose to enter the value for the clause before changing the column name. If the first column name is a number and the second column name is a string, entering a string value in the fldValue data field before changing the column name would result in a validation error, since the new value would b a string. The typical remedy for validation errors is to return False from the **Validate( )** method, which would force the user back into the data field object; so the user could not ever get to the lstColumns list box to change the column name.

You will want to validate the value in the fldValue data field just before you are about to enter it into the fldExpression multiline data field object.

■ Open the **Click( )** method of the btnAdd push button. Add the underlined code to the existing code:

```
DIM vExpression As String
DIM vValidateOK As Integer
IF dsExpression.udpColumnDatatype = "DATE" THEN
    IF ISDATE(fldValue.Value) THEN
        vValidateOK = 0
```

```
        ELSE
            vValidateOK = 1
        END IF
    ELSEIF clsExpression.udpColumnDatatype = "NUMBER" THEN
        IF ISNUMERIC(fldValue.Value) THEN
            vValidateOK = 0
        ELSE
            vValidateOK = 1
        END IF
    ELSE
    vValidateOK = 0
    END IF
    IF vValidateOK = 1 THEN
        vExpression = "The comparison value is not a valid " & &
            LCASE(clsExpression.udpColumnDatatype) & "."
        MSGBOX(vExpression, 0, "Invalid Value")
        fldValue.SetFocus()
    ELSE
        vExpression= lstColumns.Value & " " & &
            rbfOperators.upmGetOperator() & " " & &
            fldValue.Value & " "
        IF NOT ISNULL(fldExpression.Value) THEN vExpression = &
            CHR(13) & CHR(10) & &
        rbfCondition.Value & " " & vExpression
        fldExpression.Value = fldExpression.Value & vExpression
        lstColumns.Value= NULL
        rbfOperators.Value = NULL
        cbNot.Value = NULL
        fldValue.Value = NULL
        Self.Enabled = False
        rbfCondition.Visible = True
    END IF
```

In the code above, you validate the entry in the fldValue data field. If the data type of the column selected is a date, you use the **ISDATE( )** function. If the data type of the column is numeric, you use the **ISNUMERIC( )** function.

NOTE
Oracle Power Objects will automatically convert alphanumeric strings into their numeric representation. Because of this, an alphanumeric value, such as "abc123efg" or "4/4/53" will return TRUE from the **ISNUMERIC( )** function. Alphanumeric strings that

include invalid numeric characters, such as the space in "123 456", will return FALSE from the **ISNUMERIC( )** function.

Since any value can be a string, there is no need to validate an entry if the column selected is a string.

If the validation fails, you bring up a message box that informs the user of the failure. The **LCASE( )** function takes a string function and returns the string in all lowercase letters, which will make the message seem more "soft-spoken" to the user. You use 0 in the second parameter to indicate that the message box will only have an OK push button, and the third parameter is the title of the message box.

Finally, you set the *focus* of the application into the fldValue data field if a validation fails. Setting the focus into an object means setting the user's cursor into the object.

Adding Quotes to String Values

You have been able to enhance your class to prevent a major source of user error. As long as you are checking for valid datatypes, it will be easy to help avoid another source of invalid expression clauses.

As discussed earlier in this chapter, you cannot be assured that a user will know or care what the data type is of a selected column name. As a developer, you understand that a string value used in an SQL statement must have single quote marks preceding and trailing it. A user may have difficulty remembering this, so they may end up with a lot of invalid expressions due to the lack of single quote marks.

Since you can easily determine when to add single quote marks to a string value, why not add them automatically for the user, making the user's task easier and resulting in fewer errors?

■ Add the underlined code to the existing code for the **Click( )** method for the btnAdd push button:

```
DIM vExpression As String
DIM vValidateOK As Integer
IF lstColumns.udpColumnDatatype = "DATE" THEN
    IF ISDATE(fldValue.Value) THEN
        vValidateOK = 1
    ELSE
        vValidateOK = 0
    END IF
```

```
ELSE IF clsExpression.udpColumnDatatype = "NUMBER" THEN
    IF ISNUMERIC(fldValue.Value) THEN
        vValidateOK = 1
    ELSE
        vValidateOK = 0
    END IF
ELSE
vValidateOK = 0
END IF

IF vValidateOK = 1 THEN
    vExpression = "The comparison value is not a valid " & &
        LCASE(clsExpression.udpColumnDatatype) & "."
    MSGBOX(vExpression, 0, "Invalid Value")
    fldValue.SetFocus()
ELSE
    IF clsExpression.udpColumnDatatype = "STRING" THEN
        vExpression= lstColumns.Value & " " & &
            rbfOperators.upmGetOperator() & &
        " '" & fldValue.Value & "' "
    ELSE
        vExpression = lstColumns.Value &" " & &
            rbfOperators.upmGetOperator() & &
        " " & fldValue.Value & " "
    END IF
    IF NOT ISNULL(fldExpression.Value) THEN vExpression = &
            CHR(13) & CHR(10) & &
            rbfCondition.Value & " " & vExpression
    fldExpression.Value = fldExpression.Value & vExpression
    lstColumns.Value= NULL
    rbfOperators.Value = NULL
    cbNot.Value = NULL
    fldValue.Value = NULL
    Self.Enabled = False
    rbfCondition.Visible = True
END IF
```

The additional code checks to see if the column name selected is a string and adds a single quote mark to the beginning and end of the fldValue.Value in the expression clause.

NOTE
Adding single quote marks to the beginning and end of the fldValue.Value will work well with any string that does not already contain a single quote mark, which could confuse the issue. If the user has entered "Mark's" as the comparison value, this functionality will make the string "'Mark's'", which the database will interpret as a string of "Mark"—and then confusion. To make this function work perfectly, you should use the **INSTR( )** function to iteratively go through the comparison string and add an escape character to any single quote marks that are in the string.

To round out the functionality in your class, you should find a visual method to inform users of the data type.

Displaying the Data Type of a Column

In the previous section, we recalled that a user may not know or care what the data type of a column used in an expression is. This description actually covers two types of users—the ones who do not care, and the ones who would care if only they knew what the data type of a column was. Even the users who do not care may eventually tire of seeing the error message from a failed data type validation, so they may start to care about the data type of a column.

All the logical conditions are in place to let you graphically indicate the data type of the column to the user.

- Bring the clsExpression class window to the top. Move the btnAdd push button lower in the class window until it is just above the radio button frame for the conditional operators.

- Add a radio button frame between the fldValue data field and the btnAdd push button. Set the Name property of the frame to 'rbfDatatype' the Label property to 'Datatype' and the DataType property of the frame to 'String'.

- Add a radio button to the frame. Set the Name property of the radio button to 'radString', the Label property to 'String', the DataType property to 'String', the ValueOn property to 'STRING', and the ReadOnly property of the radio button to 'True'.

- Add another radio button to the frame. Set the Name property of the radio button to 'radNumber', the Label property to 'Number', the DataType property to 'String', the ValueOn property to 'NUMBER', and the ReadOnly property of the radio button to 'True'.

■ Add another radio button to the frame. Set the Name property of the radio button to 'radDate', the Label property to 'Date', the DataType property to 'String', the ValueOn property to 'DATE', and the ReadOnly property of the radio button to 'True'.

Your class should now look like this:

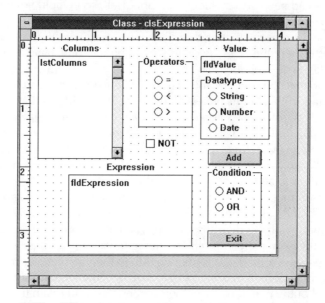

■ Add the following code to the **PostChange( )** method of the lstColumns list box:

```
rbfDatatype.Value = clsExpression.udpColumnDatatype
```

It is very simple to add a visual indicator of a column's data type for the user. All you have to do is create the visual objects to display the information, and add a single line of code to properly set the radio button frame's Value property. Oracle Power Objects automatically takes care of setting the appropriate radio button's status.

Your clsExpression class is now fairly robust. A user will be able to not only use a form based on the class to create expressions, but also be able to understand how the form works through visual indicators, rather than requiring a lot of training. In the final section of this chapter, you will learn how to leverage the work you have done on this class to create another class with all the power and slightly different functionality.

Creating a Subclass from Your Class

You have built a class that provides a high degree of built-in functionality. But you may have wondered—why did I make this a class? Why didn't I just build the form directly? Or at least make a library and use that to add a form to the application? At least a library would have also included the form itself, so I would not have had to drop an instance of the class into a form.

Because you have been creating this class in the scope of this book, you only had a single instance of the class. If you are truly going to only have a single instance of a class, you probably don't need to make a class. However, the next time you need to give the user the ability to build an expression, you will have your prebuilt class with all of its pretested functionality readily available.

Why use a class instead of a library? First of all, changes in a class automatically ripple down into all the instances of the class. If the expression builder was a library, every time you made improvements and maintenance changes in the library, you would have to recopy the library to every place where the library was used to add the new functionality.

Another reason to use an instance of a class instead of a library has to do with the *scope* of a library and a class. A library, as discussed in Chapter 5, can only be a form or a bitmap. In the Orders application, you have been using an instance of a class that takes up a complete form. In another application, you may want to use the clsExpression class as part of a form, rather than the complete form.

An even more important reason to use a class is to implement *subclasses*, which inherit all of the functionality of their parent class and retain the ability to supplement or replace any method from the parent class.

In this final section, you will create a subclass of the clsExpression class that will deliver slightly different functionality. A developer could choose whether to use an instance of the clsExpression class or an instance of the subclass in an application. Any maintenance or improvements that are applied to the clsExpression class will be automatically inherited by the subclass.

The Need for a Subclass

You have created a class that allows a user to build compound expressions with six different operators: "=", "<", ">", and the negation of each of these conditions. A user may want to use another operator in his or her expressions: the LIKE operator. The LIKE operator allows users to specify generic searches, such as finding all values that begin with 'P' with the phrase "LIKE 'P%'". The "%" sign is a *wildcard*, which can represent any number of characters. The LIKE operator will only work with character strings.

Since an approximate search may retrieve a very large number of rows or put a strain on the performance of the database, you may not want to give the user the ability to use the LIKE operator in all cases. You may also have already rolled out applications that use an instance of the clsExpression class and do not want to add this functionality to them. At the same time, you want to take all the functionality of the clsExpression class and include it in your new class, as well as ensuring that any changes or enhancements to the clsExpression class are automatically included in any applications that use the new functionality.

The solution to this problem is to create a *subclass* from the clsExpression class. A subclass is a child of a class that inherits all the properties and methods from its parent and can have its own instances. The same rules of inheritance apply to a subclass that apply to an instance of a class.

The New Functionality Required in the Subclass

You will need to add some functionality in the subclass you will create to handle the LIKE operator. Your new class will have to

- Have a new push button to denote the LIKE operator in the rbfOperators radio button group

- Hide and show the LIKE push button depending on the data type of the selected column

- Enable and disable the cbNot check box, since the operator "NOT LIKE" generally carries a very heavy performance penalty

- Make sure that the value in the fldValue data field ends with a wildcard

You won't have to worry about processing the LIKE operator, since the rbfOperators radio button frame will handle that automatically. The rbfOperators will also automatically deselect the LIKE push button when its value of the radio button frame is set to null after an expression has been successfully added to the fldExpression multiline data field.

Creating a Subclass

Your first step is to create a subclass from the clsExpression class.

- Open the application window for the Orders application. Select the clsExpression class. Choose the Edit menu from the main menu bar and select the Create Subclass menu choice.

Oracle Power Objects will create a subclass from the clsExpression class. The subclass will inherit all of the methods and properties from the clsExpression class. Oracle Power Objects will give the subclass a default Name and Label property, so you will have to make them more appropriate.

■ Change the Name and Label properties of your new class to 'clsExpressionWithLike'.

Notice how the property diamond is displayed in black, indicating that the property value for the subclass is different from the property value for its parent.

To see the power of subclasses, you can change something in the clsExpression parent class and observe the effect on the clsExpressionWithLike subclass.

■ Open the clsExpression class. Change the Label of the radAnd radio button to 'And'. Open the clsExpressionWithLike class and look at the label for the btnAnd push button.

You can see how changes to a parent are automatically reflected in the subclass as long as the changed property or method has not been overridden in the subclass.

■ Open the clsExpression class and change the Label of the radAnd radio button back to 'AND'.

Now that you have created your subclass, you can start to add the objects and functionality you will need.

Adding a New Push Button

You will have to add a new radio button to the rbfOperators group to give the user a way to specify the LIKE operator.

■ Open the clsExpressionWithLike class. Select the rbfOperators radio button group and move it up a little bit. Move the cbNot push button down a little bit. Enlarge the rbfOperators frame so that it has room for another push button. Add a radio button to the bottom of the rbfOperators radio button group. Set the Name property of the radio button to 'radLike', the Label property to 'LIKE', the DataType property to 'String', and the ValueOn property to 'LIKE'.

Since you will be using the Value of the rbfOperators frame to get the operator, and since the btnLike radio button is within that frame, you will not have to add any additional code to process the new radio button.

■   Arrange the radio buttons in the rbfOperators frame.

Your subclass should look like this:

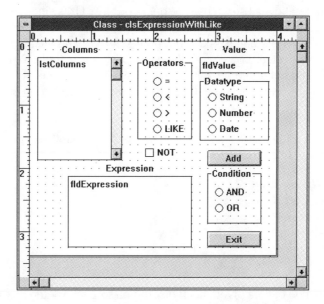

Hiding and Showing the LIKE Radio Button

The LIKE operator will only be valid for columns that are strings. To prevent a user from improperly selecting the LIKE operator, you can hide the radLike radio button when it is not valid and show it when it is valid.

■   Open the **PostChange( )** method for the lstColumns list box. Add the following code to the method:

```
Inherited.PostChange()
IF container.udpColumnDatatype = "STRING" THEN
    radLike.Visible = True
ELSE
    radLike.Visible = FALSE
END IF
```

You must first call the inherited **PostChange( )** method, which will set the value of the udpColumnDatatype property for the class. After the value is set, you can hide or show the radLike push button.

Enabling and Disabling the NOT Check Box

You do not want to allow a user to use the operator NOT LIKE, since this can result in a significant performance penalty. To prevent this, you can disable the cbNot push button whenever the btnLike push button is selected, and enable it whenever any other value is selected. You can easily accomplish this with the **PostChange( )** method for the radio button frame, which will be executed whenever the Value property for the frame is changed by the user selecting a radio button or through code in the class.

■ Select the rbfOperators radio button frame. Add the following code to the **PostChange( )** method of the frame:

```
IF Value = "LIKE" THEN
    cbNot.Enabled = False
    cbNot.Value = NULL
ELSE
    cbNot.Enabled = True
END IF
```

You set the value of the cbNot check box to null to uncheck the box when you disable it. It might be confusing to the user to see the cbNot box checked and disabled. If you are enabling the cbNot check box, there is no need to modify the value for the check box.

The btnAdd push buttons will reset the rbfOperators frame by setting its Value property to null after an expression clause has been added. The cbNot check box will automatically be enabled by the **PostChange( )** method when this occurs.

Massaging the Selection Value

Some of your users may understand that they will need a wildcard at the end of their selection value if they are using the LIKE operator, while some may not. The easiest way to handle both types of users is to check the string for a wildcard and add one if it is missing.

■ Select the btnAdd push button. Add the following code to the **Click( )** method:

```
IF rbfOperators.Value = "LIKE" THEN
IF INSTR(1, fldValue.Value, "%") = 0 THEN fldValue.Value = &
        fldValue.Value & "%"
END IF
Inherited.Click()
```

This code will add a "%" to the string in the fldValue data field if the user has not already put one there. In this case, you wanted to add the wildcard to the fldValue data field Value before performing the inherited processing for the **Click( )** method.

Documenting Your Subclass

You added the **__Documentation** subroutine to the clsExpression class to document the class. The **__Documentation** subroutine was inherited by the clsExpressionWithLike class, but the value for the subroutine is not visible in the subclass. Since future developers may be using the clsExpressionWithLike class without necessarily looking at the clsExpression class, you should copy the documentation to
the subclass.

- ■ Open the clsExpression class. Open the **__Documentation** subroutine and select all of the text in the code window. Click on the CTRL and the 'C' key together to copy the text.

- ■ Open the clsExpression subclass. Open the **__Documentation** subroutine and put the cursor into the code window. Click on the CTRL and the 'V' key to paste the text from the clsExpression **__Documentation** subroutine.

Your subclass is now properly documented. Your last step is to test the new subclass, which will be easily accomplished.

Testing Your Subclass

In order to test the subclass, you will have to add an instance of it to your application.

- ■ Bring up the application window for the Orders application. Open the frmSelectionClause form. Click on the background of the form to select the instance of the clsExpression class. Delete the class instance. Drag the instance of the clsExpressionWithLike to the form. Set the updCallingScreen property of the clsExpressionWithLike instance to 'frmOrders'.

Since the instance of the clsExpressionWithLike class is new, you will have to set the value of the updCallingScreen property.

■ Run the application to test the form.

When you run this class, you may notice that the "%" wildcard appears briefly in the fldValue data field as it is added to the value of the data field with the LIKE operator selected and before it is cleared after adding the expression clause to the expression. This happened because the concatenation of the clause took place in the code for the **Click( )** method for btnAdd push button in the clsExpression parent class. If you wanted to modify the way the clause was concatenated, you would have had to have replaced all of the code in the **Click( )** method. This not only would have involved copying many lines of code, but it would have meant breaking the inheritance link between the clsExpressionWithLike's **Click( )** method on the btnAdd push button and the **Click( )** method on the btnAdd push button of its parent class. In order to avoid this situation, you could create a new method, **udmConcatenateClause( )**, and add it to the btnAdd push button of the clsExpression class. You could put the code that concatenates the expression clause into this method. You would call the empty **udmConcatenateClause( )** method in instances of clsExpression class, and add the appropriate code to the clsExpressionWithLike class.

NOTE
Some databases allow a user to have a wildcard at places other than the end of a string with the LIKE operator. However, there can be severe performance penalties if the string begins with a wildcard. You may wish to use the **INSTR( )** function to ensure that there are no other "%" characters in the fldValue string.

By creating the subclass clsExpressionWithLike from the clsExpression class, you were able to easily add functionality to an already robust class. And, if you decide to enhance the clsExpression class in the future, the changes will automatically be in effect for the clsExpressionWithLike subclass.

You have learned a lot in this chapter. You built a complex class that you will be able to use in many different applications. In building the class, you became more familiar with implementing logic in Oracle Power Objects. And, most importantly, you learned how powerful and flexible classes and subclasses can be, and caught a glimpse of how much your productivity can be improved through using them.

CHAPTER 7

Business Rules

aken to the lowest-level of abstraction, all data is nothing but 0's and 1's on a storage medium someplace. This medium can be RAM, magnetic disk, optical disk, or several other types of storage media. If you think about what it takes to organize this data and make it usable as part of an organization's everyday business, you will have to agree that it is the *business rules*.

Business rules are those criteria that are essential to running a business. These typically have nothing to do with the data, itself. For example, if a particular organization may not accept any orders on weekends, the system has to be written to prevent order entry on weekends. This is a condition that is totally external to the data. This is a business rule that has to be implemented in the program regardless of how the data is stored and organized.

Traditionally, business rules are enforced in code and become a hardwired part of the application. However, this makes the business process that requires the hardwired rule difficult to modify. If for some reason it has to be modified, then the process of that modification could become resource intensive. Newer generation tools such as Oracle Power Objects try to give the developer many facilities to easily implement and maintain business rules.

Overview

In this chapter, we will classify business rules by type, give examples for each business rule by type, look at how each rule can be implemented, and also look at the validation processes required to implement the business rules. You will get a clear picture of how Oracle Power Objects facilitates the implementation of each type of business rule described. One of the most powerful aspects of Oracle Power Objects architecture is the flexibility it gives to partition the application in a client/server (C/S) environment. In this chapter, you will learn

- Three-layer client/server architecture
- Business rule classification
- How to implement security at the application level
- How to implement referential integrity using Oracle Power Objects
- How to enforce field-level validation rules
- How to enforce custom business rules

Client/Server Architecture

Before we begin classifying business rules, we will first set the context. This discussion will cover only *three-layer* architecture, which is a way of dividing the different responsibilities in a client-server application.

Three-Layer Architecture

A client/server application can be divided into three distinct areas (see Figure 7-1). Notice that we are talking about how the application can be divided into three layers. We are not really talking about hardware at this point. We will come to that later. The three areas are the user interface layer, the business rules layer, and the database layer.

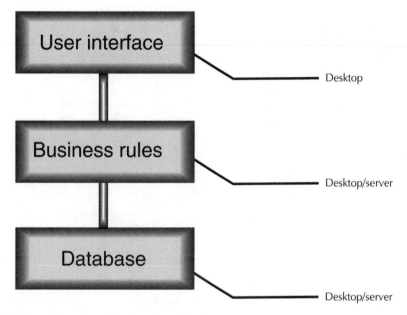

FIGURE 7-1. *The three layers of a client/server system*

User Interface Layer

This is the application's interface to the outside world. A good user interface allows users to easily find the function they would like to run. It allows them to navigate the application easily, without having to learn a lot of steps that are difficult to use and understand. It also allows the user to analyze and manipulate the data in an intuitive way. So, the user interface allows users to look at their desktop computers as enlightening windows into the data world. From his or her desktop, the user can see, manipulate, and analyze the underlying complex data. An example of this is a spreadsheet application with a custom-designed user interface to analyze sales performance. The user does not need to know how the data is organized or all the complex calculations that go into analyzing that data. He or she simply needs to know which spreadsheet to run.

Business Rules Layer

As mentioned in the introduction, business rules implement business policy. Figure 7-2 illustrates the relationships that are essential to running a business. These rules

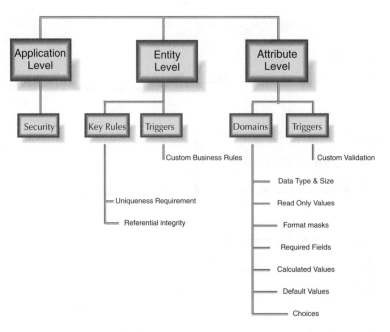

FIGURE 7-2. *Business rules hierarchy*

may have nothing to do with the data itself. They are imposed on the data as a way of doing business. For example, some business rules could be:

- Do not accept orders on Tuesdays.
- Do not accept orders from customers that have outstanding invoices that are 90 days or more overdue.

We will get into a more formal classification of these rules later in this chapter. For now, assume that there are literally hundreds or thousands of these kinds of rules that have to be programmed to implement even a simple system. Some of them are going to be handled automatically. Some of them are going to be explicitly programmed.

Database Layer

The final layer in the client/server system is the database layer. The primary goal of a database is to provide for a *secure* and *consistent* view of data. Ensuring security implies that the database never loses information and it provides access only to those people that are allowed to see the data. Providing consistent data implies that the database keeps the data time-invariant, which means that the same question when asked at different points in time would yield the same answer, provided that the underlying data remains the same. This statement may sound superfluous, but is very important. Consider, for example, an order placed by a customer three months ago. Assume that the sales tax at the time the order was shipped was 3 percent. Since then, due to legislative changes, the sales tax has increased to 4 percent. Also assume the customer has called and asked for a copy of the invoice since he or she lost the original. When you go to your system and ask it to generate a copy, it should not use the new sales tax rate, since the reprinted invoice would not match the old invoice. Ensuring temporal consistency is one of the major issues that the database designers have to deal with.

Now that we have defined three distinct application layers, the next question is which hardware components hold which layers. This is an issue of serious debate for the industry pundits. We contend that it does not matter. As long as the three layers stay distinct and separate, where they reside becomes more of a performance tuning issue. We'll look at some different configurations.

Single-User Client/Server

It may seem odd to talk about a single user client/server, because it has been drummed into your heads that a client/server system requires a client machine and a separate server machine. This is not the case. The client and the server in client/server refer to how the application is divided, not the hardware. Hardware is incidental.

Multiuser Client/Server

Most people mean a multiuser client/server when they talk about client/server systems. In fact, this also is the most common application for client/server systems. In this case, you would have several front-end machines (clients) communicating with one or more back-end machines (servers). The application layers can be divided any way you like. Again, this becomes a performance issue. We'll look at a few cases.

User Interface and Business Rules in the Client and the Database in the Server

In this configuration, most of the processing is done on the front end, and the database is only accessed for data. This would cut down on the network traffic, and thus improve performance. It would also make the application more portable, since the database is only used for storing data. This application could easily be ported to different relational back ends (assuming that a relational database is used). On the other hand, implementing all the business rules in the front end would bloat the application, making it potentially slower. It would also increase the hardware requirements for the client, possibly calling for costly hardware upgrades. It would also make it difficult to maintain and manage releases, since a change has to be distributed to several (maybe hundreds or thousands) clients.

User Interface in the Client and Business Rules and the Database in the Server

This scheme would reverse the effects described in the first option. It would be easy to maintain this configuration, but the power of a desktop would not be fully utilized. Also, some of the power of tools like Oracle Power Objects are not available on the back end and the application would not be portable across different relational back ends.

A Distributed Configuration

There are several variations of this scheme, and they all differ in the degree of distribution of the business-rule processing between the client and the server. As we said before, it does not matter where this processing goes, it is only important that each layer stays distinct and separate.

Business-Rule Classification

Business rules can be enforced at several levels in the application. Where they are enforced is determined by where the code for enforcing them is placed. This sounds obvious, doesn't it? But it is not. There are always choices to make. In this chapter, we hope to give you a basis for making these choices. Each business rule is illustrated with an example in the general sense, as well as within the context of Oracle Power Objects. Figure 7-2, shown previously, demonstrates the business rule hierarchy.

Application Level

The business rules that are applied at the application level are security related. These rules can be at two levels: the network level and the program level. The network level specifies who can access the network. For example, even though the user is authorized to run the application at his or her departmental network level, he or she may not be authorized to access it from a remote site. This type of security is set up by the network administrator. At the program level, it is typically user security, which is enforced by the user name and password mechanism.

Logon Class

When you build an application, it is usually customized for a set of users and a given environment. In this section you will build a logon class with the following assumptions. The database you will be working with is an Oracle Workgroup server database. The connect string is oracle:kasu/password@links_main. You would need to change this connect string appropriately to fit your needs. Since the focus of this chapter is a discussion of application level security, the logon class you will create will only prompt for username and password. In the next chapter, you will create a more comprehensive version of a logon form that will give users the option of specifying different databases and will prevent them from attempting to logon too many times.

There is one more thing that you need to set up. You need a session name. This can be the name of the session you are allowing the users to log on to. At startup, set this session up such that it has a user name and password that point to a dummy table. This session gets changed when the user logs on with the appropriate user name and a password password that accesses the correct database. In the example below, this is set to OPO_APP.

Based on the above assumptions, you know which database you are connecting to and the network information in the form of a connect string. The two things you need from the user are the user name and the password information so that you could check to see if this user is authorized to access this database or not. To accomplish this, you would create a logon class that can be customized for any particular application. Making this a class gives you the flexibility of using this for many applications.

NOTE

This logon form in Chapter 8 will work with either Blaze or Oracle databases.

Create Logon Class

From the Application window, click on the New Class button on the toolbar. The Class window will appear on the screen. Set the Name property to 'clsLogon'. This is like any other form. You can now add objects to this form to build a logon class. You will add a total of six objects to this class. Add two static text objects and give them the labels of 'User Name' and 'Password'. Add two Text Fields and give them the names 'txtUserName' and 'txtPassword'. Set the DataType property of the text field objects to 'String'. Arrange these four objects on the screen such that the static text objects correspond to the text field objects. These two text field objects are used to collect the user name and password information used in opening a session to the back-end database. Now add two command buttons and set their names to 'cmdOK' and 'cmdCancel'. Also, set their labels to 'OK' and 'Cancel'. Arrange the objects on the screen so they appear like this:

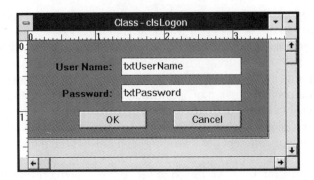

You now have to make this class into something that is aware of what it needs to do. You do this by attaching Oracle Basic code to some of the events of this form.

User Properties

The two pieces of information you need to specify when this class is instantiated are the *type of database*, and the *location of the database*. You do this by creating two user properties. With the clsLogon form active, open the Properties sheet for this form. Click on the button to bring up the Properties screen. Scroll to the bottom of the Properties screen, to the blank row. Click on the leftmost column in the row (Name column) and enter the name for the new property 'udpLogonDatabase'. This property specifies the type of database that you want to log on to (e.g., Oracle). Click in the Type column to the right of the Name column and set the type to 'Property'. Next, click in the DataType column and select the 'String' data type. Repeat the process to add another user property named 'udpLogonDatabaseAddress'. This specifies the location of the database.

This class needs a third property called 'udpLogonSuccessFul' with a data type set to 'Long'. This is used by the application to determine if the logon is successful or not. It is defined to be a variable to pass information between the logon class and the application that is using the logon class.

Now that these properties are defined, you will add them to the logon class. Simply select the udpLogonDatabase property, and drag and drop it on to the logon class's Properties sheet. Repeat for the properties udpLogonDatabaseAddress and udpLogonSuccessFul. These three properties are now available for the logon class.

Attach Code

You will now write the Oracle Basic code and attach it to the logon class so that it is available whenever it is instantiated. The code will be attached to the two command buttons that were placed in the class. The code will perform the following functions.

cmdOK   The user will enter his or her name and password in the text fields provided and click on the OK button. The code attached to the OK button will construct a connection string. Assign it to the RunConnect property of the session, and try to activate the session. If the connection is successful, it will return a value of 0 in the udpLogonSuccesFul property. Otherwise, it will return a 1 to indicate failure.

cmdCancel   The Cancel button just closes the window and returns to the calling entity with the udpLogonSuccessful property set to '2'.

cmdOK.Click( )   The code to be attached to the click events of the cmdOK push button is as follows.

```
DIM rsForm, sesCurSession As object
DIM strConnectString As String
DIM lngRetVal As Long
inherited.Click()

' Get a reference to the session object - This is in the property
'RecSrcSession.
sesCurSession = OPO_APP      ' Set the session name.
Container.udpLogonSuccessful = 0

' Try logging on to the session.
strConnectString = Container.udpLogonDatabase & ":" & &
        Container.txtUserName.Value & "/" & &
        Container.txtPassword.Value & "@" & &
        Container.udpLogonDatabaseAddress
' Set the run connect property of the session.
sesCurSession.RunConnect = strConnectString

' Activate the session.
sesCurSession.Connect()

' Check for errors.
IF NOT sesCurSession.IsConnected() THEN
        lngRetVal=MSGBOX("Problem Connecting to the Database, Please Try
```

```
Again")
        Container.udpLogonSuccessful = 1
END IF
```

Notice the way the connection string is constructed using the two user properties. Some more error checking can be done here to make sure that the user properties are specified. Otherwise, this connection could never be established.

cmdCancel.Click( )   The code to be attached to the click events of the cmdCancel button is as follows.

```
Inherited.Click()
' If the user clicked on the cancel button then closed the application.
TopContainer.udpLogonSuccessful = 2
```

The logon class is now complete. You can now incorporate this logon class into an application as described in the following sections.

Create Logon Form
With the Application window active, click on the New Form button to create a new form. Set the Name property to 'frmLogon'. From the Application window, drag the logon class and drop it onto the Form window. The logon class will now appear to be part of the frmLogon form.

Set the User Properties
Set the udpLogonDatabase to 'Oracle', the udpLogonDatabaseAddress to the location of the database (this is typically the name of the server, e.g., Links_Main), and the udpLogonSuccessFul property to '0'.

Attach Code to the Application
At this point you are ready to enable this form so that any user running the application would have to go through the logon screen to perform any work. You do this by attaching code to the OnLoad event of the application. This OnLoad event is triggered whenever the application is loaded. This means that you would make the user log on when the application is first invoked. After that, the user is free to use all the facilities provided by the application.

Application.OnLoad( )   The code to be attached to the OnLoad event of the application is as follows.

```
DIM objRetVal As Object
DO
    objRetVal = frmLogon.OpenModal(False)
```

```
      Select Case frmLogon.clsLogon.udpLogonSuccessful
            Case 0
                ' Bring up the first screen in the application.
                frmFirstForm.OpenWindow()
                Exit Do
            Case 1
            Case 2
                    Exit Do
            Case Else
                    Exit Do
      End Select
Loop
```

If you run the application now, the logon form would come up. It should look like this:

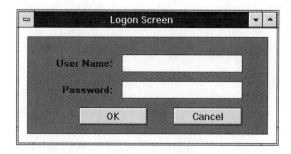

The above code opens the logon form as a modal form since you do not want the user to be able to do anything else but log on. Opening the form as modal makes sure that the user could not do any other operation before logging on. For example, in this case the user has the choice of clicking either on the OK or the Cancel button. When the form closes and returns control to the code above, the return code is checked to see if OK was clicked. If it was, then the next form is opened, putting the user in the application. If the user has clicked Cancel, then the application is closed.

The above example shows how you could use a logon class to implement a simple user security scheme. In the next chapter, you will create a different version of a logon form that will allow a user to specify different databases, will work with both Oracle and Blaze databases, and will limit the number of times a user can attempt to logon to a database.

To summarize, security at the application level is implemented as a logon class. It allows you to control the usage of the class at the application level. However, nothing prevents you from invoking this class from anywhere. For example, if you want to use a different session to run a particular report, you would have the user log on to a different instantiation of the logon class.

Entity Level

The following sections examine the enforcement of business rules at the entity level.

Security

Security at the entity level is typically enforced on the back-end database. All major relational databases provide for securing database objects via Grant and Revoke commands to control privileges. Oracle Power Objects depends on the back end to enforce this type of integrity. Recall the discussion at the beginning of this chapter about where to enforce business rules, in which we briefly talked about portability. Any time the back end is used to enforce business rules, portability suffers. This is a design decision that has to be made case by case.

The other method for enforcing security is by creating views. Oracle Power Objects supports this view creation in an intuitive and user-friendly way. See the User Guide for details on creating views.

Key Rules

There are two aspects of business rules that we talked about. One is validating the data, and the other is maintaining data integrity. There are three operations in a Relational Database Management System (RDBMS) that involve integrity issues. These are the data manipulation operations, **insert**, **update**, and **delete**. *Key rules* govern the effects of these three operations on the database. The main goal of key rules is to maintain data integrity. Key rules are enforced at the individual entity level, as well as at the relationship level.

Not Null and Uniqueness Requirements
You begin to address the integrity issues first by choosing a primary key. A primary key is chosen to satisfy two business rules:

1. A primary key must exist for each entity (*Not Null rule*).

2. A primary key must be unique for each item in the entity (*Uniqueness requirement*).

What does this mean in simpler terms? Rule 1 says that whatever column(s) you chose to represent the primary key for a table cannot be null. Rule 2 says that the values chosen to populate the column(s) chosen for the primary key must be unique in the table. These two rules together go a long way toward establishing integrity within a single entity. You will have to specify a primary key (Not Null rule), and that value must be unique (Uniqueness requirement). For example, if you chose social security number as the primary key to the customer table, then to insert a new customer, you must specify a unique SSN, as well as an SSN that was not previously used to identify another customer. We'll look at the implications of this on the three operations.

■ **Insert** You will only be able to insert new customers. Trying to insert a customer record that already exists in the table will be rejected as duplicate.

■ **Update** You will be able to update one and only one record, using the primary key. The record to be updated must exist.

■ **Delete** You can delete one and only one record using the primary key.

How Oracle Power Objects Enforces the Uniqueness Requirement

Oracle Power Objects provides a straightforward way of enforcing the Uniqueness requirement. You can define both types of constraints specified above through the Table Editor window. The Table Editor window looks like this:

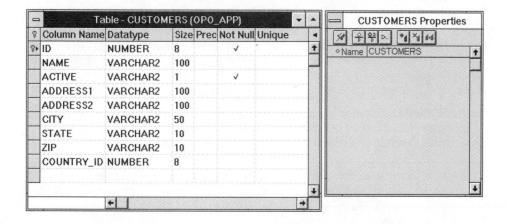

There are three values you could specify. Not Null, Unique, and Primary Key. Notice that you could specify a column to be Unique and Not Null, the same characteristics as a primary key. This is called an *alternate key*. The only difference between the primary key and the alternate key is that an alternate key could have a null value, and could still be specified to satisfy the uniqueness criteria.

Referential Integrity

While the primary key deals with the integrity issues for single entities, foreign keys deal with relationships between entities, and hence the referential integrity (RI) issues. RI can be of two types: declarative and procedural.

Declarative RI is enforced by the database manager on the back end. This is entirely dependent on the RDBMS in question. For example, Oracle 7 supports declarative referential integrity. SQLServer 4.2 does not. Again, this becomes a design issue that has to be resolved on a case-by-case basis. If you depend on the RDBMS to enforce RI, and then, switch the RDBMS, you may lose the RI capability. More and more databases nowadays are supporting this feature.

Procedural RI can be enforced either in the front end or the back end. To enforce this in the back end, the back end must support some type of language to write the required procedures. For example, Oracle Power Objects uses PL/SQL to write stored procedures and triggers. Sybase uses Transact-SQL. RI's main goal to is preserve data integrity across relationships. All these rules can be implemented on the front end using Oracle Power Objects. For the sake of clarity, we'll assume a master-detail relationship exists between PRODUCTS and ORDERITEMS. PRODUCT_ID is the primary key for the PRODUCTS table, ORDERITEM_ID is the primary key for the ORDERITEMS table. The ORDERITEMS table has the foreign key PRODUCT_ID that identifies the product record. There are three operations that affect this relationship. They are **insert**, **delete**, and **update**, and are described below.

Insert   By definition, the parent/child relationship is a binary relationship. Given that you have a parent ID and a foreign key in the child that refers to that parent ID, we have to deal with two cases: either a parent record exists or does not exist. All the cases described refer to inserting a child record.

If the parent record exists, you will have no problems at all. Go ahead and insert the record.

If the parent record does not exist, when you are inserting a child record, the foreign key in the child record will be null. There are five ways to deal with this case:

- *Restrict the insertion*   This type of integrity check is enforced by declarative RI, and it is the most common kind of insertion business rule implemented. For example, do not allow for the ORDERITEM row to be inserted unless the product exists.

- *Create parent record*   You may just create the parent record if it does not exist. This, again, is not a recommended way. For example, the user may want a new product that you do not currently have, but you know that you can get it. In this case, you simply create a product record and continue on with the order processing.

■ *Allow for insertion* This would create orphan child records, and is not recommended. For example, you may take an order when you do not have the product. See the last case for a better alternative.

NOTE
This type of insertion may be necessary when performing bulk loads, in which you do not want to execute triggers and other related processing, because it would take too long. Typically, you would turn off RI, perform the bulk load, and turn RI back on. If you do this, it is important that you make sure that the data being loaded is consistent before the load is done, or run another batch program to perform consistency checks.

■ *Insert with default value* You could specify a default parent record for any child records that are inserted without specifying the parent record. For example, if someone wants order paper and they do not specify the specific brand, you may want to use the store brand as the default.

■ *Special case processing* You may want to set the parent ID in the child record to specific values, either collected from the user or calculated from other known values. For example, you may have two different store brands, and you may want to alternate between them when setting default values.

Delete   Given the same master-detail relationship, **delete** presents a different problem. It is exactly the opposite of **insert**. In this case, we are concerned about deleting the parent and still maintaining data integrity. Deleting a child record should not pose any problems. The following five cases illustrate the various issues involved:

■ *Do not allow deletion* Do not allow for the deletion of the parent record if any child records exist. For example, do not allow for the deletion of a PRODUCT record, if that product is used by any ORDERITEM record.

■ *Cascade the deletion* Delete the parent record, but also delete all the associated child records. For example, if a PRODUCT record is deleted, then delete all the associated ORDERITEMS records. In our example, this would a very dangerous case. Imagine a thousand orders, all having an order item for Lerox bond paper. Because of some business reasons, you decide to discontinue Lerox bond paper and delete the product record. With **cascaded delete**, this operation would delete all the order items that refer to this product. It would be a disaster. Be very careful when using this option.

> **NOTE**
> The danger sign to look for is a record with more than one foreign key. This implies that the entity is involved in more than one parent/child relationship. A cascaded delete is not a good idea in this case. You may get lucky and be protected by the other relationship's RI rules. But there are no guarantees.

■ *Allow deletion* Allow for the deletion of the parent record, but set the foreign key in the child record to 'null'. This works in only a limited number of cases, and we don't recommend it. In our example, it does not work. If a product record is deleted, this rule will make the PRODUCT_ID in all the ORDERITEMS rows that refer to it null. This situation is not acceptable.

■ *Set to a default value* Allow for the deletion of the parent entity, but set any child entities to a default value. For example, if Lerox bond paper is discontinued, then replace it with some other equivalent-quality paper.

■ *Special case processing* Allow for the deletion of the parent only if certain conditions are met. For example, mark the Lerox bond paper product record as deleted so you will not be taking any orders for Lerox bond paper from this point on. When all the ORDERS that use this product have been processed, you can delete that PRODUCT record permanently.

Update   An **update** can be considered to be a **delete** followed by an **insert** if it involves the keys. When the keys are not involved, then it becomes a simple update to the values of the columns involved. Consider using key updates. (As mentioned before, **update** has the characteristics of both **insert** and **delete**, but with one caveat: you don't have to manufacture any values.)

The primary key of the parent record is changed. This is as though you have deleted the original record and have added a new record with the new primary key, so the **delete** and the **insert** rules apply. There are no restrictions on inserting a parent record, so you only have to worry about the first three **delete** rules. The others do not apply to this case. See if you can figure it out.

- *Restrict update* Do not allow for the changing of the parent record as long as child records exist.

- *Cascade updates* Cascade the update through all the child records, just as you would for a **delete**.

- *Allow update* Allow for the unconditional update to the primary key. This leaves you with many orphaned records. You should not do this for the same reasons that you should not allow unconditional deletes.

The foreign key in the child record is changed. It is as though you have deleted the old child record and inserted a new one. Again, there are no restrictions to deleting child records, so the **insert** rules apply—but only the first three cases. The rest of them do not apply.

- *Restrict update* Do not allow for updating the foreign key unless the changed item already exists in the parent table.

- *Create parent record* This is similar to the **insert** rule. When the foreign key in the child record is updated, a parent record is automatically created.

- *Allow update* Updates to the child record's foreign key are allowed, even though the parent record does not exist. This will have the effect of orphaning the child records.

How Does Oracle Power Objects Enforce Referential Integrity?

As discussed above, there are two sides to RI. One is to delete or update the primary key of a parent record, and the other is to insert or update a child record. To accomplish the first, Oracle Power Objects provides two properties at the container level. These only apply to the container holding the detail (child) recordset. These two properties, LinkMasterDel and LinkMasterUpd, are shown in the illustration below.

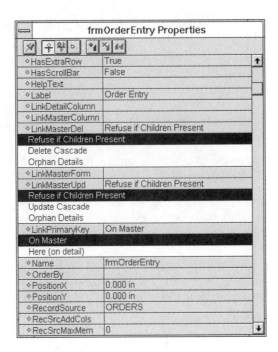

Update or Delete a Parent Record   When you are trying to update or delete the primary key of a parent record then the child records become orphaned.

LinkMasterUpd—This property determines whether the primary key can be updated by the user. It takes three values.

- 'Refuse if Children Present'   Update to the parent record's primary key is prevented if any child records exist.

- 'Update Cascade'   Update the child records to match the new primary key of the parent record.

- 'Orphan Details'   Allow the parent record to be updated unconditionally, thus orphaning the child records.

LinkMasterDel—This property determines if the parent record can be deleted. It takes three values.

- 'Refuse if children present'   Prevents deletion of parent record if child records exist.

■ 'Delete Cascade'   Delete all the child records when the corresponding parent record is deleted.

■ 'Orphan Details'   Delete the parent record unconditionally, thus orphaning the associated child records.

Notice that Oracle Power Objects only covers the first three cases of the **delete** rules. The other two can be covered procedurally with code in the events provided. More on that later.

Insert or Update a Child Record   It is nice that Oracle Power Objects provides us with an easy way to enforce RI via the setting of two properties. It literally saves you hundreds of lines of code. Now you are going to say, what about child record inserts and updates? We know deleting child records is not a problem. This is even easier to do in Oracle Power Objects. Let us see how.

Inserting a child record   The child records are usually shown in a repeater as part of a form that is showing the parent record. The two containers are linked through their primary/foreign key relationship. The application can automatically assign the foreign key of the child to be the primary key of the parent record when a new row is inserted. Oracle Power Objects always maintains the proper foreign key value for the child, once the master-detail relationship is established as described in Chapter 1.

Updating a child record   The simplest thing to do would be not to show the foreign key as part of the detail record. Even if you decide to show it, disable the control that shows the foreign key so that the user cannot change it.

Custom Business Rules

Sometimes factors other than the relationship itself influence the **insertion**, **update**, and **deletion** of records. These factors (custom business rules) have to be implemented via procedures. Consider the following examples where customized rules are necessary. Before getting into how specific rules are implemented, we'll talk about triggers and stored procedures and how they relate to methods in Oracle Power Objects.

Triggers

Recall that an *event* is an action taken by some entity in the application. For example, a mouse click. A *method* is a procedure that is executed as a result of the event that has occurred. So, events and methods follow a modified Newton's third law—every action has a reaction. The events are *actions* and the methods are *reactions*. This is true in most Windows applications. What is interesting is that it is also true for databases; but in a DBMS, they are called *events* and *triggers*. The events supported on a DBMS are confined to the data manipulation operations, **insert**, **update**, and **delete**. Different databases support different events. For instance, Oracle 7 supports triggers that are before and after DML operations. For example, an event is triggered as **BeforeInsert** and **AfterInsert**. SQL-Server 4.21 only supports a single event for triggering. For example, the **OnInsert** event. Notice that triggers are associated with a particular table in a database. There are no database-level triggers.

Triggers can be used to implement business rules at both the table and the column level. We recommend using triggers to implement custom business rules only. Declarative enforcement should be used wherever possible to save time and effort. The following section describes the three manipulation operations and the possible triggers as implemented on the back end, as well as methods implemented in the front end (Oracle Power Objects).

Insert A Child Record

Consider a business rule that says that the first 30 people to order the Lerox bond paper get a two-for-one deal. This rule has nothing at all to do with the relationship between product and order items. This is just an arbitrary business rule that is to be enforced for public relations reasons, rather than any business need. These types of rules are enforced using code. If they are enforced on the back end, they will take the form of triggers and stored procedures. On the front end they will be methods.

For enforcing this rule on the back end, you would write a trigger for the **PreInsert** event (assuming an Oracle 7 database) associated with the ORDERITEMS table. This trigger would check to see if the current order is for Lerox bond, and if more than 30 people have already ordered it. If the order count is <= 30, it would automatically insert another ORDERITEMS row, one without charge.

To enforce business rules in the front end, Oracle Power Objects provides several events. They are as follows.

InsertRow( )   This method is called whenever a row is to be inserted. It will first call the method **PreInsertCheck( )** to see if the **insert** can proceed. If the **PreInsertCheck( )** returns a True, then it will call **PreInsert( )**, followed by the **PostInsert( )** method. Notice that these methods should not be called directly from code. These methods are always invoked by the **InsertRow( )** method. For our example, we want to place the code in this method after the **Inherited.InsertRow( )** line. This code would then check to see if there needs to be an extra item inserted to comply with the business rule and would insert the new record.

PreInsertCheck( )   This method is called before the actual **insert** takes place. This event can be used to prevent insertion from occurring. For our example, there will be no code here.

PreInsert( )   This method is called when the record is inserted. You cannot prevent insertion at this point.

PostInsert( )   This method is called after the record is inserted. It can be used to update counts, etc.

> **NOTE**
> The **InsertRow( )** method calls the associated **PreInsertCheck( )**, **PreInsert( )**, and **PostInsert( )** methods as part of its default processing. These three methods are triggered before the execution returns to **InsertRow( )**. This means that any code following the **Inherited.InsertRow( )** statement in the **InsertRow( )** method executes only after the three associated methods have finished execution.

Delete a Parent Record

Consider a business rule that says that since you are discontinuing Lerox bond, substitute all the orders that haven't shipped with Mill bond. This rule is again not dependent upon the relationship between the parent (PRODUCTS table) and the child (ORDERITEMS table).

DeleteRow( )   This method is called whenever a row is to be deleted. This will first call the method **PreDeleteCheck( )** to see if the **delete** can proceed. If the **PreDeleteCheck( )** returns a True, then it will call the **PreDelete( )** method followed by the **PostDelete( )** method. Notice that these methods should not be called directly. For our example we want to place the code in this method after the Inherited.**DeleteRow( )** line. This code will then update all the records that have Lerox bond to point to Mill bond, if they have not shipped yet.

PreDeleteCheck( )   This method is called before the actual **delete** takes place. This event can be used to prevent deletion from occurring. For our example, there will be no code here.

PreDelete( )   This method is called when the record is deleted. You cannot prevent deletion at this point.

PostInsert( )   This method is called after the record is deleted. It can be used to update counts, etc.

Updating a Record

Sometimes you will need to do custom processing based on changes in certain columns of a table. They do not have to be key columns. Oracle Power Objects provides a method to accomplish this function. It is called **ValidateRow( )**. This method is the standard method provided with the bindable containers, not a control. A control has an equivalent method, which will be discussed later in this chapter.

The **ValidateRow( )** method is triggered whenever the application decides to commit changes or when the user tries to move to another row. This method is useful for checking required fields—for example, making sure that a value greater than zero is entered in the quantity field of an ORDERITEM record. This method is also useful for cross-checking attributes . For example, if a customer can order only two items of Lerox bond paper, you would place the code to check for that in this method.

The default return code from the **ValidateRow( )** method is True. Any method code added to customize this method would make this function return a False. If you want to have the method return True, then you must explicitly set the return code as follows:

```
ValidateRow = True
```

If **ValidateRow( )** returns a False, the application displays whatever message is defined in the ValidateRowMsg property of the container. If the validate row fails, then the values in the container would still display the new values. To redisplay the old values, you need to execute the **RevertRow( )** method. The following code segment illustrates this point. You would enter this code in the **ValidateRow( )** method of the container in which the fields fldDescription and fldQuantity appear.

```
' Check to see if the product ordered is Lerox bond paper.
' If yes, and the quantity ordered is not 0, and not more than 2,
' then let the order go through. Otherwise disallow the order.
'
IF txtDescription = "Lerox Bond" And &
        txtQuantity >0 And txtQuantity <3 THEN
    ValidateRow = True
ELSE
    ValidateRow() = False
    Self.RevertRow()
END IF
```

That ends the discussion on entity-level enforcement of business rules. To summarize, Oracle Power Objects supports both declarative and procedural methods of enforcing business rules. It provides a comprehensive set of properties and methods to maintain data integrity. This is one of the main strengths of Oracle Power Objects.

Attribute Level

So far, the discussion has centered on enforcing business rules at the application and the entity levels. Based on your situation, you would decide on where to implement these business rules. Attribute-level business rules, however, are usually implemented on the front end. Oracle Power Objects provides a comprehensive set of methods, properties, and functions to accomplish this.

Domains

A domain is a set of valid values for an attribute. Think of it as a set of valid logical or conceptual values that an attribute can assume. For example, consider the set of states. This set can constitute the set of values for a state attribute wherever it occurs. The best way to think of a domain is as a separate construct. There are two ways of defining domains. One way is to define the domains up front, and as you define attributes, associate the appropriate predefined domain to that attribute. The other way is to define domain characteristics as you are defining the attribute (e.g., data type and length), and at the end figure out if any of the attributes share a domain.

Domains are important because they verify that the values for an attribute make business sense, determine if the occurrence of the same value in two or more different attributes indicates the same real-world value, and determine whether various data manipulation operations (joins, unions, etc.) make business sense. For example, the domain characteristics for ORDERITEMS.ID is a number that uniquely identifies a row in the ORDERITEMS table. PRODUCTS.QuantityInHand denotes the number of units of a particular item available for sale. Both are numbers, but they represent different real-world values. In addition you could not join these two tables on the two attributes specified previously, since it does not make business sense—even though they have common domain characteristics. In the following sections we will examine the facilities available in Oracle Power Objects for defining these domain characteristics. Oracle Power Objects provides for defining the domain characteristics in two ways. One is to set a property of the bound control where the particular attribute is displayed, and other is via method code.

Data Type and Data Size
Some of the lowest-level business rules that can be enforced are the rules that specify what type of data an attribute holds and how long that data can be. Oracle

Power Objects provides two properties, DataType and DataSize, to accomplish this. DataType limits the kind of data that can be entered (long, integer, date, etc.). DataSize limits the number of bytes that are allocated for that particular attribute when displayed in a control. For example, consider the attribute PRODUCTS.Description displayed onscreen in a text field control. If you set the DataType to 'String' and the DataSize to '20', the user will be able to enter strings no longer than 20 characters into that field.

Read-Only Values

As discussed earlier, one way to prevent users from changing the foreign key in a child record is to disable the control that it is displayed in. Oracle Power Objects provides two properties for doing just that. They are the ReadOnly and Enabled properties. If ReadOnly is set to 'True', or Enabled is set to 'False', the user cannot move focus into the control, making it impossible for the user to change it. The difference between the two is the way the text in the control appears when the property is set. When the Enabled property is set to 'False', the text in the control appears gray, while setting the ReadOnly property to 'True' will make the text in the control appear normal. Using the Enabled property is better, since it gives a visual cue to the user.

Format Masks (Input and/or Output)

Format masks come in two flavors. The input format mask determines how a particular value is entered into a field on the screen. Oracle Power Objects does not support input format masks. The output format mask determines the way entered data is displayed. The format masks depend on the data type of the field displayed. It only applies to text fields and combo boxes. Oracle Power Objects provides several predefined ouput format masks, as well as the ability to define your own. See online help for a list of the predefined output format masks.

Choosing a Predefined Mask   To choose a predefined mask, click on FormatMask in the Properties sheet. A pop-up list of masks appropriate to the control's data type appears.

Defining a New Mask   To enter your own mask, click on the window next to FormatMask in the Properties sheet. In the window you have now entered, you can type the mask characters for your format mask.

Required Fields

A required field will prevent users from entering a null value in a bound control—one in which the control is bound to a field in a table, in the database, that does not allow null values. This is one of the most basic and useful constraints.

Calculated Values

Calculated values are those that are derived by applying an algorithm to some other attribute(s). For example, in the master-detail form you built in Chapter 1, the item subtotal is calculated by multiplying the unit price and quantity. This is a simple expression based on two other attributes in the same form. The expression can use all Oracle Basic numeric functions. When referring to the internal value of a control, use the control's Name property. Optionally, you can use the syntax ControlName.*Value.*

For example, to set the internal value of Field3 to the sum of the internal values of Field1 and Field2, multiplied by two, you would enter the following for the control's DataSource property.

```
=(Field1 + Field2) * 2
```

or

```
=(Field1.Value + Field2.Value) * 2
```

Using SQLLOOKUP   You can also use the **SQLLOOKUP( )** function for the derived value calculation. This is especially useful when the control needs to look up values in a foreign table (i.e., one other than the Main table for the form, as specified through the RecordSource property). For example, to display the product description instead of the PRODUCT ID for an ORDERITEM record, you can enter the following expression for the DataSource property of the control:

```
=SQLLOOKUP(OPO_APP, SELECT products.description &
        FROM products WHERE products.ID  =  + txtProductID.Value)
```

In this syntax, OPO_APP is the name of a session, and txtProductID is a text field displaying the PRODUCT ID for an ORDERITEM record.

Containers and Derived Values

When setting the derived value for a control, you can refer to any other control on the same container, or any appearing on another container within the container. For example, when setting a derived value for a control appearing on a form that also has a repeater display, you can refer to the internal values of any controls on the form, plus any controls in the repeater display. However, controls on the repeater display cannot use controls on the Main form as part of a derived value calculation.

Aggregate Functions and Derived Values

Since controls in a repeater display appear multiple times (once for every record in the repeater), you might want to use aggregate functions on the internal values of these controls. For example, you might want to sum all of the prices of line items within an invoice. In this case, the line items appear in the repeater display and the unit price of each item is represented by a text field in the repeater display. Aggregate values cannot be evaluated from within the container holding the controls whose internal values are being aggregated. For example, if you apply an aggregate function to values appearing in a repeater display, you must perform the calculation on the container holding the repeater display, not within the repeater display itself.

When setting derived values, you can use all Oracle Basic aggregate functions. In the case of summing prices for an invoice, you would create a text field on the Main form that would use the **SUM( )** function as part of its derived value calculation. When setting the DataSource property for this text field, you would then enter something like this:

```
=SUM(repeater1.price)
```

Default Values

The default value appears whenever the control is displayed and another value has not been assigned, either by user entry or querying a record from a record source. For example, the value assigned to the DefaultValue property appears in a control when the user enters a new record. If the control connects to a column in a record source, and if the column corresponding to the control has a value stored in it, then the value from the record replaces the default value for the control. In addition, you overwrite the default value as soon as you enter a new value in the control. If no value is assigned to DefaultValue, the control's default value is null. Therefore, you should always assign a value to DefaultValue if you want to avoid having null values in a control. For example, when the user inserts a new record and a check box appears on the form, the value for the check box will be null, not the value assigned to the ValueOn or ValueOff property, if DefaultValue is not set.

NOTE
Though you can enter any string as the default value for a control, the application converts this string to the appropriate data type, if the DataType property for the control is set to Integer, Float, or Date.

Choices

One way to control what gets entered in a column in a table is via pick lists. This is also known as existence checking. It means that a value is allowed to be entered into a field only if it already exists somewhere else. It also implies that that field is a foreign key. This checking can be implemented on the back end via triggers. But Oracle Power Objects provides a much more straightforward way of implementing this function.

List boxes and pop-up lists are used to display items from another table. For example, to restrict the user to entering only the products that are currently available, you would make the PRODUCTID control a pop-up list, which displays IDs from the PRODUCTS table. This effectively enforces the existence check, since the user cannot really enter anything other than what is presented to him or her in the list.

Triggers

We have discussed several different ways that Oracle Power Objects provides for implementing business rules. But there are probably hundreds, if not thousands, of instances where you need some sort of a custom business rule enforced at the attribute level. For example, consider the following business rules:

- A single customer cannot order more than 10 pieces of any item.

- The maximum discount a customer can get is 25 percent.

These types of rules can again be enforced on the back end via the use of triggers. But Oracle Power Objects provides one very powerful method to cover all cases like this, called the **Validate( )** method. Using this method, any type of custom business rule can be enforced. You would enter code in this method to check to see if the data entered by the user meets the criteria defined. The default return code from the **Validate( )** method is True. Any method code added to customize this method would make this function return a False. If you want to have the method return True, then you must explicitly set the return code as follows.

```
Validate = True
```

If the method returns True, then the values are accepted and the user can move focus out of the control. If the method returns False, then the value is rejected and the user cannot move focus out of the control until a valid value is entered. In addition, any message defined in the ValidateMessage property will be displayed in a message box. Two things must happen for this method to be triggered:

1. The user must change the value in the control.

2. One of the following events must happen:

- The user tries to tab out of the control.

- The user clicks anywhere outside the control.

- The user presses the ENTER key after editing a text field or a combo box.

- The user makes a new selection in a list box or a pop-up list.

- The user selects a control, as in the case of a radio button or a check box.

If the **Validate( )** method fails, it leaves the rejected value displayed in the control. To make this control show the value it had before the changes were made, you would call the **RevertValue( )** method before exiting the **Validate( )** method. The following example builds an address class, which as a part of its validation looks up values for the CITY and STATE fields if the ZIP code is entered.

Building the Address Class

One of most common elements of most databases is the address. It is used in several places (for example, in ORDERS record, CUSTOMERS record, and Invoice record). No matter where you encounter it, it has the same common elements: one or two address lines, CITY, STATE, and ZIP. This is a perfect example of a class where you would do the validation in one place and then use it where needed. You build an Address class in Chapter 5 to illustrate the use of classes. In the following section you will create another address class that will use the **Validate( )** method to enforce some business rules.

From the Application window, click on the New Class button on the toolbar. The Class window will appear on the screen. Set the Name property to 'clsAddress'. You can now add objects to this form to build an address class. You will add a total of eight objects to this class. Add two Static Text objects and set their labels to 'Address' and 'City/St/Zip'. Add five Text Fields and give them the names 'Address1', 'Address2', 'City, txtState', and 'Zip'. Set the DataType property of the Text Field objects to 'String'. Add a combo box to the class and give it the name 'cboState'. Arrange these objects on the screen as shown in the following illustration.

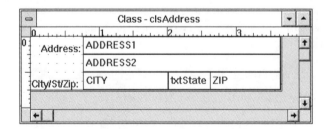

How the Address Class Works

This address class is instantiated on a form that needs the address displayed. Once the class is instantiated, you need to connect it to the right table in the database, such that data relevant to the particular form in which this class resides is correct. The requirements are as follows:

- The user must be able to specify whether he or she can look up the state from a State table.

- The user must be able to specify a ZIP code look up, by specifying a ZIPCODE table. The class must look up the city and state if a ZIP code is entered.

- If a ZIPCODE table is specified, then the State table is ignored.

- Column names in the ZIPCODE table can be specified when the class is instantiated.

Given the requirement that if a State table is specified and ZIPCODE table is not specified, you would have to show a combo box to display the state on the address class. You would do this by overlaying the combo box with a text field and showing the combo box if the State table is specified, and the text field if the State table is not specified. To support the above requirements, you would need to add the following user properties to the class.

User Properties	Description
udpStateTable	Specifies if a State table is available for lookup. Data type is Boolean.
udpStateTableName	If the udpStateTable flag is set to 'True', then this property must be set to the name of the State table. Data type is String.
udpZipTable	Specifies if a ZIPTABLE is available for lookup. Data type is Boolean.
udpZipTableName	If the udpZipTable flag is set to 'True', then this property must be set to the ZIPCODE table. Data type is String.
udpZipCityColumn	Specifies the name of the column in the ZIPCODE table holds the names of the cities. Data type is String.
udpZipCodeColumn	Specifies the name of the column where the ZIP code resides. Data type is String.
udpZipStateColumn	Specifies the name of the column where the state information resides. Data type is String.

If you don't already have a ZIPCODE table, create one with the characteristics shown here:

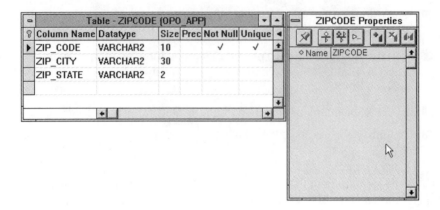

Once these properties are added, you need to write Oracle Basic code to make this class work.

frmClass.OnLoad( )
To attach code to the **OnLoad( )** method of the class and the **Validate( )** method of the Zip Text Field, use the following code.

```
' If state table is specified make the txtState control visible to display
' the state. Otherwise make the cboState control visible to
' the state. This sets up the address visual object to the
' correct format, and ready to display the address.

IF udpStateTable THEN
    cboState.Visible = True
    txtState.Visible = False
ELSEIF udpZipTable THEN
    cboState.Visible = False
    txtState.Visible = True
ELSE
    cboState.Visible = False
    txtState.Visible = True
END IF
```

The code attached to the **OnLoad( )** method positions either the combo box or the text field based on the user properties specified.

zip.Validate( )   The following code looks up the city and state if a ZIP code is entered. It defaults to the names of the columns in the ZIPCODE table if they are not specified.

```
' Look up City and State when the ZIP code is entered.
DIM strCity As String, strState As String, strSql As String
DIM strCityColumn As String, strStateColumn As String, &
    strZipColumn As String, strZipTable As String
DIM strFormattedZipCode As String
On Error Goto Err_PostChange

' Format the ZIP code if the entered ZIP code is  9 digits.
strFormattedZipCode = newval
IF Len(strFormattedZipCode) = 9 THEN
    strFormattedZipCode = Left(strFormattedZipCode,5) & "-" & &
    Right(strFormattedZipCode,4)
END IF


' If a ZIPCODE table is provided then look up State and City.
IF TopContainer.udpZipTable THEN
    ' See if column names are specified, if not use default values.
        IF NOT IsNull(TopContainer.udpZipTableName) THEN
            strZipTable = TopContainer.udpZipTableName
        ELSE
            strZipTable = "ZIPCODE"
        END IF

        IF NOT IsNull(TopContainer.udpZipCodeColumn) THEN
            strZipColumn = TopContainer.udpZipCodeColumn
        ELSE
            strZipColumn = "ZIP_CODE"
        END IF

        IF NOT IsNull(TopContainer.udpZipStateColumn) THEN
            strStateColumn = TopContainer.udpZipStateColumn
        ELSE
            strStateColumn = "ZIP_STATE"
        END IF

        IF NOT IsNull(TopContainer.udpZipCityColumn) THEN
            strCityColumn = TopContainer.udpZipCityColumn
        ELSE
            strCityColumn = "ZIP_CITY"
```

```
        END IF

    strSql = "Select " & strCityColumn & " from " & & strZipTable
& " where " & strZipColumn & " = " & Left(newval,5)
    strCity = SQLLOOKUP("Select " & strCityColumn & " from " & &
strZipTable & " where " & strZipColumn &" = " & Left(newval, 5))
    strSql = "Select " & strStateColumn & " from " & strZipTable
& &

" where " & strZipColumn &" = " & Left(newval, 5)
    strState = SQLLOOKUP("Select " & strStateColumn & " from " &
& strZipTable & " where " & strZipColumn &" = " & Left(newval, 5))

    IF NOT IsNull(strCity) THEN
        TopContainer.City.Value = strCity
    END IF

    IF NOT IsNull(strState) THEN
        TopContainer.txtState.Value = strState
    END IF
END IF

Self.Value = strFormattedZipCode
Validate = True

Exit_PostChange:
    Exit Function
Err_PostChange:
    MsgBox "Error = " & Cstr(Err) & " Formatting Zip Code "
        Resume Exit_PostChange
End Function
```

How to Use the Address Class

From the Application window, click on the New Form button. A new form will be created. Give this form the Name property of 'frmAddressClass'. Drag the clsAddress class onto this form to instantiate it. You will be passing a ZIPCODE table to this class, so set the udpZipTable property to 'True'. Set the udpZipTable name to 'ZIPCODE'. Now set the udpZipCityColumn to 'ZIP_CITY', udpZipCodeColumn to 'ZIP_CODE', and the udpZipStateColumn to 'ZIP_STATE'. Set the RecordSource property to 'CUSTOMERS' and the RecSrcSession to whichever session you are using.

Now you need to connect the data sources of the address class to the correct columns in the CUSTOMERS table. Set the DataSources of the following controls as follows:

Control	DataSource
Address1	Cust_Address1
Address2	Cust_Address2
City	Cust_City
txtState	Cust_State
cboState	Cust_State
Zip	Cust_Zip

The DataSource names are column names from the Customer table. This is all you need to do. If you run the form now, it should work according to the requirements specified above, and look like this:

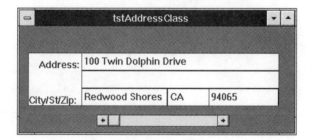

Summary

In this chapter, you have learned how to use the facilities provided by Oracle Power Objects to enforce business rules. The breadth and depth of what Oracle Power Objects provides is impressive. Two of the most difficult aspects of building a client/server system are providing easy data access and maintaining data integrity. Oracle Power Objects succeeds admirably in handling both those issues.

In the next chapter, you will examine several database issues. In particular, you will learn all about sessions and how to fetch data from a back-end database, and examine issues in transaction processing.

CHAPTER 8

Database Server Connections

In all of the previous chapters of this book, you have been concentrating on creating client applications. This emphasis is only natural, since Oracle Power Objects is a tool for creating client applications. But, as the name implies, there is more to client/server computing than just creating client applications. The server in client/server is the repository of data for the application, so any good application developer will have to understand the implications of working with a database server. In this chapter, you will learn about the purpose of the database server, how your application connects to the server, the concept and purpose of database transactions, and the different types of data retrieval supplied by Oracle Power Objects. In Chapter 9, you will learn about some of the issues involved in sharing data with other users and the interplay between protecting data integrity and enhancing client/server performance. Both this chapter and Chapter 9 will deal with the specifics of interacting with Oracle and Blaze databases, and both chapters will supply coding examples to help you address some of the issues raised by data interaction in a client/server system.

The Database Server

The term *client/server* refers to a computing architecture in which a client application works with data stored in a database server. This architecture implies that there will be a specific application interface to data. The client application will use specific calls to interact with the server data. Although a client/server system is typically installed with the client applications on a personal computer or workstation, with the server data being accessed through a local area network, a client/server system can also be implemented with a local database sharing the same machine as the client application.

Oracle Power Objects is built on a client/server model. Although Oracle Power Objects provides large increases in developer productivity by automatically implementing many of the details of server data access, it is still important to understand some of the issues involved in interacting with a database server, since the way an application converses with a database can have a dramatic impact on the performance of the application and, even more importantly, the integrity of the data.

The Purpose of a Database Server

Before getting to the specifics of how Oracle Power Objects interacts with a database server, it would be useful to review the purpose of a database server.

A database server is an application that handles the storage and manipulation of data. This single statement covers a wide range of functionality. After all, a filing system handles the storage and manipulation of data, but the concept of a database server has matured to define an application that not only stores and manipulates data, but also provides a set of functions for storing and manipulating data that make it easier for a user to access the data.

A database server provides an interface to the data it stores. Modern databases provide users with a *logical view* of their data. A logical view of data gives users the ability to identify data by referring to the data by some sort of name, rather than by the location of the data on a physical storage medium, such as a disk. The database controls the location and storage type of the data.

A database server can store, retrieve, and massage its data, and the server gives data users the ability to prescribe the storage, retrieval, and massaging of data through a set of well-defined functions. In today's computing environment, most new databases are *relational* databases. Relational databases use a standard language, structured query language, or *SQL*, to define user interactions with the database server. SQL gives a user the ability to retrieve data based on selection criteria, to specify the order that data is retrieved, to write new data to the database, to update existing records (or *rows*) in the database, and to delete rows from the database. SQL is well suited for the client/server environment because the language is very compact and an SQL query only returns those pieces of data requested by the user that fit the selection criteria. Because of this, SQL helps to reduce the amount of data that is moved over a local area network, which can help the overall performance of a client/server system.

A database system also provides different types of data *validation*. A database server validates data according to the type of the data—string data, numeric data, data that represents dates, and other types. A database system can ensure that all values in a particular data field, or *column*, are unique. A database system can provide *referential integrity*, which can be used to guarantee that a value stored in one column already exists as a value in another column. Some database systems give database users the ability to define *triggers*. A trigger is a piece of code that executes whenever a row of data is added, modified, or deleted.

You may have recognized some of these types of validation as similar to some of the validation you have already added to your application. For instance, Oracle Power Objects can automatically return an error to the user if the value entered into a data field object with a DataType property of 'Date' is not a valid date. It is often good application design to validate data before sending it to the server. If you send invalid data to the server, you will receive an error in the application, and either the application or the user will have to correct the error and resend the data to the server. You can put the old adage of "an ounce of protection is worth a pound of cure" to good use by avoiding the excess LAN traffic and user intervention by handling many common types of errors in the application.

A database system uses validation to maintain the *integrity*, or correctness, of the data. A database system also maintains the integrity of the data when many different users are accessing the data. If two users try to update the same piece of data, one user's changes may overwrite the other user's changes. A database will use *locks* to prevent users from overwriting each others' changes, and the database will use the concept of the *transaction* to determine when one user's changes are made available to other database users. The transaction is also used to give a developer the ability to implement "all or none" processing, in which a group of database actions will either all complete successfully or all be removed.

Oracle Power Objects provides a powerful level of default functionality to help you deal with these database features in an intelligent manner, as well as the ability to modify the defaults. Your application's success in interacting with the database will have a strong effect on the performance of the application system, as well as on the integrity of the data.

Sessions

As you learned in Chapter 1, Oracle Power Objects includes a top-level file object called a *session*. Your application will use a session to establish a connection between the client application and the server database. By keeping all of the information that controls the connection to the database in a separate file object, Oracle Power Objects gives you the ability to change the database you connect to without modifying anything in your client application.

How Does a Session Work?

A session uses some of its properties to control how it connects to and interacts with a database. A session uses a *connect string* to specify which database to connect to, and what user name and ID to use when connecting to the database.
    The connect string consists of three main portions:

```
database_type: [username[/password]] [@address]
```

The first portion of the connect string indicates the type of database you will connect to. This portion of the string could be 'Oracle', 'Blaze', or 'Dblib', for example. The 'Dblib' string indicates that the connection to an SQL server database will be made via the DBLIB client API. The database type must be followed by : (colon), and the string used for the database type is not case sensitive.
    The second portion of the connect string contains the user name and password The brackets around this portion of the connect string indicate that this parameter is optional. If you are connecting to a local Blaze database, for instance, you will not need to specify a user name or password. If you log into a Blaze database without a user name or password, you will automatically log in as the 'DBA' user. You can define users in some databases that do not require a password, so the password portion of the connect string is not required for this type of database.
    The final portion of the connect string indicates the location of the database you will connect to. Typically, the location for a database uses the @ (at symbol) and either a protocol indicator followed by a : and the database name, or a protocol indicator followed by a file location. For instance, if you were going to access a Blaze database file named SAMPLE.BLZ in the C:\BLAZE directory, the final portion of your connect string would be '@C:\BLAZE\SAMPLE.BLZ', with the string giving the location of the file. To connect to an Oracle database on a NetWare machine named Oracle_Server1, the final portion of the connect string would be '@x:Oracle_Server1', with the **@x:** indicating a NetWare server and the rest of the string giving the name of the server. There are some situations in which you will not have to specify the location of a server, such as when you are connecting to a local Personal Oracle7 database.

You will normally set the session that an application will use in the DefaultSession property of the application. If you designate a DefaultSession in an application, you will not have to use the AT *session* syntax whenever you access a database, such as in a Translation property for a list box or an **EXEC SQL** statement. By designating a DefaultSession in your application, you can make the application more portable, since you can simply change the DefaultSession setting to direct all database interactions to a different database.

The Three Types of Connect Strings

You may want to connect to different databases at different times. For instance, you may sometimes want to use a session directly in the Oracle Power Objects design environment to see the data structures and data in the database. You may want to connect to a different database when you are running an application in the Oracle Power Objects Designer Environment. You very well may want to connect in a different way when a user is running your application, since each user may want to log in to a database with their own user name and password.

Oracle Power Objects sessions have three different properties to control how a session connects to a database. The DesignConnect property string is used when you directly connect a session to a database. The DesignRunConnect property is used when you run an application that uses a session in the Oracle Power Objects Designer Environment. The RunConnect property is used when an application connects to a database at run time. Because of this, the RunConnect property is the only one of these three properties that can be modified at run time.

If the property that an Oracle Power Objects application would normally use is null, Oracle Power Objects will go to the next higher level connection property. For instance, if there is no RunConnect property for a session, an Oracle Power Objects application will use the DesignRunConnect property string. If the DesignRunConnect property is also null, Oracle Power Objects will use the DesignConnect string.

When Do Sessions Connect to a Database?

An Oracle Power Objects session gives you a property that allows you to specify when you want an application to connect to a database. The ConnectType property gives you three options: 'Connect On Startup', 'Connect On Demand', and 'Connect Manually'. If you specify 'Connect On Startup', the application will connect to a database as soon as the application starts running. If your application will immediately require database access when the application begins, you should use this option. 'Connect On Demand' is the default option for the ConnectType property.

When your application connects to a database on startup, the application will not be able to get any information from the user, such as their user name and password, so 'Connect On Startup' is not always an appropriate connection option. The 'Connect On Demand' option will automatically connect to a database as soon as an application requires a database connection. For instance, if a bound container needs to get data from a database, or an **EXEC SQL** or **SqlLookup( )** function needs to run, an application with the ConnectType property set to 'Connect On Demand' will connect. The 'Connect Manually' option will only connect when the application specifically calls the **Connect( )** method of the application. If you want to maintain explicit control of the connection to a database, you would use this option. You must be careful to ensure that the user will be logged into a database before your application requires any database access.

Prompting a User for Connection Information

Both the 'Connect On Demand' and 'Connect Manually' options will allow your application to interact with the user before connecting to a database. Oracle Power Objects can automatically prompt the user for connection information at run time.

To force your Oracle Power Objects application to prompt the user for login information, set the RunConnect property of your application to **?** (question mark). You can also set the DesignRunConnect property of your application to **?** if you want to be prompted for connection information when you run your application from the design environment.

When the appropriate property is set to **?**, the following dialog box will appear when your application first tries to connect to a database:

The ability to prompt for connection information is a very powerful feature of an Oracle Power Objects application. However, there may be times when you want more hands-on control of what happens during the login process. For instance, the default login dialog box provided by Oracle Power Objects forces a user to know the syntax of the connection string. The default login dialog box also does not allow you to specify your own actions in the event of a login failure. In order to give you more familiarity with the way that an Oracle Power Objects application interacts with a database, and to give you the ability to substitute your own functionality for the default login dialog box, in the next section you will create a login screen that will force a user to enter the information necessary to build a connect string that will be used to connect to a database when the application first starts running.

Creating a Login Screen

Typically, you want a user to log in to a database with his or her own user name and password, so that the database can enforce the security levels implemented by the database administrator. Since an application can set the RunConnect property at run time, you can easily create a login screen that will allow a user to specify the database they want to use, as well as their user name and password.

Setting the Appropriate ConnectType Option

Since the application you are designing requires access to a database, you want users to log in to a database immediately upon entering the application.

■ Open the ORDERSES session. Change the ConnectType property to 'Connect Manually'.

Changing the setting in a session will apply to all applications that use that session, so it is a good idea to decide on one setting for the ConnectType property as your normal default and design your applications accordingly. Since you will frequently want to use a login screen, the 'Connect Manually' option is appropriate, and you can save the login form as a library.

Your next step is to create the login form and add the necessary objects for the form.

Creating the Login Form

You will create a form that will collect the information needed to determine the connect string.

■ Open the Application window for the Orders application. Create a new form. Give the form the Name of 'frmLogin' and the Label of 'Login To Database'.

■ Add a radio button frame to the form. Set the Label property of the radio button frame to 'Database Type', the Name property of the radio button frame to 'rbfDatabaseType', and the DataType property of the radio button frame to 'String'. Add three radio buttons to the frame—one with a Name property of 'radBlaze', a Label property of 'Blaze', a DataType property of 'String', and a ValueOn property of 'BLAZE'; one with a Name property of 'radOracle', a Label property of 'Oracle', a DataType property of 'String', and a ValueOn property of 'ORACLE'; and one with a Name property of 'radSQLServer', a Label property of 'SQL Server', a DataType property of 'String', and a ValueOn property of 'DBLIB'. Set the DefaultValue property of the rbfDatabaseType to 'ORACLE'.

You could use a data field object to allow the user to enter the name of the database type, or a popup list that would give the user a list of values. However, since the user will always be required to enter a database type, and since there are probably a small, fixed number of options for the type of a database, in this particular case a radio button group is probably the most appropriate object to use.

Your login form should now look like this:

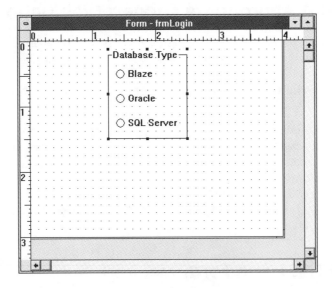

■ Add a data field object to the login form just below the rbfDatabaseType radio button group. Set the Name property of the data field to 'fldDatabase' and the DataType property of the data field to 'String'. Add a static text object to the left of the data field with a Label property of 'Database:', a TextJustHoriz property of 'Right', and a TextJustVert property of 'Center'. Adjust the static text so that it ends just to the left of the data field.

The data field object will allow a user to enter any string for a database name or location. Using a data field for this information is appropriate if a user may be using any database and the user understands how to specify a database. Typically, neither of these conditions are totally true, so you might want to consider using a pop-up list object, with the proper information for the connect string as corresponding column and a descriptive name as the display column. The disadvantage of using a pop-up list would be that you would have to either hardcode the values in the object or create a database table that would hold the two values, and that you would have to modify this information if the database changed. But the advantage would be that a user could simply identify a meaningful name for a database, rather than remember and enter a location string.

NOTE
If you were to use a database table to store the location strings and names of a database, you might want to have your DefaultSession connect to the database that would hold this information with a generic user name and password, do an explicit **Disconnect( )** from the database once the information had been retrieved, and then do a **Connect( )** once the user had entered his or her username and password.

Your login form should now look like this:

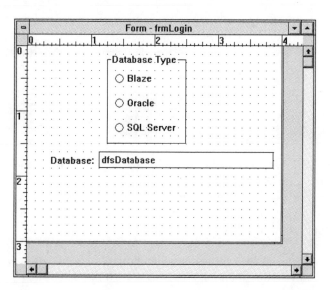

■ Add a data field object to the form just below the fldDatabase data field. Set the Name property of the data field to 'fldUsername' and the DataType property to 'String'. Add a static text object to the left of the data field and set the Label property to 'User Name:', the TextJustHoriz property to 'Right', and the TextJustVert property to 'Center'. Position the static text so that it is just to the left of the fldUsername data field.

■ Add a data field object to the form just below the fldDatabase data field. Set the Name property of the data field to 'fldPassword' and the DataType property to 'String'. Add a static text object to the left of the data field and set the Label property to 'Password:', the TextJustHoriz property to 'Right', and the TextJustVert property to 'Center'. Position the static text so that it is just to the left of the fldUsername data field.

Your login form should now look like this:

■ Enlarge your form to make it 3 1/2" high. Add a push button to the bottom left of the form. Set the Name property of the push button to 'btnLogin' and the Label property to 'Login'. Add a second push button to the bottom right of the form. Set the Name property of the push button to 'btnCancel' and the Label property to 'Cancel'.

When a user clicks on the btnLogin push button, your application will use the information they have entered and attempt to log in to the database. If a user clicks on the btnCancel push button, they will exit the application without ever having logged in.

Your login form should now look like this:

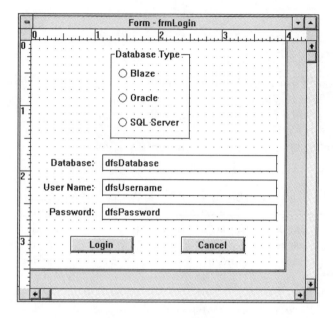

■ Modify the code in the **OnLoad( )** method of your application. If you have been creating your application as outlined in the earlier chapters of this book, add the following code to the beginning of any existing code:

```
frmLogin.OpenModal(0)
```

You want the frmLogin form to appear before any other forms in the application, so you will call it immediately upon loading the application.

■ Set the IsDismissBtn property of the btnLogin push button to 'False'.

You do not want to dismiss this modal dialog box, since there is no need for it once a user has successfully logged in or canceled out of it.

■ Add the following code to the **Click( )** method of the btnLogin push button:

```
DIM vLogin As String
IF NOT ISNULL(fldUsername.Value) THEN
    IF NOT ISNULL(fldPassword.Value) THEN
```

```
            vLogin = fldUsername.Value & "/" & fldPassword.Value
        ELSE
            vLogin = fldUsername.Value
        END IF
    END IF
    vLogin = rbfDatabaseType.Value & ": " & vLogin & &
        fldDatabase.Value
```

Since a connect string may contain a user name and password, a user name only, or neither, you will have to use the set of **IF** clauses above to set the user name/password portion of the connect string. Remember that a connect string does not necessarily need to have a database location either, so you do not need to check to ensure that the fldDatabase string contains a value.

NOTE
The login screen being described in this section is an all-purpose login screen that can handle any type of connect string. In actual practice, you will probably want to give your users a more limited choice of login options. You could use the pop-up list for the name of the database, as suggested in the previous note, and check to make sure that a user name and/or password has been entered, if they are appropriate in your situation. If an application is always going to log in to the same database, you could eliminate the fldDatabase data field entirely and use a hardcoded string for the database location.

■ Add the underlined code to the code for the **Click( )** method of the btnLogin push button:

```
DIM vLogin As String
IF NOT ISNULL(fldUsername.Value) THEN
    IF NOT ISNULL(fldPassword.Value) THEN
        vLogin = fldUsername.Value & "/" & fldPassword.Value
    ELSE
        vLogin = fldUsername.Value
    END IF
END IF
vLogin = rbfDatabaseType.Value & ": " & vLogin & " " & &
    fldDatabase.Value
ORDERSES.DesignRunConnect = vLogin
ORDERSES.Connect( )
```

Once you have set the RunConnect property of the session to the value of the *vLogin* string and call the **Connect( )** method for the session, you can reference the properties of the ORDERSES session by prefixing the property name with the ORDERSES name.

When the user clicks on the Login push button, you create the connect string from the values entered and set the RunConnect property of the session to the connect string. You can then connect to the database by calling the **Connect( )** method of the session.

After you call the **Connect( )** method of the session, you can enter the first form window of the application if the connection has been successfully accomplished.

■ Add the underlined code to the end of the code in the **Click( )** method of the btnLogin push button:

```
DIM vLogin As String
IF NOT ISNULL(fldUsername.Value) THEN
    IF NOT ISNULL(fldPassword.Value) THEN
        vLogin = fldUsername.Value & "/" & fldPassword.Value
    ELSE
        vLogin = fldUsername.Value
    END IF
END IF
vLogin = rbfDatabaseType.Value & ": " & vLogin & &
    fldDatabase.Value
ORDERSES.RunConnect = vLogin
ORDERSES.Connect()
IF ORDERSES.IsConnected() THEN
    btnCancel.Cancel()
END IF
```

The **IsConnected( )** method of a session is used to indicate whether a session is connected to a database. If the **Connect( )** method has executed successfully, the **IsConnected( )** method will return True, and you can call the **Click( )** method of the btnCancel push button that will close the frmLogin form.

You will also want to inform the user if they did not successfully log in to the database.

■ Add the underlined code to the **Click( )** method of the btnLogin push button:

```
DIM vLogin As String
IF NOT ISNULL(fldUsername.Value) THEN
    IF NOT ISNULL(fldPassword.Value) THEN
        vLogin = fldUsername.Value & "/" & fldPassword.Value
    ELSE
```

```
            vLogin = fldUsername.Value
    END IF
END IF
vLogin = rbfDatabaseType.Value & ": " & vLogin & " " & fldDatabase.Value
ORDERSES.RunConnect = vLogin
ORDERSES.Connect()
IF ORDERSES.IsConnected() THEN
    btnCancel.Click()
ELSE
    IF MSGBOX("You did not successfully login to the database.  " & &
        "Would you like to try again?", 4, "Unsuccessful Login") = 7 &
        THEN btnCancel.Click()
END IF
```

NOTE
Notice that the message for the message box is broken up into two separate strings that are concatenated together. The purpose for this was to allow the string to cover two lines, since you can only use the **&** (ampersand) line continuation character outside of a quote string.

The **MSGBOX( )** function will use both a Yes and a No push button, as indicated by the number 4 as the second parameter of the function. If the user selects the No push button, the function will return the value of 7 and you should close the frmLogin dialog box by calling the **Click( )** method of the btnCancel push button.

NOTE
If the user chooses the No push button in the message box, you are closing the dialog box without having logged in successfully. You will handle this possibility later in this chapter.

Finally, you might not want the user to have more than three login attempts for security reasons.

■ Add the following code to the Declarations section of your application:

```
Global nLoginAttempts As Integer
```

By declaring a variable as **GLOBAL** in the Declarations section of your application, you make that variable available to all objects in all forms in the application. If you were to keep track of the login attempts with a variable that you declared in the **Click( )** method, the variable would be reinitialized every time you called the method, so it would not keep track of previous failures. To give a value persistence, you must declare the variable a **GLOBAL** in the Declarations section of the application.

■ Add or modify the underlined code in the **Click( )** method of the btnLogin push button:

```
DIM vLogin As String
IF NOT ISNULL(fldUsername.Value) THEN
    IF NOT ISNULL(fldPassword.Value) THEN
        vLogin = fldUsername.Value & "/" & fldPassword.Value
    ELSE
        vLogin = fldUsername.Value
    END IF
END IF
vLogin = rbfDatabaseType.Value & ": " & vLogin & fldDatabase.Value
ORDERSES.RunConnect = vLogin
ORDERSES.Connect()
IF ORDERSES.IsConnected() THEN
    btnCancel.Click()
ELSE
    IF MSGBOX("You did not successfully login to the database.  " & &
        Would you like to try again?", 4, "Unsuccessful Login") = 7 THEN
            btnCancel.Click()
    ELSE
            nLoginAttempts = nLoginAttempts + 1
    END IF
IF nLoginAttempts > 2 THEN
    MSGBOX("You have exceeded the allowable number of login attempts."& &
        " Please contact the system manager.", 16, &
        " Too Many Login Attempts")
    btnCancel.Click()
END IF
END IF
```

Each time the user fails to log in and does not leave the login box, the value of the *nLoginAttempts* global variable increases. If the user is unsuccessful on three login attempts, the application will display a message box with a Stop icon, indicated by the 16 as the second parameter, and stop the application by calling the **Click( )** method for the btnCancel push button.

NOTE
Notice that the **&** continuation character is removed following the **THEN** in the **IF** clause where the user is prompted about whether they would like to try to log in again. If there was only a single line of code, such as btnCancel.**Click( )**, the **IF** clause can be on a single line and does not require an **END IF**. When you add a second line of

code to the clause, you have to add an **END IF** and you can remove the continuation character.

If a bad user has unsuccessfully tried to log in to a database three times, your application will look like this:

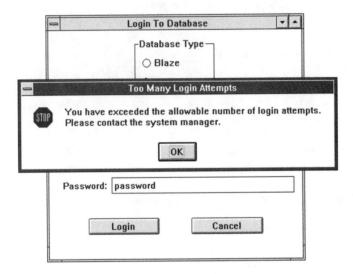

Checking for a Successful Connection

A user of this application could leave the login dialog box after successfully connecting to a database, after clicking on the btnCancel push button, or after failing to log in on three successive attempts. When you return to the **OnLoad( )** method of the application, you will have to add some code to check for a successful connection, since you will not want to run the application if the user has not successfully logged into a database.

■ Add the underlined code after the **OpenModal( )** call in the **OnLoad( )** method of the application:

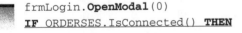

```
frmLogin.OpenModal(0)
IF ORDERSES.IsConnected() THEN
```

■ Add the following code at the bottom of the code in the **OnLoad( )** method of the application:

```
ELSE
CloseApp()
END IF
```

With this code, the application checks to make sure that a successful connection has been established. If it has not, the application will execute the **CloseApp( )** method, which will stop the application.

- Run your form and exit the frmLogin form by hitting the btnCancel push button.

You can see that you will rapidly leave the application when you return to the **OnLoad( )** method and call the **CloseApp( )** method.

You have created your own customized login dialog box, which you can use in many different applications. If you wanted to make your login dialog box more generic, you could add a property to the application that would store the object handle of the session and use that property in place of the ORDERSES qualifier.

Transactions

One of the most important functions of a database is to manage the sharing of data between different applications and users. A problem that occurs in a multiuser database is how to ensure that changes to related data all occur simultaneously, regardless of whether the data resides in the same row of the same table or not. For instance, if a user transfers money from one account to another, how can a database guarantee that the money is debited from one account and credited to the other account, or neither debited or credited?

Another problem that a database must resolve is when to make one person's changes to data available to other users. Yet another problem associated with multiuser databases is the need to protect one user's changes to a piece of data from being unwittingly overwritten by another user's changes to the same piece of data. All of these problems threaten the integrity of the data.

Relational databases use the concept of a *transaction* to address all of these issues. A transaction is a unit of work in a database. A transaction is normally automatically started when a connection is first made to a database. All changes to the database are added simultaneously to the database when the transaction is committed. A transaction can be rolled back, which means that all changes made to the database since the transaction began are discarded and the transaction is ended. A database also uses a system of data locks, which prevents other users from changing data, to protect a user's changes from being overwritten by another user; and ending a transaction, by either a commit or a rollback, will release all locks that have been applied to data used in the transaction. (Locking is an extremely important topic that will be covered at length in Chapter 9.) Typically, a new transaction will begin immediately after a transaction has been committed or rolled back. All in all, a transaction plays a key role in maintaining the integrity of data and in the operation of a database.

Sessions and Transactions

Oracle Power Objects map a transaction to a session. All methods that have a transaction as their scope, such as the **CommitForm( )**, **CommitWork( )**, **RollbackForm( )**, and **RollbackWork( )** methods, will execute for an entire session. To commit the data changes for a session, you can call the **CommitWork( )** method for the session with the syntax

```
session_name.CommitWork()
```

The *session_name* is an object handle for a session. You could use the **GetSession( )** and **GetRecordset( )** functions as described below, to represent the session for a recordset:

```
GetContainer().GetRecordset().GetSession().CommitWork()
```

If you have three different forms connected to the same session, the **CommitWork( )** method for the session will commit all of the changes in all of the forms.

Oracle Power Objects also includes the **CommitForm( )** and **RollbackForm( )** methods for a form. These methods will call the **CommitWork( )** or **RollbackWork( )** methods for all of the sessions in a form. For instance, if your form is a container for one session and the form contains a repeater display that is bound to another session, the **CommitWork( )** method will commit all changes for all bound containers associated with either session.

When you call the **CommitWork( )** method, Oracle Power Objects will automatically use a two-phase commit protocol to guarantee that changes are committed to both transactions or neither transaction. For more information on two-phase commit, refer to the documentation for your database server.

You may wish to create more than one session to access the same database in order to control how you commit or roll back changes to a database server. For instance, you might want to give a user the ability to call a comments dialog box from a form. You would want to commit the changes to the comments when the user leaves the comments form, but still give the user the ability to roll back any changes they may have made on the Main form. If you used a separate session for the comments dialog, the **CommitWork( )** method for the dialog box or the **CommitWork( )** method for the session would not affect the session used for the calling form.

There are other implications associated with the **Commit...( )** and **Rollback...( )** methods that your will learn about later in this chapter. You may want to use different sessions to avoid some of these other repercussions of the use of sessions.

Default Handling of Changes

As you have already seen, Oracle Power Objects will automatically enable the Commit and Rollback push buttons when a change is made to data on the form.

When a user changes any data in a bound object associated with a session, the **IsWorkPending( )** method of the session will return True. When there are any changes in the data for any of the sessions associated with any of the objects on a form, the Commit and Rollback push buttons in the default toolbar are enabled.

You use the **IsWorkPending( )** method to see if any of the data for a session has been changed. You can call the **IsWorkPending( )** method of a session with the following call:

```
Self.GetContainer().GetRecordset().GetSession().IsWorkPending()
```

When a user clicks the Commit push button, Oracle Power Objects will call the **CommitForm( )** function, which will call the **CommitWork( )** method for each session that is associated with a container in the form. Similarly, when a user presses the Rollback push button, Oracle Power Objects will roll back each session that has a bound object in the form.

Later in this chapter, and in Chapter 9, you will learn about other ways that transactions can affect your Oracle Power Objects applications.

Retrieval

You have been learning about how to initiate a connection from your Oracle Power Objects application to your database server, and how your database server manages transactions. One of the most important ways that a client/server system differs from a traditional, monolithic system is the impact of data retrieval on the overall performance of the system.

In a traditional application architecture, the application and the data reside on the same machine. Communication between the database server and the client application occurs through shared machine resources, such as memory, disk, and the bus between the CPU and the disk. In a client/server system, the database server is usually separated from the client application by some sort of network. The network transmits data much slower than the shared resources in a single machine, and over much greater distances. Because of this, data retrieval can create a performance bottleneck in a client/server system.

Oracle Power Objects automatically manages data retrieval. Oracle Power Objects also gives you some powerful options to help reduce the data retrieval bottleneck and improve the responsiveness of your applications.

Data Retrieval Options

Oracle Power Objects gives you the ability to set options for data retrieval as a property of any bound container, such as a form or a repeater display. You can set the retrieval option as the RowFetchMode property of the container. There are three options for the property setting:

- *Fetch All Immediately* When the RowFetchMode of a bound container is set to 'Fetch All Immediately', Oracle Power Objects will retrieve all rows that match the selection criteria to the client application immediately, before returning control of the application to the user. The retrieved rows are stored in the bound container's recordset.

- *Fetch As Needed When the RowFetchMode of a bound container is set to 'Fetch As Needed', Oracle Power Objects will only retrieve the rows that match the selection criteria to the client application as the user needs* them. Oracle Power Objects will fetch the data 10 rows at a time to minimize the amount of LAN traffic, and the returned data is stored in the container's recordset. As the user requests data that is not in the recordset, by navigating to a position in the recordset that does not yet contain data, Oracle Power Objects will automatically fetch the next 10 rows of data. The relative positioning of the scroll bar will not be accurate with this option, since Oracle Power Objects will have no way of knowing how many rows will ultimately be fetched to the recordset. The setting is the default.

- *Fetch Count First The 'Fetch Count First' option for the RowFetchMode property works in the same manner as the 'Fetch As Needed' option, except that Oracle Power Objects will determine how many rows match the selection criteria before fetching the first 10 rows from the database. The 'Fetch Count First' option of the RowFetchMode property lets Oracle Power Objects use the scroll bar to properly indicate the relative position of the current row in the entire result set.*

Which RowFetchMode Should You Use?

The RowFetchMode option you use depends on your expectations about how much data a bound container will receive in your application.

Client/server systems are user driven. One of the implications of this characteristic of client/server applications is that the user determines the selection criteria for many data retrieval actions. Oracle Power Objects addresses this issue by automatically including Query-By-Form (QBF) capabilities in all applications. But if a user is going to determine the retrieval conditions, a developer cannot always accurately predict the number of rows returned in a query. A user may define selection criteria that would return a very large amount of data to the client application. If you attempt to deny a user the ability to do this, you are also flying in the face of one of the guiding principles of client/server design—client/server applications are user driven. Your user may not know beans about the principles of client/server design, but they will definitely know if you attempt to limit their access to data.

The 'Fetch All Immediately' option of the RowFetchMode property will cause a user to wait until all rows are fetched from the database server before they regain control of the application. If a user has selected a large amount of data, the waiting period will be longer than if they have selected a smaller amount of data. In many databases, there is nothing inherent about any particular selection criteria that would indicate the amount of data that will match a selection criteria. For instance, if the user is querying the number of accounts that are past due, there might be a significantly larger number of accounts that match that criteria from one day to the next. Differing amounts of data that meet a selection criteria lead to differing response times for a data retrieval with the RowFetchMode property set to 'Fetch All Immediately'. Differing response times result in inconsistent performance, and since users do not understand the underlying reason for the inconsistencies, inconsistent performance can lead to user complaints.

To avoid receiving such complaints, the authors of this book recommend using the RowFetchMode property to either the 'Fetch As Needed' or 'Fetch Count First' for all bound containers, unless you have a good reason to believe that there will only be a limited amount of data returned. For instance, in the Orders application you have been working on, you can expect that each order will not have hundreds and hundreds of order lines. You can leave the RowFetchMode property of the repeater display set to 'Fetch All Immediately'. You will also need to fetch all of the data for a bound container whose data will be used in an on screen, aggregate calculation to ensure the correctness of the calculation.

The 'Fetch As Needed' and 'Fetch Count First' options of the RowFetchMode property deliver some significant performance improvements. First of all, a user will not have to wait for all the data to be returned to the application before continuing to use the application. Second, by spreading the data retrieval load out, you reduce the impact of a large retrieval on the database server and on the LAN itself. Finally, if a user can get the information they need without retrieving all of the data, you will have reduced the load of the data retrieval on the server and the LAN.

For the bound container of the Main form, you should change the RowFetchMode property to 'Fetch Count First'.

The 'Fetch Count First' option requires Oracle Power Objects to execute an SQL query that will return the number of rows that will eventually be returned before fetching the first 10 rows of data. There is some overhead associated with running this query, but the overhead will be fairly minimal and consistent, regardless of the number of rows that will meet the selection criteria. In the use of the application, the first set of 10 rows will take a little longer to fetch than the remaining sets of 10 rows. Since the database will have to parse and execute the SQL query when it first receives it, the initial data retrieval will take longer than subsequent data retrievals anyway, so selecting the count first will not dramatically affect the responsiveness of the application.

NOTE
You may be saying "Ah ha!, so different queries will take different amounts of time. Dang those user-driven applications!" when you think about the need for an SQL database to parse and execute queries. You will be right, but it is poor form to talk to yourself when reading a book. It is true that different queries will take different amounts of time to execute on an SQL database server. However, in a client/server system, data retrieval can take much longer than the execution of queries, so it is best to minimize this bottleneck. In addition, user-driven applications demand that users can control, to some extent, the data that will be retrieved, so limiting this control to satisfy the demands of the data will not be acceptable.

If you feel absolutely certain that you will never need to know how many rows may be retrieved, you can use the 'Fetch As Needed' option to deliver the performance benefits of incremental data retrieval without incurring the additional overhead of first determining the row count. There are times when you might want to know how many rows will eventually be retrieved, and the best and easiest way to get this information is by using 'Fetch Count First'. Later in this chapter, you will learn of a very important reason you might want to know how many rows are in the selected data.

Determining the State of Data Retrieval

Oracle Power Objects gives you functions that can help you programmatically determine how many rows are in the result set of a query and how many rows have been retrieved.

The **GetRowCount( )** method applies to a recordset. The syntax for the method is

```
recordset.GetRowCount()
```

You could use the **GetRecordset( )** function to get the recordset of a bound container. The function will return the number of rows in the recordset when the function is executed. This number will represent the number of rows that have been retrieved from the database so far.

The **GetRowCountAdvice( )** method also applies to a recordset and has the same syntax. This method is only valid for recordsets that are associated with bound containers that have their RowFetchMode property set to 'Fetch Count First', and it returns the number of rows that will eventually be returned to the recordset.

You can use these two functions to easily determine how many more rows are still on the database server that will eventually be fetched to the application. But why would you want to do this?

Incremental Data Retrieval and Transactions

In the discussion of transactions, you learned that you could end a transaction with a commit or roll back. Since SQL is a set-oriented language, a database must use some way to address individual rows in a set of rows. A transaction uses an internal pointer called a *cursor* to keep track of the current row in a result set. When the transaction ends, the cursor is destroyed, since the database server has no further need of it.

It is good practice for a user to commit or roll back the changes that they make to data as soon as possible, so that their changes are available to other users and so that the data in their client recordset is in agreement with the data in the database. But a problem can occur if the RowFetchMode property of a bound container is set to one of the incremental retrieval options. When a user commits a transaction, the cursor is destroyed on the database server, so the Oracle Power Objects application assumes that there is no more data to retrieve. This could lead to a user getting an incorrect view of their data. For example, let's say a user query selects 100 rows. The user has retrieved the first 20 rows, makes a change in the data, and commits the changes. When the user attempts to continue to scroll forward, Oracle Power Objects will not be able to fetch any more rows. The user may think that there are only 20 rows that meet their selection criteria.

It is imperative that an application not give a user incorrect results. As a developer, you are stuck with a difficult decision—deliver poor and inconsistent retrieval performance, or compromise the validity of the user's view of the data. Fortunately, you can account for this with a few lines of code.

■ Open the Properties sheet for the frmOrders form. Add the following code to the **CommitForm( )** method:

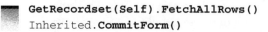

```
GetRecordset(Self).FetchAllRows()
Inherited.CommitForm()
```

The **FetchAllRows( )** method will force Oracle Power Objects to retrieve all of the rows in a query result set to the recordset of the bound container. The **FetchAllRows( )** method will have no effect if all the rows have already been retrieved. With this code, you are ensuring that all rows in the result set will be fetched to the recordset before a commit is performed.

Whenever a user rolls back the current transaction, the **RollbackWork( )** method automatically requeries the database, so you will not need to add similar code to the **RollbackForm( )** method.

This will solve your logical problem of ensuring that the user does not get an inaccurate view of the data. It could present other perceived problems, though. If an application retrieves the first rows of a very large result set, and the application has retrieved many rows when the user commits the first change to the database, there may be a significant delay in the first commit. In addition, the user might be finished working with the data from this particular query, so the application might be retrieving data that the user no longer needs.

You can address this issue by determining the number of rows left to be fetched and making sure the user wants to get them.

■ Add the underlined code to the **CommitForm( )** method of the frmOrders form:

```
DIM vRowsLeft As Integer
vRowsLeft = Self.GetRecordset().GetRowCoundAdvice() - &
    Self.GetRecordset.GetRowCount()
IF vRowsLeft > 0 THEN
    IF MSGBOX("There are " & STR(vRowsLeft) & " rows left to retrieve." & &
        " Do you want to retrieve them?", 4 + 32, "More Rows") = 6 THEN
        Self.GetRecordset().FetchAllRows()
    END IF
END IF
Inherited.CommitForm()
```

This code will check to see if there are any rows left in the result set on the server that have not yet been retrieved. The **MSGBOX** function will inform the user how many rows remain and ask for confirmation that the user wants to retrieve them. The number 4 in the second parameter of the **MSGBOX** function gives the message box a Yes push button and a No push button, while the 32 in the second parameter displays a question mark in the message box.

NOTE
The message displayed by the message box lets the user know how many rows will be retrieved, but it does not detail the implications of responding No to the retrieval question. You could pop another

message box with information about the repercussions of refusing the retrieval, you could modify the message text, or you could let the user know the full impact of refusing to retrieve all the rows. Your best solution will depend on the knowledge and taste of your user community.

Bringing up a message box disrupts the flow of an application. You might want to modify the above code so that it only executes if a significant number of rows will be retrieved.

■ Modify the underlined line of code in the **CommitForm( )** method of the frmOrders form:

```
DIM vRowsLeft As Integer
vRowsLeft = Self.GetRecordset().GetRowCountAdvice() - &
    Self.GetRecordset.GetRowCount()
IF vRowsLeft > 100 THEN
    IF MSGBOX("There are " & STR(vRowsLeft) & " rows left to retrieve." & &
        " Do you want to retrieve them?", 4 + 32, "More Rows") = 6 THEN
        Self.GetRecordset().FetchAllRows()
    END IF
END IF
Inherited.CommitForm()
```

The changed code will only bring up a message box, forcing the user to make a choice, if there are more than 100 rows left to be retrieved. Depending on the configuration of your system, you may want to increase or decrease the threshold for the user message box.

The solution described above attempts to address some of the problems surrounding data retrieval in client/server systems. Client/server applications have a new set of problems that an application must deal with. The application must be user driven, so the application cannot place limits on data retrieval that interfere with the user's ability to access data. The user may choose to access a large amount of data, either accidently or on purpose, and there is a potential performance bottleneck in retrieving data from a remote server.

When you have users trying to bring data from a remote server to a client application, you must try to find the best way to implement the system so that the application runs as smoothly and efficiently as possible, as much of the time as possible. In the above solution, if the result set that a user is retrieving from the database is less than 100 rows, the first rows will be rapidly retrieved, and there will be a brief pause after the user commits or rolls back the first change to the database. If the user is retrieving a large amount of data, and tries to commit or roll back a change to the database with many rows remaining to be retrieved, they are given the option of retrieving the rows or not. The user does not need to be bothered when it is not necessary, and the user will get a responsive application at all times.

There are further complications that come into the picture when a user is accessing data that other users will also be using. The next chapter will review the issues involved with multiuser data access and how to address them with Oracle Power Objects.

CHAPTER 9

Client-Side Database Considerations

In Chapter 8, you explored several facets of the connection between an Oracle Power Objects application and your database server, such as how an Oracle Power Objects application connects to a database server, how an Oracle Power Objects application retrieves data from a server, and some of the implications of the method of data retrieval you select for your Oracle Power Objects application. In this chapter, you will learn how an Oracle Power Objects application stores data it has retrieved from the server on the client machine and also explore some of the factors to consider in a multiuser environment. You will become equipped to handle some of the complex issues that arise in the creation of enterprise-wide applications.

The Recordset

In Chapter 8, you read the term *recordset* a few times. In this section, you will learn more about the recordset and learn how you can directly manipulate a recordset.

What Is a Recordset?

In Chapter 8, you learned that you can select the way an Oracle Power Objects application retrieves data from a database server. Oracle Power Objects can either bring back data on demand, 10 rows at a time, or bring all the data to the client machine. Oracle Power Objects uses a recordset object to store data retrieved from a database server.

When you specify a RecordSource property for a container, Oracle Power Objects will create a recordset for that container. The recordset contains a column for each derived value specified in the container. When a user asks for data from a database server, the data actually comes from the recordset for the data. When a user updates data, the updates are stored in the recordset until the user commits the changes, at which time the changes are sent to the database. By using the recordset as an intermediary to the database server, Oracle Power Objects can give a consistent data interface to the user while optimizing the interaction with the database server.

There is a RecSrcMaxMem property for all container objects. The value stored in this property controls the amount of memory used to store the recordset for the associated data. If the amount of data stored in the recordset exceeds the amount of memory allocated for the recordset, Oracle Power Objects will swap the recordset to disk. Oracle Power Objects will clean up any disk files used for recordsets when the recordset is destroyed by ending the connection to the database or closing the recordset's container. By default, a recordset uses 4K of memory to store data. You can increase the amount of memory used to store a recordset, which will improve the performance of scrolling through the rows of the recordset by the user. However, be aware that increasing the memory for a recordset will decrease the amount of memory available to other applications on the client machine and can adversely affect performance of other portions of the application or other applications.

Direct Access to a Recordset

There are times when you want to have a value in a recordset that will not need to be displayed on the screen. You have already created recordsets that contained values that were not displayed on the screen when you linked the repeater display that contained information from the ORDER_ITEMS table to a row in the ORDERS table in the frmOrders form. When you specified that the ORDER_ID column in the ORDER_ITEMS table was the LinkDetailColumn of the repeater display, Oracle Power Objects automatically included the ORDER_ID column in the recordset for the repeater display. Oracle Power Objects also knew that any changes to the value of the ID column in the frmOrders form would automatically be rippled down to the values in the ORDER_ID column of the ORDER_ITEMS table.

In the ORDERS table, there is a column called ORDER_FILLED. This column is used to indicate whether an order has been shipped or not. When a user enters a new order in the frmOrders screen, the status of the order will always be '1', which indicates that the order is a new order. There is no need to display this information on the frmOrders form, but there is a need to set the value of this column to '1' whenever a new order is created.

■ Open the Properties sheet for the frmOrders form. Scroll to the RecSrcAddCols property and set the property to 'ORDER_FILLED'.

The RecSrcAddCols property is used to indicate additional columns that will be in a recordset that will not be indicated as a DataSource for any items on the screen. Oracle Power Objects will automatically add a column to the recordset to hold any columns that are listed in the RecSrcAddCols property.

■ Add the following code to the **PreInsert( )** method of the frmOrders form:

```
Self.GetRecordset().SetColVal("ORDER_FILLED", 1)
Inherited.PreInsert()
```

The **PreInsert( )** method is executed when a user begins to insert a new record into the recordset. The **SetColVal( )** function will programmatically set the value of a column in the current row of the recordset. The first parameter of the function can be either the name of a column in the recordset or the number of the column in the recordset, while the second parameter is the value to assign to the column in the recordset. You can use the **GetRecordset( )** function as you did in the last chapter, with the **Self** keyword, to properly qualify the **SetColVal( )** method. As with most methods, you should call the inherited **PreInsert( )** method if you are adding code to the **PreInsert( )** method.

There are a variety of other methods you can use to access and manipulate data in a recordset. You can also dynamically create recordsets programmatically that are either bound to a database server or that have no connection to a database server. Later in this chapter, you will be dynamically creating a recordset to use when comparing the retrieved values in a bound container's recordset with the values currently in the database. For more information on recordsets and their associated methods, refer to the *Oracle Power Objects User's Guide*, which comes with the product.

Multiuser Integrity Issues

Up until this point, you have been creating your application without giving any thought to the fact that the data being used by your application may also be used at the same time by other users and applications. When your application is using data from a database that allows multiple users, such as a typical Oracle server, a new level of complexity is introduced. The data being used by one user of your application may be simultaneously being used by other users of the application, or even by other applications. The changes you make to the data may be overwritten by the changes made by other users, or vice versa. If this situation is allowed to exist, the integrity, or correctness, of the data may be seriously compromised.

Suppose two users read the same order. Each made changes to the order, and then each one committed the changes to the database. The second user to commit the changes could easily overwrite the first user's changes.

All databases give you a way to *lock* a record, which will prevent any other users from simultaneously making changes to the same row. Oracle Power Objects automatically implements locks on database rows and also gives you a way to easily determine if anyone has changed the data you wish to change. You can use these features of Oracle Power Objects and some Oracle Basic code to avoid compromising the integrity of your data.

What Is a Lock?

Some of you may not have worked extensively with multiuser databases, so the concept of a lock may not be entirely clear to you.

A database lock limits the access that other users have to the data that is locked. There are two basic types of access to data—read access and write access. Correspondingly, there are two types of database locks. A *shared*, or read, lock indicates that a row has been read. A shared lock allows other users to read the locked data, but does not allow users to write over the data. An *exclusive*, or write, lock indicates that a row is being written. An exclusive lock does not allow any other user some types of access to the data that is locked. Some databases use an exclusive lock to prevent all types of access to a database. The exclusive lock in an Oracle database does not prevent other users from reading the data, but it does prevent other users from writing to the row of data while there is an exclusive lock on the row. Both shared and exclusive locks are released when the data transaction that is using the locks is committed or rolled back.

Since the data in a database is used by many users and many applications, a developer must always balance the need for many users to access data, which is termed *concurrency*, with the need to preserve the integrity of the data. Locking many pieces of data can cause *contention*, which is a situation in which a user is waiting for another user to release a lock. Obviously, the more contention in a database, the more users will have to wait and the poorer the performance of applications that use the data.

In order to fully understand the implications of locking and data integrity for your application, you should know a little bit about how the Oracle and Blaze databases implement their locking schemes.

How Do Oracle and Blaze Implement Locks?

Locking is implemented in the database server. Different database servers have different ways of locking data.

Oracle uses a "snapshot" method of maintaining read data integrity. Oracle does not necessarily lock rows that have been read, but maintains a version of the data as it existed when it was read. Since there are no locks on data that has been read, another user or application could conceivably change data that has been read by an application. When a write operation, such as an INSERT, UPDATE, or DELETE, takes place, Oracle places an exclusive lock on the data row being written. The exclusive lock prevents other users from writing to the locked row, but other users can still read the row. A user also has the ability to prevent other users from writing data to data rows that have been read by using the syntax SELECT...FOR UPDATE. Other users will still be able to read this data, but no user will be allowed to change the data that has been written.

Since Blaze is exclusively a single-user database, you do not have to worry about other users changing the data in a Blaze database.

How Does Oracle Power Objects Handle Locking?

When you create an application using Oracle Power Objects, it will automatically handle locking data in the database server. Oracle Power Objects applications implement a locking strategy that makes sense for client/server applications.

Client/server applications tend to be read intensive. A read intensive application will read many more rows than it writes. In addition, client/server applications tend to have transactions that run a long time. An application will retrieve data for a user, and the user may spend some time reviewing the data before making any changes to the data. A long transaction with many pending write operations can cause a great deal of contention in a database if too many locks are held for the duration of the transaction.

Since most applications developed with Oracle Power Objects will tend to read more data than they write, Oracle Power Objects will acquire the least restrictive type of lock available when data is read. For an Oracle database, this means that the data will be read from the Oracle database and no locks will be placed on the database.

Oracle Power Objects designates two different types of locking schemes to handle writes to a database. *Optimistic* locking and *pessimistic* locking, as their names imply, make different assumptions about the possibility of simultaneous database writes taking place that could lead to a loss of data integrity. Oracle Power Objects' optimistic locking scheme places an exclusive lock on a data row just before changes to that row are being committed to the database, while its pessimistic locking strategy places an exclusive lock on a data row as soon as the user begins to change any data in the row.

Optimistic locking leaves data unlocked for a longer period of time, since it is optimistic about the chances that the data will not have been changed. Pessimistic locking is less sure that the data will not be changed, so it prevents the situation by placing a lock on data as soon as a user begins changing data.

In the current release of Oracle Power Objects, only pessimistic locking support is implemented.

Data Integrity in a Multiuser Database

In the previous section, you learned how Oracle Power Objects will implement locks on the data being used. Oracle Power Objects will not lock data when it is read, so there is still a possibility that data that has been read could have changed since it was read. If the data has been changed, and your application attempts to change it again, your changes could overwrite other changes to the data. In this section you will learn how to set up your Oracle Power Objects application to easily determine if data has been changed and how to write Oracle Basic routines to ensure that your application will not overwrite other users' database changes.

Detecting Client-Side Changes in Data

Oracle Power Objects gives you an easy way to determine if any data in a recordset has been changed and has not been committed to the database or rolled back. You can use the **IsWorkPending( )** method of a session. The syntax for the function is

```
[session].IsWorkPending()
```

The method will return True if there are pending changes to the data in any recordset for the session and False if there are not.

You can get the session identifier by using the **GetSession( )** function for a recordset. To find out if there is work pending for the current container, you would use the syntax

```
GetContainer().GetRecordset().GetSession().IsWorkPending()
```

The **GetContainer( )** function retrieves the container and the **GetRecordset( )** function returns the appropriate recordset to qualify the **GetSession( )** function.

The **IsWorkPending( )** method is useful if you want to discover whether there are any pending changes to the data in the session. The method can help you to make determinations that can affect the way your application operates. For instance, you may wish to check if there is any work pending in a session before you move to another connection to the same data. The **IsWorkPending( )** function applies to all data in a session, which may relate to several different recordsets.

The **IsWorkPending( )** method gives you a handy way to find out if there are uncommitted changes waiting in the session to be sent to the database. You may want to automatically commit the changes to the database whenever a user tries to move to a new record. When a user tries to navigate to a new record, the **GoNxtLine( )**, **GoPrvLine( )**, or **GoPos( )** methods are triggered, so you could add code to check for changes and automatically commit them. You could also add code to check for changes and prompt the user to see if he or she would like to commit the changes before moving on to the next row of data. As discussed in Chapter 8, committing or rolling back data may require additional interactions with the database. You should consider the implications of leaving uncommitted changes and the repercussions of committing changes carefully. Oracle Power Objects will automatically prevent a user from leaving any application while changes to the data are pending, so you do not have to worry about the user leaving the application without acting on any changed data.

CompareOnLock

When you are using an Oracle Power Objects application against an Oracle database, no locks are placed on data that has been read. Since no locks are placed on the data, other users may change the data between the time it is read and the time you are ready to update it. For instance, suppose that you are keeping track of how much of a particular item you have in inventory. Every time someone submits a purchase order, you subtract the amount of the item ordered from the amount remaining in inventory. If two people each read the amount left in inventory, and one person subtracts their order from the original total, and then the second person also subtracts their total from the original total, you will be left with an inaccurate inventory total. This lack of data integrity can have serious repercussions. How can you determine if a piece of data has been changed since you read it?

Oracle Power Objects gives you the ability to set the CompareOnLock property of every object that is bound to a data source. When the CompareOnLock property is set to 'True', Oracle Power Objects will automatically compare the value in the database column that is bound to an object whenever it attempts to acquire a lock on a database, which it does whenever a user tries to make changes to the data in a pessimistic locking scheme. If the data has been changed, Oracle Power Objects will let the application user know by popping up a message box. Oracle Power Objects will automatically compare any values in the recordset that are not associated with bound objects, such as columns used for linking and columns specified in the RecSrcAddCols property.

By default, the CompareOnLock property of a bound object is set to 'True'. Since protecting the integrity of your data is of primary importance, you should generally leave CompareOnLock set to 'True'—otherwise you will allow Oracle Power Objects to overwrite data updates that have occurred since you retrieved the data. An exception to this case might be very large objects that are changed infrequently, such as graphics. Oracle Power Objects has to retrieve data from the database to compare its current value with the value you retrieved, and for a large object the performance implications might outweigh the small possibility of overwriting someone else's changes.

Neither the **IsWorkPending( )** function nor the CompareOnLock property do anything to avoid the problems that may arise when the data in the server has been changed since it was initially read. Oracle Power Objects will prevent the data from being overwritten, but it will do nothing to correct the situation. The next section will give you some ways to correct any problems that may arise from a multiuser integrity conflict.

Preventing Lost Updates

Oracle Power Objects provides a powerful automatic feature that allows you to detect if the data you are about to modify has been changed since it was retrieved from the database. It is important to discover if the current value of the data differs from the value of the data initially retrieved, since writing new changes over other changes could result in a *lost update*. A lost update, as the name implies, is a change to a piece of data value that is overwritten by another change to the same piece of data. When updates are lost, the integrity of the data is compromised, and incorrect data will inevitably lead to incorrect conclusions based on the data.

If your application will be used in an environment where many people will be simultaneously updating the same data, the CompareOnLock feature of your Oracle Power Objects application will be very useful. Oracle Power Objects will automatically inform the user of an application if any of the data in the application whose CompareOnLock property is set to 'True' has changed since it has been retrieved. However, Oracle Power Objects does not give the user of the application a means to correct the difference between their retrieved data and the data currently in the database. The user could requery the database to get the new values; but if the user is looking at the 100th row of data in the results of a query, he or she will have to retrieve all 99 previous rows to get to the changed row. If your application will be deployed in an environment where there is a strong possibility that updates may be lost, or if you are very concerned about the integrity of your data, you can add logic to your application that can automatically detect any differences between the data you are about to update and the data in the database. If any differences are detected, the application logic will let the user decide whether to update the data in the application with the changed values from the database.

You will learn how to implement logic to detect and correct changed data in this section. The code you will write will accomplish several tasks. The code will

- Determine what data is bound to objects in your application container

- Retrieve the current value of the data from the database

- Determine if the current values of the data differ from the values in the container

- Prompt the user as to whether to update the data or not if changed values exist

- Prevent itself from executing when it is not necessary

You will also learn a lot more about working with recordsets in this section. The logic in this section will work with any bound container in any application. By using this logic, you can help to prevent lost data updates.

Where Should You Implement Your Logic?

Before you begin to implement the logic to detect updates, you will have to determine where you want the logic to reside.

Once your Oracle Power Objects application locks the data that will be updated, no other user can make changes in that data, since an exclusive lock on a data row or page will automatically prevent other users from writing to the locked page or row.

You will want to implement the data comparison logic as soon as a row in the database is locked. As mentioned earlier in this chapter, the current release of Oracle Power Objects only implements a pessimistic locking scheme. In a pessimistic locking scheme, your Oracle Power Objects application will lock a row as soon as you begin to make a change in the value of an object that is bound to a column in the row. After the Oracle Power Objects application acquires a lock, the application will continue through the normal processing routines.

Whenever the value of an object is changed, either by user intervention or programmatically, Oracle Power Objects will execute the **PreChange( )** method of the object. Every bound container has a method called the **ChildPreChange( )** method. This method is fired whenever a **PreChange( )** method is executed for any of the child objects for the container. If you put your logic in the **ChildPreChange( )** method, the method will be executed as soon as a user tries to change the value of any bound container in the application.

The Oracle database offers a *read-consistent* locking model. A read-consistent locking model will always be able to read a row from the database. If the row has an exclusive lock applied to it by another user who is in the process of changing the row, Oracle will return the data for the row prior to the changes. If you are using Oracle as a back-end, your Oracle Power Objects application will always be able to read a row. Unless someone else is actively changing a row, your application will be able to acquire a lock on the row. You will not be able to tell if the data in the row has been changed in the **ChildPreChange( )** method, so the logic you will place in that method will always execute.

Determining the Bound Columns

Your first task is to discover what columns in the database are bound to objects in your application.

As mentioned earlier in this chapter, Oracle Power Objects stores the data returned from the database in a recordset. There is a column in the recordset for each column in the database that is a DataSource for a bound container in the application, as well as a column in the recordset for any calculated values and for any additional columns specified in the RecSrcAddCols property of the bound container.

You can use recordset manipulation functions to determine the columns that are in the recordset for a bound container.

■ Open the frmOrders form in your ORDERS application. Open the **ChildPreChange( )** method for the form. Add the following code to the **ChildPreChange( )** method:

```
DIM vExRecSet As Object
DIM vCount As Integer
DIM vPointer As Integer
DIM vName As String
DIM vColumns As String
```

You will need each of these variables in your method. The first variable is the object variable *vExRecSet*. Since you will be referencing the recordset repeatedly throughout your method logic, you should declare a variable to hold the handle of the recordset so you will not have to use function calls to identify the recordset each time you reference it.

■ Add the underlined code to the code in the **ChildPreChange( )** method of the frmOrders form:

```
DIM vExRecSet As Object
DIM vCount As Integer
DIM vPointer As Integer
DIM vName As String
DIM vColumns As String
vExRecSet = Self.GetRecordSet()
```

You will be able to use the object variable *vExRecSet* in the rest of the method to reference the recordset for the frmOrders form. Since you are executing this code from the frmOrders form, you can use the **Self** keyword to represent the bound container.

■ Add the underlined code to the code in the **ChildPreChange( )** method of the frmOrders form:

```
DIM vExRecSet As Object
DIM vCount As Integer
DIM vPointer As Integer
DIM vName As String
DIM vColumns As String
vExRecSet = Self.GetRecordSet()
vCount = vExRecSet.GetColCount()
```

The **GetColCount( )** function will return the number of columns in a recordset. Now that you have the number of columns in the recordset, you can build a string that will contain the names of each of the columns in the database that are included in the recordset.

■ Add the underlined code to the code in the **ChildPreChange( )** method of the frmOrders form:

```
DIM vExRecSet As Object
DIM vCount As Integer
DIM vPointer As Integer
DIM vName As String
DIM vColumns As String
vExRecSet = Self.GetRecordSet()
vCount = vExRecSet.GetColCount()
vPointer = 1
DO WHILE vPointer <= vCount
    vName = vExRecSet.GetColName(vPointer)
    IF NOT ISNULL(vName) THEN vColumns = &
        vColumns & vName & ","
    vPointer = vPointer + 1
LOOP
```

The additional code is a **DO** loop that will cycle through the columns in the recordset. The **GetColName( )** function will return the name of the bound column for a column in the recordset for the column whose column position number matches the parameter of the function. As the **DO** loop cycles through the columns in the recordset, the name of the bound column is added to the *vColumns* string. A comma is also added to the *vColumns* string each time another column name is added to the string, since the list of columns that is being created in *vColumns* will be used in the next section as part of an SQL statement, where column names must be separated by commas.

The recordset contains the names of all of the columns in the database that are linked to objects in the bound container or that are specified in the RecSrcAddCols property of the bound container. The recordset also contains columns for any derived or calculated information, such as the total cost of an order line item in the repeater container. The **GetColName( )** function will return a null value for any derived columns in the recordset, so you can use the **IF NOT ISNULL( )** construct to eliminate the names of any derived columns in the recordset.

TIP
The logic described above will get the names of all of the columns in the database that are bound to objects in the container or that are specified in the RecSrcAddCols, whether they have the CompareOnLock property set to 'True' or not. The CompareOnLock property cannot be read at run time, so you cannot determine the setting for the property in your application logic. Remember that this logic will execute whether the user gets a message that the values

have been changed or not. Also remember that it is good practice for the user to know if any data has been changed in the database, so it is not such a big problem to retrieve the values for columns even if they have their CompareOnLock property is set to 'False'. The one time that comparing all the columns in a recordset could lead to unnecessary overhead is if you are retrieving bitmaps or other long columns from the database unnecessarily. You could add additional conditions to your **IF NOT ISNULL( )** construct to eliminate these columns from being included in the *vColumns* list.

Now that you have a listing of all the database columns in the master recordset of frmOrders, you can retrieve the current values for the columns in the matching row of the database.

Retrieving Current Values

You can use the list of all of the columns in your recordset to retrieve the current values for those columns for your current data row.

- Add the underlined code to the code in the **ChildPreChange( )** method for the frmOrders form:

```
DIM vExRecSet As Object
DIM vCount As Integer
DIM vPointer As Integer
DIM vName As String
DIM vColumns As String
DIM vTempRecSet As Object
vExRecSet = Self.GetRecordSet()
vCount = vExRecSet.GetColCount()
vPointer = 1
DO WHILE vPointer <= vCount
    vName = vExRecSet.GetColName(vPointer)
        IF NOT ISNULL(vName) THEN vColumns = &
            vColumns & vName & ","
        vPointer = vPointer + 1
LOOP
vTempRecSet= NEW DBRECORDSET(vExRecSet.GetSession())
```

You will need to store the retrieved values for the columns of the recordset for frmOrders. Oracle Power Objects uses a recordset to store retrieved values. You can create a recordset in your Oracle Basic code. You must define an object variable to hold the object handle of the recordset. You create a new bound recordset by using the **NEW DBRECORDSET( )** function. You must specify a session for a new bound recordset, which you can identify with the **GetSession( )** function for the *vExRecSet* recordset.

■ Add the underlined code to the code in the **ChildPreChange( )** method for the frmOrders form:

```
DIM vExRecSet As Object
DIM vCount As Integer
DIM vPointer As Integer
DIM vName As String
DIM vColumns As String
DIM vTempRecSet As Object
vExRecSet = Self.GetRecordSet()
vCount = vExRecSet.GetColCount()
vPointer = 1
DO WHILE vPointer <= vCount
    vName = vExRecSet.GetColName(vPointer)
        IF NOT ISNULL(vName) THEN vColumns = &
            vColumns & vName & ","
        vPointer = vPointer + 1
LOOP
vTempRecSet= NEW DBRECORDSET
(vExRecSet.GetSession())
vColumns = "SELECT " & LEFT(vColumns, &
    LEN(vColumns) - 1) & &
    " FROM " & Self.RecordSource & " WHERE ID = " & ID.Value
```

With this line of Oracle Basic code, you are creating an SQL statement that can be used to retrieve the current values for all of the bound columns of the recordset for the frmOrders form. The SELECT keyword indicates that the values for the columns listed are to be retrieved from the database. The **LEFT( )** function will delete the last comma from the *vColumns* string. The Self.RecordSource property identifies the table that is the source of the columns. For the ORDERS table, the ID column is the unique key. You use the value for the unique key to retrieve only the row in the database that matches your current row.

TIP
Both Oracle and Blaze database use a ROWID column. The ROWID column is a unique identifier for every row in the database. The ROWID column is always retrieved as part of a recordset when the database is either Oracle or Blaze. The **GetColVal( )** function returns

the column value in the recordset, and can take either the name of the column or the number of the column as a parameter. If you are only using Oracle or Blaze, you could make the WHERE clause of your SQL statement "WHERE ROWID = " & GetColVal("ROWID") for every bound container.

You have created an SQL statement to retrieve the appropriate data into the recordset you have created. Your next step is to execute the SQL statement.

■   Add the underlined code to the code in the **ChildPreChange( )** method for the frmOrders form:

```
DIM vExRecSet As Object
DIM vCount As Integer
DIM vPointer As Integer
DIM vName As String
DIM vColumns As String
DIM vTempRecSet As Object
vExRecSet = Self.GetRecordSet()
vCount = vExRecSet.GetColCount()
vPointer = 1
DO WHILE vPointer <= vCount
    vName = vExRecSet.GetColName(vPointer)
        IF NOT ISNULL(vName) THEN vColumns = &
                vColumns & vName & ","
        vPointer = vPointer + 1
LOOP
vTempRecSet= NEW DBRECORDSET(vExRecSet.GetSession())
vColumns = "SELECT " & LEFT(vColumns, &
    LEN(vColumns) - 1) & &
    " FROM " & Self.RecordSource & " WHERE ID = " & ID.Value
vTempRecSet.SetQuery(vColumns,FALSE)
vTempRecSet.Requery()
```

The **SetQuery( )** function sets an SQL statement to a recordset. The first parameter for the function is the SQL query and the second parameter of the function is a Boolean value that indicates whether the recordset is updateable. Since you will only be using the values in the recordset for comparison, there is no need to make the recordset updateable.

The **Requery( )** function, as the name implies, re-executes a query for a recordset. Once you have executed this function, the data for all the columns in the recordset for the frmOrders bound container will be retrieved into the *vTempRecSet* recordset. The **Requery( )** function will automatically create columns in the recordset for each column specified in the SELECT statement associated with the recordset.

You are now ready to start comparing the values currently in the database with the values in the recordset for the frmOrders form. Before you add code to compare the values, you should make sure that you will get rid of your temporary recordset when you have completed your comparison.

■ Add the underlined code to the code in the **ChildPreChange( )** method for the frmOrders form:

```
DIM vExRecSet As Object
DIM vCount As Integer
DIM vPointer As Integer
DIM vName As String
DIM vColumns As String
DIM vTempRecSet As Object
vExRecSet = Self.GetRecordSet()
vCount = vExRecSet.GetColCount()
vPointer = 1
DO WHILE vPointer <= vCount
    vName = vExRecSet.GetColName(vPointer)
        IF NOT ISNULL(vName) THEN vColumns = &
                vColumns & vName & ","
        vPointer = vPointer + 1
LOOP
vTempRecSet= NEW DBRECORDSET(vExRecSet.GetSession())
vColumns = "SELECT " & LEFT(vColumns, &
        LEN(vColumns) - 1) & &
    " FROM " & Self.RecordSource & " WHERE ID = " & ID.Value
vTempRecSet.SetQuery(vColumns,FALSE)
vTempRecSet.Requery()
DELETE vTempRecSet
```

The **DELETE** command deletes the *vTempRecSet* from your Oracle Power Objects application. Once you have completed comparing the values in the *vTempRecSet* recordset with the values in the recordset for the frmOrders form, you will not need the temporary recordset any more. You will be adding additional code between the **Requery( )** function and the **DELETE** command in the rest of this section, but it is always good practice to remember to add your cleanup code as soon as appropriate, so you do not forget it later.

Comparing Current Values and Bound Data

You have now retrieved all of the current values for the columns in the recordset for the frmOrders container. Your next step is to compare the new values in the *vTempRecSet* with the values in the recordset for the container.

■ Add the underlined code to the code in the **ChildPreChange( )** method for the frmOrders form:

```
DIM vExRecSet As Object
DIM vCount As Integer
DIM vPointer As Integer
DIM vNewPointer As Integer
DIM vName As String
DIM vColumns As String
DIM vTempRecSet As Object
vExRecSet = Self.GetRecordSet()
vCount = vExRecSet.GetColCount()
vPointer = 1
DO WHILE vPointer <= vCount
    vName = vExRecSet.GetColName(vPointer)
        IF NOT ISNULL(vName) THEN vColumns = &
                vColumns & vName & ","
        vPointer = vPointer + 1
LOOP
vTempRecSet= NEW DBRECORDSET(vExRecSet.GetSession())
vColumns = "SELECT " & LEFT(vColumns, &
    LEN(vColumns) - 1) & &
    " FROM " & Self.RecordSource & " WHERE ID = " & ID.Value
vTempRecSet.SetQuery(vColumns,FALSE)
vTempRecSet.Requery()
vPointer = 1
vNewPointer = 1
vcount = vtempRecSet.GetColCount
DO WHILE vNewPointer <= vCount
    IF vExRecSet.GetColVal(vPointer) <> &
        vTempRecSet.GetColVal(vNewPointer) THEN
    vExRecSet.SetColVal(vTempRecSet.GetColVal(vNewPointer),
& vPointer)

END IF
vPointer = vPointer + 1
```

```
vNewPointer = vPointer + 1
LOOP
DELETE vTempRecSet
```

In the new code, you have created a pointer to move through the columns in the *vTempRecSet* recordset. After initializing the pointers for both the *vExRecSet* and the *vTempRecSet* recordsets, you begin a **DO WHILE** loop that will walk through the columns in the two recordsets and compare the values for each of the columns with the **GetColVal( )** function, which returns the value of a column in a recordset. You do have to reinitialize the *vCount* variable to the number of columns in the *vTempRecSet* recordset to use for comparison, since it will contain fewer columns than the *vExRecSet* recordset. Using the existing value of *vCount* could lead to run time errors when the code attempted to retrieve a non-existent column name from *vTempRecSet*.

If the value in the new *vTempRecSet* is different from the value in the existing *vExRecSet*, your code will automatically update the value in the existing recordset.

There is one problem with the implementation shown above. As you will recall, when you retrieved the column names from the existing recordset, you did not include any columns in the existing recordset that contained derived values, since you did not need to retrieve them from the database. Because of this, the number of a column in the existing recordset may be greater than the number of the column in the new recordset. To account for this potential difference, you can add another **DO** loop inside of the existing **DO** loop.

■ Add the underlined code to the code in the **ChildPreChange( )** method of the frmOrders form:

```
DIM vExRecSet As Object
DIM vCount As Integer
DIM vPointer As Integer
DIM vNewPointer As Integer
DIM vName As String
DIM vColumns As String
DIM vTempRecSet As Object
vExRecSet = Self.GetRecordSet()
vCount = vExRecSet.GetColCount()
vPointer = 1
DO WHILE vPointer <= vCount
    vName = vExRecSet.GetColName(vPointer)
        IF NOT ISNULL(vName) THEN vColumns = &
                vColumns & vName & ","
        vPointer = vPointer + 1
LOOP
```

```
vTempRecSet= NEW DBRECORDSET(vExRecSet.GetSession())
vColumns = "SELECT " & LEFT(vColumns,
     LEN(vColumns) - 1) & &
    " FROM " & Self.RecordSource & " WHERE ID = " & ID.Value
vTempRecSet.SetQuery(vColumns,FALSE)
vTempRecSet.Requery()
vPointer = 1
vNewPointer = 1
vCount = vTempRecSet.GetColVal
DO WHILE vNewPointer <= vCount
    DO WHILE vExRecSet.GetColName(vPointer) <>  &
        vTempRecSet.GetColName(vNewPointer)
            vPointer = vPointer + 1
    LOOP
    IF vExRecSet.GetColVal(vPointer) <> &
        vTempRecSet.GetColVal(vNewPointer)THEN
        vExRecSet.SetColVal(vTempRecSet.GetColVal(vNewPointer), &
                vPointer)
    END IF
vPointer = vPointer + 1
vNewPointer = vPointer + 1
LOOP
DELETE vTempRecSet
```

Since you got the original list of columns from the existing recordset, the columns will always be in the same order in the temporary recordset, but there may be some derived columns in the existing recordset that are not in the temporary recordset. The internal **DO** loop will only execute if the name of the column in the existing recordset does not match the name of the column in the new recordset. If this condition occurs, the **DO** loop will continue to step through the columns in the existing recordset until a match occurs.

Your code now automatically updates the values in the recordset for the frmOrders bound container if the values in the recordset are not the same as the values just fetched from the database. You could leave your logic as is, but your users might get confused if they see values in their screens automatically changing when they try to change any value on the screen. To avoid this confusion, you might want to give the user some feedback about the changes in the data values.

Prompting User for Updating Values

You can keep your users from becoming confused by informing them of changed values with a message box. The message box could not only inform the user that the data for a particular column has been changed, but also inquire whether the user wants to update the value or not.

■ Add the underlined code to the code in the **ChildPreChange( )** method for the frmOrders form:

```
DIM vExRecSet As Object
DIM vCount As Integer
DIM vPointer As Integer
DIM vNewPointer As Integer
DIM vName As String
DIM vColumns As String
DIM vTempRecSet As Object
vExRecSet = Self.GetRecordSet()
vCount = vExRecSet.GetColCount()
vPointer = 1
DO WHILE vPointer <= vCount
    vName = vExRecSet.GetColName(vPointer)
    IF NOT ISNULL(vName) THEN vColumns = vColumns & vName & ","
    vPointer = vPointer + 1
LOOP
vTempRecSet= NEW DBRECORDSET(vExRecSet.GetSession())
vColumns = "SELECT " & LEFT(vColumns, LEN(vColumns) - 1) & &
    " FROM " & Self.RecordSource & " WHERE ID = " & ID.Value
vTempRecSet.SetQuery(vColumns,FALSE)
vTempRecSet.Requery()
vPointer = 1
vNewPointer = 1
vCount = vTempRecSet.GetColCount()
DO WHILE vNewPointer <= vCount
    DO WHILE vExRecSet.GetColName(vPointer) <>  &
        vTempRecSet.GetColName(vNewPointer)
            vPointer = vPointer + 1
    LOOP
    IF vExRecSet.GetColVal(vPointer) <> & &
        vTempRecSet.GetColVal(vNewPointer)
THEN
            IF MSGBOX("The value for the " & &
        vExRecSet.GetColName(vPointer) & " has changed from " & &
        vExRecSet.GetColVal(vPointer) &" to " & &
        vTempRecSet.GetColVal(vNewPointer) & &
```

```
". Would you like to update the value?", 4 + 96, &
" Updated Values Exist") = 6 THEN &
vExRecSet.SetColVal(vTempRecSet.GetColVal(vNewPointer), &
            vPointer)
    END IF
vPointer = vPointer + 1
vNewPointer = vPointer + 1
LOOP
DELETE vTempRecSet
```

If there is a difference between the retrieved value for a column and the value for the column on the screen, the application will bring up a message box identifying the name of the database column that has changed (which was retrieved with the **GetColName( )** function), the previous value for the column (which comes from the existing recordset and is retrieved with the **GetColVal( )** function), and the new value (which comes from the temporary recordset and is retrieved with the **GetColVal( )** function). The message box contains a Yes and a No push button, which gives the user the opportunity to accept the changes or not, and a question mark icon. If the user clicks on the Yes push button, the **MSGBOX( )** function returns the number 6 and the value of the data is updated.

When the message box appears to inform the user that the data in their form has been changed since they retrieved the form, your application should look like this:

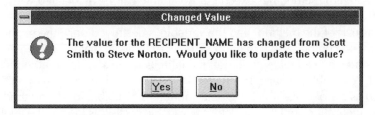

It is always a good idea to keep the users of your applications informed about changes to their data. There may be times where a changed data value is unexpected, and a user would want to refrain from updating the value of the data in his or her form. There are some significant implications if a user chooses not to update data. You might want to prevent users from having the opportunity to refuse to update data if you feel your user community might mistakenly choose this option. You might want to bring up another message box to inform users of the danger of not updating their data.

You may think that popping a message box every time there is a conflict between data in the database and data about to be changed in the form would be a hindrance to your users. In most client/server applications, there is much more data reading than writing, and the possibility of there being different data on the server will be an anomaly. If you wanted to further customize your application, you could allow your more experienced users to select an option that would set a property in your application that would disable a message box informing them of changed data. You could check the property in the application before bringing up the message box. By allowing a user to turn off information, you are still safeguarding your data by making the message box the default action while giving your user the opportunity to prevent it from occurring.

The **ChildPreChange( )** method is fired every time a child object in a form changes. Since you will be locking the data in the database as soon as the user tries to change a single value in the bound container, you should prevent the **ChildPreChange( )** logic from executing if it has already executed when the first object was changed. The next section will add this to your **ChildPreChange( )** method logic.

Preventing Your Logic from Executing Twice

Once your Oracle Power Objects application has locked the data that is to be changed, there is no need to execute the logic in the **ChildPreChange( )** method again, since no other user can modify data once it is locked.

You will not be able to use a variable to indicate that the logic in the **ChildPreChange( )** method has executed. A variable can be associated with a method. The variable is created when the appropriate Oracle Basic code is executed as part of the method, and the variable is destroyed once the method completes. You couldn't use a method variable to indicate that the method had executed, since the variable would not maintain its value after the method had completed. A variable can also be created in the Declarations section of an application as a *global* variable. A *global* variable is available to any method in any form in the application, and the value for the variable persists as long as the application is running. You could declare a *global* variable for each bound container that will use this logic, but this might become a little confusing. Since a *global* variable can be accessed from anywhere in the application without the need to qualify the variable name, it becomes harder to debug any code that uses the variable.

The optimal solution for an indicator that the logic in the **ChildPreChange( )** method has executed once would be to create a property that would indicate whether the logic had been executed once for the current changes and to reset the property when the changes are committed or rolled back.

■ Open the User Properties window by clicking on the User Properties push button in the toolbar of the Properties sheet for the frmOrders form. Scroll to the bottom of the User Properties table and add a new property with a

Name of 'udpChangesChecked', a Type of 'Property', and a DataType of 'Integer'. Drag the property from the User Properties window to the Properties sheet for the frmOrders form to add the property to the form.

You will set the value of the udpChangesChecked property to indicate that the current row in the database has been successfully checked for changed data.

■ Add the underlined lines of code to the code in the **ChildPreChange( )** method of the frmOrders form:

```
DIM vExRecSet As Object
DIM vCount As Integer
DIM vPointer As Integer
DIM vNewPointer As Integer
DIM vName As String
DIM vColumns As String
DIM vTempRecSet As Object
IF udpChangesChecked <> 1 THEN
vExRecSet = Self.GetRecordSet()
vCount = vExRecSet.GetColCount()
vPointer = 1
DO WHILE vPointer <= vCount
    vName = vExRecSet.GetColName(vPointer)
    IF NOT ISNULL(vName) THEN vColumns = vColumns & vName & ","
    vPointer = vPointer + 1
LOOP
vTempRecSet= NEW DBRECORDSET(vExRecSet.GetSession())
vColumns = "select " & LEFT(vColumns, LEN(vColumns) - 1) & &
    " from " & Self.RecordSource & " where ID = " & ID.Value
vTempRecSet.SetQuery(vColumns,FALSE)
vTempRecSet.Requery()
vPointer = 1
vNewPointer = 1
DO WHILE vPointer <= vCount
    DO WHILE vExRecSet.GetColName(vPointer) <>  &
        vTempRecSet.GetColName(vNewPointer)
            vPointer = vPointer + 1
    LOOP
    IF vExRecSet.GetColVal(vPointer) <> &
        vTempRecSet.GetColVal(vNewPointer) THEN
            IF MSGBOX("The value for the " & &
                vExRecSet.GetColName(vPointer) & " has changed from " & &
```

```
                    vExRecSet.GetColVal(vPointer) & " to " & &
                    vTempRecSet.GetColVal(vNewPointer) & &
                    ".  Would you like to update the value?", 4 + 96, &
                    "Updated Values Exist") = 6 THEN &
                    vExRecSet.SetColVal(vPointer), &
                    (vTempRecSet.GetColVal(vNewPointer)
        END IF
vPointer = vPointer + 1
vNewPointer = vPointer + 1
LOOP
DELETE vTempRecSet
udpChangesChecked = 1
END IF
```

You do not have to qualify the updChangesChecked property name since it is associated with the frmOrders form that the **ChildPreChange( )** method also belongs to.

As a final step, you will have to change the setting of the updChangesChecked property whenever the user commits or rolls back the changes to the database.

■ Add the following line of code to the **CommitForm( )** method of the frmOrders form:

```
updChangesChecked = 0
```

■ Add the following line of code to the **RollbackForm( )** method of the frmOrders form:

```
updChangesChecked = 0
```

When the user of your application commits the changes to the database or rolls back the changes, the lock on the data in the database will be released and the line of code will change the setting of the updChangesChecked property to indicate that the next time the **ChildPreChange( )** method code is called your logic should execute.

You have implemented logic in your application that will go a long way toward maintaining the integrity of your data. If there are no differences between the data in your application's bound containers and the data in the database, the method you have created will not have very much impact on the performance of your application, other than retrieving a single row of data from the database, since all of the other operations are taking place in memory. If you are working with Oracle or Blaze, even the retrieval of data will be highly optimized, since the ROWID is a unique identifier.

Client/Server Data Integrity

At this point, you may be wondering why it seems you had to do more coding to protect the data from being overwritten than you did to create the rest of the application. Why not just hope for the best?

First of all, protecting the integrity of data is not optional. The entire purpose of application systems is to gather and manipulate data. The data is then used for some meaningful purpose—to control the flow of business, to make strategic decisions, or to handle the logistics of a business or a person. If you cannot be sure that the data is correct, you cannot be sure that any actions that are taken based on that data are correct. A lack of data integrity undermines every application that uses the data.

Second, remember that the data you are using may also be used by others and by other applications. Your application may ensure that no one user will compromise the integrity of any other user of the same application. But other applications use the data, and new applications may be created in the future that will use the data in still other ways. Even if your organization proposes firm standards to control the use of data, there is still a chance that some applications may not use these standards, either through ignorance or neglect. To compound these errors with a loss of data integrity would jeopardize much more than a simple programming error.

Finally, you need to go to some lengths to protect the integrity of your data because client/server application systems use data in different ways than traditional systems. Client/server systems have a different topology, where the major performance bottleneck is data transmission from the database server to the client application. This topology, along with the fact that a client-driven application may request unpredictable amounts of data, suggests that retrieving data as it is needed is the most appropriate strategy for good throughput and performance. If you spread a transaction out over time as users gradually request data, you must not leave any locks on the data being retrieved from the database server to avoid contention problems. And as soon as you leave data unlocked on the server, any other user can, and may, change the data, which means that an application needs to check server data for changes before writing new data.

You must try to find the appropriate balance between the often-conflicting goals of data integrity and the needs of your users. The users of your application only see one type of data—their data. They do not understand the need to protect the reliability and integrity of data that may be used by many different users and applications. At the same time, one of the most valuable resources of any organization is their data. If an organization's data is compromised, the value of that data is also compromised. Organizations look to the data for guidance in making important decisions that will affect their financial health. If the data is not correct, the decision will very likely be incorrect also.

The best solution is to handle data integrity issues with care. A little bit of coding will allow your application to be more responsive to your users, which is one of the key factors in user satisfaction, while still maintaining the integrity of the data. Users may not understand the difficulty of protecting data integrity, but they will definitely not be tolerant if they find out their data is suspect. This is fortunate for you, since your understanding of these complex issues is what makes you a data-processing professional and keeps you gainfully employed. As they say about baseball, if it were really that easy, everyone would be in the big leagues!

CHAPTER 10

Reporting

In the preceding chapters of this book you have learned many different techniques for creating forms. These included creating forms to add, delete, and update records to tables; sorting records for viewing in a form; validating data in the fields on a form; and creating classes to utilize the object-oriented aspect of Oracle Power Objects. All these techniques can be applied to reports in Oracle Power Objects.

All these activities usually culminate with the generation of reports. Whether it is a sales report for the chief financial officer, an invoice mailed to a customer, a bill of lading used by a dock worker, or a simple mailing list, reports form the lifeblood of an application. Consequently, any front-end tool geared toward corporate use must have an industrial-strength reporting facility. Oracle Power Objects provides such a facility. In Oracle Power Objects, reports are very similar to forms in the sense that they are bindable containers that let you preview and print data queried from the back-end database. Many of the techniques that you have learned to use in designing forms apply to reports as well.

What Is Ahead

In this chapter you will learn the following:

- Common characteristics of forms and reports
- Differences between forms and reports
- Basic reporting concepts
- Aggregate functions in reports
- Using charts in reports
- Creating multicolumn reports using forms
- Creating dynamic reporting menus

Common Characteristics of Forms and Reports

Forms and reports share many characteristics. The process of laying out reports is the same as the process of laying out forms. This allows the user a unified way of creating forms and reports. A report container can be bound to the underlying data with the same drag-and-drop simplicity that you have learned in the preceding chapters. Reports are built on top of tables and views, just the way it is done for forms.

Differences Between Forms and Reports

There are several differences between forms and reports. The major difference is that forms are interactive, and as such are designed to provide immediate feedback on whatever operation the user is performing. They are also used to modify underlying data. Reports, on the other hand, are not interactive. They need to be self-contained and must be designed to grab the user's attention immediately. You would not get a second chance with a report. Furthermore, reports cannot be used to modify underlying data. Reports are for printing only. They are designed to fit the appropriate size of the paper being used. So it is important that the tool provide an easy way to lay out the paper's dimensions and preview the report to see how it will look like when printed. Although forms and reports are divided into specific areas like header, detail, and footer, reports have the Group by areas, which allow for creating several levels of aggregations. In the preceding chapters you have learned how to create a master-detail form. Reports use a different technique for accomplishing the same task.

Last, reports by nature are not interactive. Because of this, some of the controls that are specifically designed to interact with the user to gather information work differently on a report. For instance, a button will be a mere graphic to illustrate a point, since you really can't push a button on a piece of paper.

Basic Reporting Concepts

Reports in Oracle Power Objects are divided into several functionally distinct areas, shown in Figure 10-1.

Each of these function areas perform a different function within the report. Each of these areas are container objects. Other application objects are placed in these container objects to produce a report. These areas are described below.

ReportHeader

This area contains report-wide information (for example, the company logo). Exactly one report header is printed for each report. It appears at the top of the report's first page.

FIGURE 10-1.   *Report function areas*

PageHeader

The page header is printed at the top of each page. It contains all the information required at the beginning of each page. Sometimes the information is duplicated from the report header. In such instances, Oracle Power Objects gives you the option of turning off the page header printing on the first page.

GroupHeader

The group header is printed at the beginning of each group. This area may contain Text Fields and Static Text to clarify the use of this group. For example, if the grouping is by customer, the customer name may appear in the group header. This will have the effect of printing the customer name and all the detail records that go with the customer underneath the group header as part of the detail. A new group header is printed whenever a new value is seen in the column specified by the GroupCol property of the group header. There can be several group headers in a report.

Detail

The Detail area defines the body of the report. This area would contain Text Fields and other objects to display the information queried from the database. Any objects appearing in this area are repeated once for each record queried from the database.

GroupFooter

The GroupFooter area contains all the information needed at the end of a group. For example, a group total Text Field can be placed in this area.

PageFooter

The PageFooter area contains all the information needed at the end of a page. For example, a Text Field to display the page number can be placed in this area. This is printed at the end of each page. Again, this may have the same information as the report footer. In such a case, Oracle Power Objects gives you the option of not printing the page footer on the last page.

ReportFooter

The ReportFooter area contains all the information needed at the end of a report. For example, a grand total Text Field can be placed in this area. The report footer appears at the bottom of the last page of the report.

Most of the information in a report appears in the Detail area. The rest of the objects are used to format and group the detail information into customer-friendly reports. The GroupHeader and the GroupFooter are extensions of a report group, which is described later in this chapter.

Types of Reports

Oracle Power Objects has a powerful report writer that can be used to generate a wealth of reports. One of the most common types of reports needed is a record-per-page report. In this type of a report, information from the data table is formatted and printed as one record per page. An example would be an Order report, where information such as who placed the order, the order date, the name, and the address is printed.

Tabular reports are used to show a lot of information on a single page. For instance, the above report can be used as a tabular report to show a few salient pieces of order information for each order instead of all the information about an order. This way, you can show multiple orders per page. This is similar to table view.

Group Totals and Grand Totals reports are usually the most common types of reports found in applications. You typically total at a subgroup level (e.g., Order level), then compute a grand total (e.g., across all orders). These reports also involve master-detail records most of the time. For example, you may want to see all the order items in an order placed by a customer. You may also want to see the value of the orders placed by each customer, as well as the value of all the orders placed by all customers.

Another common type of report is a multicolumn report. A typical example of this type of report is the mailing list. A report writer needs to be flexible to be able to create this type of report, since it requires precise spacing to be able to print on label forms.

Due the nature of relational databases, most of the time the data required by a report is distributed over several tables. If data from several tables are to be combined, then you need to perform relational calculus (Selection, Join, Union, etc.) on the data to give the user the view of the data he or she needs. This is accomplished by creating views. A report writer must be able to use a view to query the data needed to generate a report.

In this chapter, you will build the following reports:

- Order Information report
- Order and Order Item report
- Order Total and Grand Total report
- Mailing list from the Customer table

To create these reports, you will use the order entry database used by the application built in the preceding chapters with Oracle Power Objects.

Order Information Report

This is a simple report that prints the information in an order. You will use the ORDERS table as the record source for this report. Two of the functional areas mentioned previously, Page Header and Detail, are used in this report. The Page Header will display a logo, which is placed at the top of each page. The Detail area will contain relevant information from the ORDERS table.

Order and Order Item Report

This is a master-detail report where the Group Header area will show the master records (ORDERS) and the Detail area will show the detail records (ORDER_ITEMS). The ORDER_ID and ORDERDATE are shown in the Group Header. Data from the ORDER_ITEMS record are shown in the Detail area.

Order Total and Grand Total Report

In this report, you will add group and grand totals for the report. You will compute Order Total for each group, and Grand Total for the whole report.

Customer Mailing List

In this report you will use the form designer to generate a customer mailing list.

Creating a New Report

A new report is created from the Application window by clicking on the New Report button or by selecting New Report menu item from the File menu. When a report is first created, Oracle Power Objects gives it a default name such as Report1. You can change this name by setting the Name property. You can also set the title for the report through the Label property. The title will appear on the Title bar of the report. Note that this title will not be printed.

Binding the Report to a Record Source

To report on the data in a database table or a view, the report must be bound to a record source. There are three ways to accomplish this. These techniques are the same that are used to bind a form to a record source.

1. Select the table or view required from the Session window. This will be used as the record source for the report. Drag and drop this icon onto the Detail area of the report. Text Fields bound to the columns in the table or view appear in the Detail area.

2. Open the Table or View Editor window. To select the columns required, SHIFT-click on individual columns, or drag the mouse on the left hand side of the editor window to select consecutive columns. Drag and drop these selected columns onto the detail area of the report. Text Fields bound to the selected columns appear in the Detail area.

3. Set the RecSrcSession property of the report to the session you will be working with to generate the report. If the DefaultSession property of the application is set, then the report will use that session as a default session. Otherwise, this property must be set. Bind the report by setting the name of a table or view in the RecordSource property. Later, Oracle Power Objects objects can be added and individually bound to the columns in the table or view.

Resizing Functional Areas

The functional areas of a report can be resized to fit the objects that are placed in them. This allows you to achieve the required look and feel for a report. Each of the functional areas can be adjusted in height individually, but their width cannot be adjusted individually. However, you can change the width of the report.

Resizing a Functional Area

There are two ways to resize the functional area of a report. They are clicking and dragging, or setting values in the Properties sheet.

Clicking and Dragging

When you click on the title of the area you want to resize, a horizontal line will appear through it. Holding the mouse down, you can drag this line up and down to adjust the height of the area. Note that a report area need not have any height at all. This means that you will not be using that area in this report. For example, you may decide that there is no need for the Report Header in your report. In such a case, you will make that area's height zero.

You can adjust the width of the report by clicking with the mouse on the double line border of the Report window and dragging it to the desired size. Notice that this will change the width of the entire report.

Setting Values in Properties Sheet

The same resizing can be accomplished in a more precise manner by setting the 'Size X' and 'Size Y' values for each of the functional areas. Again notice that setting the width ('Size X') for any of the areas changes the width of the entire report.

Adding Objects to a Report

Objects are added to a report in the same way they are added to a form. Since reports are not interactive, most of the Oracle Power Objects objects have limited use in a report. The objects are display only, thus serving as graphics to highlight a point. For example, a list box can be used to show a list of items, but you could not select any items from that list box.

Binding Objects to Data

Once the objects are added to the report, there are three ways to populate them. These are described here:

1. Bind the control to a column in a table, as explained previously.

2. Use a derived value as the 'DataSource'. This is also known as a calculated field and is usually an expression based on other fields in the report. For example, an aggregate function that computes a total.

3. Use the **SQLLOOKUP( )** function as the DataSource of a control. This function could look up data from tables other than the table or view that is being used as the RecordSource for the report. For example, you may want to look up the customer name to place in the Order report. This may be necessary because only the customer ID is carried in the ORDERS table. So, you would need to look up the name from the CUSTOMERS table.

Organizing Data in a Report

You can organize information in a report using the various functional areas. For example, you could place the company logo in the Report Header area so that it is printed once per page. A report title would go in the page header area for it to appear on the top of every page. Page numbers would go in the Page Footer area. An aggregate grand total would go in the Report Footer area. You would also use normal GUI design principles to make the report attractive by the judicious use of these functional areas.

There is one area we have not talked about yet. This is the Detail area. This is where the bulk of the report utility comes from. Think of the rest of the areas as icing while the Detail area is the cake. How would you make a cake more tasty? By layering it. You would add several layers to the cake to appeal to different tastes. In the same way, you would layer the Detail area to highlight different aspect of the report.

Oracle Power Objects provides a mechanism for layering, called *Report Groups*. A Report Group separates information according to values in one column of the report's RecordSource, such that you could see the Detail records grouped by that column. For example, you can see ORDER_ITEMS records grouped by the ORDER_ID column. When you define a report group, it adds two new areas to the report: GroupHeader and the GroupFooter. GroupHeader would contain information that identifies the group, such as the GroupBy column and other group information (for example, ORDER_ID and ORDER_DATE). You specify this column through the GroupCol property of the group header. GroupFooter would typically contain group totals information. For example, Order Total aggregate would be placed in the GroupFooter area.

Defaults

A report must provide the user with visual cues to lead him or her to the important areas of the report. It must also be attractive. One of the things you can do is be consistent in displaying objects on the report. In this chapter, you will use certain fonts and font sizes to accomplish this objective. Unless otherwise explicitly specified, the following defaults are used in creating the example reports. For Text Fields and Static Text, MS Sans Serif font with size 8 is used. All controls are set at a height of .20 inches. Static Text is also bold-faced and top-justified to align with the values in the Text Fields.

Order Information Report

In this section, you will create a new report, resize its functional areas, bind it to the ORDERS table, add objects to the report, and run it to produce a report for printing.

Create a new Report window by clicking on the New Report push button in the Application toolbar. Set the Name and Label properties of the report to 'rptOrders'. Notice that the label appears as the title of the report when it is run. In this report, you will be using two of the functional areas: Page Header and Detail. To get the effect described in this chapter, you need to set the SizeY (height) and SizeX (width) properties for each of the functional areas. By using the click and drag method, set the height of the Report Header, Page Footer, and Report Footer area to zero.

In the Properties sheet for the Report window, set the SizeX property to 6.625 inches. This will set the width of the report. Now adjust the height of the Page Header area by setting its SizeX (height) property to 1.125 inches, and set the Detail area's height to 2.125 inches.

The Report window should appear as in Figure 10-2.

One of the advantages of having classes is that you can instantiate them when you are required to use them. One such class is the logo class, supplied with the application. This is a graphic that can be dragged and dropped onto forms and reports. This logo is used on the reports that are created in this chapter.

To set the company logo on the report, drag the logo class from the Application window to the Page Header area. Select the Static Text icon from the Tool palette and place it next to the logo in the Page Header area. Next, set the properties of the Static Text box to get the same look as in Figure 10-3. Set the Label property to 'Order Information Report'. You should make this title stand out on the page, so set the FontName to Brush Script MT or choose one that you prefer. Set the FontSize to 36 to get nice large letters. Set the height (SizeY) of the Static Text box to .625 inches so that it will align with the logo. Finally, left (TextJustHoriz) and top (TextJustVert) justify the text in the Static Text box. The Report window should now appear as in Figure 10-3.

The Report window is now sized and ready to be filled with data. You accomplish this by placing objects onto the Detail area. Open the Orders table in

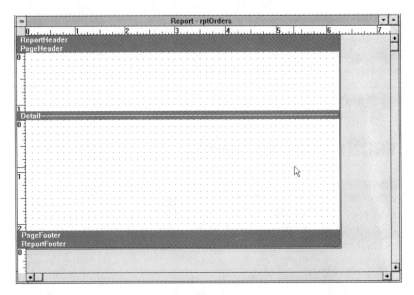

FIGURE 10-2. *Setting the width of the report in the Properties sheet*

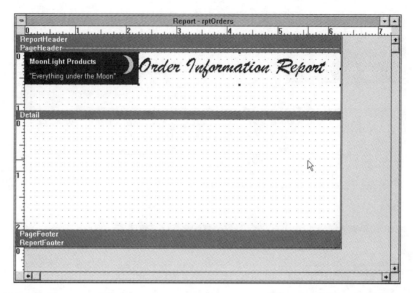

FIGURE 10-3. *The Report window with company logo*

table view. Select all the columns by dragging the mouse pointer in the selection column. Then, drag and drop the columns in the Detail section of the Report window. This automatically sets the RecordSource of the report to the table ORDERS. You may have to resize the Detail section to fit all the fields in the table. The Report window should appear as in Figure 10-4.

Rearrange the fields as shown in Figure 10-5. Set the properties for all the controls as follows. These properties can be set by selecting all the fields, by either SHIFT-clicking on each control in turn or by dragging the mouse pointer across all the required controls. Set the default values for the Text Boxes and the Static Text Fields. Once the fields are rearranged, the report Detail should look like this:

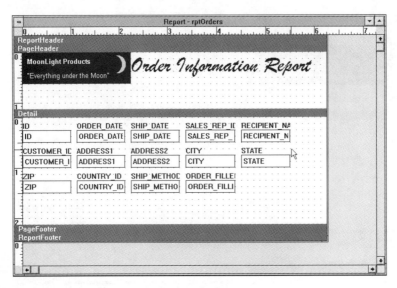

FIGURE 10-4. *The Report window with data*

Now, run the report by clicking on the Run Form/Report push button on the toolbar. The report should look the one in Figure 10-5.

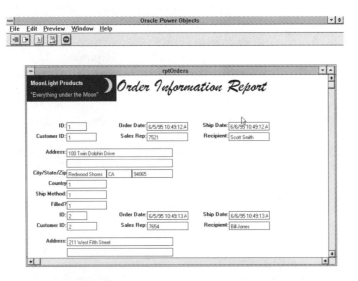

FIGURE 10-5. *The completed Order Information Report filled with data*

You have just created a simple report that lists all the information in the Orders table.

Report Toolbar

When you run the report, a toolbar appears at the top of the report (see Figure 10-5). There are five push buttons on this toolbar. They perform the following functions:

Tool	Button Name	Description
	Previous Page	Goes to the previous page in the report
	Next Page	Goes to the next page in the report
	Full Page	Toggles between full-page and screen views
	Print	Prints the report to the specified printer
	Stop	Stops and returns to the design view

Try out these toolbar push buttons to familiarize yourself with their operations. The same functions can also be accessed from the View menu.

Order and Order Item Report

While the record per page report you built in the last section was one of the more simple reports to write, the master-detail report you will be building in this section is one of the most important. Every business needs one or more of this type of report. These could be two level, as in the case of ORDERS and ORDER_ITEMS, or three level, as in the case of CUSTOMERS, ORDERS, and ORDER_ITEMS (or more, as needed). In creating this report, you will be building on the work from the previous section.

Create a new Report window by clicking on the New Report push button in the Application toolbar. Set the Name and Label properties of the report to 'rptOrderDetail'. In this report, you will be using three of the functional areas: Report Header, Page Header, and Detail. To get the effect described in this chapter, you need to set the SizeY (height), and SizeX (width) properties for each of the functional areas. By using the click and drag method, set the height of the Page Footer and Report Footer area to zero.

In the Properties sheet for the Report window, set the SizeX property to 6.625 inches. This will set the width of the report. Now adjust the height of the Report Header area by setting its SizeY property to 1.125 inches, adjust the Page Header area by setting its SizeY (height) property to 1.125 inches, and adjust the Detail area's height to 1.125 inches.

The Report window should look like Figure 10-6.

Next you should set the company logo on the report. From the Application window, drag the logo class to the ReportHeader and the PageHeader area. Select the Static Text icon from the Tool palette and place it next to the logo in the PageHeader area. Next, set the properties of the Static Text box to get the look in the illustration on the following page. Set the Name property to 'Order Detail Report'. You should make this title stand out on the page, so set the FontName to 'Brush Script MT' or choose one that you prefer. Set the FontSize to 36 to get nice large letters. Set the SizeY (height) of the Static Text box to .625 inches, so that it will align with the logo. Finally, left (TextJustHoriz) and top (TextJustVert) justify the

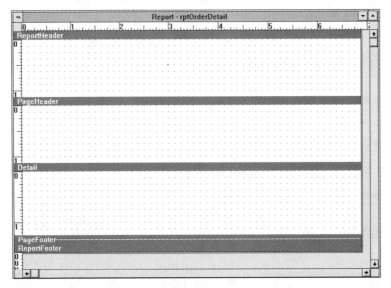

FIGURE 10-6.   *Setting the size on the master-detail report*

text in the Static Text box. The report header and page header portion of the report window should look like this:

Notice that both report and page headers are the same. This usually is not the case. They can be different. The report header is printed only on the first page. The page header is printed on every page. Here the property that prints the page header, FirstPgHdr, is set to 'False' so that the page header is not printed on the first page. Another way to accomplish the same thing is to leave the report header blank and set the FirstPgHdr property to 'True'.

You will now bind the ORDER_ITEMS table to the report by opening the ORDER_ITEMS table in table editor view and selecting all the columns by dragging the mouse pointer in the selection column. Then drag and drop the columns in the Detail section of the report window. This method is preferred over dragging the table onto the report/form, since it gives you a chance to peruse all the columns that are placed on the report/form window. You may have to resize the Detail section to fit all the fields in the table. The report window should look like Figure 10-7.

At this point, this is not a very attractive-looking report. Rearrange the controls on the window to be more attractive. First, set the default values for the Text Fields and the Static Text controls. Then rearrange the fields as shown in Figure 10-8. Notice that the Static Text Fields are moved to the PageHeader and the ReportHeader areas. This is done for the same reasons that the Logo was placed in both areas. Collapse the Detail area such that it encloses the single row of fields tightly.

Let's do a small experiment now. Let's run the report by clicking on the run form/report push button on the toolbar. The report should look like Figure 10-8.

What do you think? This report merely listed all the records in the Order Item table. This is not a terribly efficient way to look at data. What is really needed is a report that is organized as a master-detail report. In the preceding chapters, you have looked at how master-detail forms work. The form showed a master record, while the detail records were displayed in a repeater box as part of the Main form.

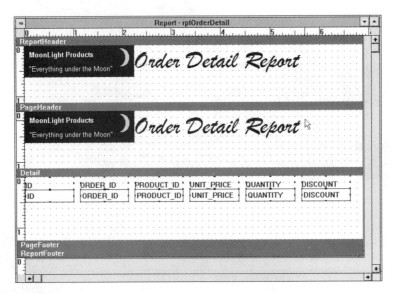

FIGURE 10-7. *Binding the Order_Items table to the report*

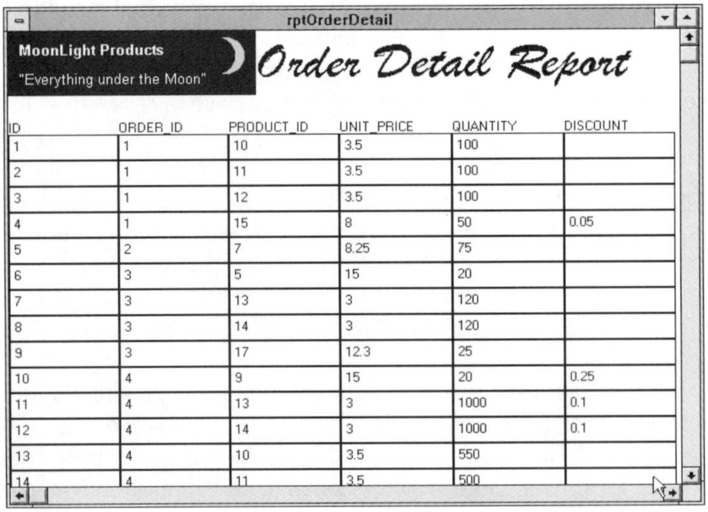

ID	ORDER_ID	PRODUCT_ID	UNIT_PRICE	QUANTITY	DISCOUNT
1	1	10	3.5	100	
2	1	11	3.5	100	
3	1	12	3.5	100	
4	1	15	8	50	0.05
5	2	7	8.25	75	
6	3	5	15	20	
7	3	13	3	120	
8	3	14	3	120	
9	3	17	12.3	25	
10	4	9	15	20	0.25
11	4	13	3	1000	0.1
12	4	14	3	1000	0.1
13	4	10	3.5	550	
14	4	11	3.5	500	

FIGURE 10-8. *Running a sample report*

This would not work in a report. You need to use a different technique to get the same sort of organization in a report.

Consider the ORDERS and the ORDER_ITEMS tables for a master-detail report. You would like this to be organized such that each page has one ORDER_ID and shipping date, followed by all the ORDER_ITEMS for that order. As explained previously, this organization is accomplished by using a Report Group.

Add a group to the report by clicking on the Report Group icon on the toolbar and clicking anywhere on the report. This will add a group header just below the page header, and a group footer above the page footer, bracketing the Detail area. That portion of the Report window should look like this:

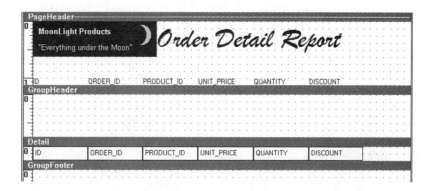

You should organize this report to show one order and its order detail items per page. Click on the GroupHeader and open up its Properties sheet. Set the PageOnBreak property to 'True'. This will cause the report writer to generate a new page whenever the value in the GroupCol property changes. Now set the GroupCol property to 'ORDER_ID'. As you may recall, we are listing ORDER_ITEMS in the Detail area. One of the columns in the ORDER_ITEMS table is ORDER_ID. You might have four items for ORDER_ID 1, five Items for ORDER_ID 2, etc. As a result of the above property settings, the report generated will have the four items belonging to ORDER_ID 1 on one page, the five items belonging to ORDER_ID 2 on the next page, and so on.

Notice that you have not done anything with the ORDERS table yet. All you did was to create a group and specify the column in the detail table that you would like to see the data grouped by. If you were to run this report at this time, you would see the order items grouped by ORDER_ID. They would be printed one per page. The following illustration shows this.

	rptOrderDetail	▼ ▲

MoonLight Products
"Everything under the Moon"

Order Detail Report

ID	ORDER_ID	PRODUCT_ID	UNIT_PRICE	QUANTITY	DISCOUNT
1	1	10	3.5	100	
2	1	11	3.5	100	
3	1	12	3.5	100	
4	1	15	8	50	0.05

This looks fine except for the fact that you do not have any information on the order itself. To get some information about the order, you need to add some controls to the GroupHeader area. This information has to come from the ORDERS table. You cannot just drag some columns from the ORDERS table onto the GroupHeader area. This will conflict with the RecordSource that is presently being used for the report, which is ORDER_ITEMS. One way to get data from a different record source is to use an embedded form. Select the Embedded Form button from the Tool palette and create an embedded form in the GroupHeader area. It should look like this:

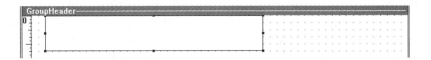

Open the ORDERS table in table view. Select the columns required—ORDER_ID, ORDER_DATE, and SHIP_DATE—and drag them on to the embedded form in the GroupHeader area. Rearrange the controls as shown and set the default properties for the Text Fields and the Static Text. Now that there is a group header, you can delete the Static Text Fields with the field headings from the ReportHeader and the PageHeader areas. Delete the Static Text Fields from the ReportHeader area, and cut and paste the Static Text Fields from the PageHeader area into the GroupHeader area. Run the report. It should appear as in Figure 10-9.

Now you need to link the embedded form to the ORDER_ID in the ORDER_ITEMS table. Notice that this is contrary to what is done for forms. In a

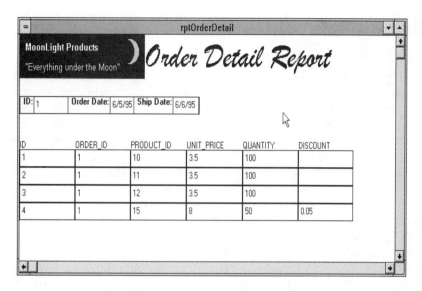

FIGURE 10-9. *The finished report*

form, the ORDERS table is the master table. The ORDER_ITEMS table is the detail table. Here, it is the opposite. It is a little confusing, but if you look at the fact that the GroupHeader is organizing the detail data by pulling together all the ORDER_ITEMS belonging to a single ORDER_ID, you would notice that this GroupHeader occurs once for a set of ORDER_ITEMS. In a sense, it is the GroupHeader that is the master here. Once you convince yourself that this is true, then things become clear. If the GroupHeader is the master record, then you can use the information in the master record (GroupHeader) to link to a detail record (embedded form) to display any data that is required from the detail form.

The information that is needed in the embedded form is the order information. This comes from the ORDERS table. You have already established the RecordSource property of the embedded form by dragging and dropping columns from the ORDERS table onto it. Now, you will link this embedded form to the GroupHeader to get the correct order data.

Give the embedded form the name 'OrderInfo' by setting its Name property. Set the LinkDetailColumn to 'ID column' of the Orders table. Set the LinkMasterColumn property to the 'ORDER_ID' column, which is the GroupCol of the GroupHeader. Finally set the LinkMasterColumn Property to be the 'GroupHeader1'. This GroupHeader1 is the default name given to the GroupHeader by Oracle Power Objects. You could have given it any name you like.

Adding Sub/Group/Grand Totals

Now you have the report organized just the way you want it. It has the company logo, a nice grouping by ORDER_ID, etc. But something is still missing. It sure would be nice to see some of the items to be totaled. For instance, how about seeing, on the OrderItem line, a single amount that shows the price of the items ordered after any discount is applied? Or a single amount that shows how much the whole order is worth? Better yet, how about a grand total that shows the value of all the orders taken?

Oracle Power Objects has built-in functionality to make this simple. That is what you are going to do now. You will add three new fields to the report. They are not bound to the columns of any table or view. They are called *derived* or *calculated* fields. They are merely expressions that use existing values from the database, simple arithmetic operators, and some built-in Oracle Power Objects functions to miraculously come up with the totals.

As before, start with the report you have just completed. Add Static Text and a text box as shown to the Detail, GroupFooter, and ReportFooter areas. Then set the properties as follows. The Sub Total field is added to the Detail area, since this needs to be computed for each line item. The Order Total field is added to the GroupFooter, since order totals are computed for each order, over all the items in that order. The Grand Total field is placed in the ReportFooter area, since grand total is computed once for all the orders in the database.

Object	Property	Value	Description
Sub Total Static Text	Label	Sub Total	Name of the static text box
Sub Total Text Box	Name	SubTotal	
	DataSource	=Quanity*Unit_Price* (1−Nvl(Discount,0))	
Order Total Static Text	Label	Order Total	Name of the Static Text box
	TextJustVert	Bottom	
Order Total Text Box	Name	OrderTotal	
	DataSource	=NVL(SUM(rptOrder Detail.Detail.Subtotal),0)	

Object	Property	Value	Description
Grand Total Static Text	Label	Grand Total	Name of the Static Text box
	TextJustVert	Bottom	
Grand Total Text Box	Name	GrandTotal	
	DataSource	=NVL(SUM(rptOrderDetail. GroupFooter.OrderTotal),0)	

The totals fields are unbound in the sense that their values do not come from any column in a table or a view. They are calculated from existing values. The formulae for calculating these values are set in the DataSource property of the control. Let us look at these formulae a little more closely.

Sub Total

The Sub Total is computed by multiplying the unit price with the number of units ordered and then discounting that by the specified discount rate, as shown here:

QUANITY*UNIT_PRICE*(1−NVL(DISCOUNT,0))

Order Total

The Order Total is computed by totaling all the item subtotals, as shown here. This is placed in the GroupFooter area, since you only want one Order Total for each order.

NVL(SUM(rptOrderDetail.Detail.Subtotal),0)

Grand Total

The Grand Total is computed by totaling all the order totals, as shown here. This is placed in the ReportFooter area, since you only want one of these per report.

NVL(SUM(rptOrderDetail.GroupFooter.OrderTotal),0)

The report should look like this:

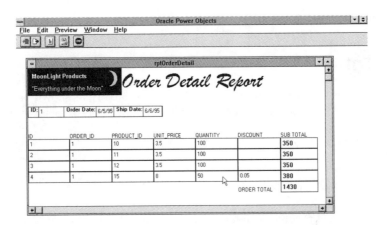

Run the report. The first page and the last page of the report are shown in Figures 10-10 and 10-11, respectively. The first page shows a single logo and the title. This comes from the ReportHeader. Remember that you have turned off the printing of the page header for the first page. Otherwise, you would have seen the logo printed twice, since the ReportHeader and the PageHeader areas look exactly the same. The last page shows the Grand Totals field. This comes from the ReportFooter.

FIGURE 10-10. *First page of the report*

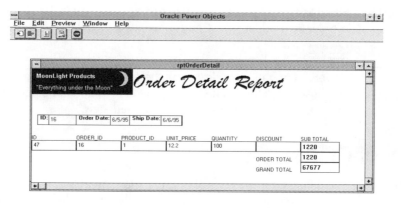

FIGURE 10-11. *Last page of the report*

Adding Charts to a Report

A typical executive, if there is such a thing, sees a mountain of paper during the course of a year. Most of it gets filed in the trash can. The objective of a report should be to grab someone's attention and keep it while trying to get a point across. Nothing is more unappetizing than rows and rows of figures to study while you are trying to get ready for a big meeting. Put yourself in the user's position. Do *you* want to spend hours studying a report? No, of course not. That is why it is important that you make your point and make it emphatically.

Charts are a good way to highlight salient points of a report. Whether it is sales by region or product distribution, charts make the presenter's life easier by driving the point home visually. You will now add a chart to our report. This chart will show the distribution of products by order.

Just as in creating totals, the range of data that you would like to display determines where you place the chart in the report. For example, if you would like to chart at the order level, the chart would go in the GroupHeader or the GroupFooter areas. If you would like to chart at the report level, the chart would go in either the ReportHeader or the ReportFooter areas. For our purposes then, the chart will placed in the GroupHeader areas.

Think of the chart control as if it is in a master-detail relationship with the GroupHeader. In fact that is how you will be setting up this chart. You will be mapping the distribution type of product by quantity. In other words, it will show the makeup of an order by product type. Charts have their own RecordSource.

NOTE

One very important point is that all the records that make up the chart must be fetched immediately. So the rowfetchmode property for the chart must be set to 'Fetch All Immediately'.

Types of Charts

Charts can take five different forms: Vertical Bar, Pie, Horizontal Bar, X-Y Scatter, and Line. Let us now proceed to add a chart control to the form. Click the chart control in the Tool palette and click the GroupHeader area of the Report window. One of the small details you have to worry about is how large you should make the chart. There are no hard and fast rules for this. The basic rule is that you want to highlight the facts, not overwhelm the user. The next rule is that you make it at least large enough to be legible. There is nothing worse than making the information you are trying to highlight into an unreadable mess. This has the adverse effect of frustrating the user, since he or she knows that it is supposed to be important, but cannot make out what it is that is so important. Size is a minor, but important, detail. Set the SizeY property of the group header to 2.115 inches, so that you can place a decent-sized chart control in it.

Now you are ready to tackle the chart control itself. First, take care of positioning the control so that it looks just right. You have already done the work, so you might as well use it. If you think it looks better somewhere else, then feel free to move it around. Remember "beauty is in the eye of the beholder." Set the SizeX property to 1.865 inches and SizeY property to 1.781 inches. Position it by setting the PositionX to 5.375 inches and the PositionY to 0.125 inches. Remember that there is no magic formula for this. It is mostly trial and error. That is why it takes a long time to develop a report. Getting the data you want to show up is easy. Getting it to look the way the user wants is what takes time. This does not mean just looking pretty, but getting the data in the right place so that it will help the user instead of frustrating him or her.

Next, take care of appearances. You want to make this a Pie chart. So set the ChartStyle property to 'Pie'. Since you will be using product names to label the different pieces of the Pie, set the ChartLabelStyle property to 'Names'. Now specify the X and Y axes of the chart. You will be charting two columns from the same table in this example, the ORDER_ITEMS table. Set the ChartXCol property to 'Product_ID' and the ChartYCol property to 'Quantity'. Set FontBold to 'True' to emphasize the labels, FontName to 'MS Sans Serif', FontSize to '8', and set the

HasBorder property to 'True' to box the chart. Give the chart a label that is descriptive, so that the user knows what he or she is looking at. Set the Label property to 'Item Distribution'.

Now the chart is positioned and is ready to display data. As mentioned before, this chart plays a *detail* role in a master-detail relationship, where the *master* is the group header. In this chart, you want to visually display data from an order to show that item A comprises about half the order, item B a quarter, and so on. So the chart must have access to the ORDER_ITEMS records. Set the RecordSource property of the chart to 'ORDER_ITEMS', and the RecSrcSession to 'ORDERSES', the same as the RecordSource and Session for the report. This is just a coincidence. There is no rule that says that they have to be the same. You know that the ORDER_ID field is a foreign key in the ORDER_ITEMS table. It actually refers to the primary key of another table, the ORDERS table (hence the name foreign key). You will group these items by this foreign key. Set the LinkDetailColumn property to 'ORDER_ID'. This detail column has to be tied to a master column in the reports record source. In our case, it is the same column since the RecordSource of the report is also ORDER_ITEMS. Set the LinkMasterColumn to 'ORDER_ID'. You want this chart to appear in the group header. Set the LinkMasterForm to 'GroupHeader1'. The GroupHeader area of the form should look like this:

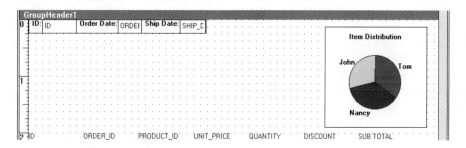

Run the form by clicking on the Run Form/Report push button. The screen should look like Figure 10-12.

Multicolumn Reports

One of the more common types of reports is a multicolumn report. This may be a mailing list, an address book, or a phone listing. Report writers in general have problems handling this type of report. This is because when you make a multicolumn report, you have to snake columns, such that when one column is complete, you have to start on the next column on the same page. Unlike a computer screen, a printed page is sequential. It is not possible to print on the left

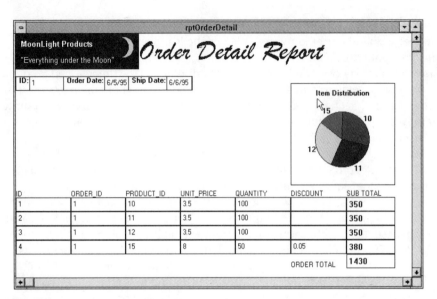

FIGURE 10-12. *The control chart at run time*

side of the page, rewind to the top, and print on the right side of the page. The page has to be formatted up front and then printed.

Oracle Power Objects has a novel way of solving the problem. In Chapter 1, you have learned to use the repeater display which is a wonderful tool for displaying multiple records on a screen. One of the nice things about Oracle Power Objects forms is that they can be printed. As mentioned in the beginning of the chapter, forms cannot be grouped like reports since they do not have all the functional areas of a report. But for any report like a mailing list, which is simply a listing of records from a database without any headers or footers, forms work well.

It must be mentioned here that Oracle Power Objects report writer is limited in the sense that it cannot handle multicolumn reports in the current release. But this feature will be added in a future release. You will build a mailing list report using a form with a repeater display, which has a very precise way of controlling spacing between columns in forms, as well as spacing between successive items on a page.

From the Application window, click on the New Form push button from the Application toolbar. Set the Name property to 'rptMailingList'. Select the repeater display icon and place it on the form. Since a mailing list requires precise spacing, you will want to use sizing properties to size the form. Standard label forms have predefined measurements. As an example, set the SizeX property to 5 inches and the SizeY property to 6 inches.

The characteristics of repeater displays were discussed in Chapter 1. There is a primary panel that can be resized, and it will cause all the secondary panels to assume the same size. On this form you should make the repeater display into a two-column display to print a two-column mailing list. You will do this first by setting the SizeX property of the repeater display to 4.75 inches and the SizeY property to 5 inches. Also set the HasBorder, HasScrollBar, and HasExtraRow properties to 'False'. At this point, the primary display would assume the same width. To display two labels across, shorten the width of the primary panel by clicking on the right border of the primary panel and dragging it to the left until two equal-size panels appear. The primary panel now would be on the upper-left corner of the repeater display. Click on the gray panel just to the right of the primary panel and drag it to the right to create a space of about .25 inches between the two. Click on the gray panel directly below the primary panel and drag it down to create a distance of about .25 inches. Set the HasBorder property of the primary panel to 'False'.

At this point the screen should look like a mailing list. Now, let us bind this to a record source. Open the Customer table in table view. Select the fields NAME, ADDRESS1, CITY, STATE, and ZIP. Drag and drop them on to the primary panel:

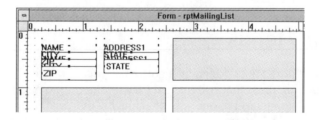

Just a few more things to do and you will be done. The fields on the primary panel look all jumbled up as they usually do when you drag and drop them. First, get rid of all the Static Text boxes by individually selecting them and deleting them. You should do this by having the Properties sheet open, successively clicking on the objects on the primary panel, and looking at the Properties sheet Title bar to see if each is a Static Text box or not. Once all the Static Text boxes are deleted, you will be left with the text fields. Rearrange these fields in a standard mailing label Name, Address, City, State, and ZIP format. Select all the text fields and set the HasBorder property to 'False'. To see how this screen would look when printed, select the Print Preview item from the File menu. The resulting screen should look like this:

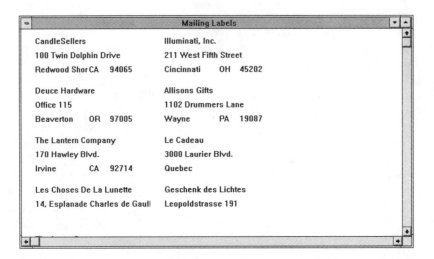

As explained before, from this preview screen you can page back and forth to see the different pages of the form, or print it to get hard copy.

Dynamic Menus

One of the nice things about designing a custom application is that you can set up the user interface in a way that will make it easy for the user to navigate the application. Custom menus are one way of achieving that goal. Oracle Power Objects provides a straightforward way of creating and attaching menus to forms. *Menus* are graphical objects you add to your application to provide lists of commands that the user can select to execute an action. Menus are contained in a Menu bar, which is displayed at the top of the Application window. Each window (form or report) in your application can display its own Menu bar; when the window is active, the associated menu bar appears in the appropriate location.

By default, forms and reports in run-time mode display a Menu bar that provides access to many common commands. You can customize the default Menu bars, either by adding custom items to the menus that appear by default, or by adding or replacing them altogether.

An Oracle Power Objects Menu bar can contain three types of menus: system default, application default, and custom menus.

System Default Menus   These are standard menus for an application in the operating system where your application is running. System default menus on the Macintosh are Apple, File, and Edit. System default menus on Windows are File, Edit, Window, and Help.

Application Default Menus   These are standard menus for Oracle Power Objects windows. Examples of application default menus are the Database and Preview menus.

Custom Menus   These are menus that you design yourself. You can add, modify, or delete components of the system or application default menus, or you can create entirely new menus.

In the Oracle Power Objects object model, there is a hierarchy for menus. At the lowest level, you have *menu items*. These are the individual lines of text you see when you drop down a Menu bar (for example, Open, Close, and Print). These are not objects. These are simply parts of a *menu object*, which is the next level up in the hierarchy. Menu objects are items you see on a Menu bar object (for example, File, Edit, and View). These menu objects are associated with a *Menu bar* object, which is the highest level in the hierarchy. Menu objects are not actually contained within the Menu bar object—you can associate the same menu object with any number of Menu bar objects.

Besides the names of commands, menus can display additional information. Separator lines group related commands within the menu. Keyboard equivalents (also called *accelerators*) are associated with commands in the menu. The user can execute menu commands simply by typing the keyboard equivalent sequence.

Disabled commands are displayed in grayed-out text and indicate commands that the user cannot select. Check marks indicate commands that can be turned on or off. You can control all of these features for menus that you create, both when you create the menu and after creation.

Create Switchboard

One of the properties of a Menu bar is that it has to be attached to a particular form or a report. This gives us a chance to illustrate three different concepts. You will create a switchboard, which is a form that is used to invoke different functions in an application, a form version of a menu. You will create a Menu bar, which essentially performs the same functions as the switchboard. You will also learn to filter records so that the user can specify a particular set of records for viewing or printing.

First you will create a switchboard. To do this, open a new form and place three buttons on the form as shown in the illustration on the following page. Give the form a name by setting the Name property to 'frmReportMenu'. Set the HasScrollBar property to 'False'. Set the Name property of button1 to 'btnOrders' and the Label property to 'Orders'. This button when clicked will run the Orders report that was created previously. Set the Name property of button2 to 'btnOrderDetail' and the Label property to 'Order Detail'. This will run the Order Detail report. Set the Name property of button3 to 'btnMailingList' and the Label property to 'Mailing List'. This button will run the mailing list report.

The screen should look like this:

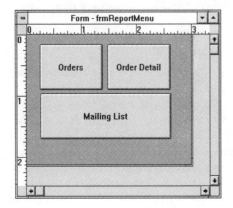

Adding Method Code to the Form

The form is now laid out just the way we want it. You now have to attach code to these buttons so that they can perform the functions required. The most common event for a button is a click event. Things happen when a button is clicked. So it makes sense to attach Oracle Basic code to the click events of the buttons on the form.

- Select the btnOrders button and open up its Properties sheet. Select the **Click( )** method to open up the Code widow. Type this code:

```
rptOrders.OpenPreview()
```

This piece of code will open the Orders report in preview mode.

- Select the btnOrderDetail button and open up its Properties sheet. Select the click method to open up the Code widow. Type this code:

```
rptOrderDetail.OpenPreview()
```

This piece of code will open the OrderDetail report in preview mode.

■ Select the btnMailingList button and open up its Properties sheet. Select the click method to open up the Code widow. Type this code:

```
frmMailFilter.OpenWindow()
```

That looks different, doesn't it? However this method does not open any of the reports that were created before. That is true. The form opened by this button has not been created yet. You will rectify that situation shortly. First a little explanation. One of the concepts that is useful is the concept of filtering. Filtering allows you to restrict the records retrieved from a database, based on a set of criteria. Speaking in SQL terms, this is like specifying a Where clause on a Select statement.

To use filtering effectively, you need some user interaction. If you hard code filtering criteria in to the method that runs the report, you have essentially defeated the purpose of filtering. So what you need is a place to collect filtering information, which you can then use to apply to the underlying recordset of a form or a report. To best accomplish this gathering of filtering information, you will create yet another form called frmMailFilter.

From the Application window, click on the New Form button on the Application toolbar to open a new form. Give it a new name by setting the Name property to 'frmMailFilter'. Drop two Text Fields, two Static Text boxes, and a button on the form. Rearrange the controls as shown in the illustration that follows. Give the Text Fields names by setting their Name properties to 'MailName' and 'MailState'. Set their corresponding Static Text boxes' Label properties to 'Name' and 'State'.

This form is going to collect either the name or state, or both, and apply that criteria to the Customer table, which is used to create the mailing list report. The Text Boxes should reflect the characteristics of the data they are collecting. Set the DataSize to '20' and the DataType to 'String' for the MailName Text Field. Set the DataSize to '2' and the DataType to 'String' for the MailState Text Field. The button that is on the form will gather the data entered in the Text Fields and will create a condition that is applied to the recordset to create the mailing list. Set the Name property of the button to 'btnMail' and the Label property to 'Mailing List'.

The form should look like this:

This is a relatively simple form that filters the records from the Customer table based on the Name and the State. Once either of these two fields is entered, the user will click on the Mailing List push button. The code shown below is attached to the click event of the push button. It will filter the records to select only the records that meet the criteria and will invoke the Mailing Label form to generate the labels.

```
DIM strWhere As string
' Check to see if anything is entered in the inquiry fields.
strWhere = ""
IF NOT isNull(MailName.Value) And Len(MailName.Value) > 0 THEN
    strWhere = "Name Like  '" &MailName.Value & "%'"
END IF
' Build the where clause
IF Len(strWhere) > 0 THEN
    IF NOT isNull(MailState.Value) And Len(MailState.Value) > 0 THEN
        strWhere = strWhere & " And " &  "State Like '" &
            MailState.Value & "%'"
            END IF
ELSE
    If not isNull(MailState.Value) And Len(MailState.Value) > 0 THEN
                strWhere = "State Like '" & MailState.Value &  "%'"
            END IF
END IF

' Set the QueryWhere Method of rptMailingList
MSGBOX strWhere
frmMailLabel.OpenPreview()
frmMailLabel.rptMailingList.QueryWhere(strWhere)
```

NOTE
When you run one of these forms, make sure that you run the application and not the individual form.

To get the switchboard to appear when you run the application, you need to place one line of code in the **OnLoad( )** method of the application. Otherwise, Oracle Power Objects will bring up a random form. Place the following line in the **OnLoad( )** method of your application:

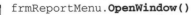

```
frmReportMenu.OpenWindow()
```

Now we will go back to creating the Custom menu for the frmReportMenu form. Creating a Custom menu bar is a seven-step process. You will go through each of the steps in the following pages. But first, take a look at Figure 10-13. It shows the various steps involved in creating a Custom menu.

Create Menu Bar

Create a Menu bar object and initialize it with the system and the application default menus. To initialize the Menu bar with system default menu only, you will use the method **MenuBar.SysDefaultMenuBar( )**. To get both system and application default menus, you will use the method **MenuBar.DefaultMenuBar( )**. In the example below, the second method is used. A new Menu bar is created by using the **NEW** command. The newly created Menu bar is referred to by the variable *mbrReports*.

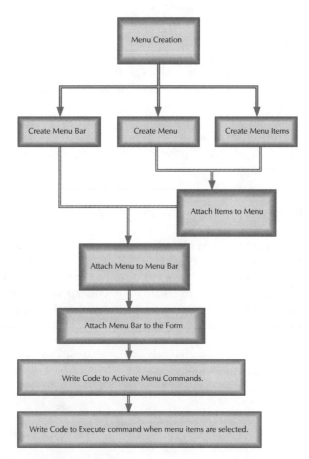

FIGURE 10-13.   *Creating a Custom menu*

Create Menu

Next you use a similar method to create a menu called Reports. This newly created menu is referred to by the variable *mnuReports*. You immediately set the Label for this menu to '&Reports'. The **&** preceding the R designates that letter as the keyboard shortcut. This menu can be invoked from the keyboard by the key combination ALT-R.

Add/Insert Menu Items

Now add the menu items to the menu by using the **AppendMenuItems( )** method. Three menu items are added with keyboard shortcuts. These keyboard shortcuts can be used once the Report menu is dropped down using ALT-R. You could also insert menu items into the menu by using the **InsertMenuItem( )** method. For details on these methods, please refer to Chapter 14 of the *Oracle Power Objects User's Guide*, which comes with the product.

Append Menu to Menu Bar

Up to this point, the Menu bar and the menu are independent. The menu can be attached to any Menu bar you choose. It also can be attached to multiple Menu bars. You attach the Reports menu to the Menu bar using the **AppendMenu( )** method of the Menu bar object.

Attach Menu Bar to the Form

Finally, the Menu bar is attached to the form by using the **SetMenuBar( )** method of the frmReportMenu form.

Where to Place the Method Code

There are two places where you can place the code that creates the Menu bar. If you would like the Menu bar to be created when the application starts up, then you would place the method code in the **OnLoad( )** method of your application. On the other hand, if you would like to create the Menu bar when the form or the report is first displayed, then you would place the method code in the **InitializeWindow( )** method of the form or the report.

```
' Declare variables to hold menu bar and menu objects
DIM mbrReports As Object, mnuReports As Object
```

To create the Menu bar:

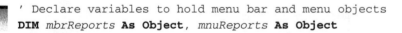

```
' Create menubar object and initialize it with system and
application default menus.
```

```
mbrReports = NEW MenuBar
frmReportMenu.DefaultMenuBar(mbrReports)
```

To create the menu:

```
mnuReports = NEW Menu
mnuReports.Label = "&Reports"
```

To add menu items:

```
' Add items to menu, including seperator lines and keyboard
equivalents
mnuReports.AppendMenuItem("&Orders", cmdRunOrders, 0, NULL)
mnuReports.AppendMenuItem("Order &Detail", cmdRunOrderDetail, 0,
   NULL)
mnuReports.AppendMenuItem("&Mailing List", cmdRunMailingList, 0,
   NULL)
```

To append the menu to the Menu bar:

```
mbrReports.AppendMenu(mnuReports)
```

To attach the Menu bar to the form:

```
'Associate the MenuBar object with the form.
frmReportMenu.SetMenuBar(mbrReports)
```

```
' Declare variables to hold menu bar and menu objects
DIM mbrReports As Object, mnuReports as Object
```

Write Code to Activate Menu Items

With that, the setup for the menu is complete. You have created a Menu bar object and a menu object, added items to the menu object, attached the menu to the Menu bar object, and attached the Menu bar to the mailing list form. Now, all that is left is to make this menu perform the actions required. For that, you have to write more Oracle Basic code. There are two aspects to handling menu selections. The first is setting the status of the menu items. This involves enabling and disabling, and checking and unchecking, menu items. The second involves actually performing the action when a menu item is selected. Oracle Power Objects provides two convenient places to place code to handle these two aspects of menu handling.

You set the status of menu items by placing code in the **TestCommand( )** method on the form. Notice that this method is available only on the Application window, the Form window, and the Report window. That is why you only can add

Custom menus to these three types of objects. Oracle Power Objects calls this method once for each item in the menu whenever the menu is pulled down. There is one argument to this method, and it is a number signifying the menu item that is to be enabled or disabled. Within the method then, you can return one of the following four values to affect the particular menu item in question.

TestCommand_Enabled   This enables the item so that, when selected, a corresponding **DoCommand( )** method is executed to perform a desired action.

TestCommand_Checked   The menu item is enabled and also a check mark is placed next to the item in the menu. This is useful for toggling a menu item, such as Ruler. In this case, the menu item is always enabled, but the check mark indicates whether the Ruler is turned on or off.

TestCommand_Disabled   This will disable the menu item so that it cannot be selected.

TestCommand_Disabled_unchecked   The menu item will appear disabled but with a check mark next to it.

Notice that these are constants that are predefined by Oracle Power Objects. If the return value is not set explicitly, **TestCommand( )** returns a 0. This causes Oracle Power Objects to check to see if there is any default processing associated with the menu item selected. If there is, then that default action is performed. But if there is no default action associated with that menu item, it is then disabled.

TestCommand( ) is usually processed using a **SELECT** statement. First, you need to define global constants to identify the menu items that were added to customize the menu. Oracle Power Objects makes this easy by providing a constant called cmd_FirstUserCommand, which follows the last constant used by the Oracle Power Objects default menus. For example, if you decided to use the system default menu, and then added the Custom menu, the first item in the Custom menu would have a value that is one more than cmd_FirstUserCommand. Go to the Application window and open up its Properties sheet. Select the Declarations and place the following code in it:

```
CONST        cmdRunOrders = cmd_FirstUserCommand + 1
CONST        cmdRunOrderDetail = cmdRunOrders + 1
CONST        cmdRunMailingList = cmdRunOrderDetail + 1
```

Notice the method of defining these constants. The first constant is defined using an Oracle Power Objects–provided initial value. Then, each succeeding constant is defined in terms of the previous constant. You could have defined these by still using the cmd_FirstUSerCommand initial value and adding 1,2, and 3 to it as follows:

```
CONST         cmdRunOrders = cmd_FirstUserCommand + 1
CONST         cmdRunOrderDetail = cmd_FirstUserCommand + 2
CONST         cmdRunMailingList = cmd_FirstUserCommand + 3
```

Now, let us say you add a new report to the Custom menu and would like for it to show up at the top of the menu. Using the first method, you would define the constants as follows:

```
CONST         cmdNewReport = cmd_FirstUserCommand + 1
CONST         cmdRunOrders = cmd_NewReport + 1
CONST         cmdRunOrderDetail = cmdRunOrders + 1
CONST         cmdRunMailingList = cmdRunOrderDetail + 1
```

Notice that you only had to change the first two lines. But using the second method, you would have to renumber all the items succeeding the changed items:

```
CONST         cmdNewReport = cmd_FirstUserCommand + 1
CONST         cmdRunOrders = cmd_FirstUserCommand + 2
CONST         cmdRunOrderDetail = cmd_FirstUserCommand + 3
CONST         cmdRunMailingList = cmd_FirstUserCommand + 4
```

If you have a long list of items, it becomes tedious and error-prone. So we recommend that you use the first method when you need to define a series of consecutive constants. Getting back to defining the code for processing the menu items, notice that in our example all menu items are active. Open the Properties sheet for the form, select the **TestCommand( )** method, and place the following piece of code in it:

```
' Enable the menu items
SELECT CASE cmdCode
    ' Enable menu item to run Order Information report.
    CASE cmdRunOrders
            TestCommand = TestCommand_Enabled
    CASE cmdRunOrderDetail
            TestCommand = TestCommand_Enabled
    CASE cmdRunMailingList
            TestCommand = TestCommand_Enabled
    CASE ELSE
            TestCommand = TestCommand_Enabled
END SELECT
```

Write Code to Execute Menu Items

Once a menu item is enabled, it can be selected by the user. When an item is selected, then some corresponding action should take place. These actions are implemented in the **DoCommand( )** method of the form/report to which this Menu bar is attached. The code can also be attached to the application object. The advantage of attaching code to the application object is that your application responds to commands in a consistent way. For example, you may have defined two Custom menus on a form as well as a report. The first item on both menus happens to be the same. In this case, you place the code for processing that menu item in the application object. This not only gives you a central location to process that code, but also gives you only one place to maintain that code. This is true with **TestCommand( )** code also.

As indicated at the beginning of this section, menu actions are performed by calling the **DoCommand( )** method. Just as with **TestCommand( )**, the menu action code is implemented with a **SELECT CASE** statement. Oracle Power Objects calls this method any time a menu item is selected and passes a constant that indicates the item selected. This constant is the same one you have defined for **TestCommand( )**. Oracle Power Objects first calls the **DoCommand( )** method of the form/report that the menu is associated with. If the command is not handled there, then it calls the **DoCommand( )** method associated with the application. If it is not handled there, then Oracle Power Objects checks to see if there is any default processing associated with it. If there is, then it is performed. If there is no default processing, then nothing is done.

In our example, each of the menu items opens either a report or a form. The code is placed in the **DoCommand( )** method of the form, since you want this menu to be active for this form only:

```
' Perform the necessary action when the menu item is selected
SELECT CASE cmdCode
    CASE cmdRunOrders
        rptOrders.OpenWindow()
        DoCommand = True
    CASE cmdRunOrderDetail
        OrderDetail.OpenWindow()
        DoCommand = True
    CASE cmdRunMailingList
        frmMailFilter.OpenWindow()
        DoCommand = True
    CASE ELSE
END SELECT
```

This task is complete. You now have two ways to run the reports—by using the push buttons from the switchboard or by clicking in the custom menu that appears at the top of the form. Run the form and experiment with the different ways of invoking these reports.

Summary

This chapter covered two important features of Oracle Power Objects: reports and menus. Starting with a simple report, you have progressed through the steps of creating a master-detail report, adding aggregate values to generate totals, including a chart to make the report functional and attractive, using Oracle Power Objects forms to create mailing labels, and, finally, running all the reports using a switchboard and a Custom menu.

The importance of reports cannot be emphasized enough. In general application, designers think of reports as something to be done last. Nothing could be further from the truth. You should think about and plan for the reports from the beginning just as you would for forms. Most designers feel that reports are easy and do not require a lot of time and resources to implement. That is true until you come across a requirement that cannot be implemented using the reporting tool on hand. Then you are in trouble. Users are a lot less forgiving about their reports than their forms. Give reports their just due, and everyone will be happy in the long run.

Let's look ahead a little. So far in this book we have been extolling the power and flexibility of Oracle Power Objects. But there comes a time when even the most powerful tool cannot handle the problem at hand. The sensible tool would give the developer access to specialized components that can be used from the tool itself. Oracle Power Objects, of course, is very sensible. It allows you to access OLE objects, DLLs, and OCXs. Sound strange to you? Don't worry, all of these will be explained in the next chapter.

CHAPTER 11

Extending the Power

So far you have seen most of the native capabilities of Oracle Power Objects in the preceding chapters. Yet there are always those times when you have to reach a little bit beyond the capabilities of a tool at hand. You cannot do all the repairs to a house with a screw driver. Some times you need to reach for a hammer, because it does a better job of dealing with the problem at hand. A good tool allows you to use other tools without having to abandon the project to do it. In that sense, Oracle Power Objects qualifies as a good tool.

Oracle Power Objects allows you to extend its native capabilities in three ways. The first is that Oracle Power Objects provides you bindable controls to access OLE (object linking and embedding) servers like Excel, MS Word, and a myriad of other programs. Second, it allows you to call dynamic link libraries (DLLs), including those that are provided with the Windows operating system. Finally, it allows you to use custom OCX controls, which are objects built using

OLE technology. With these three capabilities you have virtually unlimited customizing power when used in conjunction with Oracle Power Objects.

Overview

In this chapter we will briefly explain each of the three technologies mentioned above. You will learn what OLE automation is, What DLLs are and how to use them, and you will learn about OCX custom controls as well. You will learn step by step how to use these technologies. Although these are not native to Oracle Power Objects, they are important technologies for the short term, as well as into the future.

Object Linking and Embedding (OLE)

At the basic level, OLE is a protocol that allows two applications to communicate with each other. The terminology used with OLE is a little confusing, however. It uses the terms *client* and *server*, which are somewhat related to the client-server in a traditional sense. But the way OLE works is anything but like a client-server in the traditional sense. The following features make an OLE server different from a server in the traditional sense.

1. The OLE client and the OLE server must reside in the same machine. Future versions of OLE will support distributed OLE clients and servers.

2. OLE servers can not only save data, they can also supply the user interface that can be used to edit the data.

3. There is class of OLE servers that are known as *mini* servers. These are not capable of storing their own data. Some examples of mini servers are MS Word Spell Checker and Thesaurus, and Shapeware's Visio Express.

4. There is whole class OLE custom controls that can be considered mini servers. More on those later in this chapter.

In OLE, from the current application you can either embed an object in the current application or create a pointer that points to an object that is held by another application. The *linking* and *embedding* terms refer to where the data for the particular object you are referring to is held. Consider the example of a Word document. You can embed this Word document into Oracle Power Objects by storing it in a table as RAW data, or you can link to a Word document that is a .DOC file in a subdirectory somewhere on your machine. So, *embeded* data is in a field in a table or in a storage area specific to the application, and *linked* data is in a file in a directory.

Now that this Word document is stored somewhere, we should be able to manipulate it. Consider the document mentioned above. If it is a linked document, then you could use MS Word directly to edit the document. The next time you open your application with the linked document in it, any changes that were made would show up in it. On the other hand, if the document is embedded in it, you can only manipulate that document from within the application.

In summary, an *embedded* object maintains a reference to the application that created the object, but not the data contained in the object. A *linked* object maintains a reference both to the application that created the object and to the file that contains the data for the object.

Embedding the document objects has the advantage that a copy of the original document is saved with the container document. This data is available in the container document, even though the original data has disappeared. If you link the document, a reference to the original data file is stored in the container document. If you happen to move that document to a different directory, then you can no longer edit that document from the container application. Embedding essentially creates a snapshot of the data in the document, which then is stored locally. Thus, embedding a document is good for archiving purposes.

If you have a document that changes frequently, and the container application needs to see the latest version at all times, then linking that document is a better choice. It also saves on storage space, since only one copy of the data is kept.

What Is the Registration Database?

When you install an OLE server application, the setup utility for the new software adds entries to your registration database (REG.DAT) file. The registration database is a source of information about applications. The purpose of the REG.DAT file is to associate unique file extensions to the OLE object types. This information is used when you open or print a file from File Manager and by applications that support OLE. The registration database is set up and maintained by Windows and Windows applications, and is located in the Windows directory. This file should not be moved or deleted. Doing so may result in a loss of functionality in File Manager, Program Manager, and applications that support OLE.

Using the Registration Info Editor

The Registration Info Editor comes with two interfaces. The default interface appears when you run REGEDIT.EXE and is used for viewing and modifying registration information in the REG.DAT file that pertains to the Open and Print commands in File Manager. The advanced interface is used for accessing all registration information, including information used by applications that support OLE. To use the advanced interface, start Registration Info Editor with the /v option (regedit /v) by using the Run command in File Manager or Program Manager. We recommend that you only modify information in the registration database if you are instructed to do so by an application vendor or a product support technician (or you understand the registration information in the registration database). If you have an application that is not registered in the database, you can use File Manager to associate the application with a file name extension so that you can open files from File Manager.

Using OLE Objects in Oracle Power Objects

You can create more attractive forms and reports by adding OLE objects (such as pictures, graphs, and sounds) developed in other applications. You can create OLE objects using any Microsoft Windows–based application that supports OLE. An OLE object can be an entire file (for example, a Microsoft Excel worksheet) or part of a file (for example, cells from a worksheet). You can add these objects to a database by either linking or embedding them; they can be either bound or unbound.

Now, we'll look at some examples of the concepts described above. In the following section you will create both an unbound and bound embedded OLE object, and a linked OLE object.

Creating an Unbound Embedded OLE Object

From the Application window, click on the New Form push button to create a new form container. Give it the Name 'frmOle'. This will be the OLE container. From the Tool palette, click on the OLE control push button. Draw a new control on the form frmOle. The dialog box shown below appears:

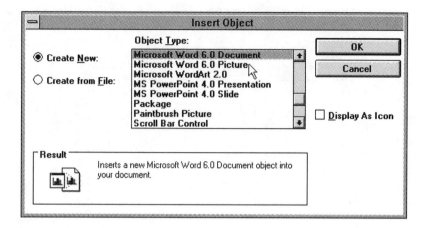

This dialog box shows all the OLE servers that are registered with Windows. You could select any one of them to work with the form. Since you are creating an embedded OLE object, select the option Create New by clicking on the corresponding radio button on the dialog box. Select the Object Type Microsoft Word 6.0 Document. Click on the OK push button.

At this point, the MS Word interface appears on the screen with the document open. Notice how the heading shows how this document is part of the form frmOle. You can type any text you wish into the document. The document will look like this:

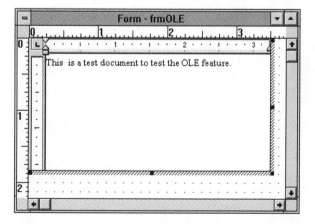

Save the text you have typed, and exit the MS Word application. The text you typed will be shown in the OLE control on the form. At this point the form will look like this:

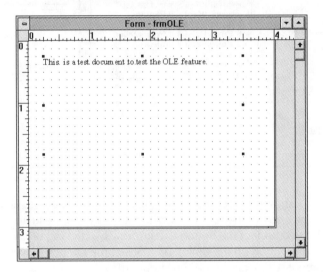

The document that is shown on the form can be edited anytime by double-clicking anywhere in the OLE control. With this example, you have essentially included MS Word as part of your application. This is a powerful feature, indeed. You can now run the form to see the OLE control and the data in it:

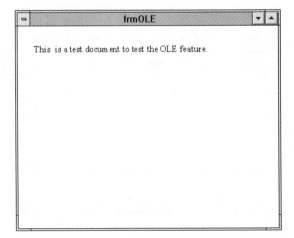

Creating an Unbound Embedded OLE Object by Pasting

Another way to create an embedded object is by pasting. With the server application up on the screen (for example, MS Word), copy the data you want to the clipboard. Then, switch to the Oracle Power Objects window. Select Edit, Paste Special from the menu. Oracle Power Objects will automatically create an OLE object and place the text from the clipboard in it.

Creating a Linked Object

From the Tool palette, click on the OLE control push button. Draw a new control on the form frmOle. The OLE server selection dialog box appears. Since you want to link to an object instead of embedding it, select the Create from File radio button. This allows you to choose an existing file containing a document and make it an OLE object in the form of your choice. Click on the check box called Link to indicate that you want this file to be linked. The selection form should look like this:

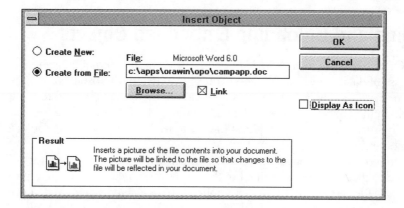

Select the file you want to be part of the form. Click OK on the Browse window. The document is opened by the server, and you can edit it as you wish. When you have finished editing, save the document and exit the server. You should be back in the Oracle Power Objects form.

NOTE

Notice how you will not be able to see the data clearly in a linked OLE control as opposed to an embedded one. This is because in a linked OLE control, the dimensions of the document are maintained by the server. In an embedded document, the sizing is done by Oracle Power Objects. Remember to size the document such that it fits in the OLE control on the form you are using.

Binding OLE Controls

So far, you have seen how to create unbound embedded and linked controls as part of Oracle Power Objects containers. Oracle Power Objects also allows you to bind OLE controls to columns in the database. Since Oracle Power Objects does not always know what type data it will be saving in the database, a generic data type is used. It is Long Raw in Oracle and Blaze and Image on an SQL server. The process of binding an OLE control to a column is the same as before. You could type the name of the column in the DataSource property of the OLE control, or you could drag the column from the table or view editor and drop it into the OLE control.

NOTE
Bound OLE objects must be embedded.

Loading and Unloading Embedded Objects

Linked OLE objects are always stored in files, using the file format appropriate to the class of data. For example, when you save a linked Microsoft Word document in an Oracle Power Objects application, the document is stored in a .DOC file in the operating system. The user can edit the file containing the data through the server application, without having to run the Oracle Power Objects application in which there is a link to the file.

Embedded objects behave differently. You can write the contents of an embedded OLE data object to a file, but they are stored in a slightly different format than "native" files created in the server application. However, you can read from and write to these files through Oracle Power Objects using the server application's interface.

Files containing OLE data objects can store only one object. If you write to an existing file, you overwrite its contents with the new OLE data object. OLE controls have two methods that control file input and output for embedded OLE data objects. These are described here.

WriteColToFile( ) writes data from the OLE control to the file. The contents of the file cannot be read from the server application. However, you can read the contents of the file into an OLE control using the ReadColFromFile( ) method.

ReadColFromFile( ) reads data from the file to the OLE control. The OLE data object in the file must have been written to the file with the **WriteColToFile( )** method.

Both methods take one String argument, which specifies the path and file names of the file containing the data object. These methods can be called from any of the valid events of the OLE control.

Use of the Clipboard with OLE Objects

There are three methods that let you copy OLE data objects between an OLE control and the clipboard:

CanPasteFromClipboard( ) indicates whether the clipboard contains an OLE data object that can be pasted into an OLE control. It returns True if there is an OLE data object in the clipboard, or False if there is not.

PasteFromClipboard( ) pastes an OLE data object from the clipboard into the OLE control.

CopyToClipboard( ) copies the OLE data object stored in the OLE control to the clipboard.

OLE Automation

OLE automation is a special protocol designed to facilitate communication between an OLE client and an OLE server. Note that all OLE clients and servers do not support OLE automation. OLE automation is what makes an OLE server behave more like a data server. For OLE automation to work, the OLE server must support the protocol. In addition, the OLE client must possess the language that is needed to manipulate the server data. OCX controls are custom controls that support OLE automation.

NOTE
Oracle Power Objects version 1.0 will not support OLE automation. This means that you will not be able to control sending/receiving data from OLE 2.0 applications. OLE automation will be provided in a future release of Oracle Power Objects.

OLE Custom Controls

An OCX control is a custom control imported into Oracle Power Objects. The OCX is defined through C code, following the guidelines for OCX controls published by Microsoft Corporation. OCX controls are available in Windows only. You must have the OLE DLLs provided with Oracle Power Objects installed to use OCX controls.

OCXs are a special variety of mini servers, called *in-process servers*, that support OLE automation and provide additional features not available from mini servers. Just like mini servers, such as MS Graph, you embed OCX objects in containers. Once the OCX is imported into Oracle Power Objects, it can be used as any other control. One major difference between an OLE server and a OCX control is that OLE servers are activated by double-clicking on the object that used the server. Whereas OCX objects are activated when they appear on their container (e.g., when the form is displayed), OLE servers usually register themselves during installation. OCXs must be imported into Oracle Power Objects to register them.

OCX Properties and Methods

When you create an OCX control, you define its properties and methods. If OCX properties or method names match those of standard properties or standard methods in Oracle Power Objects, then the Properties sheet for the control displays those properties and methods as if the control were native to Oracle Power Objects. The application applies the default processing for OCX methods with the same names as standard methods, so the OCX control does not need to replicate the method's default processing within its own code. OCX properties and methods must have the same data types for the Value property of a control, as well as the arguments and return values of methods.

Oracle Power Objects interprets an OCX property or method with a nonstandard name as something unique to that control. When the Properties sheet displays the property or method, a special graphical indicator appears next to its name. When you call a method unique to an OCX, it performs whatever processing you have defined for it. The OCX creator must define default processing for the unique methods.

Importing an OCX Control into Oracle Power Objects

Before you can use an OCX control, you must import it into Oracle Power Objects.

1. In the active Designer window for the form, report, or user-defined class selected, select the File Import OLE Control menu command.

2. In the dialog box that appears, select the path and file names of the custom control. Again, OCX controls generally have the .OCX or .DLL extension in their file names.

3. Click OK to import the selected OCX control.

The new OCX control now appears at the bottom of the Object palette.
To add an OCX control to a container, use the following steps.

1. Select a Designer window for a form, report, or user-defined class.

2. Click on the push button in the Object palette for the OCX drawing tool.

3. Draw the new OCX control on the container by clicking on the approximate location where you want the control to appear, applying a default size to the OCX.

4. Click and drag across the region of the container where you want the control to appear, then release the mouse button when it has approximately the dimensions you want to give it.

OCX Properties and Methods

You can add standard properties and methods to an OCX (for example, **Click( )** and **Value**), as well as properties and methods unique to the OCX control. In the latter case, the property or method appears on the Properties sheet with a special symbol appearing near its name, designating it as an OCX-specific property or method. This is shown in the illustration below.

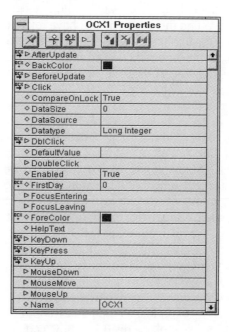

There are some important considerations about OCX-specific properties and methods:

- You can override the default processing for an OCX-specific method by adding method code to it. Additionally, you can call the overridden processing with the **Inherited.method_name( )** statement.

- OCX-specific methods cannot return object references.

- OCX controls are not bindable. Even if you add RecordSource and RecSrcSession properties to an OCX control, Oracle Power Objects will not be able to query records for the control.

Dynamic Link Libraries

Most compiled programming languages, like C and Pascal allow the developer to develop libraries of useful functions that reside in separate files from main programs. For example, C has the Standard I/O library, the Math Library, and so on. You can use these functions in your C program by declaring what are called *function prototypes.* When your program is compiled, the compiler resolves these references to external library functions by deferring them to a later stage. This later stage is called *linking.* In the linking phase, you would have to specify all the libraries that are required to find the functions you have referenced in your program. The linker would search these libraries until all external references have been resolved. At this time, the required code from the libraries would be combined with your program to generate a single .EXE (Intel platform) file, which then can be run as a stand-alone program. This is called *static linking* or *early binding.*

Windows, on the other hand, uses the concept called *dynamic linking* or *late binding.* In this scheme, you would still create function prototypes as before and go through the compile and link process as before. But the linker at this time would not pull the code into the .EXE file. It just resolves the call to the external function to a pointer that can be used to jump to the function at execution time. In this scheme, the DLL loads into the memory along with your program, and when a particular function is needed, control gets transferred there as it would for any other function in your program. The main advantage of DLLs is that they can be shared among many programs, since only one copy of the DLL exists in memory.

Oracle Power Objects supports calling external functions that reside in a DLL. The most common DLL you would be using are the Windows DLLs. You may also have a special DLL that you use that is very business specific. Oracle Power Objects gives you the facility to do that. When you want to use a function that is located in a DLL, Oracle Power Objects needs to know certain things about that function. These are the name of the function as you want to call it in Oracle Power Objects code, the name of the DLL file that contains the function, the name of the function as it exists in the DLL, the arguments and the data types you need to pass to the function, and the data type of the return value you expect from the function. You do all this by creating a function prototype in the Declarations section of the application you are building by using a **Declare** statement. The format of the **Declare** statement is as follows.

Syntax 1
Declare Sub *globalname* Lib *libname* [Alias *aliasname*] [([argumentlist])]

Syntax 2
Declare Function *globalname* Lib *libname* [Alias *aliasname*] [([argumentlist])]
   [As *type*/ Cstring]

Sub
Declaring the procedure as a Sub indicates that it does not return a value.

Function
Declaring the procedure as a function indicates that it will return a value as specified by the **As type** clause of the declaration. It means that this procedure can be used as part of an expression.

globalname
The *globalname* is the name of the procedure called. Procedure names follow the same rules used for naming other Oracle Basic variables. As mentioned above, Function procedures can be typed, and would return a value of that type. The name used must be unique within the application. If a data type is not specified for the Function procedure, it will return a value of the type declared for the procedure originally.

Lib
The Lib clause is mandatory and indicates that the procedure resides in a DLL.

libname
This part of the declaration specifies the name of the DLL. It could also specify the location of the DLL. This name is a quoted string and is case insensitive. If you are using the three main DLLs of windows, you could use the shortcuts, "Kernel", "User", or "GDI." Windows knows enough to translate these strings to their proper names.
    You could, as part of the name, include the path name where the DLL file is located. If a path name is not specified, Windows uses the default path order, current directory, Windows directory, Windows system directory, and any

directories listed in the PATH variable. It would also search any directories on the network, if they are available and are specified in the PATH.

> **NOTE**
> This search order is important. Make sure you have only one copy of the DLL on your search path. Otherwise, Windows will use the first instance of the DLL it finds. If you happen to have an older version of the DLL in the current directory and a newer version in the Windows directory, Windows will end up using the older version. The best place for the DLLs is the Windows system directory.

Alias

There are three main reasons to use aliases for DLL functions:

- Oracle Power Objects requires that the method names be unique within an application or a library. Sometimes the external DLL's name may conflict with an Oracle Power Objects reserved word or method. In those cases, you can use the Alias clause to change the name of the DLL function to suit your requirements.

- DLLs written in other languages may use certain characters in their function names that are illegal in Oracle Basic. For example C or C++ allow their variables to begin with the underscore character. This type of variable declaration is illegal in Oracle Basic, so you would have to use an Alias to map those function names to names that are legal in Oracle Basic.

- All the functions in a DLL may or may not have a name, but they all have a unique number, called the *ordinal* number, associated with them. There are two reasons not to expose the names in a DLL. One is to save storage space. Since the long string of characters signifying the name need not be part of the DLL file, it will be smaller. It also saves a lookup while trying to jump to that procedure. The second is that it makes the DLL harder to reverse engineer, since there is no name specified. So, if you only know the ordinal number, which you can get from the documentation, you can specify your own name for it using the Alias clause. We recommend not using the ordinal number if the name is exposed, especially since the ordinal numbers may change with each release of the DLL.

aliasname

An *aliasname* is a text string that identifies the name of the procedure in the DLL. This could be the name of the procedure in quotes or a "#<ordinal Number>".

argumentlist

An argumentlist is a list of variables representing arguments that are passed to the Sub or Function procedure when it is called. The format of this list is described below.

As *type*

As *type* Declares the data type of the value returned by a Function procedure. The argument type may be **Integer**, **Long**, **Single**, **Double**, **String** (variable-length only), or **Variant**. Notice that the type **Object** is missing. This data type is exclusive to Oracle Basic. Until you can generate a DLL with functions that can return an Object data type, this data type cannot be used.

Cstring

This specifies that the function returns a C-style string. These are strings that are null terminated. Oracle Basic would convert this string to its own internal format.

The way that parameters are passed to the DLL is important. They are usually passed on the stack. The DLL expects these parameters to be in a certain order and of a certain length. In the **Declare** statement, you specify the order by the parameter's position in the list, and the length by the data type. This is where the **Declare** statement plays an important role.

There are two ways parameters can be passed to the DLL. One is *by value* and the other is *by reference.* By value implies that the actual value of the variable is passed to the DLL. The DLL would not know anything about the variable that contained that value. Hence, it cannot modify it. So variables passed by value cannot be modified by the DLL. When a variable is passed as by reference, then a pointer to the variable is passed to the DLL. The DLL is now free to modify the contents of the variable. Oracle Basic provides the **ByVal** keyword to allow you to pass variables by value. If the **ByVal** keyword does not precede the variable name then it is assumed to be passed by reference.

The argument argumentlist has the following syntax:

[ByVal] *variable* [As *type*] [,[ByVal] *variable* [As *type*]] . . .

ByVal

This indicates that the argument is passed by value rather than by reference. **ByVal** cannot be used with arrays. With a numeric argument variable, **ByVal** converts the actual argument to the numeric type indicated in the **Declare** statement before being passed. When **ByVal** precedes a String argument variable, the address of the null terminated string data is sent to the procedure. When **ByVal** is not included, a string descriptor is sent to the called DLL procedure.

variable

This is an Oracle Basic variable name. If you use a type declaration character with a variable, don't use the **As** clause. If there is no **As** clause, the default data type of variable is used.

As type

This declares the data type of a variable: **Integer**, **Long**, **Single**, **Double**, **String**, **Variant**. A **Declare** statement for an external procedure can be used only in the Declarations section of an application. These procedures are then available from anywhere in the application. Empty parentheses indicate that the Sub or Function procedure has no arguments and that arguments should be checked to ensure that none are passed. In the following example, **Test** takes no arguments. If you use arguments in a call to **Test**, an error occurs:

> **Declare** Sub **Test** Lib "*MyLib.DLL*" ( )

When you specify an argument list, the number and type of arguments are checked each time the procedure is called. In the following example, **Test**1 takes one Long argument:

```
Declare Sub Test1 Lib "MyLib.DLL" (X As Long)
```

Using Windows API Functions

MS Windows 3.1*x* consists of a small executable file, WIN.COM, and a bunch of DLLs. The bulk of the Windows API functions are contained in the following DLLs. All of these DLLs can be accessed from Oracle Power Objects.

USER.EXE

This handles all the user interface functions. These include processing the keyboard input, as well as controlling the appearance of the individual windows.

GDI.EXE

This contains the functions responsible for the graphical elements that appear on the screen. It has primitives for drawing lines, boxes, etc.

KERNEL.EXE

This contains the functions that perform the operating system duties. These include memory management, loading and executing programs, and process scheduling.

MMSYSTEM.DLL
This contains the multimedia functions. These include support for sound, MIDI music, animation, and video.

Mapping C Data Types to Oracle Basic Data Types

Windows DLLs use C data types for return values. This requires that you convert these C types to Oracle Basic data types when you use these Windows functions. The following table lists the conversions needed.

C Data Type	Windows Data Type	Oracle Basic Data Type
char	char	String * 1
unsigned char	BYTE	String * 1
int, short	int BOOL	Integer
unsigned	WORD	Integer
unsigned short	HANDLE handle	Integer
long, long int	long	Long
unsigned long	DWORD tag FAR *	Long
float	varies	Single
double	varies	Double
long double	not used	none
char array	LPSTR	String

DLLs are a powerful way to extend the capabilities of Oracle Power Objects. Use them with caution, though. As with anything external, you are dependent upon someone else to make sure that everything works right. DLLs are known to cause many GPF (General Protection Fault) crashes. GPF is a type of crash that occurs in Windows when an application program clobbers system memory. This may be because of a bug in the DLL or because of a bad declaration. Recall the order of passing parameters is very important. Sometimes the DLL has no way of checking whether you passed a correct parameter or not. For example, you might forget the **ByVal** keyword in front of a variable, which will then be passed as a pointer. The DLL might modify it, which would cause problems since you are expecting it to be invariant.

Using the Any Data Type

Sometimes it is necessary to pass a NULL value to a DLL procedure. You can use the **As Any** keyword to accomplish this. In the example below you would declare the *strKeyName* parameter as **Any** data type. This allows the parameter to accept any valid Oracle Basic data type, including NULL.

Using Windows API to Modify INI Files

One way to customize your application is to provide an .INI file, which can be read and written at run time. You would use windows API calls from the KERNEL library for this. The two routines used are GetPrivateProfileString and WritePrivateProfileString.

Before these routines can be used, they must be declared in the Declarations section of the application. The declarations are as follows:

```
Declare Function GetPrivateProfileString Lib "Kernel" &
     (ByVal strAppName As String, strKeyName As Any, ByVal strDefault As
String, &
     ByVal strReturnVal As String, ByVal intSize As Integer, &
     ByVal strFileName As String) As Integer
Declare Function WritePrivateProfileString Lib "Kernel" &
     (ByVal strAppName As String, strKeyName As Any, ByVal strValue As
String, &
     ByVal strFileName As String) As Integer
```

Declare two user-defined functions called **GetIni** and **PutIni** as follows.

```
Name:          udmGetIni
Type:          Function
Parameters:          strSectionName As String, strEntry As String,
strFileName As String
Name: udmPutIni
Type:          Function
Parameters:          strSectionName As String, strEntry As String,
strWriteVal As String,
               strFileName As String
```

Drag and drop these two procedures on to the frmUtils form. Remember that the frmUtils form is the form holding all the common routines. Place the following code in each of the procedures as shown:

```
' This procedure returns a string when given the Section Name, Entry Name
and the INI
' file name.
```

```
Function          GetIni(strSectionName As String, strEntry As String,        &
                  strReturnVal as String, strFileName as String) As Long
On Error Goto Err_GetIni
Const BSIZE = 255
DIM strDefault As String
strDefault = "Default"
GetIni = GetPrivateProfileString(strSectionName, strEntry, strDefault, &
                          strReturnVal, BSIZE, strFileName)
Exit_GetIni:
      Exit Function
Err_GetIni:
      MSGBOX "Error = " & Err & " Reading INI File"
      Resume Exit_GetIni
End Function


' This procedure Writes a string, when given the Section Name, Entry Name
and the INI
' file name.


Function          PutIni(strSectionName As String, strEntry As String,        &
                  strWriteVal As String, strFileName As String) As Long
On Error Goto Err_PutIni
PutIni = WritePrivateProfileString(strSectionName, ByVal strEntry,&
                          strWriteVal, strFileName)
Exit_PutIni:
      Exit Function
Err_PutIni:
      MSGBOX "Error = " & Err & " Writing INI File"
      Resume Exit_PutIni
End Function
```

Using the above two methods you can now read and write from the INI file. For example,

```
DIM strReturnVal As String
frmUtils.udmGetIni( "Modem", "Name", strReturnVal, "Oracle Power
Objects_APP.INI")
```

would return the baud rate from the modem section of the OPO_APP.INI file. Similarly,

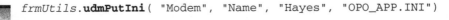

```
frmUtils.udmPutIni( "Modem", "Name", "Hayes", "OPO_APP.INI")
```

would set the Name to Hayes.

Creating Executable Applications

Once you have finished creating your application, you would like to deploy it in the field. This may be for a single user, or may be for several users. Users would be flustered if you tell them that they have to purchase Oracle Power Objects to run your application. To handle such a situation, Oracle Power Objects provides you two choices. The first choice gives you a compiled application that would require the Oracle Power Objects run-time module to run it on a client machine. This is similar to VBRUN300.DLL that you have to supply to deploy a Visual Basic application. The second choice would link in the Oracle Power Objects runtime along with your application, producing a single executable that can be run on stand-alone machines without your having to install Oracle Power Objects first.

Compiling the Application

Compiling an application makes it more efficient to execute. This does not mean that the application is compiled in the sense of C or Pascal. It simply means that all the pieces are gathered together into a single module. The application is still interpreted. The compile file uses the same name as the application, with an extension of .PO instead of .POA. For example, OPO_APP.POA when compiled will produce the file OPO_APP.PO. This file then would require the Oracle Power Objects runtime files to execute.

Creating a Stand-Alone Executable

As mentioned above, you can also create a stand-alone executable, OPO_APP.EXE, which can be run directly. This can be run without bringing up Oracle Power Objects first. One advantage of creating a stand-alone application is that it can be distributed easily. The users need not have Oracle Power Objects or the Oracle Power Objects runtime to use it.

Generating Compiled Applications

There are two ways to invoke the compiler. One is from the toolbar. If you click the Generate an Executable Application push button, the following dialog box appears:

Click on the Separate application file radio button. Click on the OK push button. This will present you with the file Browser window to allow you to choose the file to place the compiled application. The file Browser window looks like this:

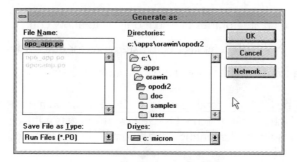

From here you can select the file name, the directory, and the drive on which this file will reside. This file will automatically be assigned a .PO extension. To run this file, you would first run the program Oracle Power Objects runtime. It will then search the current directory for all files with the extension .PO. At that point you can choose the particular application you would like to run.

You could invoke the compiler also from the Menu by selecting Run, Compile Application. The rest of the procedure remains the same.

Creating Stand-Alone Executables

In the illustration above, choose the "Stand-alone executable" radio button and click on the OK push button. The file Browser box appears. You can now choose the file name, directory, and the drive. The file will be given the extension .EXE. It will be an .APPL file on the MacIntosh.

Summary

That brings us to the end of this book. We have tried to show you the salient features of this wonderful new product, Oracle Power Objects. In a market segment that is overflowing with rapid application development tools that claim to ease client-server development, Oracle Power Objects fills a void. It separates itself from the pack by offering the following advantages:

- Drag-and-drop database connectivity along with native database drivers to provide easier and faster data access

- A facility to create libraries of visual objects to allow code reuse

- Standard ANSI basic language with extensions for quicker learning

- Cross-platform capability for standardization on a single tool

A tool cannot be all things to all people. It has to focus on a particular set of problems to be effective. We feel that Oracle Power Objects fulfills its objective of providing the means for implementing departmental client-server systems.

APPENDIX A

Oracle Basic Functions and Commands

Oracle Basic Functions

Function	Description	Example
CurDir	Returns the current path name for the specified or default volume	**CurDir[[**(*drive_id*)**]]**
Eof	Enables you to test for the end-of-file condition	**Eof(***File_number***)**
Loc	Returns the current file pointer position within the open file identified by *File_number*	**Loc(***File_number***)**
Lof	Returns the length (in bytes) of the open disk file identified by *File_number*	**Lof(***File_number***)**
Freefile	Supplies the lowest unused file number	**Freefile**
Input	Returns the number of characters that you specify from the sequential file identified by *File_number*	**Input(***n, File_number***)**
Seek	Returns the position at which the next file operation will apply for the open file identified by *File_number*	**Seek(***File_number***)**

TABLE A-1. *File Input/Output Functions*

Function	Description
Asc	Returns the numeric ANSI code for the first character in the string you supply as string_expr
Chr	Returns the character whose ANSI code is code_num
Environ	Returns the Windows environment string corresponding to the environ_string you supply (In Macintosh, returns null)
Fix	Converts the numeric expression you supply to an integer by truncating the fractional part

TABLE A-2. *General Functions*

Function	Description
Int	Converts the numeric expression you supply to the largest integer less than or equal to that expression
Rnd	Returns a single-precision random number between 0 and 1
Space	Returns a string consisting of a specified number of spaces
Spc	In a Print# command, skips the number of spaces that you specify
Systemname	Returns the name of the system on which Oracle Power Objects is running
Vartype	Returns an integer representing the data type of the argument

TABLE A-2. *General Functions* (continued)

Function	Description
Lbound	Returns the smallest permissible defined value for an array subscript
Ubound	Returns the largest permissible defined value for an array subscript

TABLE A-3. *Array/Subscript Functions*

Function	Description
Choose	Returns value selected by an Index from a list of values
Err/erl	Returns error number/line number
Iif	Immediate If statement. Returns one of two values
Isdate	Determines whether the value supplied could be converted to a Date
Isnull	Checks to see if the expression supplied is null
Isnumeric	Checks to see if the argument supplied can be converted to a number
Msgbox	Displays a message to the user
Nvl	Allows for the specification of a default value if the value of an expression is null

TABLE A-4. *Control Functions*

Function	Description
Abs	Returns the absolute value of the numeric expression supplied
Atn	Returns the arctangent of the numeric expression supplied
Cos	Returns the cosine of the expression supplied
Exp	Returns the exponential (e to the power) of the expression supplied
Fix	Converts the numeric expression to an integer by truncating the fractional part, if any
Log	Returns the natural log of the numeric expression supplied
Mod	Returns the modulus of the first value with respect to the second value
Sgn	Returns the sign of the numeric expression supplied
Sin	Returns the sine of an angle given in radians
Sqr	Returns the square root of the numeric expression supplied
Stdev	Returns the standard deviation of a set of values
Tan	Returns the tangent of the angle specified in radians

TABLE A-5. *Mathematical, Statistical, and Trigonometric Functions*

Function	Description
SqlRowCount	Returns the number of rows affected by the last statement
SqlLookup	Enables single-field queries within an expression
SqlErrText	Returns the error message text returned from the last EXEC SQL operation
SqlErrCode	Returns the error code returned by the last EXEC SQL operation
SqlErrClass	Returns an error classification for the last EXEC SQL operation

TABLE A-6. *SQL Functions*

Function	Description
Chr	Returns the character corresponding to the argument
Asc	Returns the numeric ASCII code for the first character of the string supplied
Format	Converts and/or formats number, date, or string values
Instr	Returns the character position of the first occurrence of a substring
Lcase	Converts all the letters in a string to lowercase
Left	Returns a specified number of characters from the left of the string
Len	Returns the length of the string specified
Ltrim	Trims leading spaces
Mid	Returns a substring from a string
Right	Returns a specified number of characters from the right of the string
Rtrim	Trims trailing spaces
Space	Returns a string of specified number of spaces
Str	Converts a numeric value to a string
String	Returns a string of specified length containing copies of a single character
Trim	Trims leading and trailing spaces
Ucase	Converts the letters in the string to uppercase

TABLE A-7.   *String Functions*

Function	Description
Cdbl	Converts the string or numeric value to a double precision number
Cint	Converts to an integer
Clng	Converts to a long
Csng	Converts to a single precision value
Cvdate	Converts to a date
Cstr	Converts to a string
Hex	Returns a string that represents the hexadecimal value of the decimal argument
Oct	Returns a string that represents the octal value of the decimal argument
Val	Returns the numeric value of a string of characters

TABLE A-8.   *Conversion Functions*

Function	Description
Avg	Computes the average over a set of records
Count	Counts the number of records
Max	Finds the Maximum in a set of records
Min	Finds the minimum in a set of records
Stdev	Finds the standard deviation in a set of records
Sum	Finds the sum of a set of records

TABLE A-9.   *Aggregation Functions*

Function	Description
Cvdate	Coverts a string or numeric value to a date
Date	Returns the current system date
Dateadd	Adds a time interval to a date
Datepart	Returns the time interval part of a date
Datediff	Returns the difference between two dates
Dateserial	Returns the integer values for a date, Y,M,D
Day	Returns the specific day in a month (1–31)
Hour	Returns the hour portion of a specified date
Isdate	Checks to see if the value supplied is a date
Minute	Returns the minute portion of a specified date
Month	Returns the month portion of a specified date
Now	Returns current system date and time
Second	Returns the seconds portion of the specified date
Sysdate	Same as Now
Time	Returns the current system time
Timer	Returns the number of seconds elapsed since midnight of the current day
Timeserial	Returns the integer values for time (H,M,S)
Timevalue	Returns the time portion of a date
Weekday	Returns the weekday for the date specified
Year	Returns the year portion of the specified date

TABLE A-10.   *Date Functions*

Function	Description
Ddb	Returns the depreciation of an asset
Fv	Returns the future value of an investment
Ipmt	Returns the amount applied to interest
Irr	Returns the internal rate of return
Mirr	Returns the modified internal rate of return
Nper	Returns the number of periods required for an annuity
Npv	Returns the Net Present Value
Pmt	Returns the periodic payment
Ppmt	Returns the principal amount applied
Pv	Returns the Present Value of an investment
Rate	Returns the interest rate per period
Sln	Returns the depreciation of a asset
Sum	Returns the sum of a set of values
Syd	Returns the depreciation of an asset using the sum-of-the-year's-digits method

TABLE A-11. *Financial Functions*

Oracle Basic Commands

Command	Description
Exec Sql	Sends an SQL command to a database

TABLE A-12. *Database Management/Interaction*

Command	Description
Call	Invokes an Oracle Basic procedure
Do	Repeatedly executes a set of statements while/until a condition is met.
Exit	Exits a loop/function/subroutine
For	Executes a block of statements for a specified number of times
Gosub	Transfers control to a subroutine
Goto	Transfers control to a label
If	Checks if a condition is True or False and transfers control accordingly
On	Transfers control to a specified label if a condition is met
On Error	Transfers control to a label when an error occurs
Randomize	Initializes a random number generator
Resume	Restarts execution after an error
Return	Terminates the execution of a subroutine
Select Case	Conditionally executes a block of code
Stop	Stops execution
While	Executes a block of statements repeatedly while conditions remains True

TABLE A-13. *Execution Control*

Command	Description
Const	Declares symbolic constants
Dim	Declares a variable/array
Erase	Deletes elements of static arrays, or deletes dynamic arrays
Global	Declares global variables
Let	Assignment statement
Mid	Replaces a portion of a string variable with another value
Redim	Redimensions an array
Static	Establishes variables that persist in local scope

TABLE A-14. *Variable/Constant Definition and Control*

Command	Description
Rem	Declares a comment line

TABLE A-15. *Comments*

Command	Description
Declare	Declares external procedures contained in a DLL
End	Ends a function/subroutine or an IF/SELECT block
Function	Declares a function
Sub	Declares a subroutine

TABLE A-16. *Procedure Definition*

Command	Description
Close	Closes one or more open files
Get	Reads data from a disk file into a variable
Input#	Reads data from files into specific variables
Inputbox	Displays a message and gathers responses
Line Input#	Reads a text file one line at a time
Msgbox	Displays a message
Open	Opens a file
Reset	Flushes buffers and closes all open disk files
Seek	Positions file pointer to an exact Record/Byte
Width#	Establishes the output line length in a open file
Print#	Writes values to a file with formatting
Put	Writes data from a variable to a disk file
Write#	Writes values to a sequential file

TABLE A-17. *Input/Output*

Command	Description
Chdir	Changes to the directory specified
Chdrive	Specifies the working disk volume
Kill	Deletes disk files without affecting directories
Lock	Locks a file to prevent others writing to it
Mkdir	Creates the specified directory
Name...As	Changes the name of file/directory/both
Rmdir	Deletes a directory if it is empty

TABLE A-18.   *Directory/File Management*

Command	Description
Beep	Emits a Beep sound

TABLE A-19.   *Miscellaneous Command*

APPENDIX B

Coding Standards for Oracle Basic

Almost everyone agrees that there should be standards, but almost no one seems to agree on what they are. As the saying goes, "The only problem with standards is that there are so many of them." This appendix will provide a starting point for coding standards, then it is up to you to use them as they are or modify them to suit your purposes.

Why Coding Standards?

There are two points of view concerning coding standards. One is the person developing the initial program, and the other is the person maintaining the program. These two people can be the same person.

From the point of view of the person doing the initial development, coding standards are needed for the following reasons:

- It is easier to come up with names using a standard than not using a standard.

- Your own code is more readable when you follow a consistent naming and commenting standard.

- You can come up with tools to handle standard coding segments (for example, standard headers and footers for procedures and functions).

- Other programmers will think highly of you.

Now, if you are the person that has to maintain the code that is written by someone, then standards would give you the following advantages:

- The code would be easy to read since all objects in the language (constants, variables, etc.) are named the same way.

- It is easy to find the location of various objects since the name would indicate where they are created (global, local, etc.).

- Modifications are easy to make and would fit into the scheme of things.

- It would be easy to reverse-engineer if a major change has to be made to the program.

Object Naming Standards

Most Visual Basic and Access developers would recognize these naming standards. Since Oracle Basic is ANSI-compliant, these coding standards are also based on the *Hungarian* naming conventions, named after the nationality of the creator, Charles Simonyi. This type of naming standard is used by programmers all over the world.

In this naming convention, object names are made up of four parts:

[prefix]tag Name [Qualifier]

The square brackets denote optional components. The tag and the Name are the required components. The prefix and tag are always lowercase so that your eye goes past them to the Name, which begins with a capital letter. The Qualifier also begins with an uppercase letter.

Prefix
Prefixes precede the tag to provide more information about the tag or the object. For example the tag *fld* indicates a data field.

Tag
Tags are short and mnemonic. They typically indicate the class of objects. For example, the tag *mnu* indicates a menu object.

Name
Name describes the objects in as few characters as possible, but without sacrificing clarity. Do not name objects using some artificial limitation like 8 characters, which is a bad habit left over from DOS file names. Use as many characters as needed (you have up to 30, including prefix, tag, and Qualifier). If you are using abbreviations, use the most common ones so that you don't have to keep referring back to the Declaration section to see how the name is spelled. For example, use *rpt* to abbreviate report instead of *rept*. Since most people abbreviate report as *rpt*, it is easier to remember.

Qualifier
A Qualifier follows the Name and further qualifies names that are similar. For example, in the case of two tables, where one keeps the current year's data and the other keeps last year's data, you could name them tblDataCurrent, tblDataPrevious.

File Objects

File objects need not be named with any prefixes since they have the limitation of being no more than 8 characters (DOS limitation), and since they already have an extension to indicate the type of object.

Database Objects

Database object names depend upon the back-end database. Again, if the back-end database permits long names, use the following conventions. For example, if the back-end database is Oracle, then it's a lot easier if you name the tables and columns in uppercase. In this instance, it does not make sense to have lowercase tags as part of the table or column names.

Here are the tags to use if that is what your organization requires:

Object Type	Tag	Example
Index	idx	idxCustLastName
Sequence	sqn	sqnOrder
Synonym	syn	synLastOrder
Table	tbl	tblCustomers
View	vew	vewCustOrder

TABLE B-1. *Database Objects*

Object Type	Tag	Example
Bitmap	bmp	bmpLogo
Class	cls	clsAddress
Form	frm	frmCustomer
OLE object	ole	oleNotes
Report	rpt	rptCustList

TABLE B-2. *Application Objects*

Object Type	Tag	Example
Line	lin	linClockHand
Oval	ovl	ovlEmpPhoto
Rectangle	rct	rctTelephones
Static text	lbl	lblFirstName

TABLE B-3. *Static Objects*

Object Type	Tag	Example
Chart control	cht	chtRevenue
Check box	chk	chkShipped
Combo box	cbo	cboCustList
Current row pointer	crp	crpOrderItems
List box	lst	lstStates
OCX control	ocx	ocxCalender
OLE control	ole	oleWordDoc
Picture control	pic	picCompanyLogo
Pop-up list	pop	popWeekDay
Push button	btn	btnClose
Radio button	rad	radUPS
Scroll bar (vertical)	vsb	vsbBrowser
Scroll bar (horizontal)	hsb	hsbOrder
Text field	fld	fldFirstName

TABLE B-4. *Controls*

Object Type	Tag	Example
Embedded form	emb	embCustomerInfo
Radio button frame	rbf	rbfShipMethod
Repeater display	rep	repOrderItems
Repeater panel	pnl	pnlOrderItems
Report group	grp	grpOrderInfo

TABLE B-5. *Containers*

Object Type	Tag	Example
Menu	mnu	mnuMailingList
Menu bar	mbr	mbrCustomMenu
Recordset	rec	recCustRecords
Status line	sln	slnFormStatus
Toolbar	tbr	tbrCustomToolBar

TABLE B-6. *In-Memory Objects*

In addition to the objects outlined above, you need a naming convention for variable and constant declarations. They are as follows:

Object Type	Tag	Example
Date	dtm	dtmOrderDate As Date
Double	dbl	dblCurbWeight As Double
Integer	int	intRetValue As Integer
Long integer	lng	lngRetValue As Long
Object		Depends on the object being referenced
Session	ses	sesSamples as Object
Single	sgl	sglCurbWeight As Single
String	str	strTemp As String
Variant	var	varRetVal as Variant

TABLE B-7. *Variables*

Constants

Constants are defined in all uppercase with a scope prefix. For example, a global constant would be defined as gFORM_COUNT. Notice use of the underscore. If upper- and lowercase is used in naming an object, then the use of an underscore is superfluous.

Prefixes

These are some of the common prefixes used, but you can develop your own depending on your organization's standards:

Prefix	Description	Example
g	Global	gintCustFormLoaded
l	Local (optional)	lintRetVal
s	Static	sintRecordCount
r	Parameter passed by reference	rintRecordCount
v	Parameter passed by value	vintRecordCount

TABLE B-8.   *Prefixes*

Qualifiers

Qualifiers typically depend on the application, but here are some common ones:

Qualifier	Description	Example
Cur	Current item	lngOrderCur
First	First item	lngOrderFirst
Last	Last item	lngOrderLast
Next	Next item	lngOrderNext
Prev	Previous item	lngOrderPrev

TABLE B-9.   *Qualifers*

Type	Tag	Example
Function/Subprocedure	udm	udmGetIni
Property	udp	udpZipColumnName

TABLE B-10.   *User-Defined Properties and Methods*

Comments

A program without comments is like a product without a user manual. How would you like to buy a complicated stereo system without a user manual? It is surprising how many good programmers ignore commenting their code. Comments are best done when the code is first written. Commenting after the fact becomes a chore. Here are some guidelines for commenting code.

Header Comments

Always place a header at the beginning of a procedure or a method that explains the reason for the existence of the method. Also, describe the input and output parameters and the calling sequence, if necessary. See the following example:

```
Function udmGetIni(strSectionName as String, strEntry As String, strReturnVal As
String, &                  strFileName As String) As Long
' Function:    This procedure returns a string, when given the Section Name,
Entry
'            Name and the INI file name.
' Input:     strSectionName    - Name of the section in the INI file
'          strEntry          - Name of the entry in the Section
'          strReturnVal       - String returned
'          strFileName        - Name of the INI File
' OutPut     strReturnVal        - Value returned
'          udmGetIni        - Number of characters in the string returned.

On Error Goto Err_GetIni
Const BSIZE = 255
DIM strDefault as String
strDefault = "Default"
' Call the windows API procedure to get the value of the string.
GetIni = GetPrivateProfileString(strSectionName, strEntry,
strDefault, strReturnVal, BSIZE, strFileName)
Exit_GetIni:
    Exit Function
Err_GetIni:
    MsgBox "Error = " & Err & " Reading INI File"
    Resume Exit_GetIni
End Function
```

In-Line Comments

In-line comments should be avoided. These came into being during the assembler era, and they are visually unappealing and hard to maintain. The only exception is when declaring variables. The following declaration is usable:

```
DIM     I                        ' Index for stepping thru' the array
DIM     astrLetters(1 to 26) As String    ' An Array of Letters.
```

But in-line comments in code is not recommended. For example:

```
.....
For I = 1 to 26                  ' For loop to step thru array
    msgbox astrLetters(i)        ' Display the letters. the letter
Next I                           ' Increment the Index.
```

The preferred method is

```
' Step thru the letters array and display the letters in a message box.
For I = 1 to 26
    msgbox astrLetters(i)
Next I
```

A single comment at the beginning of the loop clearly states what you are doing in the loop.

Indent Comments Along with the Code

Visual indentation is invaluable in organizing the code. Comments should not interfere with indentation. For example:

```
' Step thru the letters array and display the letters in a message box.
For I = 1 to 26
    ' Check to see if the letter is an I. If so then display it.
    if    astrLetters(i) = "I" Then
        msgbox astrLetters(i)
    End If
Next I
```

is preferred over:

```
For I = 1 to 26
' Check to see if the letter is an I. If so then display it.
```

```
if      astrLetters(i) = "I" Then
      msgbox astrLetters(i)
   End If
Next I
```

Too Many Comments

Too much commenting is just as bad as too little commenting. Do not place the entire functional spec as a part of the procedure. Always read the comments to see if you can follow the flow of the procedure by reading the comments alone, without reading the code. This is really the litmus test for commenting the code.

Index

B

E

F

G

H

I

P

Q

S

T

U

V

W

MY TOUGHEST CRITICS RIDE TRICYCLES, PLAY PATTY-CAKE, AND REFUSE TO EAT THEIR PEAS.

Hi, I'm Eric Brown. As executive editor for *NewMedia* magazine, it's my job to evaluate new multimedia technology.

As a parent, it's my job to help my kids discover the joy of learning.

from media-savvy kids like Cecilia and Isabela-- not to mention their mom

ISBN: 0-07-882083-9,
400 pages, $29.95, U.S.A.
Includes one CD-ROM.

The critics and their mother

That's why I've selected and reviewed the best 100 fun educational titles on the market in my new book **That's Edutainment!**

That's Edutainment! explores the new thinking behind the latest edutainment software and offers tips on building lifelong learning skills. It even includes a CD-ROM packed with try-before-you-buy software and demos.

It's not easy to get applause

Cynthia--but **That's Edutainment!** has earned the respect from critics who really count.

That's Edutainment! A Parent's Guide to Educational Software is available now at book and computer stores.

Or call toll-free 1-800-822-8158 and use your VISA, American Express, Discover, or MasterCard.

The NEW CLASSICS

ORACLE
DBA HANDBOOK

by Kevin Loney

**Every DBA can learn to
manage a networked Oracle
database efficiently and
effectively with this
comprehensive guide.**

Price: $34.95 U.S.A.
Available Now
ISBN: 0-07-881182-1
Pages: 704, paperback

TUNING ORACLE

by Michael J. Corey,
Michael Abbey and
Daniel J. Dechichio, Jr.

**Learn to customize Oracle
for optimal performance
and productivity with this
focused guide.**

Price: $29.95 U.S.A.
Available Now
ISBN: 0-07-881181-3
Pages: 336, paperback

ORACLE
WORKGROUP
SERVER
HANDBOOK

by Thomas B. Cox

**Take full advantage of the
power and flexibility of the new
Oracle Workgroup Server and
Oracle7 for Windows with this
comprehensive handbook.**

Covers Oracle7 for Windows

Price: $27.95 U.S.A.
Available Now
ISBN: 0-07-881186-4
Pages: 320, paperback

ORACLE:
A BEGINNER'S
GUIDE

by Michael Abbey
and Michael J. Corey

**For easy-to-understand, comprehensive
information about Oracle RDBMS products,
this is the one book every user needs.**

Price: $29.95 U.S.A.
Available Now
ISBN: 0-07-882122-3
Pages: 560, paperback

ORACLE® *Oracle Press*™

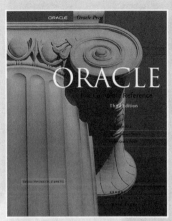

ORACLE: THE COMPLETE REFERENCE

Third Edition

by George Koch
and Kevin Loney

Get true encyclopedic coverage of Oracle with this book. Authoritative and absolutely up-to-the-minute.

Price: $34.95 U.S.A.
Available Now
ISBN: 0-07-882097-9
Pages: 1104, paperback

ORACLE BACKUP AND RECOVERY HANDBOOK

by Rama Velpuri

Keep your database running smoothly and prepare for the possibility of system failure with this comprehensive resource and guide.

Price: $29.95 U.S.A.
Available Now
ISBN: 0-07-882106-1
Pages: 400, paperback

ORACLE POWER OBJECTS DEVELOPER'S GUIDE

by Richard Finkelstein,
Kasu Sista, and Rick Greenwald

Integrate the flexibility and power of Oracle Power Objects into your applications development with this results-oriented handbook.

Price: $39.95 U.S.A.
Includes One CD-ROM
Available September, 1995
ISBN: 0-07-882163-0
Pages: 656, paperback

ORACLE POWER OBJECTS HANDBOOK

by Bruce Kolste
and David Petersen

This is the only book available on Oracle's new single/multi-user database product.

Price: $29.95 U.S.A.
Available August, 1995
ISBN: 0-07-882089-8
Pages: 512, paperback

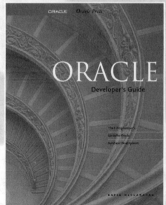

ORACLE DEVELOPER'S GUIDE

by David McClanahan

Learn to develop a database that is fast, powerful, and secure with this comprehensive guide.

Price: $29.95 U.S.A.
Available November, 1995
ISBN: 0-07-882087-1
Pages: 608, paperback

BC640SL

EXTRATERRESTRIAL CONNECTIONS

THESE DAYS, ANY CONNECTION IS POSSIBLE...
WITH THE INNOVATIVE BOOKS FROM LAN TIMES AND OSBORNE/McGRAW-HILL

LAN Times Guide to
Interoperability
Edited by Tom Sheldon
$29.95 U.S.A.
ISBN: 0-07-882043-X
Available Now

LAN Times Encyclopedia
of Networking
by Tom Sheldon
$39.95 U.S.A.
ISBN: 0-07-881965-2
Available Now

LAN Times Guide to SQL
by James R. Groff
and Paul N. Weinberg
$29.95 U.S.A.
ISBN: 0-07-882026-X
Available Now

LAN Times E-Mail
Resource Guide
by Rik Drummond and
Nancy Cox
$29.95 U.S.A.
ISBN: 0-07-882052-9
Available Now

LAN Times Guide to
Multimedia Networking
by Nancy Cox,
Charles T. Manley, Jr.,
and Francis E. Chea
$29.95 U.S.A.
ISBN: 0-07-882114-2
Available August, 1995

LAN Times Guide to
Telephony
by David D. Bezar
$34.95 U.S.A.
ISBN: 0-07-882126-6
Available August 1995

BC640SL

WHEN IT COMES TO CD-ROM...
WE WROTE THE BOOK

**BYTE Guide to CD-ROM,
Second Edition**
by Michael Nadeau
Includes One CD-ROM
$39.95 U.S.A.
ISBN: 0-07-882104-5
Available Now

Fully Revised & Expanded!

This Exclusive CD-ROM Package Includes
• Sound Clips and Clip Art
• Samples of CD-ROM Applications
• Multimedia Authoring Tools

Part buyer's guide, part standards guide, and part troubleshooter, the *BYTE Guide to CD-ROM, Second Edition* discusses all aspects of this burgeoning technology so you can take full advantage.

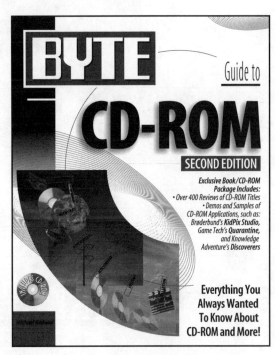

Exclusive Book/CD-ROM Package Includes:
• Over 400 Reviews of CD-ROM Titles
• Demos and Samples of CD-ROM Applications, such as: Brøderbund's **KidPix Studio**, Game Tech's **Quarantine**, and Knowledge Adventure's **Discoverers**

Everything You Always Wanted To Know About CD-ROM and More!

BYTE Guide to Telescript
by Cronder Concepcion and
Paul Staniforth
$29.95 U.S.A.
ISBN: 0-07-882119-3
Available December, 1995

BYTE Guide to OpenDOC
by David Berkowitz
$29.95 U.S.A.
ISBN: 0-07-882118-5
Available January, 1996

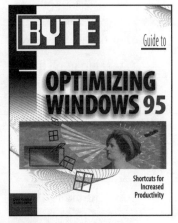

BYTE Guide to Optimizing Windows 95
by Craig Menefee and Lenny Bailes
$29.95 U.S.A.
ISBN: 0-07-882120-7
Available December, 1995

BC640SL

Roam the Globe

ART, BUSINESS, HOBBIES, HUMOR, JOBS, KIDS, MOVIES, MUSIC, RELIGION, SCIENCE, SPORTS, AND MORE...FOR EVERY USER

WITH THE
INTERNET YELLOW PAGES
Second Edition

152 categories from Archaeology to Zoology, PLUS a fully annotated list of Usenet newsgroups. Indispensable to Internet users everywhere!

A unique directory—unmatched in scope and organization—that shows you how to access thousands of free Internet resources from all over the world!

by Harley Hahn and Rick Stout

Order Today!

$29.95, A Quality Paperback, ISBN: 0-07-882098-7, 892 Pages, Illustrated

BC640SL

New Books from Osborne/McGraw-Hill Available Now

Business Degrees for the '90s

Essential Tools for Advancing Professionals

The Digital MBA

Edited by
Daniel Burnstein
Foreword by
Nancy Austin,
Coauthor of
A Passion for Excellence
Includes a CD-ROM
$39.95 U.S.A.
ISBN:
0-07-882099-5

Too busy managing a business to spend time in school studying business? If you want the management expertise you'd gain with an MBA without spending thousands of dollars, check out this book/CD package. Packed with "MBA-ware," this book will teach you how to use the interactive software on the CD-ROM for analyzing and running your business.

NetLaw: Your Rights in the Online World

by
Lance Rose
$19.95 U.S.A.
ISBN:
0-07-882077-4

Whether or not you have a J.D., cyberspace presents a changing legal frontier to maneuver through new obstacles at every turn. Discover your rights and the risks of online communication as you explore such topics as copyrights, the First Amendment, searches and seizures, sexually explicit materials, and more.

AND DON'T FORGET...
Osborne's Best-Selling

The Internet Yellow Pages
Second Edition
by Harley Hahn
and Rick Stout
$29.95 U.S.A.
ISBN:
0-07-882098-7

More Than 700,000 Copies in Print!

BC640SL

ORDER BOOKS DIRECTLY FROM OSBORNE/McGRAW-HILL

For a complete catalog of Osborne's books, call 510-549-6600 or write to us at 2600 Tenth Street, Berkeley, CA 94710

Call Toll-Free: *1-800-822-8158*
24 hours a day, 7 days a week in U.S. and Canada

Mail this order form to:
McGraw-Hill, Inc.
Customer Service Dept.
P.O. Box 547
Blacklick, OH 43004

Fax this order form to:
1-614-759-3644

EMAIL
7007.1531@COMPUSERVE.COM
COMPUSERVE GO MH

Ship to:

Name _____

Company _____

Address _____

City / State / Zip _____

Daytime Telephone: _____
(We'll contact you if there's a question about your order.)

ISBN #	BOOK TITLE	Quantity	Price	Total
0-07-88				
0-07-88				
0-07-88				
0-07-88				
0-07-88				
0-07088				
0-07-88				
0-07-88				
0-07-88				
0-07-88				
0-07-88				
0-07-88				
0-07-88				
0-07-88				
	Shipping & Handling Charge from Chart Below			
	Subtotal			
	Please Add Applicable State & Local Sales Tax			
	TOTAL			

Shipping & Handling Charges

Order Amount	U.S.	Outside U.S.
Less than $15	$3.50	$5.50
$15.00 - $24.99	$4.00	$6.00
$25.00 - $49.99	$5.00	$7.00
$50.00 - $74.99	$6.00	$8.00
$75.00 - and up	$7.00	$9.00

Occasionally we allow other selected companies to use our mailing list. If you would prefer that we not include you in these extra mailings, please check here: ❑

METHOD OF PAYMENT

❑ Check or money order enclosed (payable to Osborne/McGraw-Hill)

❑ AMERICAN EXPRESS   ❑ DISCOVER   ❑ MasterCard   ❑ VISA

Account No. ⬜⬜⬜⬜⬜⬜⬜⬜⬜⬜⬜⬜⬜⬜⬜⬜

Expiration Date _____

Signature _____

In a hurry? Call 1-800-822-8158 anytime, day or night, or visit your local bookstore.

Thank you for your order   Code BC640SL